Trust, Politics, and Revolution

Trust, Politics, and Revolution

A European History

Francesca Granelli

I.B. TAURIS

LONDON • NEW YORK • OXFORD • NEW DELHI • SYDNEY

I.B. TAURIS

Bloomsbury Publishing Plc

50 Bedford Square, London, WC1B 3DP, UK

1385 Broadway, New York, NY 10018, USA

BLOOMSBURY, I.B. TAURIS and the I.B. Tauris logo are trademarks
of Bloomsbury Publishing Plc

First published in Great Britain 2020

Cover design by Adriana Brioso
Cover image © Macrovector/shutterstock
Cover background © sorendls/iStock

A catalogue record for this book is available from the British Library.

A catalogue record for this book is available from the Library of Congress.

ISBN:	HB:	978-1-7883-1472-5
	ePDF:	978-1-7883-1573-9
	eBook:	978-1-7883-1574-6

Typeset by Integra Software Services Pvt Ltd.
Printed and bound in Great Britain

To find out more about our authors and books visit www.bloomsbury.com
and sign up for our newsletters.

Contents

Figures   vi

1 Introduction   1
2 What is revolution?   11
3 What is trust in the twenty-first century?   25
4 Power, control, and trust   51
5 Ancient revolutionaries   61
6 Medieval Europe's rebellious nature   81
7 Renaissance Man – A revolutionary?   95
8 Convulsions, then rupture   117
   Interlude   145
9 A new revolutionary paradigm?   151
10 Conclusion   163

Notes   168
Bibliography   245
Index   320

Figures

1   A rudimentary imagined trajectory of trust and distrust
    in revolution   7
2   Facets of trust   26
3   What is trust? (Part 1)   27
4   What is trust? (Part 2)   28
5   Changing relationships of trust   37
6   Schematic depicting the continuum of power   53
7   The relationships and interplay between trust, power, and control 58
8   Ancient Greek framework of trust   63
9   The networks of trust in Ancient Greek society   69
10 The Roman Republic's framework of trust   74
11 The Roman framework of trust during the *Principate*   78
12 The developing framework of trust   85
13 The developing framework of trust in the late medieval period   88
14 Early Renaissance framework of trust   97
15 The framework of trust after the Protestant Reformation   111
16 The evolving framework of trust in seventeenth-century England 128

1

Introduction

With the fall of the Berlin Wall in 1989, which brought an end to the Cold War, the future looked bright as liberal democracy triumphed over communism. Yet today we seem to be entering another period of marked uncertainty: mass migration creates huge stress and major social divisions; religious fundamentalism paves the way for terrorism; transnational organizations and the 'benefit scramble' challenge the State from above and below and also challenge institutions[1]; the rise of China shifts the axis of global influence; the re-emergence of Iran upsets the regional equilibrium; Russian posturing and aggression threaten European security; globalization exacerbates the divide between rich and poor; and ongoing debt crises undermine growth and stability.

The fragility and volatility of the Middle East – epitomized by the hopes and dreams of the Arab Spring quickly turning to despair and dismay – are played out to a global audience, against the backdrop of a 'crisis of trust' in governments and institutions that appeared long before the Brexit decision and the Trump presidency.[2] This increasingly popular refrain has become a central concern for politicians and regimes in the twenty-first century.[3] For without trust, institutions fail, regimes fall and societies falter.

This is the backdrop for an emerging new paradigm in revolution. It is driven in part by communication. Advances in technology have played an important role in twenty-first-century revolution – with instant connectivity (collapsing time and space), many-to-many messaging, and the ability to combine multimedia channels while simultaneously managing vast amounts of data and reducing costs. Traditional and digital media now grow and inform each other. The result has been an explosion in networks of trusts, the conclusion of which we have yet to see. Messages and images move virally and at an exponential rate along these networks[4]; unconstrained within the digital world, they mirror and distort, support and challenge, shape and disrupt both the political mediascape and social attitudes. Underpinning all of this is a critical component: trust.

Research focus, significance, and originality

The present work traces and explores the interplay between trust and revolution. It aims to chart the changing nature and forms of trust against a parallel development in revolution. The underlying questions are: how do we comprehend a particular concept or idea, how was this understanding achieved and how has this influenced our awareness today?

Arguing that trust is a powerful lens through which to interpret revolution, the principal objective of this book is to trace the relationships and networks of trust in Western European revolutionary situations across the *longue durée*, from the Ancient Greeks to the French Revolution and beyond. The theoretically informed historical account draws on contemporaneous discussions and practices of trust and revolution. The initial chapters serve to highlight changes and contextualize trust in contemporary revolutionary situations. This evaluates the ways in which the two concepts have shaped the diverging trajectories of contemporary uprisings.

Few doubt the importance of trust; few doubt the significance of revolution. Although literature on both is widely available, they have yet to be combined in one study. No book-length historical study of the interconnection of trust and revolution exists to date. When mentioned at all, trust has been subsumed into the concepts of solidarity and collectivism; yet, at best, this deals with one facet of the interplay of trust and revolution. I have set out to contribute to the wider scholarship, by unpacking the multi-faceted meaning of revolution, and the changing nature and networks of trust embedded within Western society.

Methodological perspective, approach, and sources

This book employs historical methods. It sets out to excavate the concepts of revolution and trust across time and space, recognizing that they embody so much that they cannot be unambiguously defined.[5] By marrying the *history of ideas* with a *longue durée* approach (as opposed to traditional, event-focused history found in much of the existing literature on revolution), the role of human agency is maintained. Furthermore, the concept of revolution lends itself to a focus on discontinuity; an objective of the book, informed by the *longue durée*, is to rehabilitate continuity so that it might apply to revolution as clearly as it does to trust.

In combining these approaches, each of the chapters dealing with historical and contemporary events notes the analytical importance of a specific revolutionary conjuncture. From these, longer-term historical trends and tendencies can be sourced, which lay the foundations and parameters for subsequent developments. We must nonetheless recognize contingencies of social agency, through relationships of trust. Although not uncontroversial, such an approach is made possible by the theoretical and methodological bridges built between the history of ideas and the *longue durée*, which McMahon labelled: 'The Return of the History of Ideas?'[6] Revolution is a prime candidate for such an approach, whereas a history of trust has yet to be written.

No study is without limits: it is beyond the scope and ambition of this book to provide a comprehensive and continuous history of trust and revolution. At most, the following discussion tours a familiar archipelago, comprising acknowledged inflections in both concepts. Using trust to focus on these perceived periods of change provides an alternative perspective on continuity and discontinuity. Drawing on primary sources, each chapter faces its own shortcomings: from the limitations of the literature available to the disjunction between the period and a teleological eye. It repeatedly raises questions of: who authored the source material – elites, historians, theorists, or practitioners, and what were their intentions? All the time, we must minimize the risk of universalizing Western history as seen through Western eyes.

The remainder of this chapter justifies the approach taken with reference to the relevant literature outlined in the methodological sections.

La longue durée

I have set out to explore the concepts of revolution and trust across 2,500 years: from the Ancient Greeks and Romans to the contemporary revolutionary situation in Egypt. In so doing, I am using trust to analyse revolution at various periods and at different scales, a venture that differs markedly from traditional linear, cause-and-effect history. The latter is not the only way to approach such a task: in the words of Braudel, 'it is one which by itself can pose all the great problems of social structures, past and present. It is the only language binding history to the present, creating one indivisible whole.'[7] Its methodological shortcomings are addressed by drawing from, and carefully combining, the approaches of a number of theorists as outlined in the following paragraphs.

Braudel's idealized multi-layered theory of time: of the *longue durée* (long-term), the conjuncture (medium-term) and episodic history (short-term) – or geographical, social, and individual time – emphasizes the primacy of longer-term, structural trends over momentary events and contingencies in a rather determinist fashion.[8] However, 'its preoccupation with the structural scaffolding of history means that the role of individual events and human agency tends to assume an epiphenomenal one, consigned to the marginalia of history'. Individuals in the *longue durée* are merely the 'foam cresting on the waves of history'[9] – a point acknowledged by Braudel.[10] Having fallen out of fashion, a return to the *longue durée* necessitates revision, especially in its conception of the structure–culture relationship.

Another issue arises when an historiographical approach is applied to concepts: is it justified to speak of the *longue durée* of a concept if its meaning has changed significantly? What does continuity of a concept require?[11]

Furthermore, by referencing Koselleck, 'who has fathomed the *longue durée* problem for conceptual history', revised forms of duration can be understood and applied.[12] Just as Braudel sought interdisciplinary collaboration, Koselleck combined history and sociology as a way of going beyond mere historicism but, while his account tended towards the *longue durée*, he disputed the achievability of *histoire totale* and instead offered that history is represented through language. He distinguished between two different 'layers of time' (*Zeitschichten*), the 'natural conditions that allow our specific anthropological experiences of time', and 'structures of repetition' that 'individuals consciously adopt, ritualise, culturally enrich and level to a degree of consistency that helps to stabilise a society'.[13] In so doing he frees the *longue durée* from the confines of Braudel's naturalistic and structuralist method.

Repeated human activity and practices are underlined throughout this book. With it, 'different patterns of repetition are conceivable [as] certain phenomena may exist continuously or be interspersed by breaks, repetition may be desired, forced by external constraints or simply exist as a result of inertia'.[14] This approach can accommodate highly individualized situations: while composed of different layers of time, each moment may be interpreted as an instance of a broader trend – such continuity, based on repetition, allows for variation and gradual change.

History of ideas

The history of ideas is a contentious and fiercely debated area of historical enquiry. A key task is to identify its terrain and the methodology used to navigate it, as practitioners use a variety of labels, often interchangeably, such that definitions are hard to come by and consensus easy to conjure.[15] Despite these differences, there remain two common threads.

First, concepts shape and are shaped by the world around them. Often value-laden, they are used as tools or weapons in the argument. As Syrjämäki argues, 'this theoretical insight leads to explanations of conceptual change and its relationship to social changes; dissolving the sharp distinction between theory and practice to study conceptual history is to study a form of cultural, political and social change'.[16] Second, the meaning of a concept must always depend upon the specific historical context.[17] This raises the question: how are we to study concepts in order to understand them? There is no Archimedean point from which to grasp an objective meaning; they only ever have a contextualized meaning that depends on how the concept is applied, by whom and with what result.

The approach taken here is to draw from primary sources to trace the use of, and interaction between, the concepts of revolution and trust, spanning a variety of periods throughout European history.[18] It reunites the *longue durée* (once unreceptive to the questions of meaning and intention) with the history of ideas and in so doing reintroduces the role of human agency (which had been side-lined) back into the mix.[19] This is a fruitful reconciliation, which has reinvigorated both schools of thought. By drawing carefully from Koselleck, Skinner, Neustadt and May, respectively, this research is able to overcome many of the criticisms directed at Lovejoy's traditional history of ideas.[20] By using a time-bound methodology, and connecting separate contexts while maintaining the 'synchronic specificity' of those contexts,[21] it avoids the dangers of reification and the denial of agency inherent in Lovejoy's abstract, atemporal theory.[22] Moreover, it counters the criticism levelled at the traditional history of ideas by emphasizing the mechanisms connecting these moments rather than assuming that ideas travel materially and institutionally across time.

In Bevir's words, the approach suggested here defends 'against both reductionists who dismissed ideas as mere epiphenomena [by-products] and canonical theorists who approached texts as timeless philosophical works'.[23] However, these theorists are not without their critics. Skinner is criticized for his restrictive approach to ideas through verbal language, since ideas can also emerge in non-linguistic media or genres.[24] To avoid similar criticism, a combination of language and daily practice is interwoven through each chapter and further supported by references to evolution in the arts. This book follows the approach of intellectual history, placing the concepts of revolution and trust in a broader context.[25]

Together, these theorists provide the theoretical and methodological framework that underpins this book. Recognizing that history is constrained by primary sources, the book acknowledges that even the best sources are typically representative of elites. Nonetheless, these historical and philosophical texts were not written in isolation but by historians, commentators, philosophers, and theorists who took an active role in the political and social debates of the day. By overlaying the discourses from these texts with the daily practices, rituals, and norms of the day, this book seeks to paint a rounded picture. By employing a contextualized approach, it attenuates criticism of conventional methods which can distort the meaning of texts and ideas with hindsight and present-day insights.[26]

The journey

Even with the growing interest in the concept of trust found within the social sciences and, indeed, the recent resurgence in the study of revolution, the former concept has yet to receive the attention it deserves. The rationale of this book is that trust, in its multiple forms, provides a lens through which to analyse and understand revolution. Trust has been overlooked to date, with power the traditional focus of study. In isolation, however, power represents just one dimension in the interplay of factors influencing individual choice; trust offers another. These concepts not only co-exist but are socially conferred and constrained.

Older, rudimentary views of trust and distrust assume they are separate and opposite and, consequently, would be understood as bipolar constructs in a revolutionary situation (as illustrated in **Figure 1**).[27] However, the lack of trust is not the same as distrust. The relationship between trust and revolution is even more complicated.

What seems like a simple concept becomes rather less so after a literature review.[28] Trust, while conveying so much, sits at the crossroads. It is 'a term with many meanings' which incorporates cognitive, affective, and behavioural components to varying degrees.[29] 'Not a singular or simple concept',[30] the notion of various types of trust is widely accepted. Yet, to date, fewer researchers have developed typologies of trust.[31] Of those who have, the majority are informed by a single discipline.[32] By contrast, this author supports a cross-disciplinary approach. Perhaps more importantly, there is no history of trust.

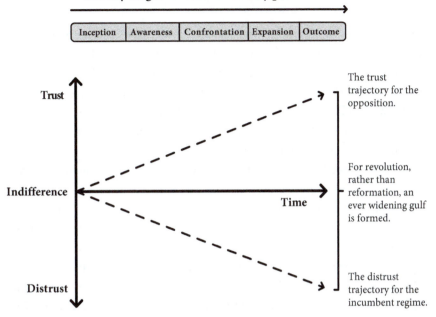

The key stages of a revolutionary process

| Inception | Awareness | Confrontation | Expansion | Outcome |

Trust

The trust trajectory for the opposition.

Indifference

Time

For revolution, rather than reformation, an ever widening gulf is formed.

Distrust

The distrust trajectory for the incumbent regime.

Figure 1 A rudimentary imagined trajectory of trust and distrust in revolution.

'Developing an integrated model of trust is particularly difficult, given the vagueness and idiosyncrasies in defining trust across multiple disciplines and orientations'.[33] However, it is necessary to capture the nuances of trust/distrust that are played out simultaneously between parties in the never-ending human drama. Concentrating on studies of trust in psychology, sociology, and philosophy, the typology used in this book draws on, and adds to, the interdisciplinary work of McKnight and Chervany in seeking to categorize different types of trust; it does so by capturing its disposition, intentions, perceptions, and behaviours.[34]

It quickly became apparent that using a contemporary typology of trust for an historical study was inappropriate. It compared modern apples with historic pears. Trust, as with revolution, is dynamic and ever-changing; the very notion adapts to the needs of individuals and their society. Despite the lack of a history of trust on which to draw, I have outlined the evolution of trust and the emergence of different types in revolutionary situations. This study covers how different types of trust are created, maintained and sustained. It further adds depth and understanding to the feedback mechanism inherent within trust – and may replace the more simplistic, one-directional models used in much research to date.[35]

Situating trust and revolution within society

The social world is unlike the natural world, in that it cannot be determined with mathematical precision. A collage rather than a system, it is a jumble arising from the thoughts, emotions, interactions, and activities of individual actors. Society is representative of the social world. It is crafted from a pattern that gives it form and structure, limiting and delimiting 'acceptable' thought and behaviour.[36] It is not a closed system but is reflective and responsive, changeable, and adaptive; it encapsulates both agency and structure.

A metaphor worth considering for the reaction, maintenance and reordering of society is that of a continuous woven tapestry.[37]

The interweaving of many different threads, representing each and every actor, adds richness, colour, texture, and decoration. As many manuals on knitting techniques describe, different types of threads and needles achieve a plethora of knitted or interwoven materials, each giving the final piece a different weight and integrity. Other factors that affect the end result include the needle's shape, thickness and malleability – as well as the thread's fibre type, texture, and twist. These represent social structures, traditions, norms, and habits. Each stitch is representative of an action, interaction, or experience that gradually builds into something larger, constantly evolving, which is never finished. The continuity of the threads suggests how these details become part of a seamless whole and the overall shape evolves throughout the process, as new threads and/or pieces are continually being woven into the design. It can sometimes look like the reverse-side of a tapestry, being nothing more than a jumble of tangled, frayed, and knotted threads, seemingly random yet a pattern ultimately emerges. As with society itself, not only is there the opportunity to repair and replace older, tattered pieces of the weave, through a symbiotic relationship between materials, processes and ideas but also a weave can be completely unravelled, the threads recycled and the process begun again anew. In such a situation, the threads carry with them a *memory* built up over a lifetime of repeated action, interaction, and experience and, in a subtle and nuanced way, they shape and influence the new design. With little discernible visual impact, the *memory* of recycled yarns can be felt.

With a 'deliciously rich history of political subversion', the association of knitting and revolution is nothing new[38]: the *tricoteuse* in *A Tale of Two Cities* can attest to this.[39] She not only knits her vengeance into her pieces but also, for good measure, sews into her work the names of the victims of Madame la Guillotine.

By looking through the lens of trust, the spatial and temporal depth of the relationships that connect us to people, communities, society, actions, and places becomes apparent alongside our understanding of revolution. Accumulating in uneven ways, this web of trust becomes a tightly woven skein. It is not merely information learned, but an acknowledgement of prior relationships, tied to experience, emotion, past, place and sociability.

The next two chapters provide both an overview and a review of the existing literature on revolution and trust, respectively. This contextualizes the original contribution of this study. Chapter 2 frames the discussion by presenting a concise European etymology of revolution, while Chapter 3 asks the question: What is trust? The latter, in outlining the five dimensions that are present in instances of trust, distinguishes trust from semantically similar concepts as well as notions of belief, ideology, solidarity, and social capital. By defining different forms of trust, understood to be emotional, logical, and inclusive, this chapter lays the foundation for the book. This typically overlooked, and often obscured, notion provides an alternative view on the past, identifying long-term patterns and major historical transformations.

In seeking to redress the focus on power in traditional scholarly interpretations of revolution, Chapter 4 outlines the interplay of trust and power, the traditional focus in the study of revolution. Then, by drawing on the etymology of 'revolution' set out in Chapter 2 to frame the discussion, the next four chapters (Chapters 5–8) focus on noteworthy revolutionary periods: from transformations in antiquity in Chapter 5, medieval Europe's rebellious nature in Chapter 6, revolutionary Renaissance Man and the Reformations in Chapter 7, to seventeenth-century convulsions and eighteenth-century rupture in Chapter 8. Rather than blindly embracing the terminology used to describe and define events, each chapter simultaneously questions and challenges their contemporaneous meanings, demonstrating the changing meaning and day-to-day practice of trust, as well as the evolving understanding of revolution. These chapters are based on primary and secondary English-language sources, in addition to translations of relevant documents in ancient and other European languages. By setting these discussions in context, each chapter highlights the interplay of trust and revolution.

Chapter 9 highlights the emerging themes before linking the notion of 'modern' revolution, which first emerged with the French Revolution, to contemporary revolution. Chapter 10 focuses on the twenty-first century; it highlights the most recent shift in revolution and reveals the changing role of trust. It argues that trust is a powerful tool with which to interpret revolution, since it is the changing nature of trust that defines revolutionary change. Unifying historical frameworks of trust once maintained traditions, thereby limiting the outcome of revolution and visions for the future; today, by contrast, increasingly fragmented and individualized networks of trust allow one to envision multiple outcomes. It is the interplay of these different forms that further explains the divergence of revolution in the twenty-first century.

In addition to summarizing the book, Chapter 11 draws some overall conclusions.

2

What is revolution?

The concept of revolution

Until the emergence, between 800 and 500 BCE, of the Greek city-states,[1] revolution was indistinguishable from revolt or rebellion. While there were many documented uprisings and rebellions, the idea of statehood did not exist, thus the concept of a revolution, as an action to challenge the State, could not exist, for 'men cannot do what they have no means of saying they have done'.[2] The term 'revolution' is found in every major language with a diverse legacy that incorporates a wide variety of cultural settings and experiences;[3] what they all share is the idea of marked change. Over time it has become a general term deployed in many areas and across many fields, from the political, historical and social to the industrial, technological and economic. It is theory and practice, ideal and material, fiction and fact. Revolution sits at the pinnacle of other forms of collective engagement within the field of contentious politics. It has, from time to time, been imbued with a significance which distinguishes such action against wider notions that could be mistaken as similar to it: revolt, rebellion, uprising, coup, independence, war, contest, solidarity, movement, partnership, participation or protest.

For the concept of revolution to be meaningful, rather than merely a hyperbolic trope, it must mirror the society of the day, reflecting and responding to its structures and institutions, while demanding changes to, or within, a regime together with the rules, norms and habits within the population at large. Consequently, when looking back at historical revolutions, they should not be seen by contemporary commentators to carry today's meaning; that should in no way undermine their impact or significance but should recognize that social concepts such as 'the State' and 'revolution' are not static but constantly evolving. 'Revolution' as a concept has been 'deeply revolutionized' and radicalized over time.[4]

Radicalizing revolution: A concise European etymology of revolution

Though the early Greek writers such as Herodotus, Thucydides, Plato, and Polybius recognized the concept of revolution, they had no single word for it.[5] Instead they spoke of uprisings (*ἐπανάστασίς*),[6] changes of constitution (*μετα-βολή πολίτείας*)[7] and transforming the State (*νεωτερίςειν την πολιτείαν*),[8] often driven by the actions of an emotionally charged unruly mob that quickly escalated, radicalizing in intent and increasingly brutalizing in deed.[9] It was not until Aristotle's *Politics* that a more delineated and methodical approach was taken, providing a definition and systematic explanation for the causes of revolution. For him, revolution (*μεταβολή*) is political in nature, with all revolutions,[10] whether originating from democracies, oligarchies, aristocracies, kingships, or tyrannies, being the result of inequality through the separation of political and economic power.[11] Representing an interruption, it is one method available to rebalance and regain the equilibrium of power. Revolutions, therefore, had identifiable causation – described and understood in terms of before and after. He describes two types: (1) a complete change from one constitution to another and (2) a modification of an existing constitution.[12] Examples include the 508/7 BCE Athenian Revolution which established democracy in Athens and the events of 411 BCE, where, during the Peloponnesian War, the Athenian democratic government was briefly overthrown and replaced with an oligarchy, known as the Four Hundred.[13]

This period witnessed the development and expansion of states. Kinship and tribal loyalties were exchanged for the bond of citizenship that created a direct relationship between citizen and State.[14] While commonalities existed, the privileges of citizenship differed across the city-states[15]; nonetheless, all were relatively narrowly distributed, ensuring mutual understanding and trust.[16] Universal laws were established by citizen assemblies and interpreted by citizens' courts; citizens participated (in varying degrees) in all areas of civic life from voting to active service in government, and they fought together in citizen militia to defend their city-state. This was an age when 'science detached itself from myth and philosophy from religion', requiring a form of trust in abstract systems including democracy, money, and rhetoric. [17] Against this backdrop, the revolution was understood to be a natural, cyclical, though not an inevitable process, since with equality, justice and good governance, such events could be avoided.[18] However, the term itself continued to be used interchangeably with a broad spectrum of other terms, denoting political unrest.

In medieval times in the West, an age defined by hierarchical social structures, where the Church and Christianity played a central role in everyday life,[19] together with the doctrine of the divine right of kings,[20] the term 'revolution' had fallen into disuse.[21] Loyalty between vassal and lord became the dominant social bond, created with oaths and reinforced by ceremony.[22] By accepting risk, a lord offered protection in return for reliable and steadfast servitude. Meanwhile, trust was placed in the affluence of banks,[23] the influence and power of religion, and the might of armies. These notions coalesced with the resulting effect that political unrest was often regarded by elites as a social device for relieving societal pressures.[24] It was an attempt to improve conditions rather than change the political and social order, directed at corrupt advisers, '*evyll* governing' and 'traitors'.[25]

Rebels were portrayed as disobedient and illegitimate, and therefore their actions were referred to as a revolt, or rebellion, rather than a revolution against a divinely appointed monarch. So while the Peasants' Revolt (1381) in England called for the removal of the King's senior officials and the law courts,[26] across Europe other events sought to limit the role of the sovereign.[27] The leaders of the 1381 rebels were either killed summarily or executed subsequently for treason,[28] a crime which conformed to the Ancient Greek definition of revolution,[29] though no references were made to 'revolution' by contemporary chroniclers.[30]

This was not the first attempt to limit the powers of the monarch but drew on a tradition that was formalized with the sealing of the Magna Carta by King John in 1215. While in practice the charter did little to limit monarchical power in England until the English Civil War, it was a symbol encouraging movements for constitutional government in Britain and around the world. Although a revolutionary response, it was not revolutionary in effect or intent.[31] However, it did become a beacon, four and five centuries later, for the notion of liberty and revolution in Britain, America and France. Later it would be referred to, by Lord Denning, as 'the greatest constitutional document of all time – the foundation of the freedom of the individual against the arbitrary authority of the despot'.[32] This document marked a move away from bonds of loyalty by developing the notion of a contract between two parties. It posited that the liberty, security and freedom of individuals were inviolable.[33]

In the sixteenth century, or late Renaissance period, a new European concept of revolution emerged and became established.[34] It was first applied in the natural sciences, only drifting later into political use. This period of 'rebirth' combined the knowledge, derived from rediscovered ancient texts, with new ideas and New World discoveries. It coincided with a 'scientific revolution' – the focus of which became inventive experimentation, observation, measurement and critical reasoning.[35] This produced coherent empirical evidence to support the scientific advancements of the age.[36] Trust in the sciences was for the first time, in many cases, underpinned by rational and critical scientific methodology. Concurrently, the widespread use of the printing press in Europe most importantly allowed for the rapid dissemination of new ideas far and wide.[37]

Derived from the Latin *revolver* (to revolve), Copernicus used the term scientifically in his 1543 treatise on the movement of the planets around the sun, *De revolutionibus orbium coelestium*. His theory presented a paradigm shift moving from the Ptolemaic model to a heliocentric one. Originally employed in the context of astronomical observations, 'revolution' was used to denote a continuous circularity of action: events are not only regularly repeated but also outside man's control; thus 'these marvels (like all marvels) are mere repetitions of the ages ... verily there is nothing new under the sun'.[38] Shakespeare even used the term to denote the law of nature, the law of cyclical change,[39] when he wrote, 'whether we are mended, or whe'er better they, or whether revolution be the same'.[40]

Nonetheless, 'revolution' is more often used by those who witnessed the violent challenges and seizure of power first-hand.[41] For example, Villani applied the term to the events in Siena in 1355, when its oligarchs were overthrown by popular action[42]; Nardi used the term to describe the events of 1494 and 1512, when the Medici were deposed in Florence,[43] and Varchi referred to the *Tumulto di Venerdi* of 26 April 1527, which was a violent precursor to the revolution a few weeks later.[44] In these examples the term was used as a metaphor; it applied to a repeating pattern of dynastic change subject to the 'wheels of fortune'. Revolution in such scenarios was conservative and limited both in effect and intent.[45] It did not seek to bring about dramatic social or political change but a return to the previous legitimate and more inclusive system of governance. Yet despite such examples, the uncommonness of the term is emphasized by its near absence in Machiavelli's *The Prince* (1513) which is seen as an important and essential practical guide to the exercise of raw political power.[46]

By the early 1600s a political meaning was seeping into the usage of the term, although it did not erase its scientific use in the wider discourse of the day.[47] It was not only used to describe the complete overthrow of government but was also employed as an alternative to the terms 'revolt' and 'rebellion' which carried with them the notions of disobedience and illegitimacy.[48] This change in meaning was a reflection of the changing notion of the State, in part a result of the Peace of Westphalia in 1648.[49] The abstract concept of the 'State', which we currently recognize, began life in the seventeenth century with the publication of Hobbes's *Leviathan* in 1651.[50] Building his ideas of the State on a scientific foundation, his treatise posited that the State was a separate entity from the powers of its ruler. For him, an individual owed a duty and allegiance to the State itself; it was the highest authority, singular and absolute.[51] Where previously the ruler and State had been synonymous, they were now increasingly separated.[52] The 'right to rebel' against an 'unjust' ruler was appropriate,[53] even called for, in protection of the State and its peoples for 'the obligation of subjects to the sovereign is understood to last as long, and no longer, than the power *lasteth* by which he is able to protect them'.[54] Although Locke also argues, in the *Two Treatises of Government*, for the right to rebel, his views differ noticeably from Hobbes.[55] Locke states that 'men' are by nature free and equal with various natural rights (life, liberty and property) and obligations (to pay taxes, to follow the law). While governments exist by the consent of the people to protect these rights, governments that fail to do so can be resisted and replaced with new governments.[56] Locke, however, rarely used the term 'revolution', preferring to use 'resistance' – a rebellion by the people against executive power. Kiefer goes a step further when he opines, in *Ethics and Social Justice*, 'it seems to me that the *duty* to rebel is much more understandable than that *right* to rebel, because the right to rebellion ruins the order of power, whereas the duty to rebel goes beyond and breaks it'.[57] The result, an enforced regime change, could be legitimate.

Consequently, both the Restoration of Charles II in 1660 and the Glorious Revolution in 1688 were described, although contested by commentators and historians, as revolutions.[58] By linking such events to nation states, the wider understanding of revolution was subtly to change. They were both seen as conservative, political in nature, a return to the past (a reversion or reversal of fortune) to paraphrase Copernicus, a scientific certainty to their outcome, a revolution.[59] Described by the Earl of Clarendon, as 'full compassing' they restored Englishmen's ancient rights and the kingship to its legitimate heirs.[60] They are seen as the first national revolutions in Europe. However, the events of 1648–9 (the introduction of a parliamentary government and the execution of Charles I) were described by Englishmen as 'the late troubled times', 'the troubles', 'distractions', 'unnatural, cruel and bloody wars', and more commonly referred to as 'the Great Rebellion', not a revolution.[61]

It was not until the French Revolution, 'when men's actions and ideals were aligned', that the first truly 'modern' revolution was experienced.[62] The people claimed the term 'revolution' to describe their seizure of power and their right to their mode of government. Until 1789 there were no words to describe such a transformation.[63] Where previously the two uses (scientific and political) of the term 'revolution' existed side by side, now 'an almost metaphysical category' was created, 'an invented social concept that bore little resemblance to actual experience'.[64] The very notion of revolution changed, born out of new horizons of expectation. It came to be seen as a permanent, violent rupture, a break with the past from which there was no going back. It no longer represented a rebalancing. Revolution came to signify more than simply political or constitutional change, requiring mass participation to gain control of the State. It became inevitable, man-made, rather than brought about by the cruel whims of fate, driving forwards towards a utopian future, both a political and social statement of intent, aspiring to nothing less than the creation of a new social order: the term was radicalized, becoming synonymous with the violent overthrow of monarchical government and purposive social change.[65] This action came to embody the idea of revolution, irrespective of ultimate successes and failures, simultaneously defining it politically and socially while mythologizing it in both the arts and in literature.

Following the French Revolution, the very notion of revolution is seen as a way to accelerate time – a meta-historical concept. Revolution became a political event on the horizon which promised a decisive change in conditions and to the social order. This was radical revolution – a 'new daring intellectual idea: a late Enlightenment paradox'.[66] Within the revolutionary consciousness it was seen as a means of realizing the utopian vision of the future more rapidly.[67] The revolutionaries, with their differing visions of the future – including the constitutional monarchists such as La Fayette, the democratic republicans allied to Thomas Paine, and the authoritarian populists, such as Robespierre – saw their actions as necessary for the betterment and liberation of all mankind. They were not limited by borders or the confines of the State. Thus, the French Revolution was as much defined by the separation and conflict between the various revolutionary groups as it was about overturning a remote and outdated system of monarchical government.

Its impact was long felt across Europe and America. With the violence it incited and the radical social changes it brought about, welcomed and abhorred in equal measure, the use of the term 'revolution' greatly increased. Controversial, stirring widespread philosophical debate, the opposing views of the day are summarized in the legendary exchanges between Edmund Burke and Paine.[68] It reignited the fear of crowds.[69] These rioting and 'unruly mobs' have been depicted throughout history as terrifying, destructive and deadly.[70] Often depicted, in art and literature, as spontaneous, emotionally charged, they act with universality of purpose, lacking any responsibility, in response to a perceived grievance or incident. Consider Shakespeare's portrayal of the mob in *Julius Caesar*; using the immortal words, 'Friends, Romans, countrymen, lend me your ears', Mark Antony turns the citizens of Rome against the initially feted perpetrators of Caesar's assassination by stirring up emotions of remorse and pride.[71] The crowd, now an enraged mob, pursues the conspirators who flee in fear.[72] Although a constant feature throughout history, following the French Revolution, mobs were becoming inseparably linked to class conflict.[73]

By the late eighteenth century, the pace of economic change and scientific innovation had exploded, and the concept of revolution widened still further. It was the age of iron, steam, and money; the first 'industrial revolution' had arrived.[74] Although few would dispute that Britain experienced the first 'industrial revolution', the term was first coined in France. The *révolution industrielle*, an economic counterpart to the political *révolution française* some years earlier, produced social changes every bit as far reaching.[75] This quickly merged into the 'technological revolution' (or second industrial revolution) around 1850 with the advent of steel, electricity and mass production. The term 'revolution' was used to describe the radical discontinuity marked by a shift in power: from manual labour to machines. The rapid innovations and advancements in the science and technology of the age had a profound effect on the socio-economics and cultural conditions, impacting every facet of daily life. The exact date of the 'industrial revolution', its effects and speed of change are contested, being the subject of debate amongst twentieth and twenty-first-century historians.[76] However, economic historians are in agreement on the importance of the process in the history of humanity.[77]

Arising out of the Industrial Age and in tandem with the birth of sociology and political economy emerged the professional revolutionary. These intellectuals and radicals devoted themselves to the study, design, and instigation of revolution as a means of responding to the social changes, inequalities and deprivation brought about by industrialization. This was a period of convergence of social ideals, rapidly changing economic conditions and technological advancements. It was also the age of sociopolitical theorists, of revolutionary thinkers such as Marx and Darwin and of idealistic men willing to make it not only their lives' work but also the next generations' inheritance to realize their alternative vision for society's future.[78] Using reason and science to gain knowledge and understanding, they did not draw from the past, or blindly from religion, but with a notion of modernity, provided a moral critique of society and the social relationship of production. This was vital to Marx's theory of history, for those relationships of production gave society its fundamental character, whether it was capitalist in nature or something else.[79] A wide spectrum of theorists fomented, presented and debated new and varied notions about how mankind could, and should, live together.[80] These spanned the more accepted and reforming social liberals to the more radical Marxists and anarchists who sought the irreversible transformation of society.[81] Revolution evolved; it was no longer a historical event but came to be understood as an ongoing and permanent process: no longer eruptive, but man-made, if conditions were right. Throughout this process the old order would be discredited, and the new was made legitimate by mass support and involvement. Such actions, it was thought, could ultimately bring about the demise of the State itself; for as society matures, it repeatedly has to break the overbearing constraints that impede its development.[82] Central to the notion of permanent revolution was a change in temporality away from a reimagining of historic political idylls,[83] to conceiving of one's own time as being politically, socially and technically distinct.[84] In this period of revolutionary politics, individuals thought of themselves, and of their position in the State, as revolutionary. Revolution now required a new vision of society rather than simply 'uproot[ing] parts of the culture of society to lay new foundations and establish new values'.[85] The revolutionaries' aim was to overturn the world; their method was violent revolution and their target audience was the working class.[86]

We are left with three distinct conceptions of revolution as 'a political phenomenon … an abrupt social change … and as change in the entire social order',[87] ranging from a simple yet narrowly defined change in the location of sovereignty, or power, heralded by Bodin, to a broader definition which includes other forms of social upheaval (religious, economic, industrial, and political).[88] First, revolutions, as described by Le Bon, are 'all sudden transformations, or transformations apparently sudden, whether of belief, ideas or doctrine' which are driven by moments of madness and crowd action.[89] Second, for Ellwood, revolution is abrupt, violent, social change.[90] He posits that political revolution represents just one form of revolution, possibly the most visual and visceral, yet he considers it might lack the long-term impact of social and/or scientific revolution, which changes both an individual's way of life together with society in its rules, norms and outlook. The third and most inclusive conception of revolution, defined by only a minority of writers, involves change at the most basic and underlying social structural level, which in turn impacts upon all aspects of social life.[91] Hyndman is the most explicit when he states 'revolution, in its complete sense, means a thorough economic, social and political change in any great community', and therefore all aspects of social existence must change for revolution to be complete.[92]

The theories and method of revolution were rigorously united in the twentieth century, which witnessed the 'classic' Russian and Chinese Revolutions amongst others.[93] Once again, the concept of revolution changed and fragmented; it became understood as a way of making a new (utopian) society and of forging an instrument to achieve power. Revolution was the 'sticky business' of one class violently overturning another to make a new society.[94] It is a necessary struggle through which people were transformed and became 'fitted to found society anew'.[95] 'Professional revolutionaries', such as Lenin and Mao, developed their techniques and tactics into a science for revolutionary success.[96] Through their writings, and by example, they provided 'blueprints' for victory which were exported around the globe.[97] Arguably 'as influential as he was in life' as a leader, 'Lenin may have been more so in death' as 'the teacher of the peoples of the whole world', inspiring Castro, Mao and Ho Chi Minh's successful revolutions, 'as well as countless other revolutionaries in countries full of oppressed and powerless people'.[98] Even now 'in China, Mao is widely viewed as filling the roles of both Lenin – generator and theorist of the revolution – and Stalin – the harsh but effective implementer of the socialist revolution', his revolutionary tactics continuing to be used today.[99]

However, it was not until the second half of the twentieth century that academic research into, and the study of, revolution increased exponentially, producing a constellation of definitions and theories. This was, in part, a response to the sheer number and increasing frequency of revolutions. Although revolution was widely understood to take place within the boundaries of a state (a discrete national political entity), its influence in shaping, and being shaped by, the international system was profound. International factors (such as trade, migration, resources), and the influence that can be brought to bear on the global system of states, are now increasingly acknowledged in promoting revolution. Revolutions, almost without exception, promote the transformation of other states; this is the result of ideological belief, and self-preservation through homogeneity, or simply by example.[100] This recognition further changed the interpretation of the concept of revolution. From 1789 onwards, the relationship between states and revolution became a definitional focus; revolutions were seen as a way to rapidly and permanently transform existing states into something better, while the revolutionaries themselves often aspired to transformation at a global level.[101] Revolutions, always the focus of political conflict, now increasingly came to be seen as the battleground of two oppositional ideologies, involving the wider international community.[102] The result was that 'much of the drama of world politics between 1945 and 1989 was played out through the processes of revolution and counter-revolution'[103] at the edges of a bipolar world which pitted East against West, communism against capitalism, an ideological and physical confrontation, the outcome of which had the potential for mutually assured destruction communicated through proxy wars and the Cold War.[104] This period produced multiple strands in our understanding of the term 'revolution'. These included the idea that revolution produced the following: paradigmatic change in knowledge and capabilities, more often seen in science and technology[105]; profound radical and widespread social transformation, such as the 1960s–80s' sexual revolution[106]; dramatic violent social and political disruption, as witnessed with the Russian Revolution; and simply the promise of something new, as was commonplace in advertising.[107] Together with written and rewritten histories,[108] the multiple definitions generated within academia have been used to demarcate the concept, influencing and colouring perceptions of revolution.[109] The term 'revolution' is seen, experienced and understood to operate on a graduated scale, from a definitive rupture to merely a hyperbolic trope.

The current prospects for dramatic, all-encompassing, social and political revolutions are limited. Capitalism has become globally dominant, and overturning a regime is very different from overturning the modes of production. However, this increasing uniformity on the political free-market landscape means that many regimes now face a growing challenge from militant religious fundamentalists, who aim to topple governments and seize political power in a religious *jihad* (a holy war).[110] Political Islamists are not new and neither is their desire to appropriate the institutions of power, either through peaceful social activism or violence.[111] However, 'in tone and syntax, this type of Islam is different from Muslim politics of the 20th century and the revolutionary Iranian variant'.[112] Creating a theocratic republic in Iran (the 1979 revolution) was not only unexpected, lacking the customary causes (defeat at war, a financial crisis, peasant rebellion or disgruntled military), surprisingly quick, relatively non-violent and hugely popular; it was unusual in terms of revolutionary theory and praxis.[113] An outcome, as one scholar described it, 'that had to be explained'.[114] It was 'in some ways quite anomalous' and 'unique'.[115]

Notwithstanding these developments, a persistent notion of revolution remains – one which recalls the Russian experience. With the collapse of the Soviet Union in 1989, the all-encompassing social and political revolution that delivered an alternative vision for society died, and with it the modern 'classic' template. Instead, the 'Autumn of Nations',[116] and the later 'Coloured Revolutions', sought to bring about popular non-violent regime change by assuming that change could be achieved through a 'reforming non-violent revolution'.[117]

Both Vaclav Havel, in Czechoslovakia, and Adam Michnik, in Poland, pursued legal and electoral options.[118] In an almost carnival atmosphere, they have been described as 'present[ing] the most sweeping demonstration[s] so far of the power of "politics" without violence'.[119] Such examples produce so-called 'corrective', 'conservative', 'negotiated' revolutions or 'transitional' democratic reforms, stretching and conflating the concepts.[120] However, this underplays the history of thought, deed and sacrifice it took to reach these points. In the discourse on revolution the *event* has once again become the focus whereas in reality it is the *processes* that happen afterwards that are the revolution. In focusing on the replacement of despotic political regimes as the revolutionary event, the extant systems of governance have been left intact. For systemic change they need to be dismantled and new ones constructed.

Similarly the recent events in the Middle East and North Africa (MENA) region, popularly referred to as the 'Arab Spring',[121] represent what, at first glance, appear to be popular spontaneous uprisings but were in fact co-ordinated and well-organized actions by large numbers of disparate groups in society working together to form cross-class alliances to bring about change.[122] Typically they were directed by underemployed or unemployed, well-educated urbanites protesting against repressive regimes and their apparatus of control.[123] These events have resulted in a variety of outcomes not envisaged in Lenin's template for revolution.[124] While the Arab Spring briefly raised hopes that the oppositional forces of autocracy and jihadi, in the region, had been overtaken and made irrelevant by reform, they were soon disappointed. With their limited, if not definitional, failures, these so-called revolutions[125] are having a profound impact on our understanding of both revolution and reformation, reopening debate around their causes, trajectory and consequences.

A counter to this view can be seen in the 'Jihadi Spring',[126] a collective term which is used in reference to the various militant Islamic groups that are fighting a, perceived, 'holy war' against non-believers. In the late twentieth century, new groups of neo-traditionalist *Salafis*[127] sought a radical break, a political, social and religious revolution.[128] Their stated aim is to create an Islamic caliphate, while their goal is for the Qur'an to dominate a new world order; in so doing Islam has been militarized and weaponized. By uniting religion and politics, any divide between the public and the private spheres is removed, while simultaneously reconfiguring the political and social order and uniting all Muslims under a conservative global theocracy.[129] Referred to collectively as a 'Jihadi movement' it is fragmented and disparate with groups operating from a local to global level.

At the pinnacle the stated aim is not only revolutionary, in both action and intent, but goes past traditional revolutionary theory, beyond the notion of 'international' communism[130] and the Iranian theocracy.[131] Ultimately it is to remove revolution from the confines of the State, which has so defined revolution, while simultaneously giving primacy to religion in this social, political phenomenon.[132] The goal is to create the worldwide *ummah* (an Islamic supranational community).[133] It is 'cherished both as memory and ideal'; it is 'seen through the prism of centuries with all the rough edges smoothed over'[134]; its reinstatement is a 'holy trust' (an obligation) for all Muslims.[135] However, while attractive to many, drawing recruits from around the world into multiple conflicts in Iraq, Syria, Kenya, Somalia, Afghanistan, Yemen, and Nigeria, they are not the popular, highly participative and democratic mass movements seeking freedom from tyranny, oppression and corruption that are widely associated with the classical model of revolution. Instead they represent new twenty-first-century forms of global religious revolution, supported by few, feared by many. To date such action has brought about mass migration, enforced conversion, extreme violence and brutality and a determined counter action (by Kurdish forces, Gulf State alliances and the West). More reminiscent of past religious wars, from the Crusades (*c.* 1095–1291, 1396–1456) to the European Wars of Religion (*c.* 1524–1648), their intent is more far-reaching; they plan to seize power, not simply at state level, but to ultimately create a new global caliphate governed by Sharia law, redrawing the political world order. This is the very definition of fundamental transformation: a revolution!

At the start of the twenty-first century the age of revolution was considered by many politicians and academics to have ended. These recent events have not only confronted but challenged that notion.[136] Although strongly contested, events in Tunisia (2011), Egypt (2011), Ukraine (2014), and Syria (ongoing) have all been referred to as revolutions and so they are subtly altering the meaning of revolution in conflicting and oppositional ways.

Understanding revolution

For some, the revolutionary dream of forcibly overthrowing the government and reordering society in favour of a new system remains an ongoing battle, while for others, revolution is an ideal: the embodiment of the spirit of resistance. Conceptually, these liminal examples of revolution sit at opposing ends of a continuum, referred to as revolution. This raises the question of whether the concept of revolution is being overstretched or whether this is simply the next stage in both its development and our understanding of the notion of revolution.[137] Is the concept so wide that it can comfortably contain both the complete transformation of State and society and reflect the partial transformation, or, as described by Aristotle, the modification of an existing regime?[138] Is it the case that the concept has represented, and will always represent, the ideal while the reality of revolutionary action, and revolutionary situations, is geographically, conditionally, politically and contextually specific? And will the search for a universal theory of revolution remain elusive as we focus on the component of revolution rather than exploring the underlying processes influencing the interactions and interconnections within the revolutionary theatre?

A kaleidoscope of factors, conditions and characteristics is used to define and explain revolution and yet the concept of trust has been overlooked; viewed as a necessary ingredient rather than an explanatory element, it remains in the shadows. Often implicit, in an interconnected web of concepts that support co-operation and collaboration between individuals, it enables all forms of social and political collective action. However, while current theories of revolution have proven inadequate in explaining the evolution of the meaning of the term, the requirement for trust remains; it underpins the shared alternative vision of society necessary for creating and maintaining support in the revolutionary movement. While its role within the ideology and leadership leads to unity of action, in an age of apparent organizational fluidity, it is trust that increasingly binds people and groups together, while simultaneously, in its negative sense, weakening incumbent regimes. In this field of study, the explanatory nature of trust has, to date, been subsumed to such an extent that its effects within the process have been obscured, its role simplified rather than mapped out in detail across the multiple interactions and interconnections within the revolutionary theatre. This book explores the intersection of revolution and trust, arguing that trust is the critical determinant of the outcome of revolution.

The meaning, action and intention of revolution continue to evolve as it embodies past understanding, and the experiences of revolution, while simultaneously reflecting the contemporary society from which they emerge. Repeatedly compared, contrasted, measured and judged against those of the past, in a never-ending social and political narrative which shapes and influences individuals, institutions and the society they create, each instance and iteration impacts upon what constitutes future revolution. All the while the use of the term has increased.

As both a theory and praxis, revolution is understood and interpreted individually but it can only be created, implemented and maintained collectively within a society. It has become increasingly complex over time, as the web of interactions and network of connections within society has multiplied. Trust, in its multiple forms, is a necessary building block of society. As a result, trust, a key component in interactions, whether between individuals, organizations, institutions, systems or concepts, is increasingly relied upon. Although the process of trust is inherent in each and every action, interaction and connection, its explanatory value, when exploring revolutions and the revolutionary theatre throughout history, has been subsumed and overlooked.

What is trust in the twenty-first century?

So, what is trust?

Trust involves risk: the acceptance of vulnerability in the expectation of certain outcomes and/or behaviours in a specific situation (and time). To operationalize this working definition, we need to augment the three widely accepted *components* of trust with a further two, before outlining three *approaches* to trust in the literature: rational, trust building, and social practice. It is then helpful to distinguish trust from several *interlopers*. Together, considering the components, approaches, and interlopers enables us to identify multiple types of trust and more easily to navigate its terrain.

A starting point

The concept of 'trust', along with 'truth', an etymological cousin, remains one of the most elusive and complex concepts in the English language, despite (or in part a result of) the substantial and multidisciplinary corpus of literature and research.[1] This includes sociology, economics, philosophy, history, anthropology, evolutionary biology, social psychology, and psychology.[2] In psychological terms, trust is an internal experience drawing on an individual's willingness to accept a degree of vulnerability and his or her appetite for risk.[3] The history of its scholarship is rooted in philosophy and ethics, in debates over its strategic or knowledge-based and moral value.[4] Elaborated upon by sociologists such as Luhmann and Barber, trust is presented 'as an irreducible and multidimensional social reality', inherent, functional and fluid in each and every one of our social interactions.[5]

The following definitions represent a small sample of the many versions of trust to be found in the literature, emphasizing that there is no one definition of trust.[6] With multiple definitions it is understood, theorized, and measured in many different ways 'with remarkably little effort [made] to integrate these different perspectives or articulate the key role that trust plays in critical social processes'.[7]

A noun and a verb, 'trust is itself a term for a clustering of perceptions'.[8] Definitions range from a personality trait to a structural phenomenon.[9]

Commonalities can be identified across the wide-ranging definitions in use, from their foundations (disposition, morals, and need), the terms used (for example: expectations, exchange, interaction, and vulnerability) and the necessary attributes required (such as competence, goodwill, benevolence, predictability, honesty, and reliability) which in turn highlight the multiple facets of trust.[10] Definitions rely upon similar and closely associated concepts (as illustrated in **Figure 2**) which are often conflated with trust in daily

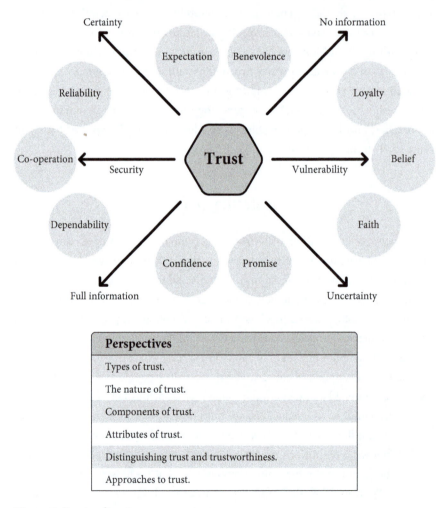

Perspectives
Types of trust.
The nature of trust.
Components of trust.
Attributes of trust.
Distinguishing trust and trustworthiness.
Approaches to trust.

Figure 2 Facets of trust.

discourse. Overlapping, these concepts can, in certain circumstances, assist in the creation, development and maintenance of trust or alternatively are the result of trust.

It is not my intention to provide an exhaustive cross-disciplinary survey of the trust literature here but rather to explore different approaches to trust, focusing on the philosophical (social), psychological and sociological. In the process the study distinguishes trust from semantically similar concepts, while simultaneously highlighting the great many types of trust in use.[11] This review, therefore, necessarily depicts the thinking of those whose work has had an effect, most directly, on this book and the work presented here.

Studying trust

Irrespective of the lens through which it is studied, there are two links, or common factors, which underpin the study of trust. First, trust is discussed as part of a society and second,[12] there is wide acceptance amongst scholars that trust involves a combination of cognitive, affective, and behavioural components, as shown in **Figure 3**.[13]

'A trusts B to do X'

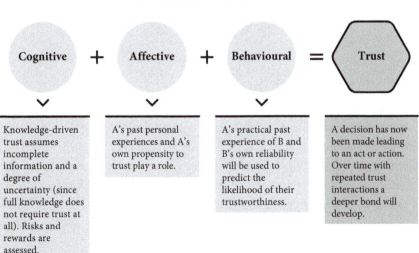

Cognitive +	Affective +	Behavioural =	Trust
Knowledge-driven trust assumes incomplete information and a degree of uncertainty (since full knowledge does not require trust at all). Risks and rewards are assessed.	A's past personal experiences and A's own propensity to trust play a role.	A's practical past experience of B and B's own reliability will be used to predict the likelihood of their trustworthiness.	A decision has now been made leading to an act or action. Over time with repeated trust interactions a deeper bond will develop.

Figure 3 What is trust? (Part 1).

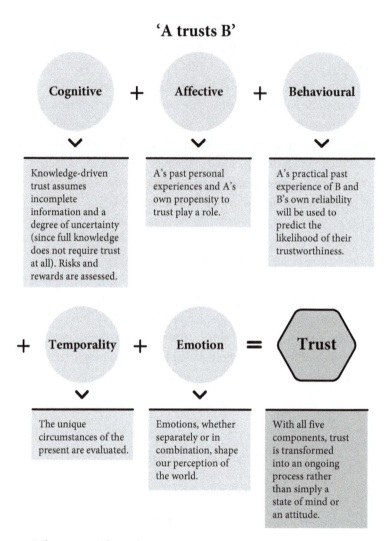

Figure 4 What is trust? (Part 2).

Figure 4 depicts the three commonly recognized dimensions of trust and provides a starting point for further discussion. Although all three dimensions are present in instances of trust, the qualitative and quantitative mix changes to reflect the specific situation and the individuals involved, all set within the wider social environs (including local, cultural, and social norms). However, it is by understanding both the temporal nature of trust (the combination of past experiences of the actors involved, together with the present conditions and available information/knowledge that are used to envisage the future) and the emotional component that the unique nature of trust, as a process, becomes apparent, as illustrated in **Figure 4.**

The influence of affect, feeling, and emotion on trust

These terms, although often used interchangeably, are distinct. Conceding the difference is more than pedantry, as it will enable a deeper and more nuanced insight into the process of trust.[14] To clarify, affect is pre-personal, an experience of feeling (a personal and biographical sensation) or emotion (social projection or display of feeling).[15] Affections are deep and long-lasting, providing intensity; always resulting in action, they involve the mind, will and feelings, and should not be confused or conflated with emotions which are fleeting and superficial; they often fail to produce action as they are disconnected from the mind and will.[16]

In this book, trust is therefore understood to be an emotional (exposing our vulnerabilities to others), logical (by assessing risks, rewards, and competency) and inclusive (by accounting for distrust) process. It is a deliberative action that an individual chooses to make, create, build, maintain and sustain. Once created, trust quickly slips unseen into the background; yet to endure, it requires constant attention, and, as such, it becomes a talent or skill to be learned and practised. It is fluid, changeable in both form and function, while also uniquely situational; reflecting the past, it takes place in the present, yet it is only in the future that the outcome is sometimes assessed and understood. Trust, therefore, cannot be reproduced or replicated in the same way that the moment contained within a photograph or recording can never be exactly recaptured.

Schools of thought and approaches to trust

Rational choices, and theories of exchange, have dominated the slim but growing literature on trust, while influential philosophical treatments have assumed that the actions, of both trustee and trustor, can be understood through the lens of instrumental rationality. This places a rational egotist at the heart of its construction of trust. As discussions about trust have continued to unfold in sociology, philosophy, economics, law, marketing, and other social sciences, it is unsurprising that an increasing array of competing conceptions exist, relating to the nature, function, structure, and emergence of trust.[17] I shall analyse three approaches: rationalist, emotional, and process.

Rationalist approaches

Coleman provides the most austere version of this approach, reducing the concept to simply a rational deliberation, an action. He asserts that 'the elements confronting the potential trustor are nothing more or less than the considerations a rational actor applies in deciding whether to place a bet'.[18] In trusting, therefore, the individual is exposed to risk, and within the framework of the theory of rational choice, the action of trusting becomes a simple risk-and-reward scenario for the parties involved. Yet this approach not only ignores situations where trust is latent but also ignores those where the 'ABC of psychology' is found.[19] In Coleman's search for a universal definition, trust has been reduced to a simple calculation of risk.

In contrast, Baier, in claiming 'when I trust another, I depend on her goodwill towards me', was one of the first philosophers to describe an affective (state of mind) approach to trust.[20] She is by no means alone in taking this stance.[21] This attempt at a universal definition cannot withstand the many instances where goodwill (a favourable disposition or attitude towards another person) is neither necessary nor sufficient. O'Neill demonstrated this shortcoming with the doctor–patient scenario; while one may trust a doctor personally as a friend or colleague, one trusts their medical judgement and professionalism based on their years of training, their professional qualifications, and the rules and regulations they operate under together with the checks and balances that maintain the integrity of their profession,[22] while recognizing they bear their patients no particular good- or ill will.[23] While Holton highlighted that a reliance on goodwill does not necessitate trust, a conman may actually rely on his victims' goodwill but never trusts them.[24] Consequently, stressing the general, and often optimistic, nature of trust is vulnerable to additional criticism when used to simply describe a rational calculation between two parties.[25]

Holton provides us with another equally influential approach when he regards trust as being laden with normative expectations. 'When you trust someone to do something, you rely on them to do it; and they regard that reliance in a certain way: you have a readiness to feel betrayal should it be disappointed, and gratitude should it be upheld,' but, as with the affective approach, this definition is unable to account for the wide variety of instances of trust and the different positions of the parties involved.[26] It implies an obligation which is often not present and reduces trust to a matter of reliance.

By regarding trust as a cognitive act, and as a three-part relationship: A trusts B to do X, it is, perhaps, Hardin, who presents the most consistent and systematic account of trust in his theory of encapsulated interests.[27] He clearly distinguishes between trust (a cognitive act), trustworthiness (a moral quality), and distrust (a rational strategy in appropriate circumstances). Hardin's theory is predicated on the exclusive application of rational choice theory; when 'A trusts B because A thinks it is in B's interest to take his or her own interest in the relevant matter seriously', which in turn means that B values an ongoing relationship with A.[28] Trust is, therefore, based on the calculated interests and preferences of others set in context (that is, the parties involved have a specific role to play which in turn dictates their specific preferences and particular behaviour in any given scenario). On this basis, Hardin's theory can be seen to negate the very need for trust since, with sufficient information about the interests of others, one can make an informed rational decision: there is no need for trust.

Therefore, as with other rationalist theories of trust, the 'concomitant conception of agency portrays rational mono-dimensional actors whose behaviour is calculable if sufficient knowledge about incentives, objectives and preferences are [*sic*] known'.[29] Consequently, the actors become interchangeable, provided the external factors are fixed and stable.[30] In the search for a universal definition of trust, these simplistic and reductionist approaches do little to further our understanding of trust and only highlight the paucity of a purely rationalist account, which ignores the complexity of decision-making and the interpersonal nature of trust.[31] As Mercer states, 'rationalists drain the psychology from trust by turning it into a consequence of incentives … emphasising incentives as the basis for trust eliminates both the need for trust and the opportunity to trust'.[32]

Similarly, by using rationalist theories to explain the emergence of trust either spontaneously by a *leap of faith* or over time through small incremental exchanges,[33] it is relegated to a reaction or response rather than an innate action in, and of, itself. In describing situations of 'spontaneous trust', rather than this action being a precondition to building trust, it is simply the result of trust that is already present. Trust does not emerge because of a leap of faith but reflects an existing attitude; confidence and reliability are increased over time through repeated positive interactions. While the rational approach still dominates, supported by empirical data, it is criticized for conflating co-operation and reciprocity with trust.[34] Research by Henrich does, however, highlight that the notion of trust and the levels of trust differ significantly within different societies.[35] There is a growing sentiment amongst some academics that 'trust will remain elusive if we fail to grasp its emotional basis' and a call for its inclusion in a more multidisciplinary approach to trust.[36] It is this very human factor which I argue not only distinguishes trust but holds the key to unlocking it.

Trust building

Given its value, we constantly seek to recreate or reproduce trust, to gain a competitive advantage, improve social cohesion or resolve a conflict, hence the constant need to reduce it to a conscious decision, a choice, made under identifiable circumstances, which we can replicate. By changing both the question and the methodological approach, it is the nature and emergence of trust which become the focus. An illustration of such an approach would be a trust-building model used in conflict situations.[37] For example, two countries overcome their hostilities by a combination of mutually reassuring steps and actions (exchanging prisoners, a ceasefire, demobilizing forces), together with the implementation of an agreed system of transparent checks and balances (independent monitors). These small, but often symbolic, steps are discussed and agreed upon between the parties and provided these are adhered to, over time, confidence is built.

The relationship between Brazil and Argentina over their nuclear facilities has been described by Wheeler as such an instance of successful trust building.[38] Public expression of trust regarding each other's peaceful nuclear intentions, and a co-operative agreement signed in 1980, laid the foundations, while the personal commitment of both presidents (Raul Alfonsin and Jose Sarnay), throughout the mid-1980s, led directly to transparent *confidence and security building measures* including military-to-military contact, scientific and technical exchanges, and a joint nuclear policy committee set up in 1985, resulting in reciprocal nuclear site visits in 1987.[39] In another work he also discusses India and Pakistan and their nuclear capabilities, describing the steps taken as a leap of trust and stressing how politically risky Vajpayee's (India's Prime Minister) symbolic gesture was by travelling on the inaugural Delhi to Lahore bus on 20 February 1999.[40] Through this signalling of his intent, together with the reciprocity shown by Sharif (Pakistan's leader), the two men were able to build personal chemistry and trust, enabling them to temporarily circumvent the traditional routes of interstate negotiations. Unfortunately, the effects were short-lived due to the Kargil Crisis in May 1999.[41]

However, increased transparency, incentives, and a formalized system of interactions do not constitute trust, as in such circumstances trust is neither present nor required. As Mercer pithily put it, 'if trust depends on external evidence, transparency, iteration, or incentives, then trust adds nothing to the explanation'; such arrangements, in fact, 'eliminate the need for, and the opportunity for, trust'.[42] Whereas Booth and Wheeler point out that the spontaneity or leap of faith required to start this process may be an expression of already present trust, the additional steps taken may help to maintain it.[43] However, such theories will continue to be criticized – not only for their functional nature, underpinned by a broadly rationalist approach, but also for their inability ultimately to explain how and why trust emerges. Consequently, the role of human agency becomes either a simple reflection of the risk profile of the participants or a readily available explanation when trust-building exercises fail. Trust is a performative action which emerges from interpersonal exchanges and will continue to 'escape simple attempts of rational calculation' and, therefore, 'cannot be derived from a decision-making process in which we simply judge the risks and opportunities involved', even when a token human element is added.[44]

'Interlude: Adding emotions'

Psychological profiles have been used to add emotional feelings,[45] as opposed to affective states of mind,[46] to trust; this acknowledges that individuals are unique, different in both the degree to which they trust (from naivety to paranoia) and how they view risk. Thus, while the propensity to trust and the appetite for risk are relative to both the individual and the situation in question, they are difficult to measure, offering little to aid one's understanding of trust, yet framed as one more facet underpinning an individual's actions.[47]

When asked to describe when and why we trust at the personal and interpersonal level, we usually fall back on trite remarks, such as 'because she has never let me down in the past'. At best these are approximations; at worst we are seeking to rationalize our behaviour after the event. So how can one incorporate emotions into an approach to trust? Michel has suggested a phronetic approach.[48] MacIntyre points out that the unpredictability of human beings and human life requires a focus on practical experience, while Flyvbjerg describes phronesis as an approach to knowledge that is action orientated and which looks at practical knowledge and practical ethics.[49] 'Trust then appears as a form of emotive coping that involves practical wisdom[50] on the part of the trusting agent rather than an abstractly reasoned and technically implementable decision.'[51] Such an approach bears witness to the marked difference between relying on an individual's role in expectations together with forms of supervision or control, and the softer, subtler implicit measures which surround personal and interpersonal trust.[52] There is a clear distinction between the types of trust being outlined and the quality of the trust involved; the first is functional in nature; the second is emotive and more than simply the sum and outcome of rational decision-making.[53] As Lahno has described, 'Genuine trust is an emotion and emotions are, in general, not subject to direct rational control.'[54]

The wider debate between pursuing a rational approach and an emotional one, when studying social interactions, mirrors the tension, highlighted above, and will continue to do so while we focus on the abstract nature of trust rather than focusing on the practical, coping experience which trust provides.[55] Given that the decision to trust is more often taken in an instant and unconsciously, it seems improbable that rational abstraction will provide us with any further deep insight. It is argued 'that trusting is performatively enacted rather than deliberately decided upon'.[56] From Plato's doctrine of a tripartite soul, Western thought portrays emotions as dysfunctional and irrational, something we must control.[57] However, there is an alternative viewpoint that not only suggests emotions are wise and not to be ignored, but that they are a form of rationality (not the classic notion of rationality) and are rational much of the time.[58] The debate continues, yet some of the most vocal proponents are those advocating a more integrative view by arguing that emotions are a type of perception and have a crucial role to play in rational beliefs, desires and decisions circumventing the impasse of pure reason.[59] In such a scenario the emotional component of trust comes to the fore and trust is, therefore, 'necessarily tied to a particular perception of the world, or some part of the world', influencing the way we think and act, and, therefore, 'cannot be understood as the immediate result of rational calculation'.[60]

It is in pursuing the role that trust plays in interacting with, refreshing, and altering our perceptions of the world that there may be found a unique and nuanced insight into how social change takes place and how the unfamiliar becomes familiar. Such an approach situates human agency inescapably in context; there is no abstraction, no outside theoretical view.[61] Pursuing an ontological understanding, individuals are no longer already formed 'rational monads' but individuals interacting freely within a constantly evolving world, opening up infinite possibilities and avenues for action.[62] In such a scenario, uncertainty which involves risk takes on a philosophical quality of its own with trust providing a coping mechanism.[63]

Trust as a social practice

Helpful material can be found in the work of some contemporary sociologists, who regard trust as a social practice.[64] Drawing on our nexus of norms, habits and traditions is part of what makes trust a social practice. Theorists also stress the way in which the commitment of both parties facilitates trust.[65] Trust in such an approach 'is historical, but it is not so much tied to the past as it is pregnant with the future'.[66] For the creation, development and maintenance of trust can be a form of agency.[67]

Dmitry Khodyakov has defined trust as 'a process of constant imaginative anticipation of the reliability of the other party's actions based on (1) the reputation of the partner and the actor; (2) the evaluation of the current circumstances of action; (3) assumptions about the partner's actions; and (4) the belief in the honesty and morality of the other side'.[68]

It is part of our human nature to imagine, evaluate, and assess the various options available to us against a backdrop of past experiences, norms and traditions – in combination with our hopes and aspirations for the future – all the while recognizing risks and uncertainty. Trust is necessary precisely because humans lack full knowledge; accordingly, it is always future-oriented. Understood as a social practice, trust goes beyond the dominant rational-choice perspective by incorporating the emotional, often indefinable, human element in the recognition of risks and uncertainty.

Niklas Luhmann's work offers insight into the social practice approach to trust; while his writings are not easy to grasp at first reading, they are rich and rewarding. He argues that society actually 'consists of meaningful communications' rather than of people and objects[69] – all of which are underpinned by the 'irreducible and multidimensional social reality' that is trust.[70]

Luhmann differentiates between personal, impersonal, institutional and system trust but rightly emphasizes that emotion unites them all.[71] As Jocelyn Pixley notes: 'Personal trust is based on familiarity and rests on emotional bonds (the embeddedness thesis), whereas system trust, for example, entails taking a conscious risk by "renouncing" further information and taking a "wary indifference" – hardly non-emotional'.[72]

Luhmann identifies three limiting factors that specifically apply to communicative efficacy. First, meaning is ambiguous: 'only in context can meaning be understood, and context is, initially, supplied by one's own perceptual field and memory'.[73] Second, 'it is improbable for a communication to reach more persons than are present in a concrete situation, and this improbability grows if one makes the additional demand that the communication be reproduced unchanged'.[74] Third, 'even if a communication is understood by the person it reaches, this does not guarantee that it is accepted and followed'.[75]

It helps to locate Luhmann's writing in the agency-structure debate, where trust takes centre stage as an essential ingredient for the smooth functioning of society. For without trust, only very simple forms of human co-operation – effectively, those which can be fully transacted on the spot – are possible.[76] His 'theory of trust presupposes a theory of time', because trust has 'a problematic relationship with time. To show trust is to anticipate the future. It is to behave as though the future were certain'.[77]

Trust is therefore the means whereby an uncertain future is given the semblance of certainty so that otherwise unachievable outcomes are attained.[78] Accordingly, a few contemporary sociologists view trust as a process, arguing against the utilitarian view that trust is either a dependent or independent variable. Rather than seeing trust as the 'glue' or the 'cement' in society, they take the two-way process of trust one step further and posit trust to be both a social practice and process.[79]

A few contemporary sociologists view trust as a process, arguing against the utilitarian view that trust is either a dependent or independent variable. Rather than seeing trust as the 'glue' or the 'cement' in society, they take the two-way process of trust one step further and posit trust to be both a social practice and process.[80] In so doing, these academics stress that it is both parties' responsibility and commitment within the trust relationship that makes social change possible.[81] Trust in such an approach 'is historical, but it is not so much tied to the past as it is pregnant with the future'.[82] Viewed in this way as a process, the creation, development, and maintenance of trust can be seen as a form of agency.[83]

It is part of our human nature to imagine, evaluate and assess the various options available to us against a backdrop of past experiences, norms and traditions in combination with our hopes and aspirations for the future, though lacking full knowledge and yet recognizing ever-present risks and uncertainty: trust is always future oriented.[84] In pursuing such an approach, trust goes beyond the dominant rational choice perspective by incorporating the emotive, often indefinable, human element in recognition of the risks and uncertainty we perpetually face in the fast and ever-changing environs in which we live.[85] With this in mind, Khodyakov has defined trust as 'a process of constant imaginative anticipation of the reliability of the other party's actions based on (1) the reputation of the partner and the actor; (2) the evaluation of the current circumstances of action; (3) assumptions about the partners' actions; and (4) the belief in the honesty and morality of the other side'.[86]

'Money – a case study'[87]

'Trust as a social practice'

Money: the 'creator and destroyer of trust'.[88] As money and the banking system have evolved, so too has the nature of our trust in it, moving from a simple tripartite relationship of trust to a dense networked relationship, as illustrated below in **Figure 5**.[89] With this transition, the nature of money has also changed, from a thing of value in, and of, itself to 'a panoply of possible futures',[90] 'money is [now] minted freedom, hence for men deprived of freedom, it is ten times more valuable'.[91]

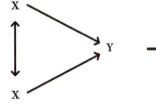

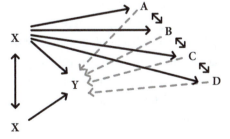

A personal trading relationship between two points (X) using commodity money (Y). Trust relationships are simple and direct.

An impersonal trading relationship between two parties (X) using fiat money (Y) in an open environment. Trust relationships are multiple, varied and overlapping. While trust is placed in other areas, they interconnect and underpin trust in money. They are also repeated for both parties involved in the transaction.

Figure 5 Changing relationships of trust.

Currency has taken many different forms over the centuries; 'they all work as money because people placed trust in them when they were used in transactions'.[92] Initially a commodity,[93] it was controlled by those in power; it became symbolic of both trust and power.[94] Even when crude coinage was first introduced in Lydia in *c.* 687 BCE,[95] it was of recognizable, if not universal, value.[96] An impersonal trust was created and maintained as a result of its inherent intrinsic value[97]; gold, in particular, became an 'intermediate token of trust',[98] with its widely accepted system of exchange. Trust was widespread, enabling exchange to flourish, yet susceptible to manipulation by those in power, with immediate, direct and measurable effect.[99] There was a direct and close relationship between an individual's trust in commodity money, the banking system, and the political elite, namely those with power and authority.[100]

In parallel to the evolution and use of money, the system of exchange evolved, as institutions sprang up to facilitate it.[101] Simple reputation based on personal exchange (or trade) was quickly replaced as markets and trading routes developed. As the demand for goods, unavailable locally, grew, so trade necessarily involved interaction, not only with strangers but also with disparate races and cultures. Greif has suggested that in this transition to impersonal exchange, underpinned by credit and central to economic growth, the 'community responsibility system' offered an intermediate step.[102] These reputation-based self-governing communities shared trading liabilities and were therefore motivated to dispense impartial justice, adding a degree of confidence to fragile trust between those trading. They also provided the time needed to develop the cornerstone of trust structures of trade and finance while simultaneously laying 'the foundations for its own replacement by an overarching system of law based [and institutionally supported] exchange'.[103] These structures include an enforceable legal system, available and reliable information, and the means to assess risk, banks, stock markets, insurance and government.

The introduction of tangible legal documents, supported by a functional and trusted legal system, created a degree of certainty in an uncertain world (of robbers, epidemics, unpredictable weather, patchy information and changing conditions). Supporting trust, they provided reassurance and boosted mutual confidence. Meanwhile the creation of banks provided security, transferability and interest on monies deposited; in return they provided credit, based on an assessment of risk, ability to repay, security and experience, to trusted and trustworthy customers.[104] These structures combined to create relatively stable conditions for more and larger companies to emerge, many with an increasing appetite for debt to fuel their growth.

At this point, in the fifteenth and sixteenth centuries, while individuals and companies had ready access to credit, monarchs and states did not. They experienced difficulties raising the necessary funds for war as they lacked a reliable system for collecting taxes; they controlled the courts and the law and could easily renege on their debts.[105] However, the concept of tradable bonds,[106] in particular government bonds, was about to change the situation, underpinning the expansion of credit not only to merchants but also to monarchs (and the State). Britain led the way, under Lords of the Treasury (Walpole and Pelham) by whom a parliamentary guarantee was introduced which ensured the interest due on government loans took the first call on monies collected through taxation.[107] They were absolutely trustworthy and as such offered a lowly 3 per cent interest rate return.[108] Supported by a relatively efficient legal and taxation system,[109] with little inherent corruption or abuse, the government quickly increased its debts, enabling it to create an effective 'fiscal-military' state.[110] The British navy, in particular, benefited.[111] Credit had now 'shifted from reliance on personal reputation and obligation to an impersonal nexus of financial institutions and underpinning them was the government involvement in the financial markets in London'.[112]

This period saw a number of converging factors, which led individually, and in combination, to a network of trust that supported the commercial, financial and state institutions which underpinned widespread trust in money. These included the introduction and popularity of coffee houses[113] and improving literacy rates together with an explosion in printed text (in particular, newspapers and pamphlets).[114] This encouraged the spread of new ideas and commerce and, together with an awareness of probability theory, allowed for a deeper assessment of risk.[115] Furthermore, the increasing use of insurance policies provided security and bolstered confidence while the Royal Exchange introduced restrictions for the 100 licence fee-paying brokers,[116] and penalties for those trading without a licence, which maintained a close-knit community, affording respectability and responsibility to those investing.[117]

Simultaneously, in the seventeenth century (in Western Europe),[118] the notion of representative money, in both coinage and paper notes, emerged.[119] Widespread impersonal trust was maintained and sustained, as the system itself was unchanged. The monetary system of exchange remained recognizable and universally accepted as monetary notes could be reliably exchanged for their value in gold. Paper money was a promissory note with a direct and fixed relationship to the commodity (typically gold), held within the banking system and matching its full value.[120] Therefore with a sound method of regulation in place, together with the obvious advantages of representative money, trust in the monetary system increased.[121] Yet, as a result of this evolution, there was ever-increasing reliance on the system in place (people had impersonal trust in the banking system), though there was a continuing element of personal trust within each individual transaction.[122] To maintain the stability and integrity of the system, trust was required in the increasing regulation surrounding both money and the banking system. The recognized maxims of the 'Square Mile' (City of London's financial district), which held that a man's word is his bond and a handshake to seal the deal and that had been relied upon for centuries, were being replaced.[123] From the 1970s, with increasing interconnectedness, facelessness and complexity, increasing reliance was, and is, placed on laws and regulations. Although such regulations were designed to be universal and consistent, in practice this was not always the case.

With the development and widespread adoption of paper notes, all money had ultimately become 'fiat' money.[124] Declared legal tender, by a government, fiat money has no intrinsic or fixed value and there is no legal requirement to redeem it against gold or silver; it is, therefore, useless without the consent of the currency user. Its value reflects the ability, integrity and reputation of the issuing government, together with the stability and prospects of the country's economy. This step has resulted in further separation and an increase in the depth of impersonal trust in the monetary system. It now represents such a complex amalgamation of factors that it is beyond most people's comprehension or understanding.[125] Described as 'a collective act of imagination', money is 'a thing which we have invested our credence in and it works because we do'.[126] With this separation and depth comes the ability to withstand discrete instances of failure.[127] Although disappointed, possibly outraged, with unmet expectations, our very reliance on the system strictly limits our available responses to its shortcomings and failures. However, if there is a combination of factors which affect multiple areas within the monetary system, trust can quickly be lost and the effects can be catastrophic.[128] If mishandled, it can rapidly destabilize a regime, creating a revolutionary situation: because 'there is no subtler, no surer means of overturning the existing basis of society than to debauch the currency'.[129] History bears constant witness that currency debasement invariably leads to inflation and ultimately hyperinflation: from the Roman Empire[130] to the Weimar Republic in Germany,[131] Argentina and most recently Zimbabwe, where hyperinflation peaked at 7.96 billion per cent.[132]

Types of trust

Not only is everyone an expert on trust, with their own ideas of what trust is,[133] making it difficult to define, but there are also a great many types of trust.[134] Therefore, 'perhaps one way of making progress' in further understanding revolution 'is to distinguish various kinds of trust'.[135] Both personal and impersonal in nature, trust is a feeling, an attitude and a relationship and as such can be interpreted in the following ways: structurally; as a disposition; an expectation; an intention; and/or behaviour. As personal trust has been discussed earlier in the chapter, the focus below is on impersonal trust, trustworthiness and distrust. These different types of trust (an illustrative typology is included as Figure X) can operate in isolation (context and situational specific), working independently of each other as well as in combination.

Type of Trust	Description
Dispositional: ability to, experience of and the expectation of trust	
Rudimentary	This reflects our predisposition to trust, established in childhood (Erikson 1963). The result of family interaction and nurturing, it is unreflexive, but forms the basis for an individual's entire 'trusting' personality or 'ontological security' (Laing 1969). Nonetheless, research has found one fifth of Americans do not have it (Solomon and Flores 2003, p. 40). It is high risk, exposing the trustor to much vulnerability.
Background	More of a feeling or an emotion, it is based on the familiarity of a situation, such as repeated actions and outcomes; as such, it could be considered immature. It simplifies the complexities of life by relying on norms, habits, traditions and rules together with a belief in social order.
Personal: attitudinal, intentional and functional	
Interpersonal	Situational and contextual, here trusting is both an action and a process based on expectations, intentions, behaviour and emotion. The product of experience and commitment, it is self-conscious in its questioning and consideration. Though it involves risk and vulnerability, both are better understood and accounted for. It is optimistic and transformative both to the parties involved and to others. It underpins communication, requiring a level of mutual understanding and cooperation.
Self	In accepting that trust is an emotional skill, which requires continuous learning and effort to develop, self-trust is confidence in one's own ability. Vital for all forms of trust, it is self-conscious and self-critical. See Lehrer's (1997) analyses of self-trust.

Type of Trust	Description
Blind	As with rudimentary trust, blind trust is high risk and makes one vulnerable. Actively denying distrust, it is purposefully self-deceptive; it is therefore a necessary ingredient of cults and religious fanaticism.
Conceptual	A significant component in how actors construct knowledge and make sense of the world through language. Combining knowledge, experience, paradigms, and judgement, it draws on the mental interconnections and associations we use to make sense of the world (Paiget 1952; Vygotsky 1962; Posner *et al.*1982; and Strike and Posner 1992).

Impersonal – Structured and functional, impersonal trust describes the connection between individuals and the institutions and systems that are meant to represent them; it is this trust from which they gain legitimacy. A shadow of the trust which exists between individuals, it typically lacks the same depth and nuances but is vital to coping with the complexities of everyday life; as such, it is unconscious and ongoing.

Political	Contains a greater conceptual element, relating both to the regime in power and its 'legitimate' alternatives. Examples include communal, direct, representative, monarchical and authoritarian regimes. It simultaneously tapes into and feeds off one's wider belief system.
Institutional	Marries the individual and society, history and experience, agreement and penalties – while addressing the need to reduce the complexities of everyday life. Examples include the police, military, UK National Health Service, civil service, schools and universities. It is closely associated with the notions of reliability, expectation, responsibility and competence.
Systems	Similar to, but distinct from, institutional trust, it encompasses a complex process rather than discrete components. Examples include legal, banking, welfare and honour systems.
Ideational	Differs from personal conceptual trust in that such trust is built on socially constructed and widely accepted notions. Examples include the notion of the State, national identity and religious symbolism.
Non-Betrayal	Represents a shift in institutional trust over time and the removal of emotion and value judgements from trust; it is a dilution of institutional trust as a result of increasing reliance on bureaucratization and legalism within governments. It marries experience with sanctions. It is closely associated with the notions of reliability, expectation, responsibility and competence.

(Continued)

Type of Trust	Description
Other types of 'trust'	
Distrust	While distrust remains a separate concept to trust, it is often interpreted as simply the negative mirror image, with the same categories (or types) of trust. The process referred to as 'trust' takes account of both trust and distrust, the balance of which determines whether, all things considered, one trusts or distrusts in a particular situation.
Mistrust	Mistakenly used as a synonym for distrust, this is incorrect: mistrust is misplaced trust. Unlike trust and distrust, which take account of the past in the present to look forward, mistrust is something retrospective. It is judgmental. It is considered as 'either a former trust destroyed, or former trust healed' (Sztompka 2000 p. 27). It is important to note that distinguishing between trust and mistrust is the first stage of Erik Erikson's theory of psychosocial development, which is essential in the formation of rudimentary trust.

Impersonal trust

Impersonal trust is the connection between individuals and the institutions that are intended to represent them; by this trust, institutions are legitimized.[136] It differs from trust between individuals as it presupposes 'no encounters at all with the individuals or groups who are in some way "responsible" for them'.[137] At times referred to as 'political trust',[138] 'systems trust'[139] and/or 'institutional trust',[140] it is separable, distinct and multilayered. A shadow of the trust which exists between individuals, it lacks the same depth and nuances.[141] However, it is vital to us as a coping mechanism, simplifying the complexities of everyday life. In trusting in institutions we expect certain behaviours, actions and outcomes which in turn provide us with a degree of certainty in a complex and uncertain world. It enables us to look forward more optimistically, plan for, and invest in the future and make long-term commitments. If there is a high degree of uncertainty, we focus on the short term, affecting, amongst other things, our actions, the economy, and government strategy.

Trust, in institutions, is therefore understood to be a reflection of 'their perceived legitimacy, technical competence, and ability to perform assigned duties efficiently' and, therefore, it is a rational decision rather than 'true' trust.[142] Therefore, impersonal trust can easily be shaken and lost when expectations of service, integrity and perhaps even value for money are not met.[143] Nevertheless, it is sometimes the case, at an individual level, that we distinguish between the failures or shortcomings of a particular individual and the institution itself.[144] In addition, the lack of impersonal trust in a particular institution does not necessarily result in a boycott; for this to happen there would need to be a widespread breakdown in the regime's power, authority, and perceived legitimacy.[145]

Individuals are all born into some system of governance,[146] even those in so-called failed states or geographically isolated communities, which they must come to understand and interact with from an early age, absorbing an understanding and appreciation of the institutional structures and systems and, through use, reinforcing them. 'We learn the rules of the game and we play it.' We cannot step outside our reality to objectively evaluate or challenge what is in place as our reaction to it is shaped and coloured by it.[147] Yet even in the twenty-first century, states are being created and the potential for revolutionary regime change remains. Both situations would require the creation or development of impersonal trust in the newly formed institutions.[148] Understanding how impersonal trust is first created is, therefore, vital in state building and rebuilding.

There are two competing schools of thought, subdivided within each at the micro and macro level. Cultural theorists posit that impersonal trust is learned; interpersonal trust is projected or superimposed onto political and other institutions.[149] For them impersonal trust is determined by cultural norms, habits, and socialization. In contrast, institutional theorists link impersonal trust to satisfactory performance.[150] Trust is a rational consequence of expectations met. While antagonistic, these approaches are not mutually exclusive. Instead they complement and reinforce each other, sharing 'the fundamental assumption that trust is learned and linked at some level to experience'.[151]

In the West, during the twentieth and twenty-first centuries, individuals have relied more and more on institutions in their everyday lives,[152] changing the relationship between government and citizen[153] and the boundary between the 'public' and 'private' spheres.[154] In the nineteenth century individuals had few expectations of their governments beyond basic provisions (defence, law and order, currency management, trade support); participation in politics was restricted and referred to as a prize not a birthright, while the relationship between government and society was limited: government provided a framework but society ran itself. However, with a combination of national and international pressures (including, but not limited to, a changing political and social landscape, the pressure of war, internationalization and globalization, demographic growth, and scientific advancement), expectations of and demands upon the State increased significantly in the century that followed.[155] In seeking to account for and improve on rapidly changing societal conditions, the State has expanded its role, encroaching on the private sphere. With this larger role, governments have increasingly been criticized, in the late twentieth and twenty-first centuries, not only for their shortcomings but also for creating 'servile' or 'nanny states', a 'something for nothing' culture which has changed the perception of citizens' rights.[156]

However, somewhat counterintuitively, while governments necessarily require trust to function effectively and to grow, recent polling data suggests that impersonal or political trust is diminishing.[157] The introduction of new policy initiatives designed to increase transparency and the response to calls for greater accountability have become a popular panacea for this issue. Yet this option may actually increase the distance between the individual and the institution: the concomitant form filling reduces human interaction and, moreover, overloads individuals with data they cannot hope to digest. It reduces the need for trust while increasing expectations. An alternative is to increase the dialogue between individuals and institutions, to view impersonal trust, as with interpersonal trust, as a process requiring creation, development, and constant maintenance.[158]

Trust and trustworthiness

We have a natural disposition to trust and to judge the trustworthiness of others, yet in the employment of these terms they can be misused or misinterpreted; the result of unthinking substitution or exchange, they are conflated.[159] More often than not, in literature the use of the word 'trust' represents an account of the opportunities, characteristics, and/or difficulties with trustworthiness; trust is merely inferred.[160] Whereas trustworthiness can be demonstrated, proven by reason and evidence, trust must be given by A to B. We recognize it as a virtue,[161] a 'good thing', a positive character trait (reflecting a willingness and ability to take responsibility, perform a duty or discharge an obligation).[162] Conversely trust is dependent on our psychological profile, our attitude, and personal experience, and although we all trust to some degree, to trust is specific and episodic (A can trust B to do X next week but not today or A can trust B to do X but not Y). Trustworthiness is a constant whereas trust is more ambiguous; we can trust blindly, foolishly, and immorally but by being trustworthy we are being honest and dependable.[163]

Hardin proposes a clear distinction between trust and trustworthiness, stressing the importance of differentiating these terms while simultaneously recognizing their interconnectedness.[164] He has focused much of his work on trustworthiness, pointing out that it is trustworthiness rather than trust (seen by him as a capability), which is required in an effective, well-functioning society, and stating that 'trust by itself constitutes nothing' and 'without [trustworthiness], there is no value in trust'.[165] However, as Luhmann[166] points out, Hardin fails to recognize that this dialectic works both ways and that there is also no value in trustworthiness without trust. This point is reiterated by Flores and Solomon who describe trust and trustworthiness as two sides of the same coin.[167]

Trust and distrust

Similarly, distrust has held limited attraction for researchers to date. As with trust, it has already produced multiple definitions and meanings. Both trust and distrust can reside in an individual simultaneously, interacting to reduce the complexities of daily life, shaping and colouring our perceptions, aiding us in making decisions, enabling us to assess the risks and uncertainty against a backdrop of incomplete information and knowledge.[168] However, where trust can be seen to be optimistic in nature, distrust is pessimistic. Although often portrayed as polar opposites, Worchel and Rotter have argued that they sit together, two extremes of the same dimension, simultaneously being weighed and taken into account as part of the trust process (distrust must be overcome in order to trust); as such, distrust is not a lack of trust or a precursor to trust.[169] Similarly Jones has posited that trust and distrust are contraries not contradictories.[170] However, the general consensus now reached amongst trust theorists is that trust and distrust are separate and opposite social constructs.[171] For example, the word 'not' separates Barber's definitions of trust and distrust.[172] Lewicki and his associates support this approach with three reasons: (a) they are empirically separate, (b) they coexist and (c) they have different antecedents and consequences. All the while they position their definitions as 'movements towards certainty'.[173]

The distinction between trust and distrust is essential, as is a balance between the two, while politically, as well as in life, distrust is as useful as trust. The measure and combination of the two are not consistent or universal but will reflect an individual's psychological profile (representing different sides of the personality it is based on a different concept of human nature). It is the specifics of the situation being faced. For example, 'the culture of trust developed within a democracy is due precisely to the institutionalisation of distrust within its construction'.[174] Distrust is inherent in the structural foundation of democracy:[175] given man's Fall,[176] a system of government needs this ultimate check on the actions of the ruler. Consider the rise of fascism in Germany and Italy in the early twentieth century.[177] Too little trust and too much distrust have the opposite effect. The importance of balancing trust and distrust sits behind the maxim 'trust but verify', used by the president of the United States of America, Ronald Reagan, in regard to the Intermediate-Range Nuclear Forces Treaty signed with Soviet General Secretary, Mikhail Gorbachev (8 December 1987), and 'trust in God but keep your powder dry' used by President Clinton, in 1997, pleased at the prospect of bipartisan co-operation to reach a balanced budget agreement.[178]

Interlopers

It is helpful to end by contrasting trust with related, but distinct, concepts.

Trust versus reliance

The difference between trust and reliance is well documented. Trust is more than mere reliance. While individuals accept a degree of vulnerability in both cases,[179] what distinguishes them is the depth of that vulnerability and its long-term effect, actual or potential. For instance, one relies on the postman to deliver our mail but we trust him not to read it.[180] If a letter is undelivered, one is disappointed or even angry – but if it is read, one feels betrayed.[181] Betrayal is a deliberate and sometimes calculated action, yielding an emotional response that greatly exceeds the feeling of disappointment; not only does the emotion run deeper, but an act of betrayal presents an existential challenge to the relationship in which it occurs.[182]

Disappointment is a fact of life that facilitates learning, development and maturity; by contrast, betrayal can shake the 'very foundations of our relationship to the world or parts thereof' and thus presents 'a much deeper and [more] serious challenge in our everyday lives'.[183] To re-establish trust, we may have to reinterpret and recreate our world.

Trust versus co-operation

As Robert Axelrod demonstrated in his seminal work, *The Evolution of Cooperation*, co-operation requires neither rationality nor trust.[184] Karen Cook, Russell Hardin and Margaret Levi have argued more recently that mutually beneficial co-operation is possible without trust, highlighting a variety of mechanisms that expedite co-operation in its absence; these include facilitating mutually beneficial conditions, monitoring, sanctions, and legislation.[185]

For co-operation to work, the parties need simply to be able to identify each other and recognize that potential benefits outweigh any potential costs – something often easier between peers rather than citizen and state. A commonality of interest provides the motive to cooperate; moreover, the parties need not benefit equally, so long as the benefit is sufficient for each party to co-operate. This might involve maintaining a communal resource, building a joint asset, collaborating in political activity or simply being civil to one another. The parties act within defined boundaries, in turn situated within a social system that can incentivize, coerce or enforce co-operation.

Trust, belief and ideology

Trust and belief are quite different, but used interchangeably by many who adopt a rational, reductionist approach. Beliefs enable us to approach and understand the world around us, shaping our perceptions and our reality. They are often neither irrefutable nor incontrovertible, but rather persistent, inflexible, and delusional; they do not rely on personal interaction.[186]

Ideology is a logically coherent system of beliefs.[187] Increasingly, research suggests that ideologies – in thought, behaviour, and language – function 'as pre-packaged units of interpretation that spread because of basic human motives to understand the world, avoid existential threat, and maintain valued interpersonal relationships'.[188]

Trust is easier when individuals can identify commonalities, such as ideology or beliefs, for this reflects – or even generates – a sense of social solidarity.[189] Trust is 'constructed out of a relationship [… and is] the product of communication in that relationship'.[190]

Trust is …

Five dimensions (cognitive, affective, behavioural, emotional, and temporal) are present in instances of trust, although the qualitative and quantitative mix changes to reflect the specific situation and the individuals involved. These are all set within the wider social environs (including local cultural and social norms). Distinguishable from semantically similar concepts such as reliance and co-operation, trust is separable from the notions of belief, ideology, solidarity, and social capital. While there are many different types of trust which can operate in isolation (context and situational specific), working independently of each other, the real value of trust lies in the mutually supportive web, or network, formed when the different types work in combination, overlapping, intersecting, and complementing multiple connections and interactions simultaneously. Trust is defined as 'the willingness to accept vulnerability based upon positive expectations about another's (individual, group, and/or institution) future behaviour'.[191] In this book, it is therefore understood to be an emotional (exposing our vulnerabilities to others), logical (by assessing risks, rewards, and competency) and inclusive (by accounting for distrust) process.

Power, control, and trust

Traditional narratives and discourses that surround revolution have focused on power and control, and have been shaped and analyzed on this basis. The 'forcible transfer of power over a state',[1] and 'the struggle for state power',[2] revolutions are seen by many theorists as the outcome of power struggles between competing interest groups.[3] 'Revolutionaries do not make revolutions! The revolutionaries are those who know when power is lying in the street and when they can pick it up. Armed uprising by itself has never yet led to revolution',[4] while 'power is not a means; it is an end. One does not establish a dictatorship in order to safeguard a revolution; one makes the revolution in order to establish the dictatorship', to seize and maintain control. 'The object of power is power'.[5]

An obsession and preoccupation, power is ubiquitous, 'present whenever and wherever social pressures operate on the individual to induce desired conduct'.[6] Foucault's statement that power is all-pervasive was pivotal in furthering this obsession. It is 'intentional and non-subjective', 'operating from the top down and also from the bottom up', 'exercised on the dominant as well as on the dominated'.[7] It is an overarching concept used to encompass notions of control, authority, coercion, violence and influence.[8] One of the 'central phenomena of human social life, no sooner does one begin to reflect what power itself means than one is confronted by a fundamental problem: it becomes unclear whether power is a positive or negative feature of human social relations' and nowhere more so than in the revolutionary space.[9]

However, an overemphasis on power has resulted in 'the assumption that power is the decisive factor … it has eaten deep into our routine accounts of social structure. The salient aspects of social life are analysed through relationships of domination and submission – or periodic revolt!'[10] Yet 'the consent of men, united in society is the [very] foundation of power'.[11] How this consent (control and/or influence) is generated and sustained needs to be investigated and better understood, opening the door to trust. I suggest power represents just one dimension in the interplay of factors influencing individuals' choices, in particular within a revolutionary situation. Power emerges from relationships operating within the constraints of a societal structure that intersect implicitly and at times explicitly, with trust. In so doing trust provides an additional explanatory element to both the operation of power and the choices made. Although some trust literature recognizes that the 'two are closely, directly or inversely, linked ... that link is not usually specified'.[12] Similarly the interaction of trust and authority and trust and control is outlined but has yet to be referred to and considered in the full context of revolutionary space.[13]

Power[14]

'Few problems in political [and social] science[s] are more perplexing than the problem of social power; ... yet, despite widespread use, power remains a slippery and problematic concept'.[15] Diverse and often contentious,[16] there is no one way of understanding power,[17] and this is underlined by significant definitional differences between disciplines and schools of thought.[18] It can take on negative connotations,[19] and yet 'the measure of a man is what he does with power'.[20] 'That some people have more power than others is one of the most palpable facts of human existence. Because of this, the concept of power is as ancient and ubiquitous as any that social theory can boast'.[21] Both a perception and a prerogative, power is defined as 'the ability to exercise one's will over others'.[22] Omnipresent and processual, power is 'dynamic, relational and multidimensional, changing according to context, circumstance and interest'.[23] Its expressions and forms can range from domination and resistance to collaboration and transformation'.[24] Affecting personal relationships, it also shapes social groups, organizations and governments.[25] It has long been a subject of study in the political and social sciences. Traditional social science emphasizes power as influence and control, often treating it as a commodity or structure divorced from human action.[26] More recent scholarship has revolved around the enabling nature of power; constraining human social action, it also makes action possible.[27]

Power and control

Whereas power, authority and influence are separable concepts which,[28] while mutually reinforcing, can act independently of one another,[29] power and control have a deeper interrelationship.[30] **Figure 6** seeks to illustrate their relative positions.

One definition of control is 'to direct, to influence, or to determine the behaviour of someone else',[31] while another describes control as 'any process in which a person or group of persons or organisation of persons determines i.e. intentionally affects, what another person or group or organisation will do'.[32] Although both definitions emphasize the notion of influence, they primarily focus on the actual or kinetic process involved. Therefore, when combined with a definition of power (the ability/potential to influence others), intention, and action are united.[33]

While 'power is nothing without control', Fiske theorizes 'power is essentially control'.[34] This is underscored by the following definitions of power: 'the ability to exercise one's will over others'[35]; 'the ability of one party to change or control the behaviour, attitudes, opinions, objectives, needs and values of another party'[36]; and 'an individual's relative capacity to modify others or states, by providing or withholding resources or administering punishments'.[37]

By conceptualizing power 'as influence and social control, the former reducing and the latter reinforcing authority', discussions of power naturally

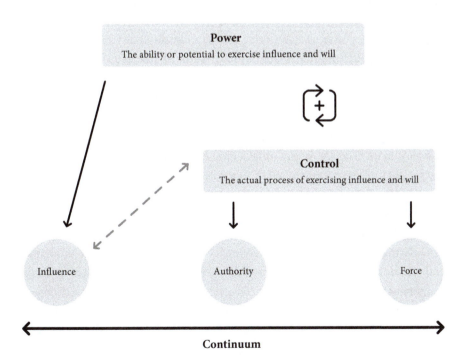

Figure 6 Schematic depicting the continuum of power.

consider authority and vice versa, with a proportion of the literature given over to comparing and contrasting the two notions.[38] Weber defines power as 'the probability that one actor within a social relationship will be in a position to carry out his own will despite resistance' while he defines authority as 'the probability that certain specific commands (or all commands) for a given source will be obeyed by a given group of persons'.[39] In contrast, Buckley defines power as 'control and influence over the actions of others, to promote one's goals; without their consent, against their will or without their knowledge or understanding', and authority as 'the direction, or control of the behaviour of others, from the promotion of collective goals based on some ascertainable form of their knowledgeable consent'.[40] Yet it is Cicero who succinctly distinguishes between the two: '*cum potestas in populo auctoritas in senatu si*' (while power resides in the people, authority rests in the senate).[41]

Authority is typically used to refer to a legitimate and formal power to act,[42] conferred on an individual to enable him or her to fulfil his or her responsibilities.[43] It is usually fairly well defined in order to limit or restrict an individual's power.[44] Dahrendorf elaborates by arguing for 'the important difference between power and authority … we are concerned exclusively with relations of authority, for these alone are part of social structure … these are not the product of structurally fortuitous relations of power'.[45]

Alternatively, power and authority can be understood as two opposing end points on a scale.[46] Barnard's definition of authority suggests the difference: 'authority is the character of a communication (order) in a formal organisation by virtue of which it is accepted by a contributor to, or "member" of, the organisation, as governing the action he contributes … '.[47] Highlighting the properties of authority differentiates it more clearly from power.[48] It is consensus and the pursuit of collective goals that legitimize authority, as opposed to power's private-goal-driven nature exercised in a range, from force and manipulation to rewards. So, while authority and hierarchy are typically associated, authority is, in fact, associated with the *right* to make decisions which are binding on actors in a social system; that *right* can be, and is, sometimes removed.[49]

Differing from authority, social influence occurs when a person's thoughts, outlooks or actions are changed through interacting with others.[50] Recognizing in humankind a need to conform, Deutsch and Gerard have focused on an individual's need, not only to be right (referred to as informational influence or social proof),[51] but also to be liked (normative social influence) as the underlying psychologies driving this.[52] Although many factors affect the strength of social influence,[53] it is ever-present, with mankind living in an environment increasingly filled with influencing forces and constraints. Its effects are strongest when the group, executing a form of 'influence', is consistent and committed.[54] Similarly, drawing on an individual's credibility as an expert will carry more weight in specific scenarios. Culture also plays a significant role, as do emotion and disposition.[55] When successful, social influence can reduce the need for controls, making force or physical coercion unnecessary.

Therefore, authority can be theorized as the more formal, static, structural aspect of power, whereas influence is the informal, dynamic, tactical element. The difference between the two lies in their formal and informal natures, respectively. Influence carries the inferences of informal procedures involving persuasion, inducement and constraint[56] and can therefore be multi-directional while authority is circumscribed, being bounded and limited to a particular context. It more usually, and stereotypically, flows downwards in a superior–subordinate relationship.[57] Therefore, while the concept of power is larger than the notions of authority and influence, it is also in the service of both.

The interplay of trust, power and control

By approaching these three separable and distinguishable concepts as mechanisms of social control,[58] often used interchangeably (co-ordinating interactions and controlling the dynamics of social relationship),[59] the number of commonalities they share is highlighted.[60] The brief discussion which follows outlines the opposing theoretical views which seek to explain the interplay between these three concepts, all of which are recognizable as:

- fundamental psychological human needs[61];
- the properties of social relationships, not attributes of individual actors[62];
- relational and context specific;
- constantly evolving processes that arise from and are formed in relationships;
- having both positive and negative effects despite the safeguards put in place[63];
- ways of managing, or reducing, complexity, and uncertainty. They largely seem to operate on the basis of the same principle – that of influence.[64]

Trust and control

Trust and control are complex processes.[65] They are essential to the effective functioning of individuals, teams, groups, organizations, regimes, and society, and are central features of social cohesion and order.[66] These two are elusive concepts that almost always co-exist, although there is little consensus on how they relate to each other.[67] 'While concepts of *trust* and *control* have been present in academic discourse and organisational practice for generations, this does not mean they are well understood or unproblematic'.[68] Viewed, in turn, as either forms of control or trust,[69] or substitutes[70]; supplementary and complementary,[71] or simply sharing common features, they are more than just 'different sides of the same analytical coin'; there is an interrelatedness about them.[72]

Without an agreement, much research on trust and control now assumes an essential dualism. Das and Teng's *dualism*,[73] focusing on perceived risks, states that 'trust and control are two separate routes to risk reduction in alliances', albeit with 'distinct linkages'.[74] In contrast, in Möllering's *duality*,[75] they 'each assume the existence of each other, refer to each other and create each other, but remain irreducible to each other'.[76] Both reframe and emphasize the interplay of trust and control but differ subtly. Das and Teng define separately an actor's expectations towards another (trust) and the level of constraint imposed on the other (control). Möllering, by reframing the problem, argues that an actor, when forming expectations of others, simultaneously takes the influences of both structure and agency into account.[77] Trust is tied to the influencing behaviours of social structures, while control is built on, and expects, generalized benevolent agency – creating a 'duality' spiral.[78] Each assumes the existence of the other and 'cross-references' backwards and forwards. They evolve and adapt over time, with every experience and system change (regulations, rules, norms); in so doing, the interconnected nature of trust and control reproduces and reinforces behaviours and practice.

This duality does not preclude a betrayal of trust, a challenge to control, or fundamental change. 'People behave predictably not despite, but by virtue of the choices they make. Nevertheless, these are choices and they might be made differently and so predictability is never total'.[79] Similarly, 'control is always imperfect – however powerful an actor might be' while 'resistance and unintended consequences may – and probably will – occur'.[80] Each and every individual has a psychological need for both trust and a sense of control.[81] They are tools for managing uncertainty and risk. With trust and control, actions, events, and processes become more predictable; decisions can be made, and futures planned. However, most people have little direct control in their lives and must counter-intuitively cede control to family, friends, employers, governments, and even strangers, to ultimately gain a *sense* of control.[82] However, just as there is strength there is a weakness in trust and control: trust leads to a ceding of control yet wielding that control can lead to a loss of trust and ultimately control. Such betrayal can elicit an extreme response as control is reclaimed. Personal values, cultural and social norms, rules and regulations, knowledge, and experience, all provide a framework shaping the response – from restoration to punishment and destruction.

Trust and power

Defining power as 'the capacity to implement' suggests it is broad enough to allow it to mean domination, authority, influence and shared power or 'power with'. It is this definition of power as a process occurring in relationships that 'opens the door to trust'.[83] Separable concepts both crucial to human co-operation, the relationship between trust and power has been poorly investigated,[84] and is often ignored, as research has focused on one or the other. There is no consensus, and the interplay of power and trust remains controversial, although the majority of researchers acknowledge that power and trust co-exist.[85] For some, power 'drives out trust',[86] negating co-operation[87]; it is the opposite of trust.[88] Differing viewpoints posit trust as either a 'tool' of power or as a substitute for power.[89] Some view power as a requirement or precondition for trust[90] while others view power and trust as supportive and complementary of each other,[91] working in combination[92] or functioning as an embedded decision.[93] Ultimately, by understanding the 'interplay' of trust and power, a deeper and more nuanced insight into relations, within and between, individuals, groups, organizations, social movements, and the institutions of the State, is gained.

Traditionally power has been represented as control over resources, like an abstract commodity which exists outside of social relationships.[94] However, power and trust represent different ways of influencing others. As the vast majority of social interactions are based on a combination of both,[95] a blend of the two is usually necessary to achieve co-ordination, co-operation, and social control. Trust and power 'allow social actors to link their mutual expectations with each other and to coordinate (re)-actions between them'.[96] As Bachmann notes, both co-ordinate social interactions efficiently and, by co-operating, enable relatively stable relationships to develop. Like trust, power has its risks and safeguards, and while it may not remove risk completely, it can diminish it considerably. 'It emerges from group formation, social organisation and the shared beliefs, theories, and values (the culture, ideologies, etc.) which shape social and personal identity and perceived self-interest'.[97] The power of leaders and groups depends on these foundations which are always being built up or torn down, 'being developed creatively or deteriorating in indifference, as a function of partisan interests, collective experience, new tasks and problems and endless battles between belief and reality'.[98] Trust plays a vital role in both underpinning and undermining these foundations.

However, there still remains a lack of knowledge and little empirical research into how trust and power relate to one another, while the research undertaken has produced contradictory results,[99] fuelling a lively and controversial debate. In response, such debates have proposed more fine-grained conceptualizations with the inclusion of the role of time.[100] Huber and Hurni's research offers one such example.[101] They were able to identify 'different types of power and different types of trust [which] interact differently with each other'.[102] They also witnessed seemingly systematic and causally connected patterns of interactions, with one acting as a necessary precondition for another to emerge. Thus, power and trust, at their extremes, may be both complements and substitutes (dualisms of sorts) producing ever-spiralling interactions of power and trust.

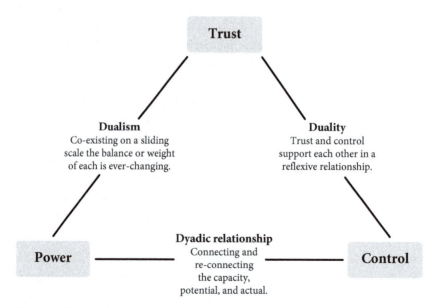

Figure 7 The relationships and interplay between trust, power, and control.

Although traditional narratives and discourses that surround revolution have focused on, been shaped by and are analysed on, the basis of power, the discussions set out in this chapter have sought to emphasize the interplay of trust, power and control and thereby challenge this obsession with power. In isolation, power represents just one dimension in the interplay of factors influencing individuals' choices while trust offers another. These conceptions not only co-exist but are socially conferred and constrained; by focusing on the interplay between them, not only are their explanatory powers increased but a fuller picture is presented. **Figure** 7 summarizes this chapter's discussion on the interplay of trust, power and control, as mechanisms of co-ordination.

Ancient revolutionaries

Ancient Athens

Ancient Athens, as with other city-states, was a strictly stratified society.[1] The superiority of its citizens was unquestioned; their status a natural endowment.[2] Domestic hierarchy mirrored this public stratification, where citizenship was available only to the elite, masters (*kyrios*) of each household and later their sons, categorically excluding women, slaves, and those foreign-born.[3] It was also reflected in the assumption of natural inequality reinforcing this structure. As in nature, everything had a place, a purpose, a pre-ordained order. For a long period of time, citizens were the only literate and sophisticated orators in society; they were the elite, the priests and magistrates whose necessary skills were nurtured and taught from an early age. They also had to demonstrate military prowess and leadership. Citizenship was by turn a ritual and public theatre; it was demanding with no time or recognition for physical/commercial labours. As such the decisions they made and the actions they took were understood to contain, and embody, a powerful rationality found lacking in their subordinates. There was no constraint or system of oversight; citizens were simply born to rule, and everyone else to obey. It was their reasoning that guaranteed action and, therefore, the very notion of human agency was shaped by the structure of society.[4]

So how, one might ask, within such a rigidly hierarchical society, where action was dictated by reason,[5] was revolution possible or even perceived? The revolution in 508/7 BCE is widely described in modern literature as extraordinary[6]; it instituted a democratic system of governance (of 'political power wielded actively and collectively by the demos' – 'direct democracy') lasting nearly two centuries.[7] Two days and two nights of rioting replaced tyranny and made way for dramatic, far-reaching political change.[8] These actions represented a continuing widening of citizenship,[9] though by no means universal or all transforming to Ancient Greek society.[10] Briefly interrupted, on two separate occasions in 411 and 404 BCE by oligarchic revolutions which established short-lived dictatorships, this period is regarded as the Classical or Golden Age (508–322 BCE)[11]: a period (nearly 200 years) of Athenian political hegemony, prosperity, and power,[12] echoed in its monuments, art, philosophy, architecture, and literature.[13]

The 'revolutionary' importance of creating such a democracy is virtually unquestioned in modern literature.[14] Not so in Ancient Greece. There was no single word for revolution and no expression translates straightforwardly into a contemporary notion of revolution.[15] The actions, which transformed the governance of the city-state, were typically referred to in the antiseptic language of 'constitutional development',[16] reflecting the changes to the constitution and citizenship base. In a similar vein, the actual moment when Athenian democracy was overthrown, by the '400' counter-revolutionary aristocrats, in 411 BCE, simply described the actions taken without elaboration or embellishment.[17]

These changes, wrought by revolution in 508/7 BCE, were not driven through with the power associated with tyranny, but by the agreement and consensus of the citizenry,[18] and a respected 'leader and champion of the people', Cleisthenes.[19] His success and position were dependent upon the will of the people, by drawing on an interlocking framework of trust, together with its interconnecting concepts (each an implicit or explicit carrier of trust), to gain consensus (see **Figure 8**).[20] Cleisthenes's system of governance was built and sustained on the customs and practices that had for so long generated strong networks of trust amongst its citizens, underpinned by their shared values and ideals in a constantly repeating feedback loop.[21] These customs and practices included communal meals, rituals and notions of legal liability. These created relationships that encouraged responsibility in those liable and reliance on those holding them liable, hence a type of trust. Another practice, resolving disputes, where the tripartite system of two opposing speakers and their audience created a distrust of the speakers, helped to regulate the system by producing a generalized trust in each other. The development of this framework of trust is explored in more detail throughout this chapter, highlighting how the conceptions, implicit and often explicit carriers of trust, were shaped and in turn shaped society.

Consensus was paramount as the Athenians were aware they were at 'war' with Sparta and needed to create a military force to defend themselves.[22] Having recently experienced tyranny and civil war, they were united in their desire for freedom and equality. The energy and momentum that were created merged social and political reforms into an overt demonstration of Athenian community, of mutual trust between its citizens.[23] The *polis* was supported by the aspiration of

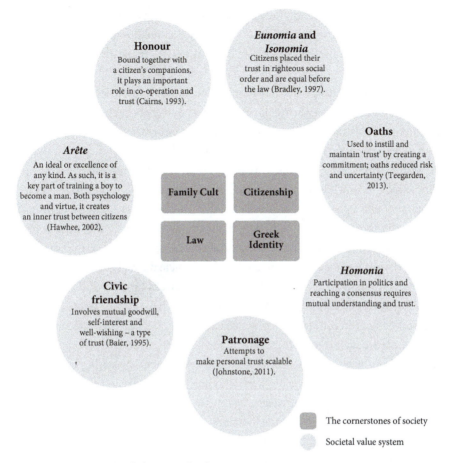

Honour
Bound together with a citizen's companions, it plays an important role in co-operation and trust (Cairns, 1993).

Eunomia* and *Isonomia
Citizens placed their trust in righteous social order and are equal before the law (Bradley, 1997).

Oaths
Used to instill and maintain 'trust' by creating a commitment; oaths reduced risk and uncertainty (Teegarden, 2013).

Arête
An ideal or excellence of any kind. As such, it is a key part of training a boy to become a man. Both psychology and virtue, it creates an inner trust between citizens (Hawhee, 2002).

Family Cult

Citizenship

Law

Greek Identity

Homonia
Participation in politics and reaching a consensus requires mutual understanding and trust.

Civic friendship
Involves mutual goodwill, self-interest and well-wishing – a type of trust (Baier, 1995).

Patronage
Attempts to make personal trust scalable (Johnstone, 2011).

The cornerstones of society

Societal value system

Figure 8 Ancient Greek framework of trust.

commercially wealthy Athenians to become citizens and, desirous of its protections and privileges, they were both willing and able to shoulder its obligations.[24]

Reframing the revolution as an issue of trust further highlights the processes which made possible such a change in governance and how society was subsequently reconstituted into a model which spread far and wide. Cleisthenes's democratic reforms became the outcome by which to navigate special and political changes. With them, local forms of trust were challenged by a more unified and widespread form of trust.[25]

While an enormous amount of literature exists on the history, philosophy, law and economics of Ancient Greece, little has been written about trust, one of the most fundamental aspects of social and political interactions within Ancient Greek society. Although this does not purport to be an exhaustive case study, as an exploration into trust and revolution in Athens in the fifth century BCE, its limitations are further compounded by the nature of texts available, the authors' styles, their own bias and its function (a history, a contemporary description, a play or judicial proceedings) and may need to rely on translations rather than the original text.

Found in the writings of Herodotus, Thucydides and Aristotle, the exact meaning of trust (*pistis* – Πίστις) is often unclear and changeable.[26] Herodotus,[27] for example, uses the term to mean 'treaty' or 'covenant made by exchange of assurances and oaths',[28] on occasion describing the forming of the bonds of friendship through blood rites.[29] At other times it is a virtue easily betrayed. Thucydides, meanwhile, oscillates between referring to trust as the credibility of the speaker and a guarantee, promise or oath.[30] However, it is Aristotle, defining trust in the fourth century BCE, who explicitly argues that rather than being univocal in nature, there are many types of trust. Furthermore, in the work of Theognis, trust is sometimes associated with the Ancient Greek idea of excellence of body and mind: an ideal.[31] 'This idea is the subjective aspect of *homonoia*,[32] and as such is social and political; the trust citizens have for one another is the inner psychological counter-part of social harmony'.[33] He, however, contrasts this notion of trust against a more pessimistic view in his 'how to' manuals (where he advises young men on morals, politics and deportment) by stating 'don't trust anyone, they'll just betray you anyway': thus, he highlights the tension within the role of trust in Ancient Greek life.[34]

While little reference was made to whom, what, or why the Greeks trusted or distrusted, a philological study tells us that trust was only personal in nature.[35] The Ancient Greek writers did on occasion hint at more, for example, when Antiphon writes about his court case and similarly, when Isocrates describes the teacher–student relationship.[36] There is also some limited evidence of 'trusting' impersonal systems. For instance, Demosthenes writes, 'What, then, do we rely upon, and what security do we get when we risk our money? We rely upon you, men of the jury, and upon your laws, which ordain that all agreements into which a man voluntarily enters with another shall be valid'.[37] While in Aristotle's analysis of 'friendships of utility' (one of three forms of friendship) trust acquires a technical legal meaning, as a credit or a guarantee between people – a form of civic friendship,[38] when those involved seek mediation through the law, rather than through their relationship as friends.[39]

However, it was not only the concept of trust (*pistis*), but also the 'carriers of trust' and their day-to-day practices, which were interwoven into the life of Ancient Greece.[40] They were based on cultural values, such as the notion of natural inequality, honour and obligation,[41] regard for the law and their conception of a Greek identity, which are communicated and reiterated in narrative form through language and practices within society.[42] They created a framework of 'trust', which underpinned both a citizen's (and his inferior's) relationships and those which made up the *polis*. Changing and developing over time (as highlighted below), they were often subsumed or rewritten within the networked relationships of trust, internally and externally within the *polis*.

These demonstrations of trust (included within the patron–client relationship, citizenship, *homonoia*, civic friendship and oaths) which overlap and entwine themselves are not only the basis of, but also fundamental to, a functioning society. In Ancient Greek literature, these conceptions ('carriers of trust') were used more frequently than trust itself. This book does not attempt to articulate a totalizing model of trust but focuses on the key pillars of Ancient Greek society, namely law,[43] the family cult, citizenship and Greek identity, and how the unfolding history of trust in Athens shaped its society and enabled revolutionary change.

Initially conceived around the notion that family was paramount, society in Athens represented the association of families rather than of individuals, as we have come to perceive of society in the West.[44] The family was the smallest unit of measure and was the first social institution in the prehistoric period.[45] Through ancestral worship around the hearth, and under the auspices of the head of the family (typically the eldest male) in the ostensible role of judge and cleric,[46] a family's identity was created and constantly reinforced.[47] Roles were determined, duties and obligations dictated and behaviour constrained. Around each hearth, the family alone worshipped their own unique gods.[48] 'The ancient Greek language has a very significant word to designate a family'.[49] It 'signifies, literally, that which is near a hearth'.[50]

With a common language, and shared history, the worship of the family cult was transmuted through extended families, clans and tribes to the formation of city-states. 'As the scale of association increased, the gods of nature, or polytheism, became more important – for these were gods who could more easily be shared … gods associated with the forces of nature rather than with divine ancestors'.[51] Extending the family cult resulted in the development of a priesthood, assemblies and rituals. As larger associations developed so did the cult of the family, moving from a solely domestic setting into a public one: it became a foundational pillar for laws and political institutions. However, the domestic heart and hearth retained their primacy, creating an impenetrable boundary. 'Justice within the family remained basically a matter for paterfamilias, not the city'.[52]

Running in parallel to the expansion of the family cult was the development of a 'Greek' identity. Its foundations were constructed, in part, of myths and legends, together with commonly held social customs.[53] They drew on families' ancestral heroes, turning them into demi-gods, and, in so doing further mingled religious beliefs into everyday life. The cult of the family remained supreme within the private sphere; however, the safety, welfare and continuity of the city were paramount in the public. As such, the cult was a mirror image projected onto the larger public canvas. It ultimately gave its citizens their communal identity (to rule and be ruled) and responsibility, indivisibly tying them to their gods.[54] In this situation, an extinguished hearth was synonymous with a family's destruction; so too if a city was defeated and enslaved.[55] When ancient citizens defended their city, they were defending their gods and their ancestral lands. Piety and patriotism were one and the same for Ancient Greek citizens and defending one's city, the highest virtue.

The city was governed by a small number of aristocratic families (the *eupatridae* or 'well-born'), who had superseded the earlier kings (*basileis*) together with nine magistrates (*archons*),[56] who shared the religious, military and judicial functions once discharged by the king, together with the Council of the Areopagus.[57] Athens, in the early Archaic period, was organized according to a law-based constitution (initially in oral form then written) with a set of core values, designed to unite an increasingly diverse population.[58] Despite the many changes in its social make-up and the administration required to meet the growing needs of the city, the governance of Athens remained broadly a religious affair, in the hands of its citizens and at the whim of its gods.[59] The wider populace had virtually no political voice.

By the sixth century BCE, these aristocratic families faced increasing unrest and challenges to their rule.[60] Fearing further revolts,[61] as circumstances increasingly highlighted the asymmetrical relationship in place between citizens and their inferiors, pre-emptive actions were taken and membership of this 'superior' class was widened. Notably, Draco (621–620 BCE) and Solon (594 BCE) introduced a number of reforms. Renowned for their harshness, Draco's laws and a new constitution on the one hand gave political rights to those Athenians 'who bore arms',[62] while on the other, the death penalty was prescribed for all and every crime.[63] This did little to redress the imbalance between the wealthy and the poor that was threatening the stability and prosperity of Athens. Solon's reforms, 'led by moral concern about justice and a prudent conviction regarding the necessity of change',[64] were more far-reaching; they cancelled all debts and abolished the practice of giving loans with a citizen's freedom as collateral (which created slavery)[65]; took the authority for interpreting the law away from the magistrates (*Archons*) and placed it in the hands of more democratically selected citizen juries[66]; and elected a short-list of candidates for the Archonship (thereby removing the stranglehold which a small number of aristocratic families had on the position). Solon, with the tacit support of the *ecclesia* (the Assembly in which every citizen could participate), the *Boule* and the *Areopagus* introduced many elements that would later form part of the 'revolutionary' democracy.[67] By widening the citizenship base, he 'replaced extreme oligarchy with ancestral democracy' and by spreading the practice of civic duty he helped to develop a sense of communal citizenship.[68] Aristotle, writing later, described the traits necessary for communal citizenship as sharing values and common interests, possessing a sense of justice and capacity for prudent judgement, being temperate and exercising self-control, and being able to put the public good above personal interests and advancement.[69]

These reforms, however, could not mitigate the 'class' struggle in Athens. The aristocracy railed against the curbing of their power and the dissatisfaction stemming from their financial losses, while the wider citizenry, newly conscious of their empowered political position, demanded land reforms and greater benefits from the taxes they paid. Factions formed, alliances were made and broken as their self-interests vied for position and power. Eventually, Peisistratus seized power by an elaborate trick,[70] establishing himself as a relatively benign tyrant.[71] His reign was described by Thucydides thus: 'the city was left in full enjoyment of its existing laws, except that care was always taken to have the offices in the hands of [a member] of the family'.[72] He was succeeded by his sons Hippias and Hipparchus (the epitome of oppressive tyrants), whose tyranny only came to an end in 510 BCE, brought about by the aristocratic Alcmeonidae family backed by a Spartan army.[73] Thus, the scene was set for the Athenian Revolution. The governance of the city-state had been corrupted and a foreign power occupied Athens. For the citizens, it was a trusted duty to Athens and each other to bring about constitutional change and to restore *homonia*.

Herodotus and Thucydides,[74] in their analyses of revolutions, theorized that the destructive force necessary for revolution was only possible after the decay of the fundamental moral and religious tenets of society.[75] Closely associated with injustice, economic collapse and moral decline, it had the potential to destroy the *polis*. In such a 'diseased' community, individuals, groups or factions would become angry and self-interested and ultimately revolt. Revolution provides cover for all manner of selfish acts (revenge, elimination, expropriation).[76] As Walsh posits, the revolutionaries' goal was not to establish justice, but to seize the power and honour they felt due to them. Such actions, Thucydides reasoned, distorted both the individual's traits of character and virtues and the community's values.[77] Over time such actions became the 'fodder' for the comedies and tragedies of the age.[78] It was not until the era of Aristotle and Plato that the notion of civic friendship was used to look beyond strife to its absence and what unified a *polis*.

Nevertheless, the Athenian democratic revolution avoided the *stasis* (civil strife) which marked so many other revolutions.[79] Rather than a destructive force, changes were brought about through the widespread acceptance of, and trust in, a communal identity.[80] A revolutionary process rather than a specific revolutionary moment, the notion of collective responsibility, a central message of Cleisthenes's reforms, brought with it a new phase in Greek history.[81] The far-reaching effects of this revolution reflect the changing patterns of thought, speech and action together with changes in social relations and political authority.[82] These events stand in such stark contrast to Thucydides's description of the revolutions that took place at Corcyra during the Peloponnesian Wars.[83] Examining those revolutions he concludes that 'human nature, always rebelling against the law and now its master, gladly showed itself ungoverned in passion, above respect for justice, and the enemy of all superiority',[84] whereas those who rebelled in 508/7 BCE were able to agree upon what they regarded as fundamental, upon their attitude to their gods, to their solemn oaths, their obligations and the security and independence of their city, putting these matters ahead of personal goals and desires.

Revolutions, as observed and recorded by Herodotus and Thucydides, were often compelled by man's self-interest, by unequal and unjust regimes, or by changes to their constitution. Revolution was a means to redress the balance.[85] To contemporary historians this was a familiar and recurring theme; and with it repeating itself the very notion of revolution became cyclical.[86] Thus, the democratic revolution is distinguished by the fact that it both represented the 'ideological hegemony' of the ordinary citizens and benefited their well-being as a whole.[87]

To establish the changes wrought by the Athenian Revolution and give them the opportunity to become ingrained, Cleisthenes drew inspiration from, and connection to, not only Athens's mythical and heroic past, but also past practices and traditions. He called upon the framework of trust underpinning society. (See **Figure 9**.)

For instance, in creating ten new tribes he simultaneously broke the traditional tribal allegiances and recreated them anew around loyalty to the State. By

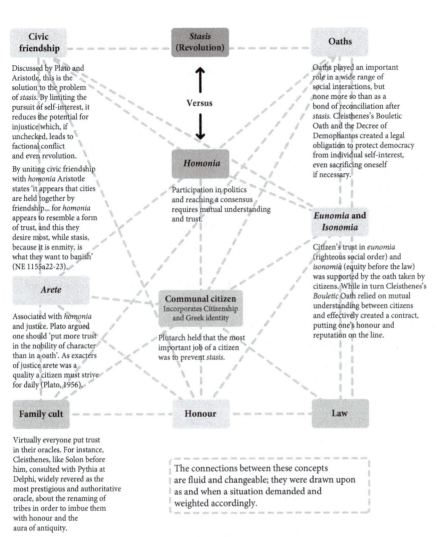

Figure 9 The networks of trust in Ancient Greek society.

abolishing patronymics in favour of demonymics (a name given according to the *deme* to which individuals belong), an individual came to identify with the State rather than their family, clan, or tribe.[88] Using the notion of a tribe but 'substituting locality for kinship' provided a sense of familiarity; an individual could draw on their own experiences and history.[89] Its purpose remained the same, a commitment to the tribe; only its focus changed. Consulting with the *Pythia* at Delphi, who was widely revered as the most prestigious and authoritative oracle in the Ancient Greek world, the tribes were named after local legendary heroes to give them an aura of antiquity and imbue them with honour.[90] An individual could feel proud by association and moderate their behaviour accordingly. Aristotle says that Cleisthenes created ten new tribes 'so that more men should have a share in the running of the state'.[91] The number of citizens now involved in the governance of the *polis* was considerable, each with a vested interest in the continued survival and success of Athens.[92] This also reduced the powers of the traditional aristocracy, ending old jealousies and curbing factional strife while consequentially expanding upon the notions of citizenship and state.[93] It was each tribe's responsibility to deliver public services, levy soldiers, and candidates for office, and in so doing it emphasized the equality of its members and reinforced tribal loyalty and commitment, creating a bond of brotherhood.[94] Having already been created, the tribes constantly maintained and reinforced an Athenian communal identity, rather than an individual one. With clearly delineated roles and obligations, the system institutionalized a trusting relationship with the State. Reinforced by publishing its workings and decisions, it ensured transparency and accountability.

The concept, together with the 'carriers (networks) of trust' and associated practices, was all operating within the spaces of the revolutionary theatre, simultaneously linking the past, present and future.[95] However, rather than a flat universal playing field it is a textural landscape, changeable and multi-varied, contracting and expanding, as different forces are applied and removed. The closer an observer looks, the more details emerge, constantly connecting and reconnecting, each containing its own narrative, its own reality. Despite being powerful, language itself is affected at the time of *stasis*; for example, Thucydides describes how 'people exchange the valuation of words'.[96] Their meaning did not change but their values did, altering the relationship between words and reality.

Throughout the transition from monarchy to aristocracy, through tyranny to democracy, a citizen's privileges were rule-bound; his role and obligations were dictated by the needs of the city and the political process was sacrosanct. Society operated within a rigid framework of trust which provided stability (*homonia*) and purpose (independence and continuity): it was built on the acceptance of natural inequality, on the pillars of the law, honour, family, and community. Within the domestic sphere the κύριος was the master: he represented the family in the public sphere. It was underpinned by a system of worship, which simultaneously initiated and claimed authority over an individual's (citizens in particular) thoughts and action.[97] This extended to dress, deportment, marriage, sport, education, and even ambition; all were dictated by rigid rules. An inevitable consequence of family cult worship, they strongly influenced and shaped the creation of a communal Greek identity for its citizens. It was this identity, created through a social revolution and underpinned by trust, which enabled the far-reaching political reforms of Cleisthenes.[98]

These dynamic networks of the interwoven and overlapping concept and conceptions of trust are mirrored in 'the prevailing image of the citizen-statesman, as a weaver' and similarly reflected in classic Ancient Greek art.[99] Concerned not only with the law, and all that belongs to the life of the community, the citizen-statesman wove these disparate strands into a unified whole.[100] Amongst the Ancient Greeks, the concept of trust with its everyday practices and the various conceptions ('carriers of trust') became the backbone of an emerging and evolving system of impersonal trust necessary to cope with the 'revolutionary' developments of society, the State, its culture, and influence. Trust became a means to an end not an end in itself.

Ancient Rome

In a harsh world where only the fittest survived, Rome was no more militaristic or warmongering than the states surrounding it, yet it became one of the largest and most enduring empires in world history. Stretching at its height from north-western Europe to the Near East, its self-image and pioneering understanding of citizenship stood out.[101] Where the Greeks spoke of communities made up of people, with their participatory politics and crushing conformity, the Romans spoke of the city and its building,[102] their antagonist politics[103] and the flexible vision of *romanitas*.[104] From its foundational legends, Rome was shaped and inspired by its passionate sense of a sacred mission to conquer.[105] Romans attributed their success to their collective piety (*pietas*) and in maintaining good relations with the gods,[106] while 'their traditions of origin stressed the progressive incorporation of outsiders'.[107] It transitioned from monarchy, to republic, to an all-inclusive Empire, and then a Christian Empire, as the need arose. With each revolution Rome returned to the notion of trust (*fides*), recreating itself by combining the old with the new.

Where the Greeks referred to rule by one, the few and by the many in their theory of *anacyclosis*,[108] Polybius (whose work *The Histories* describes the rise of the Roman Republic) spoke of a cycle of six forms of government.[109] The Romans understood 'revolution' as political constitutional change despite famously having no written constitution.[110] Although conquest and colonization produced rebellions, slave revolts and officer-led coups, these lacked the necessary 'revolutionary' element (in effect constitutional change or modification).[111] Revolution, when experienced, took a number of forms: the forcible substitution of a ruler; a new political system; and modification of the system by the Roman elite, with the action and support of the people. In 509 BCE revolution replaced the Etruscan monarchy with the Roman Republic,[112] while those in 494, 449 and 287 BCE sought greater protection and power for the people,[113] and that of 133 BCE transferred power from a corrupt oligarchy to one man. Called the Roman Revolution,[114] following the assassination of Caesar and subsequent civil war, the Republic became the Empire (*Principate*). Although constitutionally slight in effect, it was by no means a meaningless shift.[115]

Cyclical in nature, both the Ancient Greeks and Romans theorized that there was a natural order in which constitutions changed. Heavily influenced by the seasons and the cycle of birth, growth, and death, the chief cause of constitutional change was the moral decay and corruption of its citizens, meaning they were no longer able to make wise and balanced judgements.[116] 'Permanence was provided by the cycle itself'.[117] However, this was to change following a marked period of transition, when a moral and social 'revolution' resulted in a new way of life. Christianity, an equally powerful paradigm of change, was depicted by the earliest propagators and later apologists as a radical revolution. Although Greco/Roman culture and Christianity were sometimes violently oppositional, strong intellectual continuities can be identified within this transformation.

Under the monarchical Etruscan rule for over 200 years, by 509 BCE Rome had established itself as an independent republic (*res publica romana* – the 'public thing of the Roman people') lasting for over 450 years.[118] Tarquinius's tyranny ended after Lucretia's rape and suicide which resulted in a rebellion that led to the overthrow of the monarchy.[119] In simultaneously seeking to maintain power but curb the ambitions of the few, the *Curia* (one of Rome's legislative assemblies made up of aristocrats) agreed to a provisional constitution under which two Roman consuls acted as a joint executive, swearing never again to let a king rule Rome. Needing to acquire the assent of the people, they were summoned to the forum for a general election. Under this new political system of representative government, the City was able to grow into an empire. Built on the notion that Romans should act as one, prioritizing the city over themselves, they developed a strongly centralized sense of identity.[120] A constant work in progress driven by tensions between the aristocracy and ordinary citizens, the constitution evolved and with it, a new *patricio-plebeian* nobility emerged which made Rome's success possible. Reinforced by the Roman notion of trust and the trust-building foundations it laid, its written and codified laws (beginning with its Twelve Tables)[121] divided the responsibilities and duties amongst various governing representatives (power was limited and checked through a collegial system),[122] and the alliances it made,[123] together with the extensive building programmes (used to dominate and pacify; to control and welcome, to glorify and Romanize).

Rome's first revolution resolved to build a new state in which Romans would be secure and free. Paradoxically these building blocks of isolationism led to expansionism divinely ordained by the gods,[124] underpinned by the Roman notion of trust and their networks of honour, *mos mairorum* (custom of the ancestors) and civic duty.

Worshipped by the Romans as a goddess, trust was also an all-important and all-encompassing concept for Roman law and business; oral contracts were common.[125] Her temple on the Capitol held important documents and treaties signed by the Roman Senate. She was also worshipped as *Fides Publica Populi Romani* (public trust of the Roman people). In everyday use it was an essential constituent element of all social and political transactions; it was described by Cicero as truth and reliability in words and actions.[126] It meant reliability with good faith between two parties being mutually reciprocal; it implied privileges and obligations on both sides. In a society where oaths, personal credibility and the value of a citizen's word held sway,[127] reputation was important and seen as a virtue.[128] 'Not strictly social, religious, or moral ... *fides* was an ethical principle that divinities guaranteed';[129] it embodied the concept that a citizen's word would be kept under all circumstances and that their actions were transparent; to fall short risked the wrath of the gods.

Often used interchangeably with *fides*, in ancient sources, *fides publica* was a norm of law governing relationships across the legal spectrum. Regarded as the general standard of behaviour, 'public trust' promoted the notion of the public good. In Cicero's view serving the common interests above one's own was a 'sacred trust'. Understood not as a technical or legal term but through meaning,[130] it served as a guiding principle and was the foundation of justice itself.[131] Underpinning all aspects of Roman social life 'trust, as ... the Romans see it, is central to all the business of society: buying, selling, hiring, letting, in trusteeships, partnerships, and commissions. Trust is also the foundation of *amicitia*, that special brand of friendship and loyalty linking together groups of members of the senatorial and equestrian orders; and of the patron–client relationship between these notables and those from a lower station. Any violation of trust threatens to undermine the whole of social life'.[132]

Broadly synonymous with the Greek *pistis*,[133] Hebrew *ĕmūnāh* and Arabic الإيمان, the notion of *fides* differs greatly from modern ideas of trust.[134] Culturally and specifically constructed, the notion of trust (*fides*) reflects the specific interconnected and entwined combination of ideas, values, and day-to-day practices of the age (see **Figure 10**).

In use and context, throughout Roman literature, the term is understood to vary its meaning to include: fidelity, trustworthiness; faith; trust; a promise; and reliance, and this was in a risk-filled environment that made sense of uncertainty and misfortune through ideas of fate, providence, and luck. Practical in nature, the moral connotations carried within the notion of trust evolved in time under the influence of Christianity.

Under the Republic, the first public building opened was a temple (the Temple of Jupiter)[135]; linked to conquest, the City's growth was sanctioned by the gods even if its kings were gone. This pattern was repeated, yet subtly altered, under Empire and Rome's conversion. Woven into their social fabric, gods were a common,

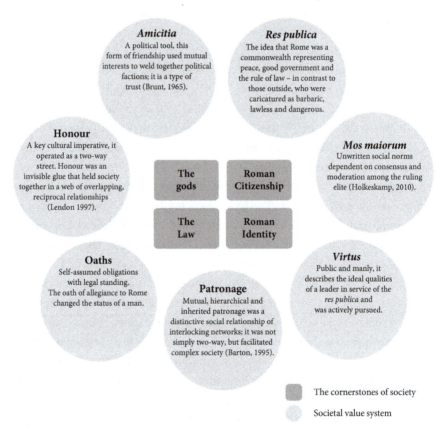

Figure 10 The Roman Republic's framework of trust.

flexible and meaningful presence in all Romans' lives in the growing *imperium*. Built on slavery, loot, tribute and taxes, Rome grew through an ever-changing combination of hard and soft imperialism (military might and Romanization), divinely ordained by the gods.[136] Without doubt Rome could be violent and savage but induced by the benefits, and swayed by the 'gift' of citizenship, many tribes wanted to become part of Rome,[137] trusting it would act responsibly, carefully and mercifully, with its power restrained and exercised responsibly.[138] Its incorporation and establishment of permanent relationships with conquered towns and tribes stood in stark contrast to those around it even though, idiosyncratically, Roman imperialism was never consensual.[139] In this way Rome's power was founded on people power; increasingly successful, it became ever more sacred.[140]

Although Rome experienced periods of upheaval and unrest under the Republic, its transition to *Principate* marked another revolutionary turning point. It 'transform[ed] political and military structures, the government of empire, appearance of the city of Rome and the underlying sense of what Roman power culture and identity were all about'.[141] This change was mirrored by the conversion of Gaius Octavius from insurgent to Augustus Caesar, founding father and longest-serving ruler.[142] Although 'cataclysmic violence and trauma' accompanied this transition, it was arguably Augustus' manipulation of religion that was most far-reaching. Combining the old and the new he gave Rome's emperors a new status as 'gods', creating the imperial cult. By co-opting religious powers, rebuilding shrines and dedicating gifts, he not only renewed religious practice but forever tied it to Rome's emperor.[143] His ability to transfer the 'trust' which the Romans had for their gods to himself was staggering.[144] Under the Empire and the emperors the city became ever more holy while Romans began to call it the 'Eternal City'.

Although this transition ultimately reflected the inability of the Republic to reconcile the various social interests at work, the revolution was personal, played out on Rome's public stage against a backdrop of corruption, cynicism and self-interest. The inability of the Roman constitution to keep up the pace and a growing need for land reform, coupled with the increasingly competitive elite (supported by their own armies), raised the spectre of change as mob violence, treachery and murder became the new tools of Roman political life.[145] After a century of constant civil strife, and sometimes open warfare, the question arises: how did Augustus transform the Republic into an empire under his control? Alliances played a key role, securing near total military power within the Republic. He then appointed provincial governors throughout the empire, loyal to him, while leaving the Republican institutions intact. He reorganized and purged the Senate of its unreliable and untrustworthy members and in so doing restored peace, stability and the law to Rome, benefiting both his network of loyal patrons and the wider populace. Like those before and after, Augustus used both religion and propaganda to unify, stabilize and strengthen the Empire. Using the people's trust he redirected the focus to himself as he became son of a god (*divi filius*), becoming both the bridge between the people and their gods and the basis of Rome's success. By subtly balancing the hard and soft tools he had to hand, he gave the impression of returning power to the senate; they in turn moved to entrench his authority even more. His outward respect for *mos maiorum* enabled him to maintain the facade of a republic while establishing himself as emperor. Consolidating authority, power and influence, the imperial foundations he laid were consolidated by his successors. Just as the republic created its republicans, 'the empire created the emperors' but despite the differences, Rome rested on the same basis.[146]

Thus under the Empire, trust (*fides*) became almost a Roman 'buzzword'.[147] Universal in its application, the term held a prominent place within Roman ideology.[148] It sat at the heart of political and diplomatic discourse, both internally and externally; it was used as a term to cement a new regime or to demonstrate that Rome was now on a good-faith footing with an ally or newly conquered territory.[149] Images of *fides* (as a goddess or as clasped hands) featured prominently,[150] notably on coinage and inscribed for posterity on monuments[151]; it was also depicted in a variety of forms in literature.[152] Its breadth of usage throughout Roman society and culture reflected its complexity. It defined the relationship between patron and client, Rome and newly subjugated foes and now relationships with one's former 'enemies', being thus multi-faceted, ethically and morally charged.[153]

In stark contrast with the Ancient Greeks, the notion of *fides*, and in particular *fides publica*, was explicitly referred to and called upon in revolutionary situations. This fundamental Roman notion was based upon a deep-rooted ideological concern that public welfare was always of paramount concern. It took precedence over private interests and personal gain. In the politically turbulent times before the Roman Revolution, Julius Caesar grounded his legitimacy primarily in a traditionally republican notion of trust,[154] to persuade his audience he was justified in leading his army across the Rubicon and instigating a civil war. In documenting the political crisis of 50–49 BCE, Caesar sets the 'good' *fides* of his friends and allies, the necessary 'good' violence which his camp inflicted, together with the respective impact on the armies and on civilian communities in each theatre of conflict, against the 'bad' of Pompey's.[155]

Comparing themselves favourably to others, Romans took particular pride in being people of trust.[156] An important narrative, it shaped the edifying tales of *fides publica*[157] (although of dubious historical accuracy, they illustrated a system of values) which were intended to communicate and widely diffuse an important public ethos, the violation of which was deemed a stain on Rome's and the individual's reputation.[158] After the republic became an empire, the use of *fides publica* was subtly altered. By anchoring it to an Augustan past (renowned for the restoration of public morals and an end to corruption which undermined the late republic), it was used to reinforce a regime, often used symbolically (on coins, in literature) after a period of civil strife, demonstrating Rome was back on a good-faith footing.[159] It later fell 'into abeyance during the *Dominate*,[160] as private loyalties and family ties replaced *fides* as the guiding principle of public law and morality'.[161] The resources, power and might of the Empire were no longer considered a public trust but the personal property of the emperor.

As Rome,[162] an 'empire of trust', came to dominate Western Europe, centralization replaced local autonomy. Rather than the Greek notion of communal citizenship, with its daily obligations, citizenship was legalistic in nature; it focused on private interests and their protection. Under the Empire, citizenship no longer involved taking part in public discussions, decisions and law making[163]: it was a case of '*civitas sine suffragio*' or 'citizenship without the vote' while standing armies became the primary defenders of the city, replacing a citizen-soldier's duties.[164] Necessarily, the definition, distinctions and rights of citizenship changed. As a result, the legal and political communities separated.[165] Citizenship became a tool of foreign policy and control, helping to assimilate an increasingly diverse population.[166] Men were no longer constrained by their prescribed 'natural' roles. The more aristocratic connotations of citizenship, its superiority and rationality, were replaced by birthright and conformity. Citizens under imperial rule were subjects of the law; ruled by it rather than ruling themselves. This notion of citizenship was reflected in a subtly different, yet widespread, understanding of the notion of trust in its various guises (see Figure 11).[167]

Commanded at will under the Empire (the will of an often-distant emperor, military might and the law), submission and obedience were common practice within society. With relentless imperial conquest and colonization, new challenges arose. One amongst many was the increasing religious diversity across the Empire and within its cities.[169] Over time, polytheism lost its dominance, as both ancient (Judaism) and new religions, including imported mystery religions,[170] attracted converts. With 'the image of a single, remote and inscrutable god dispensing his laws to a whole people',[171] these monotheistic religions were able to be experienced by those subjugated to the Roman Empire. This radical shift was reflected in the beliefs and practices of Judaism

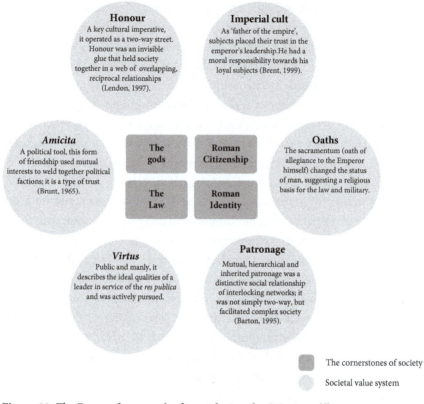

Figure 11 The Roman framework of trust during the *Principate*.[168]

in which God's will was privileged; it could not be reasoned with but must be obeyed.

Seen essentially as a private, local and personal matter, the Romans, rather pragmatically, tolerated and accepted most religions and cults.[172] However, this did not extend to the Baccanals, Druids, Jews, and Christians who faced persecution, banishment and sometimes death, though as a matter of 'political policy', rather than 'dogmatic zeal'.[173] This did not seem to hinder the Christian expansion but, instead, created martyrs for a growing audience to venerate.[174] They provided an alternative to victorious Roman military heroes and the superstars of the arena, the gladiators. Ancient heroes were previously aristocrats, portrayed over time as demi-gods; their exploits weaved into a family's cult worship, providing the foundation for polytheism and the ideal Greek and Roman traits to aspire to, but now birth and privilege no longer mattered. Christian martyrs stood alone. They provided a real and tangible example of individual free will, founded on consciousness: a model of self-respect open to all.

Despite the threats and challenges, monotheism (in particular Christianity) slowly gained ground in the vacuum largely left by the displacement of ancient communal citizenship. It had a profound effect on the highly socially differentiated and overly status-conscious Roman society, infusing it with early Christian beliefs (moral equality and charity).[175] In combination with Christian conceptions of individual agency and will, it reshaped this deeply pious, highly superstitious society, built upon an unshakeable belief in natural inequality and an irresistible fate. It resulted in a moral and intellectual revolution.[176] A new sense of unidirectional time went together with the awareness of free will.[177] As linear time replaced the cyclicality once understood, the repeating pattern of corruption undermining political constitutions was exchanged for successive moments progressing from creation to salvation. 'Time [now] had a beginning and an end; it was a narrative, whose triumphant conclusion would come in the future. From this insight came a new conception of men and women as individuals with unique destinies'.[178]

As these teachings spread, utilizing the Roman's road network, the notion of faith became firmly entwined with the concept of trust and those associated conceptions, which were implicit and often explicit 'carriers of trust'. It became synonymous with 'religious belief', subsuming the meaning 'to abide by a specific (religious, ethical, political) law'.[179] As *fides* became firmly established as meaning both a guarantee and a Christian belief, so its use increased exponentially in both literature and everyday use. Previously a Roman virtue, the notion of trust now carried within it the Christian principles and teachings necessary for salvation.[180] Similarly the notion of revolution would be seen to evolve, in time, to reflect these notions.

Towards the end of the Roman Empire, Roman rulers could no longer ignore the effects and influence of Christianity.[181] It challenged the governance of the Empire and its social structure. Thinking of themselves as highly religious, their collective piety a key to Roman success, it was, therefore, the duty of the government to maintain favour in the eyes of the gods.[182] Religion was practical and contractual in nature; it relied on knowledge, ritual construction and performance rather than faith or dogma.[183] It was a source of social order, one that Christianity threatened, with their now extensive organization and parallel teachings of love, charity and mercy.[184] It became increasingly apparent that the two could not co-exist without altering the existing social order.

By leading his troops into battle at Milvian Bridge in 312 CE under the protection of God, Constantine dramatically transformed the fortunes and status of the early Christian Church.[185] The policies he subsequently introduced, by their very nature, were transformative as ultimately they changed the Roman

Constitution,[186] fusing Church and Empire.[187] The Edict of Milan,[188] 'the Magna Carta of religious liberty', first 'put Christianity on an equal footing with paganism'.[189] It was followed by further decrees which favoured the Christians. Up to 323 CE the aim of these decrees was to maintain equality and toleration, thereafter they actively promoted Christianity. 'Henceforth bishops became men of power and influence in political and well as religious life'.[190] Most politically significant, however, was Constantine's participation in, and influence over, the Council of Nicaea: in relinquishing the right to self-government, the Church's teachings were in turn integrated into government (a *quid pro quo*).

The marriage of the Church and Empire came about gradually, as did the acceptance of Christian teachings and beliefs amongst the wider population. Conversion became fashionable as the Church gained influence and status; for many, it was a pragmatic decision rather than a religious one. The age of Constantine possesses all the ambiguities of a period of violent transition. Those ambiguities were dramatically epitomized in the person of the emperor himself. He is perhaps unique in enjoying the distinction of being deified as a pagan god, while simultaneously venerated as a Christian saint.[191] While an important political and psychological event, Constantine's conversion was a stepping stone in a more far-reaching moral and social revolution, one that supplanted both the social order and traditional Greco-Roman values.[192] Unable to offer the Empire a unifying religious ideology, paganism, once the beating heart of Rome, was replaced by the Church. Where once Roman emperors persecuted Christians in the name of their pagan gods, they were now represented as the agents of God on earth. Christianity provided a much stronger pillar to both unite and uphold the legitimacy and authority of the Empire against its enemies. Over time the Church and Empire became interdependent, becoming virtually inseparable; their union ushered in an ecclesiastical era.

Within this slowly but ever-changing environment, local communal identities were first replaced by a Roman identity (as a citizen of the Empire), before religious conversion reshaped them again. These changes similarly impacted upon the wider interconnected and interlocking framework which underpinned Roman society, from the notions of honour and Rome itself, to patronage and the law. Slowly evolving, they were in turn shaped by and shaped each other. Though not the only factor, by focusing on the impact of Christianity, changes in the function and operation of Roman society are clearly illuminated, with its new ideas (or threads) being gradually interwoven into the conceptions of trust and revolution.

Medieval Europe's rebellious nature

In Western Europe, from the eleventh century, there was a period of relative stability following the chaos and upheaval (threats of invasion, internal hostility, violence, and bloodshed) experienced in the vacuum left by the collapse of the Western Roman Empire. Medieval social order, during this period, although supported by a rapidly developing ecclesiastical structure and a rising monastic culture, was predominantly influenced by feudalism and manorialism.[1] Christianity was a strong unifying factor, particularly amongst the peasant, and later the artisan and commercial, classes. Principally instructed through music, art and architecture, as levels of scholarship and literacy were low, Christian values infused the virtues of loyalty, courage, and honour. This period saw the gradual process of medieval state-building[2]; representing a major institutional change, it moved away from a kinship-based model, to one ordered around the 'power' exercised by the monarch over their defined territories, with a variety of outcomes.[3] Intellectual activity increased, with the rediscovery of Aristotle, and with it, developments in philosophy and theology were systematically fused together in scholasticism.[4] Scholars also began to teach the complex and sophisticated Roman law. Its impact was profound, on both secular and canon law, and led to the recording and standardization of legal codes throughout Western Europe.[5]

This transformation, between c. 1000 and 1200 CE, has been termed the 'feudal revolution'.[6] It is used, by some academics, somewhat controversially, to describe the 'construction of a new civilization', being seen as 'the secret revolution of these centuries' that created 'the new social order'.[7] However, it has been suggested that the social origins of feudalism can be traced to the differential mixing of Roman and Germanic elements centuries earlier[8]; the debate continues as to whether it was the result of an extended period of transition or 'the first European Revolution'.[9] For Moore, 'profound changes in the economic and political organisation of the countryside amounted to a permanent transformation in the division of labor, social relations, and the distribution of power and wealth' in which elites 'found it necessary to reorganise themselves into a new social order, and to distribute power and authority among its branches by means of new techniques, and according to new definitions'.[10] In contrast, Barthelemy and White, in analysing French societal developments, *c.* 900–1200 CE, theorize that these display considerable continuity rather than change.[11] Regardless of their differing views, all agree, feudalism produced a co-dependency built on obligation, trust, and mutual benefit. Within this consciously ordered system everyone had their place; taxed in return for protection, this divinely ordained hierarchy brought social order and stability.

However, in Western Europe, this stability was increasingly threatened in the late medieval period (*c.* 1300–1500), as it bore witness to war, famine, and plague, religious conflict and scholarly exploration. Calamitous and disrupting, the Great Famine (1315–7), together with the Black Death (1347), reduced the population by more than a third compared to the previous century, while, at the same time, rising strong royalty-based realms waged war, extending their territories for profit.[12] Threatened from within, by both the Papal Schism (1378–1417) and a reaction against scholasticism,[13] the Church continued to face 'heretical' threats from John Wycliffe and Jan Hus.[14] Meanwhile, a commercial revolution (which saw the rise of merchants and craftsmen and the decline of agricultural dependency,[15] combining the role of key individuals with geopolitical, monetary and technological factors), coincided with various revolts and rebellions which included: the peasant revolts in Flanders (1323–8), the Ciompi Revolt in Florence (1378), the Peasants' Revolt (1381) in England, the Cabochien Revolt in Paris (1413) and the Rebellion of the Remences (1462 and 1485).[16]

Before the fourteenth century, kings were subordinate to the law,[17] and responsible for the common good; their multi-stranded role, containing elements that were not easily reconciled, was often conflicted. Theirs, necessarily, was a co-operative and collaborative rule[18]; guided by their knights and counselled by their clerks, commoners enabled their reign which is vividly illustrated in the *Piers Plowman* prologue.[19] Although exalted, the monarch's will was subordinate to the law of the land; the rebellions they faced were genuine, legitimate and often successful means of political action.[20] In key documents of the age (the Magna Carta, the Golden Bull of Hungary and Spanish jurisprudence),[21] it was actually the stated duty of those within the realm to use collective force against the king in just cause; this reflected a broad concern for the common good of the realm. Such actions have been described as 'good rebellions'.[22] However, the 'Crisis of the Middle Ages' marked a striking transition. It was a time of increasing uncertainty and dramatic change, with the tripartite social order under threat, as the shared understanding between the monarch and the three orders of medieval society began to fracture.[23] Monarchs sought to rule unchallenged, exercising their 'power' through the political institutions of state (their 'right arm') and the bureaucracy of the Church (their 'left arm'). As co-operative governments were swept away, mass movements and popular uprisings emerged. Although not unknown, discontent, which was previously limited and localized, became common and widespread, challenging the monarch and the interdependent social order; in response, rebellion became a treasonable offence.[24]

Modern scholarship, on these medieval rebellions and revolts, typically superimposes modern structures of analysis which are self-evident in the language used and the conclusions drawn.[25] However, while there is a rich vein of contemporary medieval literature discussing 'rebellions' and 'revolts', in both practical and theoretical terms, the term 'revolution' is conspicuous by its absence.[26] Instead of 'change' or 'transformation', contemporary chroniclers' discussions on revolt and rebellion are more often linked with proper kingship, the obligations of power and the common good. They highlight the failures of the powerful to govern adequately and justly, but confine themselves to operating within society's hierarchical structure, rather than threatening to overturn it. As such, in extremis, the individual (the king) could be replaced by his titled nobility with an alternative, while the system itself remained intact. Based on mutual 'trust' and benefit, the king's relationship with his titled nobility (and between the nobility and those below them) required both strength and subtlety. The nobility were not a group of 'anaemic, helpless' men as described by McFarlane, but 'fully rounded and fleshed-out nobles with their own collective and individual traits and interests'.[27] They were used to controlling the country, and kings who ignored, misread, or directly challenged the nobility did so at their own peril, while successful kings demonstrated acumen for political management, their patronage being both 'judicious and targeted'.[28]

Such actions were recorded for posterity by contemporary chroniclers. As Sizer argues, the key to interpreting these contemporary texts (including chronicles, poems, government documents, sermons, and political discourse) that discuss revolutionary activities lies in determining what revolt meant to those who lived through it.[29] However, as they are exclusively written by elites, the voices of peasants and labourers are mediated when they are heard (typically in judicial records). Their thoughts and feelings are obscured – and, in times of unrest, characterized as irrational and barbaric, disobedient, and illegitimate.[30] Such portrayals were in turn used to discredit the rebel cause; show allegiance to the writer's benefactor or king; and shape the ongoing intellectual debates amongst competing elites (such as royalty, nobility, clergy, bureaucrats, and scholars). Regardless of the reason or bias, these texts sought to reposition and reinstate the very relationships that these 'rebellions' and 'revolts' challenged.[31]

Recording actions and events rather than thoughts or ideas, the historiographical texts of the age were mediated by unsympathetic observers whose *Weltanschauung* was shaped by the same social and cultural hegemony[32]; they came with a set of beliefs about the role of the history of human action and 'rebellion' or 'revolt', within that history.[33] Described as violent, chaotic, vengeful and illegitimate, as evidenced by the terms used, 'rebellion' and 'revolt' were, however, an acceptable way, in the late medieval period, to restore good kingship and government.[34] Using academic theory, legal treatises and political precedent, the 'rebels' differentiated and legitimized the use of force, while the medieval understanding of violence, as a political tool, helps to explain the frequency of revolts.[35] Personal, direct and visceral, Brown describes the violence as endemic. Its effects are described in great detail; as a force for evil it was chaotic and lawless but it could also be a tool of right and justice, a weapon of protection and an aid for the faithful.[36] Rebellions and revolts in the late medieval period were, therefore, understood to be a moral choice, where honour and virtue existed in actions: a performance rather than a political act.[37]

Life, in the Middles Ages, was seen as a series of moral dilemmas, through which individuals must chart an appropriate course of action, set within a variable and changeable set of circumstances, created by the social world. Oaths,[38] rituals and chivalric codes of behaviour were used to regulate behaviour and so develop a sense of solidarity between the nobles, and thereby reduce uncertainty. Thus, the chronicles, which vividly captured the rebellions and revolts of the age,[39] recorded human action, judging, reflecting and grading those actions according to their perceived moral worth. Morality took the role that reason does in the modern period, and together with the concept of fortune,[40] proper kingship, governance and religion were vital in defining the role of 'rebellion' and 'revolt'.[41] Underpinning and connecting these concepts was the notion of trust (*fides*).

Representing both trust and Christian faith in late antiquity, *fides* was firmly established as the primary term for Christianity in the medieval period. Although the meaning of *fides* as a guarantee and reliability was more important in antiquity, it no longer dominated its use. Increasingly applied to a wide range of parallel uses, other terms began to replace its non-Christian functions.

Analysing the language in use is further complicated across Western Europe, since many areas operated multi-lingual systems.[42]Latin was the language of the educated. It was typically used for official documents, scholarly and liturgical texts. French was the language of chivalry and kingly courts, while the vast majority of the population spoke a variety of vernacular languages.

The word 'trust' itself, from the old Norse *traust*, first appeared in the thirteenth century. References are found throughout medieval literature: in contracts and court documents[43]; in secular, philosophical and ecclesiastical texts[44]; and in *chanson de geste*, songs and poems of chivalrous deeds and courtly love.[45] However, even with written evidence, it is difficult in practice to extrapolate exactly what was trusted, in what form and to what degree. Meanwhile, instances of the simultaneous distrust of individuals, while trust was maintained in institutions and societal structure, highlight that trust stretched beyond merely an interpersonal and local level. Contemporary evidence suggests that the values of medieval collective/communal society, as illustrated in **Figure 12**, were underpinned by the ideals of trust, loyal service, faith and 'just' governance. These notions were strongly tied to a perception of legitimate government and natural social order: 'a just and harmonious

'Just' rule
The king took an oath to defend the Church, uphold the law and rule justly. He relied on his nobles to legitimize their rule through a reciprocal system of duties, rights and obligations; requiring mutual trust (Valente, 2003).

Oaths
Symbolized the creation of a politically significant interpersonal bond, forming collaborative strategic alliances. However, they were often simply a routine part of conveyancing a transaction (Reynolds 1984).

Natural inequality
Governance through a just and harmonious hierarchy was perceived as legitimate and trusted throughout early medieval society (Siedentop, 2014).

Rota fortuna
Limiting 'fate' through virtue, courage, and reason became a popular idea in medieval instructive guilds, which were full of moralistic and aspiring tales. They had a practical use, educating and regulating behaviour (Patch, 1928).

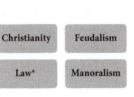

Christianity   Feudalism

Law*   Manoralism

The common good
Used by medieval writers to express a set of values, including trust, that transcended the collectivity of individuals. It acted as a loose bond that kept political communities united (Sizer, 2008).

Amicitia
Typically regarded as contractual, with utilitarian goals (such as economic or military), it was seen as a permanent agreement that could form part of an inheritance (Scorpo 2014).

Patronage
Elision between piety and patronage was a dominant motif in the Middle Ages. Articulating one's status, the elite had a responsibility to the wider community (Caskey, 2013).

The cornerstones of society

Societal value system

* Decentralized jurisdiction, often based on local customs

Figure 12 The developing framework of trust.

hierarchy – an Aristotelian monarchy rather than tyranny or, in towns, an Aristotelian aristocracy rather than oligarchy'.[46]

In a society which, through the Christian teachings of the Church,[47] simultaneously accepted the equality of each and every soul in heaven, and the inequality within the prevailing social order on earth, it was, perhaps, a natural step to 'trust' in a king anointed by God. Governing under feudal and manorial systems, the king was distant, unseen and unknown by most.[48] To maintain local customs, and a semblance of law and order, it was vital that each and every one was 'trusted' to perform their appointed duties.[49] This rigid structure was formalized through oaths of fealty, bound together by pairs of reciprocal obligations[50] and regulated with harsh penalties. However ineffectually or severely enforced, it paled in comparison to the defencelessness and anarchy of the alternative – this offers a possible explanation for why no demands were made for extending participation in government or equal rights in the vast majority of revolts and uprisings in this period.[51]

In an insecure risk-filled medieval world, of tight and wary alliances, 'trust' was at once cherished, rare and precious, especially as everyone needed to co-operate to survive. It contributed to a strong sense of community, not in the Ancient Greek sense, as a single entity, but as a constellation of memberships in different kinds of groups: households, neighbourhoods, villages, parishes, guilds and workshops, as well as counties, regions and kingdoms. The feeling of security and mutual support this created was supported by a notion of 'trust', promoted through feasting together, celebrating Carnival and other festivals (typically a combination of Christian, pagan, and local customs), attending religious ceremonies and the provision of mutual benefits (e.g. burial and mass for the dead).[52] This did not inhibit individuals from striving for personal gain, or preclude distrust or betrayal; nevertheless, in accepting a certain degree of regulation, examples of mutual support and collective activities were commonplace. These included the lay management of common lands, the building and maintaining of roads and churches and the judging of local lawsuits and crimes.[53] This local and somewhat inward-looking focus, reinforced through the 'common box', parish rituals and 'beating the bounds',[54] often resulted in a distrust of outside influence – of strangers, foreigners, and royal and seigniorial officials. They became scapegoats when times were hard, when crops failed, or diseases spread, and taxes were high.[55]

These social values, at differing times in different scenarios, not only built and maintained social bonds, but could also create barriers and divisions. For example, referring to the guilds and fraternities (including Freemasons),[56]

Reynolds argues that 'they relied first and foremost on affective bonds ... reinforced by oaths, and maintained by the collective jurisdiction over their members that all collective groups tend to assume ... they would drink together, swear solidarity and pledge themselves to mutual good works'.[57] In fact, Pooley notes, the trade elements in these guilds were 'not at first apparent',[58] but evolved generations later, while all guilds retained a religious orientation until the Reformation.[59] For example, embodying the idea of brotherhood (occasionally sisterhood), Italian guilds supported their members through acts of charity, prayers and burial.[60] However, 'Jews, always a marginal element in medieval society, were universally excluded', as women often were.[61]

As for villages, Reynolds states that they acted 'collectively in running their agriculture, their parish churches and fraternities, their local government and perhaps a good deal more besides ... united partly by subjection to the same lordship, but partly by their common rights and duties as farmers, parishioners and neighbours'.[62] However, although some individuals chose voluntary exile, becoming missionaries and pilgrims, others were excluded as outlaws, together with the religious equivalent which included those excommunicated,[63] witches, prostitutes, and perjurers,[64] the legally 'unfree'[65] and the physically impaired.[66] They were seen as a threat to communal cohesion and a coherent society.[67] It is manifest, from medieval literature,[68] that before the late medieval period (*c.* 1300–1500), both government and society in general depended upon the collective activities of a wide cross-section of people, in support of, and in opposition to, local governance and government. Founded on 'a very homogenous set of values, [they] combined acceptance of inequality and subordination with a high degree of voluntary cooperation'.[69] As late as 1311, barons in England regarded themselves as defenders of the 'community of the realm' and in so doing demonstrated the sense of collective duty and obligation that ran through all levels of society. However, even as these values coalesced, uniting medieval society both vertically and horizontally within its rigid structure, they were slowly transforming against the backdrop of the late medieval period.

The transformation followed in the footsteps of the Papal Revolution,[70] and took many forms. Both the pillars of society, and the value system uniting it, changed quite dramatically (illustrated in Figure 13), from the changing notions of kingship, societal structure, and risk,[71] to more centralized governments, the beginnings of administrative bureaucracies, and a professional system of law: all key elements in what John Watts has characterized as 'the making of polities'.[72]

These changes were felt most keenly in the late medieval period and, with them, the socio-political and economic focus of society shifted away from

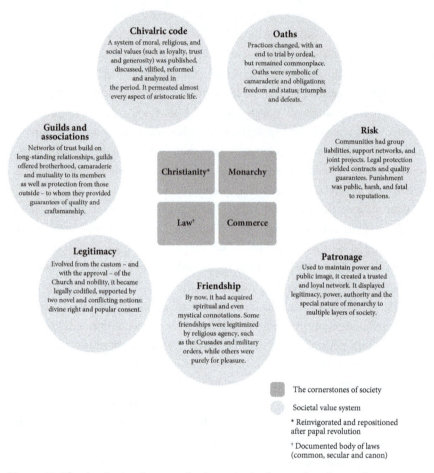

Figure 13 The developing framework of trust in the late medieval period.

extreme localism, community, and structure, to one of interconnecting and overlapping communities, good order, and legitimacy. Although hard to substantiate on the available evidence, assumptions can be drawn, in part, from changes in behaviours and subsequent actions.

Consider, for example, the early medieval system of law and justice, typically rigid and ritualistic, it relied on proof[73] and on the 'Judgement of God' through oaths and ordeals.[74] Constantly referring to what is just and right, these practices were neither uniform nor consistent. They usually equated, explicitly, to local 'customary law' (common law) but jostled for jurisdiction, in every community, with canon (ecclesiastical) and Roman law.[75] Legitimized by royal grants, local justice was dispensed by locally appointed officials, who typically knew the parties involved, understood the local feeling and the consequences of the judgements pronounced. Although sometimes appealed, it was more often preferred to outside influence. Nevertheless, by the thirteenth century, the practice of law was dominated by professionals, available only to those who could afford to pay. Increasingly esoteric and less transparent, it often rode roughshod over local community customs. When after 1215, in England, trial by ordeal was replaced by trial by jury, the connection between perjury and the 'fires of hell' was broken.[76] A community's widely held trust in the local appointee, local customs, and in the system of oath-taking and ordeal, fortified by Christian beliefs, was inevitably replaced (as communities could not function without some recourse to the law) by an unavoidable 'trust' (reliance, expectation) in the body of laws, in its systematic application and the knowledge, skill and cunning of lawyers. Supported by burgeoning administrative bureaucracies, the use of written evidence increased and testimonies were recorded. In fact, such documents, in particular manorial court rolls, became important targets during the popular uprisings of the fourteenth and fifteenth centuries and many were destroyed.[77] Also noteworthy, alongside this development of the law, was the crucial role friendship occupied within it[78]; with its 'changing concepts and practices [characterising] the intellectual, social, political and cultural panorama of medieval Europe'.[79]

Similarly, as the shared understandings (the mutual duties, rights and obligations between the hierarchical levels in society and the common good) within feudal society broke down under the mounting pressures of the age (warfare, including the Crusades, disease and famine), the acceptance and framework of trust which sustained them were simultaneously reformulated so the foundations of political order could be restored. At its heart sat an older conflict between the natural laws and natural rights of the individual and the personal will of the monarch, often in direct opposition to one another. The changes this wrought contributed to a government, in the fourteenth and fifteenth centuries, that was not 'arcane or remote, something handed down by officials; [but] something in which [its] subjects were involved, something they learned to manipulate, criticize and even change'[80]; 'self-government at the king's command'.[81]

Kings were the first to recognize the advantages of sovereignty free from traditional feudal constraints. They had, for some time, looked enviously at the Church and sought to mirror its self-governing system and structure. Increasingly able to consolidate their territories and amass wealth through the systematic collection of taxes, and, when possible, conquest, together with the 'infantry revolution',[82] monarchs no longer needed to rely on the services of their nobles.[83] In fact, kings might have argued that increasingly they had to keep their rich and powerful nobles in check. Previously itinerant kings gradually settled at court which led to the further development of administrative and bureaucratic systems. When combined with the sovereign's monopoly on war-making, and the feudal laws of primogeniture,[84] this resulted in a sharp increase in the number of independent knights (professional soldiers)[85] available for hire; nobles were no longer guaranteed a role in governing the realm. These changes inevitably led to a redefining of a king's relationship with his nobles. These traditionally 'voluntary' relationships,[86] built on mutual trust and reinforced by honour-bound oaths of allegiance, became a competition for position and status within a government increasingly built around the royal court. Networks of communication and trust were extended through this system of patronage and incorporated into developing states. During this period, nobles, governing in the king's name, often became the focus of dissent, or rebellion, and therefore it was their removal, not the king's, that was called for.[87] At the same time, the sources of legitimacy which ultimately gave a king the authority to rule changed in both their component parts and balances. They shifted by degrees, from clerical consultation (about what was customary, right, and just), in combination with the approval of both the Church and the 'great men of the kingdom', towards the opposing notions of divine right[88] and popular consent.[89]

Although this shift is suggestive of a move away from affective interpersonal trust towards a more abstract notion that united individuals' 'trust' into a practical and useable whole,[90] parallels can be drawn with the way that rapidly growing medieval towns and boroughs (communes)[91] redefined their relationship and interdependence with the countryside. They became independent marketplaces, money-based economies with the freedom of movement and security needed for trade, rather than merely administrative centres or places of leisure. Although in the majority of cases, with the possible exception of northern and central Italy, they were never able to replicate the fully independent city-states of Ancient Greece, they produced an alternative model for society, one that acknowledged the underlying freedom and equality (under the law) of all its inhabitants. They were independent of local lords; although under the indirect influence of the Church, the secular management of these communes was left to its inhabitants. For those governing, their primary concern, while balancing the threat of factions against the threat of mob rule,[92] was to ensure the interests of all groups were represented while maintaining a sense of unity within their commune. Having already formed self-governing trade associations (guilds and houses),[93] these became the nucleus of the new urban government. Typically, it was the more experienced and wealthier who were elected to represent the community on the council. Over time, there was a tendency towards oligarchy, and unless they governed unjustly or corruptly, there was little or no complaint or demands for democracy and equal rights.[94] Gradually communes petitioned, struggled and fought[95] local feudal oppressors, both secular and ecclesiastical, for further rights to legislate, impose taxes and even make war![96] If successful, charters were ratified by ritualistic oaths,[97] often supported by kings as a method of curtailing the power of feudal lords. Regarded as 'peace treaties',[98] these symbolic documents created new legal entities, 'self-governing corporations',[99] which in turn created not only a new legal system[100] but also a new 'class' outside the traditional feudal system, one founded upon the increasingly subversive notion of equality (moral and legal).[101]

Within these communes the traditional feudal hierarchy, with its vertical framework of trust, was usurped by overlapping relationships of trust, both personal and impersonal. These included communal oaths to the brotherhood within guilds, reliance on the law and mutually shared exposure to risk and liability. Communes, although not without their problems, demonstrated a practical and workable alternative to a feudal society.

As Reynolds has stated, despite these changes, 'protests and rebellions were fairly clearly against individual acts of oppression or individual rulers, rather than the [institutional] structures they represented'.[102] For throughout most of medieval Europe 'monarchy was not simply the best possible form of government; it was almost the only conceivable form'.[103] It survived, in part, because of its sanctity, influential vested interests and a perceived capacity to separate the individual (the king) from the institution itself, together with its ability to unite people under one government.

It was a time when the government (in whatever form) had the authority to control but not monopolize the legitimate use of physical force and to coerce their subjects, provided it acted justly and in accordance with custom.[104] What did change was the frequency, make-up and reach of these revolts/rebellions in the late medieval period[105]; transforming over time from localized rural uprisings in the defence of traditional customs, rights, and obligations or against the unjust behaviour of a noble or king, to instances of communal emancipation, civic emancipation, and widespread popular rebellion.[106] This is demonstrated by both the transition, in England, from the Magna Carta, in 1215, to the Peasants' Revolt, in 1381, and the changing pattern of urban rebellions in medieval Flanders.[107] When successful, although often limited, these later revolts/rebellions meant more than simply one elite replacing another as in the ancient Athenian model;

they radically reshaped city-state [and commune] constitutions, ushering into power a new social class that sat uncomfortably and uncompromisingly outside the rigid feudal hierarchy. This happening, under Aristotle's definition, was revolutionary. Although the direct results were typically localized, their influence and effect were far-reaching.

The crisis of Magna Carta, unlike previous revolts in England over dynastic issues or the personal concerns of individual nobles, sought to impose and defend the supremacy of the law and a specific government. Essentially a peace treaty, it was issued by King John as a practical solution to a political crisis. Previously, ruling using the principle of *vis et voluntas*, or 'force and will', the nobles and many contemporary writers argued that monarchs should rule in accordance with traditional custom, the law and with the counsel of the 'great nobles' of the realm. Obligated, not just to God but to his people, a monarch should rule justly for the common good. King John broke these bonds and so his nobles took up arms; in the process they took an oath to 'stand fast for the liberty of the church and the realm'. This charter, although quickly annulled, formed a wider proposal for political reform and formally recognized the means of collectively coercing the king.[108] It never threatened the institution of monarchy, nor did it seek to change the societal structure, but instead sought to legitimize and defend traditional customs, rights and obligations within the rigid feudal hierarchy.

As society changed over the next 150 years, together with its underlying framework of trust, rebellion evolved, and both its scope and reach extended. Depicted, by Thomas Walsingham, as a 'confused series of events happening simultaneously in many places'; perpetrated by 'filthy' *rustici*, 'uncouth and sordid' serfs, and 'ribalds and whores of the devil',[109] the Peasants' Revolt was not the rabble of disgruntled 'commons' described by contemporary chroniclers, but rather they were diverse, articulate and aspirational. Compared to the Jacquerie in Paris, in 1358,[110] the rebels included wealthy townsmen, gentry and even members of Parliament.[111] Articulating a set of political ideas and aims (some revolutionary such as the abolition of *villein*),[112] within the contemporary language of protest they continually proclaimed their loyalty to the king, their maxim: '*wyth whom haldes yow? Wyth Kynge Richarde and wyth the trew Communes*'. Well organized, they co-ordinated their actions and sought to target their violence; it was certainly not indiscriminate, as they 'were lovers of truth and justice, not robbers and thieves'.[113]

Although for Moore, this period began with the *First European Revolution*, the traditional view of the medieval period is one filled with uprisings, revolts, and rebellions, but none that were revolutionary. Our present-day view of this period has long been coloured by the bias of contemporary chronicles of the age: the reshaping of medieval history during the Renaissance (when it was referred to as a period of darkness and decay)[114]; the Reformation (when Protestantism wrote of the Middle Ages as a period of Roman Catholic Church corruption)[115]; and its subsequent revival in the Victorian Age (when it became the inspiration for creative expression in romanticism, the gothic revival and Pre-Raphaelite art, as well as the Arts and Crafts movement).[116] Yet, in the rebels' own words, demands and wider discourse, the feudal social order was almost never challenged in these revolts and rebellions; instead, these so-called rebels sought concessions, concrete improvements and, at times, constitutional reform. They wanted to improve institutions, or at least gain the right to participate in them.

Changing over this period, the revolts/rebellions represented collective resentment of excessive exploitation, the loss of traditional rights and customs, the groundswell of bad governance and general oppression, whether localized or more widespread. In a cyclical pattern reminiscent of the Ancient Greeks and Romans, the constitutional changes sought could be considered revolutionary; however, the rebels were also greatly influenced by Church doctrine. Sometimes acting with the support of the Church, sometimes against, the rebels did not wish, through most of this period, to risk the fires of hell by defying the divinely ordained social order. It was not until both the relationship between the individual and the Church, and secular institutions shifted, that social and political revolution was possible. In describing these ever-expanding administrative and bureaucratic systems, Moore states that 'the capacity developed by both secular and ecclesiastical powers to penetrate communities of every kind vigorously and ruthlessly, overriding the restraint of custom and enlisting or destroying men of local standing and influence in the name of order, orthodoxy and reform'.[117] Such changes are reflected in both the ever-evolving framework of trust underpinning society and the revolutionary changes in the nature and type of personal and impersonal relationships. Together they played a fundamental role in the commercial, military, scientific, and cognitive revolutions of the medieval period.[118]

Renaissance Man – A revolutionary?

Florentine Renaissance (1330–1550)

A period of transition, the Renaissance is considered a bridge between the medieval period and modernity, traditionally defined as an era of discovery, both geographically and scientifically, of the world and of man.[1] Witness to a variety of 'revolutions' across many disciplines (including the arts, science and technology, religion, learning and communication, philosophy and politics, trade and finance), this period in European history often experienced turbulent social and political upheaval.[2] There was a decline in the influence of the Church while the value and agency of man were deified as classical learning was revisited in a milieu of historical infatuation. This period, however, was not strictly 'rational' or 'secular', (and neither did a full-blown individualism emerge), 'instead, [it] is characterised by the uneasy co-existence between traditional themes and the plurality of new approaches.'[3] Rather than a break with the past, the Renaissance, in many respects, is part of an 'uninterrupted series of scarcely perceptible improvements' towards modernity,[4] with many of its achievements tracing their roots to the Middle Ages and cross-cultural interactions with the East.[5]

At the same time, 'Renaissance men' (and women)[6] sought to distinguish themselves from their medieval counterparts, who had lain 'half-awake beneath a common veil woven of faith, illusion, and childish prepossession through which the world and history were seen clad in strange hues.'[7] Regarded as a standard, Renaissance Man was a paragon, an ideal of society.[8] 'Designed to make people marvel at him, to transform himself into a beautiful spectacle for others to contemplate', Leonardo da Vinci was archetypal, a man of 'unquenchable curiosity' and 'feverishly inventive imagination.'[9] Seen as a celebration of the spirit of the Renaissance, Marlowe's *Doctor Faustus* is an extreme example: he deliberately rejects God's power and control over his life to gain his own power and wealth; he is successful but at what cost? For Heller, this conception of Renaissance Man was 'rooted in the process by which the beginnings of capitalism destroyed the natural relationship between the individuals and community, [it] dissolved the natural bonds ... his "ready-made" place in society and shook all hierarchy and stability, turning social relations fluid'.[10] However, enmeshed in a network of obligations and commitments, which limited and dictated action, the extent of the Renaissance Man's individualism and social freedom has, in the past, been overstated.[11]

This self-conscious cultural movement, in 'which humanity rediscovered its own identity',[12] began in Florence in the fourteenth century,[13] overlapping with what is regarded as the late Middle Ages, before quickly spreading across Europe in the fifteenth century, via travel, trade, art, print and marriage among the European elite.[14] A golden age, a rebirth,[15] this popular view, increasingly contested by academics,[16] was shaped by the historians, Burckhardt and Michelet, when they 're-discovered' the Renaissance in the nineteenth century.[17] Yet irrespective of the continuing academic debates as to the nature, extent and exclusivity of the European Renaissance, those involved in this movement believed they were living in new times,[18] a sentiment captured by Manetti who stated: 'Everything that surrounds us is our own work, the work of man: all dwellings, all castles, all cities, all the edifices throughout the whole world ... Ours are the paintings, the sculptures; ours are the trades sciences and philosophical systems.'[19]

While mindful of these wider intellectual debates, using the term 'Renaissance' provides a useful shorthand, invoking an immediately identifiable picture of Western Europe, *c.* 1300–1650, in which to continue this study of trust and revolution. The intention is to examine what qualities compose both trust and revolution in the Renaissance, to investigate how they differed across varied factors such as religious, social, and political life, and to consider how they were manifested in the different systems of governance across Europe. Open to various interpretations, and remarkably adaptable at creating multiple outcomes, the core value system of the Renaissance is illustrated in **Figure 14**.

The Italian Renaissance (*c.* 1300–1550) was a period of autonomy, ensuring the existence and survival of many self-governing societies,[20] while the aspirations and values of these 'free' cities, such as Florence, Siena and Venice, 'made them workshops of politics and government, engines of wealth, and innovative centres of culture as no European cities had been since antiquity'.[21] These societies, and their associated institutions (social, political and economic), were firmly rooted in their medieval communal experience and 'explicable only by understanding the deep structural impact of the medieval civic *mentalité*'.[22] Often beginning as little more than mutual

Set within an age of exploration, and discovery, abound with technological and scientific advances

Virtù

Often referring to manliness, its focus was leadership and courage but had no connotation of moral excellence. The active citizen who preserved independent government was applauded (Hexter, 1979).

Patronage

The key to social status, patronage enabled the impossible. It played an influential edicated with an oath, it created powerful srole in both secular and sacred matters. Often docial bonds and shaped personal identity.

Liberty

Consisting of *virtù* and *participazione*, liberty ensured honour, glory and fame for those willing to defend it. Together with individualism, it formed a symbiotic relationship with the thoughts and ideas of the early Renaissance (McConnell, 2013).

Fortuna

Appearing throughout Renaissance culture in a surprising variety of guises, some belief belief in *fortuna* may have been 'almost universal'. Contemporary theorists paired it with *virtu* (McLean, 200 and Witt, 1983).

Christianity

System of Governance*

Law

Commerce

Humanism

More interested in the human than the divine, there was a new willingness to question authority, to examine knowledge and to reinterpret understanding. Man, and his individualism, was firmly centre stage.

Oaths

Men of all classes swore great oaths and curses. Used in the judicial system as an affirmation of truth, oaths were not taken lightly. As with oaths of allegiance many were sworn to God.

Great Chain of Being

Universal orderliness and interdependence, with everything having its 'place'. This remained a widely held premise, even though the theme of disorder was much in evidence.

 The cornerstones of society

Societal value system

* Monarchies, republics, and principalities all included a degree of representative government

Figure 14 Early Renaissance framework of trust.

defence pacts between neighbours, these medieval communes, first recorded in the late eleventh and early twelfth centuries, are considered some of the earliest examples of civic society.[23] Focusing on Florence as an example, although never democratic in a present-day sense, what had once provided a practical and workable alternative to feudal society was increasingly beset by a seemingly endless cycle of feuding factions.[24] This created 'a veritable cauldron of suspicion, mistrust, and envy, fuelled by the struggle for wealth, status, and reputation.'[25] Over time, the asymmetrical balance of weak central authority and powerful families, with wealth and an exaggerated attitude of 'amoral familism',[26] transformed this commune into a republican oligarchy[27] that was continually reinforced by the strong social bonds of patronage. This was a predictable outcome of the collaborative solutions employed to end the ceaseless violence and prevent Florence from collapsing into seigniorial rule or anarchy in its infancy. The social, the economic, and the political had to be woven into one practical and integrated framework, creating a vibrant tapestry with trust as the common thread, for the city-state to survive.

Notwithstanding wars, disease and revolution *Firenze* flourished to the extent its florin quickly became the preferred coin for large trading transactions in Western Europe. To ensure the economy continued to thrive, the electorate revised their electoral procedures, which underpinned their system of governance to limit the worst excesses of these hegemonic mercantile families and so ensure that governance was for the common good.[28] Their solution was to employ *fortuna* (chance) to compensate for the corruptibility of man and the shortcomings of their inherited electoral system, braced by laws to reduce factional alliances[29] and a system of preferment that offered groups outside the ruling elite (the patricians)[30] a modest stake in the regime.[31] Born of distrust and paranoia,[32] the complex electoral system that was instituted, however, still relied on trust, not in the individual, but rather in the institutional procedures drawn up for the distribution of offices and honours.[33] This stood in sharp contrast to the fiduciary trust which had developed between merchants. Incorporating the notion of chance was, for them, a means of limiting the effects of 'human nature' and influence.[34]

The Florentine process was known as the *squitinio* (scrutiny)[35]; as a position became vacant a name was drawn at random from a list of eligible candidates.[36] It was formed by intersecting two organizing principles: guilds and neighbourhoods.[37] This 'diffusion of sovereignty between a multitude of councils based upon neighbourhood, profession, and political tradition meant that responsibility was divided and not located in any one particular group'.[38] It created a *res republica* of elected officials in contrast to hereditary positions under feudalism, emphasizing the 'freedom'[39] and 'free will' of a city-state's eligible citizenry to test their civic virtue and exercise their political power. The system instituted was rigidly designed to be communally held in check, obligating the governing class to act collaboratively and for the public good; it left much to chance![40] In reality, public interest typically emerged from balancing the clash of personal interests, and by the fifteenth century, the civic ideal was *unimitas* (unanimity), 'the convergence of a multitude of wants and aspirations into a single will'.[41] A patrician's participation in political life was essential in this often toxic political environment, where motives underlying behaviour, such as envy, avarice, haughtiness and malice, were ubiquitous.[42]

For Renaissance humanists and political theorists, who contemplated the individual and their role in civil society,[43] civic virtue was an obsession. In practical terms, for patricians, it equated to the acquisition of public office.

However, with an insufficient number of prestigious positions to sate the aspiring honour-hungry contenders, it created an often poisonous political culture, which contemporaries identified as the root cause of division and conflict within a city-state.[44] This was illustrated in Compagni's account of Florence (1280 to 1312), which reported that 'the city was ruled with little justice, and fell into fresh danger because the citizens became divided by competition for offices, each one hating his rival.'[45] Balancing this threat and its effects had a profound impact upon Renaissance justice and put a chronic strain on the body politic. Drawing upon and continually reinforcing relationships of trust and sealed with oaths of allegiance, the factional alliances of powerful patricians not only built on their complex networks of patronage and marriage, but also relied on their interconnected memberships of confraternities[46] and guilds.

Despite the perceived virtues of fairness, justice, republicanism and good administration depicted in the *Allegory of Good and Bad Government* in Siena,[47] Florence was not immune from the sweep of revolts that spread across Western Europe following the Black Death. In 1378, the lowest stratum of the Florentine working class overthrew the governing elite and instituted a 'revolutionary' regime which lasted for over three years. Modern proponents[48] of the Revolt of Ciompi discern 'a remarkable political consciousness for working men in an emerging capitalist society,'[49] while their opponents describe the 'Ciompi revolution' as little more than a 'Florentine *imbroglio* (tumult).'[50] However, the contemporary view, reported in often patchy and contradictory fashion, was markedly different. It was described, in turn, as 'impoverished criminals' whose 'only goal was plunder [and] slaughter,'[51] instigated by the devil, manipulated by intrigue and conspiracy, and a divine punishment for the sins of the city and its citizens.[52] The majority of contemporary chroniclers showed them little sympathy. Machiavelli, writing over 120 years later, was ambivalent towards the revolt but described the movement as unambiguously political.[53] He was the first to highlight the causes and motivation for the revolt.[54] At its heart was the *popolo minuto*'s (the 'little people's') claim to equality, to the protection of guild membership offered and their participation in governance. Initiated by the sound of bells, the 'little people' resorted to violence and in turn became 'princes of the city.'[55] This was a reflection of, and provoked by, the continual power struggle between the elites and between the seven major and fourteen minor guilds, which had been a fixture of Florentine politics since the late thirteenth century. The Ciompi's political and social demands were modest: they created three new guilds but remained within the framework of the medieval corporatist system. Even these achievements were quickly undone when the oligarchic elite regained control: it was the aspiration of the revolt that would endure. Yet, just as the political process underwent change to assimilate the lessons learnt, so the shift in cross-class relationships[56] wrought by this tumultuous political event, when combined with new mathematical techniques, made possible the 'powerful multivocal conception of credit'.[57]

Florence, the 'birthplace of financial capitalism',[58] was a mercantile economy based on commodity exchange. The commercial fortunes created quickly replaced inherited land-based wealth, redrawing and reshaping its society. Its political development was inextricably bound with the city's elite. Operating under the jurisdiction of the Church,[59] Florence was the dominant financial centre for European banking,[60] which sat at the heart of the city's considerable cultural influence. To the city's great advantage, though set against a distrustful political landscape, Florentine merchants managed to establish *fiducia* (trust) between one another. Others could only marvel 'at the ability of the Italians to do business without money'[61] which they used to great effect, creating flexibility and liquidity in the market.[62] As a French satirist noted 'one never sees or touches any money; all they need to do business is paper, pen and ink'.[63] Based on more than mathematical techniques,[64] reputation and the understanding of a handshake, the Florentines constructed a cross-cutting lattice of dense and multi-textured relationships which overlapped other social networks namely patrilineage, marriage, neighbourhoods, patronage, political office-holding, social class membership and factional affiliations.[65] 'Cooperative with and helpful towards their "competitors", Florentine merchants were deeply personalistic.'[66] As skilled communicators they developed a 'language of trust', which demonstrated their willingness and ability to trust and which 'obviated the need to resort to the blunter instruments of enforcement'[67]: the very notion of the trust they developed kept its participants in line.[68]

However, as the city's wealth and reputation grew, so the distinction between its 'governors' and those governed grew. Financial devices, such as the *monte*,[69] became the central financial institutions of the republic and with them the control of the city's finances necessarily developed while the distribution of fiscal burdens correspondingly changed.[70] The experts who were employed proved remarkably competent, maintaining their fiduciary integrity and trust; however, as financiers came to dominate, there was a heavy political cost. This enabled 'a pragmatically empowered oligarchic regime' to emerge, which in turn led to the creation of an increasingly rigid political and social hierarchy.[71] As this hierarchy hardened, it recast many of the networks of influence which crisscrossed the city.

In what was still essentially a risk-filled face-to-face society, loyalty and trust were in high demand.[72] The Republic of Florence was often spatially defined (city and countryside, political ward or parish) and mutually determining (guilds congregated on specific streets).[73] The connections formed not only created 'a stage for local social dramas of solidarity and enmity' but also connected, negotiated and overlapped with other networks of influence.[74] Each offered its own sense of identity and belonging, alongside the sense of being Florentine,[75] while 'confraternities provided the single most important lesson about cooperation of any Italian civic institution'.[76] In combination with the Renaissance system of patronage, the Medicis were able to indirectly influence and control Florence for over 300 years.[77] Operating like the modern-day Italian mafia, they not only controlled a major bank but in the background they exerted considerable influence and pressure over the city's governance and judiciary.[78] Cosimo the Elder and his grandson, Lorenzo the Magnificent, were consummate practitioners of politically (and socially) motivated patronage. Cosimo, through his patronage of art and learning, created a wise, pious public image; perceived of as a benevolent leader, he justified his influence and control over the city and *Signoria* (its government),[79] through a two-pronged approach in which learning shaped ideology, interpretations and discourse, and the arts offered a physical manifestation of power. It was used to gain support and please the citizens of Florence. Public art, commissioned to display civic pride and/or devotion to the Christian faith, was able to transform the public sphere and open spaces of the city.[80] Cosimo was so successful that 'within a few years the Medici party was so strongly rooted – if always loosely knit – and so firmly identified with the interests of Florence as a whole, that Cosimo had no need to suppress the voices of opposition.'[81]

To ensure wider ongoing civic engagement (orderly and fiscally) of a city-state's citizenry,[82] in particular those with little or no political influence, medieval communal co-operation was remodelled and reinforced. This resulted in a collaborative rather than coercive solution to the problems of political violence and division. Success relied not only upon the institution of complex electoral systems, but also upon the ability of those governing to employ less elitist, and easily transferable, processes to focus and unite the wider populace. Simultaneously, used to control and change behaviour, this process drew on an idealized notion of unanimity, uniting refined manners,[83] with religious[84] and judicial practices,[85] to sustain and underpin these long-standing civic societies.[86] It was also used to narrow the gap between the city and its hinterland (*contado*). Labelled a 'civilising process',[87] a more generally widespread literary culture proved advantageous in disseminating influential models of personal deportment ('civilising texts'),[88] while the ubiquitous presence of the law brought due process and regularized procedure. Combined with the rituals and reverence of religious practices, they evoked a change and regulated behaviour, which was shaped, altered and adapted as circumstances dictated. 'These culture forms found institutional expressions, but, most importantly, cultural practices and institutions reinforced each other, creating ways of behaving, in institutional settings, that made collaboration against divisive violence possible.'[89] By believing in the same core set of socially constructed principles, a universal and efficient system of mutual trust evolved, a key component of a city-state's identity[90] (each distinct and usually idealized) and the solidarity of its citizenry, which created a collective consciousness.

The ideals of civic unity, expressed in political rhetoric and the literature of the day, were, in practical terms, a myth. Florence 'functioned atop a grid of patron–client relationships, through what looks suspiciously like corruption,'[91] their electoral safeguards no match for the machinations of the wealthy and determined, in their never-ending competition for reputation. Of all the Italian city-states, the Venetians came closest to achieving political and social unanimity and eliminating political violence.[92] However, for Florence, primarily under the control of the Medicis during its long transformation from republic to principality, political violence continued.[93] Despite providing the stability essential to state manoeuvring within the Italian state system, and operating indirectly,[94] they faced charges of tyranny. Their survival depended on maintaining their interconnected networks of influence and patronage.[95] When the Medicis were deposed in 1494 and restored in 1512, the contemporary chronicler Nardi uses the 'wheel of fortune' as an allegory for this repeating pattern of dynastic change.[96] This revolution to overthrow the crypto-oligarchic regime in 1494 was widely approved, even by the family's supporters.[97] 'Everyone agreed that Savonarola's new government 'was the true form of Florentine public life, more than ever before' and elections were met 'with sweet happiness, seemingly a popular and more communal government'.[98] However, their desire to transform Florence, through moral reforms, into a 'City of God', was short-lived.[99] Savonarola's 'bonfire of vanities'[100] was ill-suited to Florentine identity and was quickly replaced by Soderini and his republican government. Eloquent, with a passionate personality, Parenti considered Soderini a neutral candidate, and he had the support of the less passionate and ideological citizenry.[101] Phillips argues that he 'muddled his chance to reform by [ultimately] chasing his own self-interest'[102] and so the cycle of corruption and redress repeated itself.

When a successful *coup d'etat* restored the Medicaen power in 1512,[103] it ended Machiavelli's political career. Turning his attention to writing, he became preoccupied with the military weakness, instability, inadequate justice, factionalism and absence of leadership that both dogged and undermined the Republic over his fourteen-year career. Meanwhile, the Medici family effectively brought the Papal States and Florence into a personal union.[104] Their replacement by Savonarola in 1527 ushered in a new conception of revolution.[105] In the sixteenth century, the more egalitarian civic republicanism was replaced with the defence of an independent Florence and its office-holding class. The distinction between these two regimes was small, owing more to continuity than to change. However, while Baker has gone to great lengths to de-emphasize the notion of revolution, downplaying the radical nature of this change in status, it was difficult to mask its political and cultural poignancy. Shaped by the experiences of the Italian Wars (a series of conflicts from 1494 to 1559), Florentine's political culture had irreversibly changed, particularly amongst the office-holding class, psychologically shifting the concepts of *virtu* and liberty[106]; where previously the notions of an individual's and a city-state's freedom had co-existed, the latter prevailed. Contemporary chroniclers exposed the tension between different ideas and evolving notions of liberty[107] 'in the deconstruction and reconstruction of terms and ideas. Blood was shed, fortunes were lost, and lives destroyed. People fought and died in the struggle over the political culture of the city.'[108] As continually restoring the stability and security of Florence was paramount, with a mixture of honour, loyalty and self-interest, members of the office-holding class were persuaded and cajoled into assisting and participating in this dramatic reorganization of political institutions. Transforming themselves into courtiers was seen as a way of preserving traditional values and republican traditions.[109] Baker summarizes this transformation in the changing symbolism of the traditional icons of the city. Michelangelo's *David and Goliath*, placed in the Piazza della Signoria in 1504, and associated with republican *virtu*, by 1549 was associated with Cosimo 1's ability to preserve the liberty of the 'State'. 'David was no longer a communal symbol but an avatar for the Medici prince.'[110]

For Florence, the Renaissance period was a constant drama filled with change, challenge, disorder and revolution. Outwardly preserving but stealthily eroding the ancient foundations of communal government, it transitioned from a secular to a religious republic, before becoming a Medici-dominated principality.

To achieve this final transition, the underlying societal system of trust was used against itself. It inverted the notion of liberty in a deliberate and determined fashion, in sharp contrast to the 'revolutions' of 1494 and 1527. As Rinuccini warns, 'These exotic signs and words clash with the facts'[111]; liberty was used to dazzle and deceive. Florentine's notion of liberty was associated with the city's open republican system of governance, and not simply the city's independence. Symbols of liberty,[112] often as ambiguous as the concept of liberty itself,[113] were on display throughout the city. However, just as the city was not averse to disguising its own expansionist intentions under its self-proclaimed role as defender of republican values and champion of liberty, the city's elite masked their own self-interest by returning to an earlier and singular understanding of liberty,[114] appropriating these symbols for themselves. Through their patronage of the arts and humanist thinkers, together with their influence and indirect control of the governing elite, the Medicis increasingly subverted the narrative of liberty.[115] Cosimo was the first to cast himself as the defender of liberty.[116] Thus when the question of protecting Florence's independence arose in the sixteenth century, an office-holding class, obsessed with civic *virtu*, actively aided and participated in the transition. The result of this planned (long and slow) social and cultural revolution was a relatively smooth transition from republic to principality and from citizen to courtier. Despite Rinuccini's earlier warning that the freedom of citizens to participate on an equal basis in government was being eroded few put up a fight.[117]

Instead, by subtly subverting, from the top down, the core values which underpinned this society, a political revolution was brought about. This relatively peaceful transition was, to a large extent, the direct result of actively engaging with the overlapping networks of trust, traversing both the city and its increasingly rigid class hierarchies, and in understanding their ever-changing attitude to, and appetite for, risk.

The Protestant Reformation

Even more far-reaching was the impact of the Protestant Reformation,[118] which began in the Holy Roman Empire (present-day Germany)[119] during the Renaissance (*c.* 1400–1600). Traditionally assessed in terms of the rise of the modern nation state, the Reformation is particularly associated with the 'birth hour of the German nation'.[120] Until recently it was given a privileged position in German history, 'analogous in some ways to that of the Civil War in American historiography, as the crucial and (in a quite literal sense of the term), epoch-making event, by which the nature of an entire national community and of its history has been defined'.[121] On the other hand, the dominant narratives of the

English Reformation have been divided into two competing schools of thought, set within the context of two rival historical narratives, Protestant and Catholic.[122] The French viewed this period of civil and religious war as a direct consequence of political rivalries, academics only recently focusing on the social and cultural issues, in particular the competing 'truths' which each religion presented.[123] This plurality of interpretations is reflective of the plurality of religious beliefs held in the sixteenth and seventeenth centuries and is a lasting legacy of the Protestant Reformation.

Simultaneously as an urban, rural and communal event, the Reformation started a chain reaction which destroyed European social, political and intellectual hegemony, dividing and sub-dividing the 'universal' system of trust (see **Figure 14**). Dominating the latter half of the period, the composite set of ideas and actions which made up the Reformation was predisposed to multiple interpretations. Internally conflicting from the outset, Protestant factions sought to balance the tensions between authority and equality, radicalism and conservativism; while encouraging free thought, this actively encouraged dissent. This was dramatically played out during the Tudor and Stuart reigns. At its most uncontested, it questioned the Pope's stranglehold on the Bible, and therefore the word of God. Considered 'a second renaissance', this profound 'revolution' sought to 're-assert the original faith'.[124] In so doing, it fundamentally challenged the nature and structure of the papacy, and ended the universal alliance between the Church and government, which had acted as an instrument of unity and stability across Europe for centuries. The Roman Catholic Church had come full circle.[125]

It was not the first attempt to reform the Roman Catholic Church,[126] but it was the first to benefit from the widespread adoption of the printing press.[127] It started on 31 October 1517 when Martin Luther, an Augustine monk and professor of theology, nailed his *95 Theses* to the door of the castle church in Wittenberg, Germany. He first used the term 'reformation' in a letter, to Duke George, dated 1518. 'The other name frequently applied by Luther and his friends to their party was "the gospel". In his own eyes the Wittenberg professor was doing nothing more or less than restoring the long-buried evangel of Jesus and Paul.'[128] Luther's vehement attack on the sale of indulgences (the selling of salvation) had popular and widespread support. Rapidly spreading and diversified, the Reformation was soon beyond Luther's control.[129] It became a 'revolt against the divinely instituted authority' of the Church of Rome, permanently dividing Christian Europe and reshaping the once shared, social, moral, and intellectual values. As popular prejudice was woven into both a state's identity, and an individual's religious beliefs, Protestants and Catholics became mortal enemies. This divide highlights the paradox of religion. It simultaneously expands and creates boundaries, uniting and dividing, creating trust and distrust.[130]

Despite the rhetoric, the Reformation was not entirely theologically motivated.[131] As Holborn notes, 'Everywhere the secular authorities tried to counter papal policy and they found support even among the devout, who felt that a papacy devoid of its universality and ridden with secularism, could not guarantee the common welfare.'[132] Set against a backdrop of a growing sense of nationalism, for many monarchs and princes, the adoption of socially conservative Protestantism was more pragmatic.[133] Political, economic and personal considerations more often outweighed religious belief as those who were able took advantage of the rapidly unfolding situation.[134] Henry VIII, once the 'Defender of the Faith', became a 'predatory Crown on the prowl'.[135] It was political threats and dynastic issues, combined with pride, lust, greed and opportunity, not moral indignation nor a devout religious calling that led to England's conversion.[136] A monarch/state's conversion became a way, not only of avoiding high papal taxes,[137] but also of seizing the vast clerical wealth within their kingdoms.[138] It also offered the appealing position of supreme head of state, free from papal challenge or interference. Religious belief and its practice were now subject to a monarch's will; they became a measure of individuals' loyalty, abjurers could be beheaded as traitors or burnt alive as heretics. Families were divided by faith and conflicting loyalties to their god or their king. This became a particularly challenging situation for the English who faced seventy years of religious (and political) uncertainty under Tudor rule.[139] England's Reformation is, for some, an enigma,[140] producing a 'Protestant nation, but not a nation of Protestants'.[141] It is viewed as an expression of popular as well as divine will[142] and 'a piece-meal, contingent, and top-down imposition of an unpopular religious agenda on a populace largely happy with late-medieval Catholic piety'.[143]

Viewed, by Catholics, as a 'dangerous plague of heresy', a 'poison', a 'pestilence', a 'contagious evil', Luther's ideas had spread to France (1519) and England (1520), where they were outlawed in 1521.[144] An unwitting and unwilling revolutionary, he nevertheless embraced the logic of his reformation.[145] He was excommunicated by the pope, and after he refused to recant at the Diet of Worms,[146] the Holy Roman Emperor Charles V declared him an outlaw and a heretic. A statement was issued: 'We have given him (Luther) twenty-one days dating from April 15 … When the time is up, none is to harbour him. His followers also are to be condemned. His books are to be eradicated from the memory of man.'[147] However, in challenging these traditional hierarchies,

Luther came to symbolize a new social order (one of social equality) and a series of revolts quickly followed. First, the German knights driven by greed revolted; they were defeated, and their castles destroyed.[148] The Peasants' Revolt (1524–5) followed,[149] with Luther thundering a warning for elites to heed: 'The sword is at your neck, though you think that you are firmly in the saddle. This conceit will break your necks ... not the peasants but God himself is set against you.'[150] The peasants, too, were thwarted by Protestant conservatism: 100,000 killed on the altar of social equality. Despite his rhetoric, the socially conservative Luther allied himself with the princes,[151] and in so doing Protestants suppressed Protestants as Luther's new church came to 'serve' a secular authority.[152]

In response to the threats it faced,[153] and in concert with those monarchs and Catholics who remained loyal, the Catholic Church initiated the counter-reformation. Composed of four key elements,[154] it began in earnest at the Council of Trent (1545–63). This Catholic resurgence, or revival, lasted until 1648, a period characterized by armed conflict linked to religious preferences. No longer confined to ecclesiastical debate, increasingly incompatible 'religious' movements repeatedly clashed. This period was 'dominated by insecurity, civil war and brutal repression as the tension between entrenched, defensive Catholicism and the new dissident Protestantism' grew,[155] further undermining not only papal but, as time went on, secular authority[156]: what had started as a conservative religious reaction developed into a radical political movement. As Carroll puts it, the Reformation became 'a life-or-death attack on Humanism' and 'Renaissance man'[157]; it became 'the ultimate affirmation of rebellious individualism'.[158] As intolerant, religious divisions grew across the patchwork of city-states, principalities and monarchies of Europe, a war of religion broke out, culminating in the devastating Thirty Years' War.[159]

In keeping with the age and the essential role of patronage, the most vivid battlefield for people's 'hearts and minds' rested within its art and architecture.[160] Associated with the Northern Renaissance,[161] Protestant art reflected the plainer, unvarnished, more personal Christianity of the Reformation movement, with their houses stripped bare and all ornament removed,[162] whereas the Roman Catholic south experienced the serenity and luminosity of High Renaissance art in its churches and public spaces. The split between the two schools was starkly visible and contributed, in part, to the dismantling, for some, of the Roman Catholic mental universe. A 'cultural revolution' was born out of this emotionally charged conflict, as was the wave of religious iconoclasm.[163] Creating new art forms, art was valued for its own intrinsic beauty, as the 'real world' became the artists' muse. No longer, for most, a vehicle for salvation, art became a symbol of prestige, a commodity to be widely collected and displayed.

This divide was further emphasized during the Baroque period[164] when the papacy 'self-consciously decided to resort to seduction to win back the masses'.[165]Baroque art portrayed 'a world of superhumans, extremely muscular and showing superhuman fortitude, within an environment fitting such beings'.[166] This was a marked shift, not only in style but also in intent; it sought to draw in and involve the viewer in the unfolding drama depicted. For Catholics, art was a stepping stone on the tricky path to salvation; for Protestants it was an anathema.[167] 'Through nine centuries almost all European art was inspired and financed by the Church' and now, running in parallel, were rival artistic movements each with their own embedded narratives.[168] Before the Reformation the purpose of music, art and architecture was to educate the unlettered, instruct the laity and inspire the masses. But rather than a unifying force, 'culture' became increasingly used as a tool of propaganda and division – a defining identity.

Over the years this Protestant awakening has been referred to as a reformation, a revolt or a revolution, their differing meanings as complex as the ideas and actions of the early Protestant movement. Yet, 'such labels are, in a large measure, propaganda terms presupposing fundamental assumptions and lines of reasoning not entirely supported by fact.'[169] As one might expect, 'the general picture given of the Protestant Reformation is unvarying.'[170] Protestant historians have generally defined Luther's work as a reformation, while Roman Catholic historians have referred to it as a revolt or revolution. In describing these sixteenth-century reformers, Weidenkopf states, 'they really were not about reforming the Church, but they really wanted to overthrow it, and destroy it, and replace it with something different ... and that's a revolution.'[171] This choice of the modern use of the term 'revolution', as with 'the French Revolution or the Russian Revolution, implies a violent reaction against existing authority that results in far-reaching and fundamental change'.[172] It 'places the centre of gravity in economic, political, and sociological forces and assumes that they are more influential in shaping the course of events than theological difference'.[173]

Luther himself sought 'to liberate Germany from the economic and political bondage of the Roman See' and by 'his statement of the priesthood of believers', he destroyed 'the whole medieval concept of division in society', by definition a revolution.[174] However, the 'real' 'revolution [Luther] desired to effect was neither social political nor ecclesiastical, but theological'.[175] He demanded 'change' (*mutation, Aenderung*), an end to the misuses wrought by the papacy. He sought to return the Church to its original purity and in so doing 'wage[d] war against the tyranny of error and sin on behalf of what he understood by "the truth".[176] And so what was branded a revolt (*Aufruhr*) by his contemporary opponents, Luther vehemently argued was a spiritual revolt (*geistlicher Aufruhr*).[177] Although no doubt conscious of provoking 'revolutionary change', being socially conservative, Luther did not support civic or secular revolt: as he held that it was 'not proper for Christians to bear the temporal sword or to be a ruler'.[178] At most a reluctant revolutionary, reflected in his own often contradictory rhetoric, Luther was overwhelmed by the pace of both change and ultimate outcome. Arguably, the Protestant Reformation was not a revolution in either intent or outcome. It was not characterized by the explosive change and rapid overthrow of traditional secular authority that is normally associated with the word 'revolution', and as alluded to by Weidenkopf. However, beyond control, it overturned centuries of religious authority and theocentric vision; it was a reformation of the mind, with truly revolutionary results.

Given its complex nature, most approaches analysing the Reformation separate out the religious, economic, political and social implications of the Protestant Reformation; however, I would argue that in doing so, something is lost. Religion was all-pervasive, permeating every aspect of life and experience, from the social, economic, legal and scientific,[179] its 'sacred' beats marked time,[180] irrevocably intertwining all aspects of society in Western Europe in a way that much of present-day Western society would find unimaginable and unconscionable. It is less a question of theology than shared values, traditions and interdependency. Just as 'religious observance had always received much of its meaning from its invocation of properly constituted authority; going to church could not be divorced from its "civil" functions, reinforcing community, hierarchy and obedience, any more than the state could function without its divine sanction.'[181] In questioning old certainties, challenging old loyalties and interrogating old practices, the Protestant 'revolution' permanently undermined and destabilized this union. It 'dissolved the glue that held together the familiar coherence of the social world ... [which] sent violent shock waves through even the most seemingly stable communities and institutions.'[182]

It brought with it a new age of fear and persecution as secular rulers sought to enforce their choice of official religion, equating religious dissent with treason and immorality.[183] For Henry VIII, patriotism and Protestantism were two sides of the same coin. Anti-Semitism also grew during these tumultuous times, as both Catholics and Protestants placed heavy restrictions on Jews.[184] Within this milieu a bewildering variety of non-conformists emerged, referred to as 'Radical Reformers'[185]; differing in beliefs and practices they were unified through their grass-roots communalism.[186] Sectarianism grew.[187] Despite the subordination of religious authority to political authority, following the Reformation, religious legitimacy was far from irrelevant.[188] Religiosity remained high, whether simply practising or fervently believing; the Reformation forever changed an individual's relationship with both God and the State. The notions of equality, local autonomy and community control (provided in conjunction with local religious authority and organization) were replaced with absolute non-resistance, centralized control and national security. Those out of step, unable or unwilling to adapt or conform, faced a fearful future; this contributed to the mass migration witnessed across Western Europe. This transformation necessarily broke down and then recreated new frameworks of trust, which in turn 'redefined the nature of society and its constitutive relations'.[189] This change was amplified within the Radical Protestant and Puritan movements which emerged, many of whose proponents later emigrated to America[190]; their aim to create colonies 'conceived and established as plantations of religion'.[191]

While, in the twenty-first century, the Protestant–Catholic religious division appears to have dissipated entirely in Western Europe (with the exception of Northern Ireland where such polarities persist),[192] during the Renaissance even subtle changes in belief altered political and social dynamics in important and tangible ways. They changed people's relationships, not only with the State, the sacred and judicial system, cornerstones of society, but also with almost all aspects of the value (trust) framework, which underpinned it (see Figure 15).

Within these emerging 'modern' states,[193] social regulation and welfare, previously under the purview of the Church, came under direct government control, as politics and administration were combined across all levels in these highly personalized institutions of State, while it was the local officials ('middling sorts'),[194] who, in connecting an increasingly centralized government with the locals and by enforcing the law, became the primary architects of the early modern State. In many cases it was these networks of trust which replaced the traditional frameworks of pre-Reformation Europe.

Notwithstanding shifting theological emphases, doctrinal and ceremonial changes not only impacted upon every aspect of society, in both practical and demonstrative terms,[195] but also challenged the traditional social order, for, as Luther maintained, 'every baptised Christian [was] a priest already, not by appointment or ordination from the pope or any other man but because Christ himself has begotten him as a priest in baptism.'[196] Celibacy, it was argued, did not bring one closer to God; instead the privileged position of priests, nuns and monks was eroded, replaced by family as the foundation of religion.[197] In

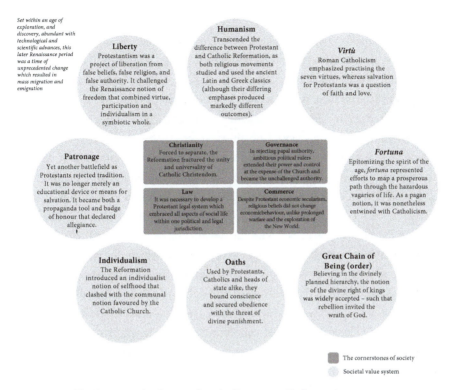

Set within an age of exploration, and discovery, abundant with technological and scientific advances, this later Renaissance period was a time of unprecedented change which resulted in mass migration and emigration

Humanism
Transcended the difference between Protestant and Catholic Reformation, as both religious movements studied and used the ancient Latin and Greek classics (although their differing emphases produced markedly different outcomes).

Liberty
Protestantism was a project of liberation from false beliefs, false religion, and false authority. It challenged the Renaissance notion of freedom that combined virtue, participation and individualism in a symbiotic whole.

Virtù
Roman Catholicism emphasized practising the seven virtues, whereas salvation for Protestants was a question of faith and love.

Patronage
Yet another battlefield as Protestants rejected tradition. It was no longer merely an educational device or means for salvation. It became both a propaganda tool and badge of honour that declared allegiance.

Christianity
Forced to separate, the Reformation fractured the unity and universality of Catholic Christendom.

Governance
In rejecting papal authority, ambitious political rulers extended their power and control at the expense of the Church and became the unchallenged authority.

Fortuna
Epitomizing the spirit of the age, *fortuna* represented efforts to map a prosperous path through the hazardous vagaries of life. As a pagan notion, it was nonetheless entwined with Catholicism.

Law
It was necessary to develop a Protestant legal system which embraced all aspects of social life within one political and legal jurisdiction.

Commerce
Despite Protestant economic secularism, religious beliefs did not change economic behaviour, unlike prolonged warfare and the exploration of the New World.

Individualism
The Reformation introduced an individualist notion of selfhood that clashed with the communal notion favoured by the Catholic Church.

Oaths
Used by Protestants, Catholics and heads of state alike, they bound conscience and secured obedience with the threat of divine punishment.

Great Chain of Being (order)
Believing in the divinely planned hierarchy, the notion of the divine right of kings was widely accepted – such that rebellion invited the wrath of God.

The cornerstones of society

Societal value system

Figure 15 The framework of trust after the Protestant Reformation.

England, the dissolution of the monasteries, often willingly accepted by their bishops, had a profound effect on local economies and the social fabric.[198] Similarly, the Latin mass, saints' day processions and the myriad festivals of the Catholic liturgical year were stopped on the State's conversion to Protestantism.[199] These once communally shared and cohesive experiences,[200] facilitated through instantly recognizable visual images and symbolism in a familiar atmosphere set to music,[201] that bridged the gulf between the literate and the illiterate, were made redundant.[202] Where traditional Catholicism had depended on the unity and invocality of the Church and State, the Reformation forced the issue of authority and obedience. It interrogated every belief and practice, criticizing the papacy for its integration of Roman and pagan traditions and its reliance on 'sacred traditions'. Trusting in the word of God, Protestant doctrine centred on *sola scripture* (scripture only) and *sola fide* (faith only). Such changes in attitude, practices and ritual invariably altered the long-held networks of trust, undermining the familiar and challenging tradition, as demonstrated by Henry's break with Rome, in 1533.

The English Reformation may be viewed against a backdrop of nationally cohesive spirituality rather than in the corrupt, exploitative and superstitious atmosphere described by Henry's commissioners,[203] an exaggeration perpetuated by the Tudors and beyond.[204] Henry's England remained a vibrant Catholic society built around local parishes, which had a distinctly community feel. There were small 'radical' or 'heretical' movements (Lollards, for example) and pockets of Protestantism, but they posed no threat to the distinctly English-flavoured Catholicism of the early sixteenth century.[205] Driven by a combination of desire and necessity, inventive steps were taken: Catholicism was outlawed,[206] denigrated and maligned while those who objected were executed. The dissolution of the monasteries (1536–41) brought an end to monastic life and a qualitative difference to society[207]: pilgrimages ceased with the destruction of shrines and relics[208]; the cult of saints was removed, depriving workers of between forty and fifty 'holy days' (holidays) per year; the great mystery plays (moral dramas in English), sponsored by religious guilds, were declared illegal and destroyed[209]; and the cult of death (abolition of purgatory) was derided.[210] These changes ruined communities, and to a great extent charity, medical care, scholarship, education, and patronage were curtailed, while art and books were obliterated,[211] history was discarded. Cut off from the familiar, invisible to their ancestors, their memories attacked, many were left confused, isolated, and bereft. Trust was lost, betrayed by Henry's 'truths'.[212] With effective control of the public forums,[213] the government was able to propagate these unified messages (acts of persuasion) on a grand scale.[214]

Historians' traditional view, although increasingly challenged, of riots and rebellions in this period is one of conservatism and constraint.[215] They were a customary response to the violation of traditional obligations woven through society, negotiated within traditional frameworks of deference and paternalism,[216] yet despite such familiarity, society's elites feared such action. This was a reflection, in part, of the powerful role prophecies played in every major rebellion of the Tudor period.[217] While now considered irrational, 'prophecies emerged from a larger worldview in which magic and religion overlapped'[218]; contemporaries accorded them a degree of respectability.[219] With a venerable tradition in England, prophecies were understood to be expressions of God's will, evoking fear and obedience. 'A tool to make or control popular opinion', by the 1530s prophecies had arguably been transformed into 'a source of power and authority for popular protest', used to challenge authority and withdraw obedience; they threatened order.[220] Their multiple meanings and interpretations inherently subverted authority. As popular elements of political culture, prophecies 'enjoyed near universal acceptance'[221] and represented a 'popular' form of political engagement in post-Reformation society.[222] They simultaneously drew from, and illustrated, the popular anxiety regarding questions of religion, succession, the economy (enclosure protest and agricultural crisis), and played a role in the international power struggles of the age. While 'those in positions of power sought out knowledge of the future themselves in order to guide their decision-making', they also demonized, criminalized and trivialized them.[223] The resurgence of these oblique predictions with 'no single truth' reflected the ideological tumult of the age.[224]

Even as subtle changes in belief altered political dynamics in important and tangible ways, they also changed people's relationship with the law. In Germany, the Protestant Reformation inevitably brought an end to the two-court system (ecclesiastical and civil), compelling the development of a legal system which embraced all aspects of social life within one political and legal jurisdiction. However, in spite of this transformative 'revolution', the law remained religiously grounded, just as in the Papal Revolution (1050–80) before it.[225] But now the Ten Commandments became the focus not only of how to live but also as the basis for law. In practical terms, the demise of ecclesiastical courts rather than secularizing civil law marked a 'spiritualization' of the erstwhile temporal jurisdiction, certainly for German princes.[226] Reflecting Luther's notion of two kingdoms, the civil and ecclesiastical were separated. In effect there was no longer one common and easily identifiable Western legal tradition underpinning Western European states and their societies. In Protestant states, a citizen's responsibility to obey its civil authority was paramount; it was part of God's plan, just as monarchs were God's representatives with a monopoly of political power[227] and, therefore, disorder and rebellion were mortal sins.

Although the Reformation in England took a very different course, the introduction of the 'notorious' Tudor laws on treason and sedition reflected the image-conscious Tudors' design for a strong centralized English State under their rule,[228] in turn re-emphasizing the role of legislation and a unified legal system. A few contemporary lawyers voiced their theoretical concerns regarding the tensions between maintaining order, political obligation, and the liberty of subjects, but cognizant of the political realities of the age, they supported their monarch.[229] Some even developed the connection, between the rule of law and the need for obedience, into a theory of divine right monarchy. Crompton, for one, argues that the laws of God, nature and the realm demand absolute obedience, even in the face of injustice and tyranny.[230] Such a position caused Pole to state that 'the realm now had no more than "a memory of its pristine liberty" despite its best men's efforts.'[231]

Set against a Reformation backdrop of the expanding notions of liberty (free from false beliefs and arbitrary authority), and individualism (to embody freedom of conscience), the notions of authority and obedience increasingly clashed. In particular, the conflicting loyalties of those out of step with a state's religion needed to be carefully balanced, as by enforcing compliance, in the defence of national security and to reinforce the monarch's authority, increasing numbers were persecuted and executed. With both sides of the religious divide creating martyrs, anxieties about the relationship of the individual with the State, and about justice and the legality of violence, increased.[232] A violent response proved counter-productive in the case of 'Bloody Mary', so named after her persecution of Protestants during her short-lived restoration of Roman Catholicism in England (1553–8); it exacerbated anti-Catholic and anti-Spanish feeling.[233] Exposed for public scrutiny, in vivid and gruesome detail, in Foxe's (1563) *Book of Martyrs*, this popular book is said to have done more to embed Protestantism into the English psyche than oaths of allegiance and vernacular bibles ever did.[234]

This simultaneously raised the question of the lawfulness of oaths; where they had once provided a legal incentive to tell the truth they were now being used to enforce conformity and root out heresy; often abused, they became instruments of betrayal.[235] Oaths, for both Protestants and Catholics, remained 'vital gateways through which human society was able to experience God'[236]; they played a central role in post-Reformation society, with churchmen and citizens required by oath, test, or formal declaration to swear allegiance to their monarch.[237] 'Upheld as binding promises, undergirded by the sanctity of God and his holy name'[238] oaths were arguably 'the primary means through which royal supremacy was implemented' in England.[239] The Tudor government relied upon the binding nature of oaths (individuals risked the wrath of God) to actively promote compliance and conformity. However, controversy continued to build over the *ex-officio* oath,[240] which became known as the 'cruel trilemma'.[241] Gray insists that such oaths were only used where the issue was acquiescence and obedience, loyalty and allegiance, a necessity, as no government, especially one with such limited policing powers as the Tudors, could govern without a measure of consent.

Historians are quick both to debate the extent of government reforms, or revolution,[242] of this period, and to argue the alternative notions of religious evolution, or conversion.[243] However, it was the interdependence and combined effects, when interacting across all the strata of English society, which resulted in a 'revolution', with trust being, simultaneously, a cause and effect. It was not simply a process of conversion or changing bureaucratic procedures, but rather the change in the way individuals interacted and 'trusted' within, and between, societal institutions. Often intrinsically divisive, these changes, which dramatically altered Church and State, created a dualism, fracturing societal unity. This was a 'revolution' of trust, which ultimately reordered and redrew key relationships, adapting many of the networks crisscrossing society and, in doing so, necessarily reflected the changing attitudes to risk within society. Whether the changes wrought in government and the Church were imposed from above for political, economic or 'national' reasons, or were the result of a groundswell of popular opinion, or a collaborative effort, in combination they took time to take hold, to embed. While in legal and practical terms, changes were relatively quickly and peacefully conformed to, daily communal practices, rituals and traditions proved slower to adapt or eradicate.

However, in the face of unified and orchestrated acts of persuasion, combining both 'the carrot and the stick', the stage was set to change the framework of trust underpinning the political and social landscape. By controlling the medium of print[244] and continuously preaching across the length and breadth of the country, the regime not only employed the existing relationships of trust to influence, threaten and co-opt, but actively coached people to trust, and in turn to generate trust in these new discursive practices and narratives which carried with them the weight of authority and the obligation of obedience.[245] The English Reformation simultaneously utilized and subtly altered the existing framework of trust which brought about a fundamental revolution that reshaped the English political, social, theological and psychological landscape. It rewrote the history of Catholic England and continues to colour its cultural heritage. Arguably (and temporarily) reversed during the reign of Mary I (1553–8),[246] the process regained its momentum under Elizabeth[247] (and continued under the Stuarts). By combining the power of an increasingly centralized government, combined with the perceived threat, recriminations and Marian examples of Catholic violence, any hope of reuniting the Catholic Church and the English monarchy in a relationship of equals was ultimately extinguished. This was a lengthy and complicated process, the outcome of a series of challenges, conflicts and crises which varied throughout England.[248]

Across Europe, the Protestant 'revolution' of the sixteenth century threatened the very structure of society and led to decades of conflict and strife.[249] As revolutionary and far-reaching as the Roman Empire's conversion to Christianity, rather than an instrument of unity and stability, Protestantism challenged authority and obedience, resulting in pluralism and fragmentation.[250] It split the

Church asunder and redrew the political map of Europe, reshaping the identity of states and Western culture.[251] It forever altered the tripartite relationship between the individual, God and State, which had operated unchallenged for over a millennium. A state's religion was now imposed upon the many at the monarch's command, more often driven by pragmatic rather than religious concerns. Few had the luxury to choose, while religious allegiance or conversion became a matter of expediency for a state's political elite. New frameworks of trust were needed to heal the deep divisions, to rebuild and maintain social cohesion, but with no unifying thread to connect them, the once remarkably adaptable core value system fractured. Despite the almost endless warfare, by 1648, the religious map of Europe had barely changed in nearly a century, although the dominance of the Holy Roman Emperor had been severely curtailed,[252] and the authority of the Pope had all but been eliminated. A new system of the political order had been established, with the Peace (and treaties) of Westphalia,[253] and so began Europe's era of absolute monarchy. Once filled with the sacred in thought and institutional practice, the new, post-Reformation political theology of obedience to, and authority of, the monarch dominated Europe.[254]

Convulsions, then rupture

England in the seventeenth century

In 1603 the three kingdoms (England, Scotland and Ireland) were united, for the first time, under Stuart rule.[1] However, in stark contrast to the united, peaceful and prosperous Britain depicted in Drayton's elaborate illustration for his topographical poem, *Poly-Olbion*, this was a period of conflicting notions and redefinition, of religious, scientific, political, domestic and cultural upheaval, and of ferment.[2] These ideas were further stimulated by self-reflection and the analysis of an individual's personal life. Set against a backdrop of population growth and a burgeoning economy, England was no longer isolated, on the periphery of Europe; it was part of Europe and the world as it expanded its overseas possessions and trading posts.[3] Britain in the seventeenth century was deeply divided by separate political, legal and ecclesiastical systems. Moving from an 'Age of Faith' to an 'Age of Reason', this period was marked by conflicting pressures and transition in which armed insurrection was commonplace[4]: this reflected not only a fear of popery, but also conflict between English Anglicanism and Scottish Presbyterianism, tensions within English Protestantism and the fragmentation of Puritanism into numerous competing sects.[5] Added to this was the struggle for power between the monarchy and the English gentry. The resulting breakdown in government order, mid-century, was exacerbated by social inequality, and compounded by periods of economic hardship (high inflation and poor harvest), while a growing cohort of 'masterless men' further endangered social cohesion. It created a volatile cocktail which had profound implications for English society and its culture.

Predominantly rural,[6] the English population expanded significantly during this period[7]; but rather than the stereotypical insular communities imagined, migration and mobility were commonplace, affected by changing economic circumstances,[8] growing inequalities and the lure of London.[9] Not the only unsettling force at play, the popular and widespread belief in folklore, superstition and pagan rituals, which had sat relatively peacefully alongside shifting Christian traditions, was increasingly challenged by the Puritan movement. Once relatively homogeneous, rigid patriarchal and hierarchical English communities produced profoundly different responses to this combination of pressures. Some emphasized tradition, cooperation and unity, others, moral discipline and the 'reformation of manners'.[10] These responses mirrored the growing divisions within the English Protestant Church, in particular between Laudianism and Puritanism.[11] In contrast to earlier historical periods explored in this book, rather than uniting society 'the passions and principles, ideas and values which creatively fermented in the cultural and political life of early Stuart decades' had a more polarizing effect.[12] Neither geographically nor structurally defined, they criss-crossed society. Although with only ever a small committed minority in each 'camp', there were larger groups who supported and sustained them for varying and disparate reasons. These diverging responses were a precursor and contributing factor in the English Civil War, continuing throughout the Restoration and beyond. It was perhaps the most tumultuous period in English history. During this period, political theorists inextricably intertwined the notions of revolution and trust. But, with multiple definitions in use, their exact meaning and intent were often obfuscated. Overlaid on one another, their particular use was often politically motivated. Intended to court popular support and manipulate public perceptions, simple oppositional messages were effectively conveyed across an efficient and rapidly expanding communications network.

Affordable print (with both text and images)[13] effortlessly inserted itself into the pre-existing and often complex oral networks which transmitted information throughout England.[14] By sharing imagery, format, dialogue and themes, oral communication, and print were able to work together to disseminate the news, rumours, gossip, and important social information of the age. For instance, upon 'entering a coffee-house one would be greeted ... by the cry "what news have you?" and then look for a space at a long table covered with papers of various kinds'.[15] The written and spoken word quickly became entwined, in turn, encouraging new forms of communication (pamphlet, newspaper, periodical, journalism) as well as altering those already in existence.[16] Facilitating new forms of polemic debate, print arguably gave rise to the formation of public opinion.[17] It transformed the public's ability to understand and participate in English political life in the seventeenth century; and connected the elite with the world 'beyond Westminster'.[18] This was built on the pre-existing foundations and tradition of widespread participation in local government to create 'common politics'.[19] 'The idea that political life became both popular and shared, even if it was not necessarily equal'.[20]

Words as weapons

'The civil wars of the 1640s were the most heavily reported conflict the British peoples had yet undergone. What historians have termed "the print explosion" from 1641 played a critical part in circulating information – and misinformation – to a public thirsty for news'[21] – 'Parliamentarian propaganda tended to capitalize upon anti-Catholic and xenophobic prejudices to portray the Cavaliers as violent, libertine plunderers ... The royalists countered with their image of the low-born, socially subversive rebel, intent on levelling all authority and wealth'.[22] Reporting the news of the day, popular newspapers/pamphlets also featured strong religious images or bitter parodies of the 'gracious king' holding hands with Heresy but swearing commitment to Truth.[23]

In combination, affordable print, a growing sense of sociability and an emerging 'public sphere' quickly ensured information was disseminated, interpreted and then actioned.[24] While dismissed by some as mere 'bum fodder' – described as 'infectious swarms' of 'guilty sheets' observed 'walking the streets', the 'cuckoos of our time', they were bemoaned as 'gall and bitterness and devilish calumnies' – most contemporary commentators recognized this power and potential.[25] They 'united in trying to grapple with what effect it would have on political life and popular participation',[26] raising the question of what should, and could, be done. Earlier monarchs had sought to strictly control their public image, and governments to manage the flow of information, with 'official and authorised' publications, but the costly failures of the early Stuarts brought an effective end to such monopolies. After the Restoration, 'the British had secured the right, albeit assumed and unprotected by legislation, to read the news of their troubled country'.[27] And so rather than attempt to suppress or prevent the news, the later Stuart government, having learnt from their predecessors, sought to manipulate it.[28] As a result, this period produced literature of such extremes, in celebration of, or reaction to, the Restoration of Charles II.

With an unprecedented array of information and news now available to those in society who wanted it,[29] and matched by the public's insatiable desire for it, political participation grew. Now open to all, it 'connected the local and the national; the centre and the periphery; elites and non-elites; and the discrete genres of print to the public sphere and popular mobilisation'.[30] With their diverse readership, pamphlets, often accompanied by woodcut prints, not only reflected the political, social and religious controversy of the age, becoming an ideological battleground for competing forces, but also emphasized man's complicated relationship with, and interest in, power and politics, leading to an 'explosion of print' at crisis points throughout the century. As each and every side of the debate was seized upon in print, it reflected political division, exacerbating it by constructing 'otherness' and 'opposition'. It played a pivotal role in constructing religious, political, provincial and national identities. By drawing on powerful symbolic images,[31] ideas and characters, it not only helped to create, mould and enforce these identities but also introduced them to a wider audience. Despite popular misconceptions, these identities and the news in general were not accepted without question. Contemporaries rightly feared the credibility of printed news and so, through experience, devised strategies/ tactics to engage with it. In this way seventeenth-century readers were able to 'use print carefully, pragmatically, purposefully and strategically', aware of both the industry's structural dynamics and the intervention and manipulation by interested parties.[32]

The quality of seventeenth-century media should, therefore, be seen as both 'informative and polemical, idealistic and instrumental, accessible and discriminating, reasoned and Babelish, and through these dichotomies, the appetite of the popular reader for not only ideas and identity, but 'political opinion and debate, was fed'.[33]

English rebellion, revolution and war

Within this milieu, with little or no consensus amongst contemporary commentators as to the nature of the ongoing civil strife, no single term could be agreed upon to describe, or define, such actions and events. Meanwhile, the terms ('rebellion' and 'revolution') themselves became increasingly politicized, as Adamson notes, 'after 1660, it was difficult to refer to events of the mid-century crisis without the very choice of words becoming an implicit declaration of Civil War allegiance'.[34] Most contemporary historians writing or publishing before 1702 could be clearly labelled as Royalist, Parliamentarian or Whig.[35] By turn, they alluded to the period between 1640 and 1660 as 'the late troubled times', 'the troubles', 'distractions', referring to 'internecine wars' and 'unnatural, cruel and bloody wars',[36] while the king's ardent supporters labelled it 'the Rebellion' or even 'the Great Rebellion'.[37] Notably, it was Guizot, in 1826, who first referred to this particular action as an 'English Revolution'. In his work he explains, 'the analogy of the two revolutions is such, that the first [the English] would never have been understood had not the second [the French] taken place'.[38] Revisiting and reinterpreting historical events was nothing new.[39] It is a reminder that 'each generation has its own troubles and problems, and, therefore, its own interests and its own point of view' and that 'it follows that each generation has a right to look upon and re-interpret history in [their] own way'.[40] However, it raises questions over influence, distortion and the possibility of manipulation. In sharp contrast, both the Restoration of Charles II and the overthrow of King James II in 1688 were (in advance, and at the time) referred to as revolutions.[41] In such high-stake situations descriptions are influential and persuasive; carrying symbolic and political weight they confer legitimacy on or deny it to those involved.[42] Perhaps it had never been truer than in these conflicts that language was one of the first casualties.

While there already existed a double meaning of the term 'revolution',[43] by the seventeenth century it had a variety of meanings and uses. It had evolved from 'a simple, rather obscure, Latin word' – *revolvo* – 'to a widely used and complex doctrine of political action'.[44] It was, nevertheless, its astronomical (scientific) meaning which dominated the wider discourse of seventeenth-century England, as contemporary dictionaries can attest.[45] However, as one might anticipate, in 'the first modern age of English literature',[46] poets and playwrights quickly appropriated the term 'revolution', expanding and popularizing its use.[47] Political commentators, by drawing more widely from contemporary literature and from recent events in Europe,[48] slowly began to use the term to describe such political reversals of fortunes (the Restoration and the overthrow of James II).[49] Furthermore, in 1664, the phrase, 'the Revolution of the twelve years' was first used to describe the period between Charles I's execution and the Restoration. It was incorporated into contemporary political discourse, correspondence, and diaries – for example, Ascham's discourse (1648) – Evelyn's diary (1620–1706) and Hampden's testimony before the House of Lords (1689)–in the latter half of the seventeenth century, as a way of describing and interpreting recent events. Lexicographers, such as Kersey (1715), Philip (1720), and Johnson (1755), however, did not assign the term a political meaning until the early eighteenth century.

Contemporary evidence, therefore, suggests that the term 'revolution' 'was used rather loosely to describe various types of political and social changes which took place within the monarchical form of government'.[50] And, as in the present day, it meant different things to different people in different situations, including a change in the form of government, dynastic change, dynastic restoration or wider socio-economic changes. As events unfolded, the labels given to these actions continually changed. Perceptions, knowledge and understanding altered in an environment of rapidly emerging feedback loops.[51] In the seventeenth century, despite the various interpretations, the contemporary notion of revolution meant a complete circular political movement to most.[52] For many this reflected the 'wheel of fortune'[53] or divine intervention.[54] Neither permanent nor progressive, revolution simply referred to a transfer of power and a recasting of government.[55] It should, therefore, not be feared but regarded as a natural and justifiable cycle, a rebalancing, which upon completion returns itself to 'the original'.[56] And yet this period can be distinguished from earlier revolutionary cycles by the presence of so many fundamental and far-reaching ideas, a time of unmatched pluralism. Individuals labelled themselves as 'radical'[57] and 'challenged the fundamental political, religious, or social axioms of the day'.[58] However, a lack of widespread 'trust' (legitimacy) and innate conservativism was able to temporarily corral these ideas such that by the end of the century 'it was the State and the Established Church that defined what was radical and not the Dissenters'.[59]

This was an age full of stark dichotomies. It was a time in which kings had a 'divine right to rule' but Charles I was executed, and James II was expelled. In this 'century of revolution', these actions needed to be understood, reflected upon and justified. Two political theorists stood out: Hobbes (1588–1679) and Locke (1632–1704).[60] In an age of such upheaval, with the underlying unity of a Catholic Europe shattered, their differing views of the world (the state of nature and human nature) mirrored the division and fragmentation they saw in the society around them. The oppositional views they developed reflected not only their own positions, experiences and influences during these turbulent times,[61] but also brought their notions of man's individuality and self-interest to the centre of political analysis. Hobbes was the first to 'revolutionise' the concept of political revolution.[62] In rejecting the ideas of his contemporaries, he purposefully rejected the notions that corruption inevitably afflicts all forms of government, that Fortune shapes events, and that God directly intervenes. In his writings as a physicist, Hobbes 'combined the language of the otherwise distinct intellectual practices of political and scientific speculation' in his theory of revolution.[63] However, rather than define the term, he characterized the entire period of 1640–60 as a revolution,[64] and instead focused his attentions on his science of 'equity and justice' which alone could stop civil strife, ending the cycles of revolution.[65]

As with the age in general, Locke's response to issues of revolution 'reveals a mixture of radicalism and conservatism, idealism and practical politics'.[66] In contrast to Hobbes, he unequivocally defended the 'right' of revolution, although he rarely used the term, instead preferring 'resistance'[67] by which he meant a rebellion by people with executive power. In line with his contemporaries, when he referred to revolution, he incorporated its scientific meaning, namely as a completed circular motion,[68] describing how the political cycles, experienced in England in the seventeenth century, ultimately returned to their original constitutional point. In doing so, he drew attention to the rebels' innately reactionary nature,[69] while underlining that the complete cycle (after the Restoration) constituted a revolution. Writing in the wake of the Exclusion Controversy, Locke, in a 'revolutionary' argument, outlined how this cycle of revolution was a direct response to a betrayal of *trust*. It occurs, for example, if the legislative assembly refuses to preserve property and liberty or if the monarch refuses to call Parliament, hinders its freedom, interferes or obstructs free elections or substitutes his will for the law-making process. He contended that if either a legitimate monarch or duly elected representative betrays the 'trust' placed in them, it is they who are the true rebels and revolution is justifiable. The king, in particular, exposed himself to the threat of justifiable revolution as he had a 'double trust' as both executor and initiator of the law-making process. Revolution for Locke was, therefore, a backward-looking and reactionary movement. It was a purposeful action designed to return to a position of mutual trust.

While these contrasting ideas and shifting discourses undoubtedly influenced later generations, at the time of their publication,[70] the broader population would have been largely unaware of Hobbes's and Locke's controversial tomes and the ideas they contained.[71] For while print had increased dramatically, such literary and academic works were published in low numbers; expensive in comparison to pamphlets, they took time to write and longer to publish; furthermore, because they were shaped by patronage they had, at the time, limited audience and appeal.[72] To the wider audience, revolution was a transfer of power, while rebellion was increasingly seen as a precursor, or its failure. Divisive, violent and repetitive, revolution was often disappointing as individual liberties recently won were quickly curtailed by conservativism.

Building on earlier ideas associated with revolution, revolt and rebellion, both Hobbes and Locke continued to shift the emphasis, by degrees, towards the notion of 'trust'. Both their works included specific references to trust, and the betrayal of trust.[73] 'Hobbes presented a case for the essential fatuousness of interpersonal trust in a world without an unlimited authority to enforce contracts.[74] Yet he had a deep trust in the good moral fabric of the sovereign and his ability to act in the best interest of all men. He was also conscious of the necessary development of trust between political parties to build viable societies.[75] Locke, on the other hand, 'assumed a comparatively high degree of trust within civil society, concentrating instead on forming and maintaining a government that is worthy of civil society's trust'.[76] For him trust was binary – imperative for political society and government but, if neglected or opposed, it was forfeited.[77] Before considering this issue further, it may be helpful to examine what the term 'trust' meant when used by Hobbes and Locke.

With a rich nexus of meaning in seventeenth-century English usage,[78] 'trust' was ubiquitously referred to in contemporary political discourse throughout the century. Yet it held two distinct meanings. First and foremost, it was understood as an unsecured expectation that a promised undertaking would be performed. Second, it meant the focus of political discourse as a legal instrument. Analogous to the private law of trust, it evolved from the notion that government was a trust instituted by God. As such, God was understood to have granted the trust of government to the king, as the trustee, for the benefit of the people.[79] A cornerstone of the divine right of kings, it became an integral component in the century's most divisive debate. It was called upon by those who argued that royal power was absolute by the laws of God and Nature, and by those who sought to limit it. With no consensus to unite these opposing factions, both sides in the civil war 'maintained, apparently sincerely, that they were fighting for the King, the law, and the established religion, but each side turned out to be loyal to different understandings of these concepts'.[80] Against this backdrop, 'trust' became the rhetorical weapon of choice, appropriated by both sides.

Using trust as a legal instrument, these ongoing debates, which drew not only from new ideas but also from historical precedents and traditions, questioned the fundamental basis of society and government. These debates between the educated elite coincided with literary writers' conceptions of England, or its nascent colonies, as an *Oceana*, or a *New Jerusalem* and, so-called, 'radical groups' experimental visions for a new society.[81]

Writing on the question of obedience and allegiance, contemporaries such as Sir Edward Coke wrote that they are due to the monarch 'by the "Law of Nature", the "Law of God" and the "Moral Law"', which he understood to be absolute and incontrovertible.[82] However, the issue at stake, from as early as the fourteenth century, was 'if the King do not demean himself by reason in the right of his Crown' are his 'lieges bound by oath to remove [him]'.[83] This became a particularly vexing issue during the Engagement Controversy (1649–51).[84] Royalists such as Edward Bagshaw argued 'ligeance being a corporeall service is to be done to a visible, corporeall, and local person; not to a thing invisible, [and] incorporeall'.[85] Similarly, John Cleveland, asserted 'the body politick, ... is an invisible nothing, and can neither give nor take homage'.[86] George Buchanan, meanwhile, theorizing seventy years earlier, distinguished between the office of king and the man who exercises the office.[87] He argued that despite any and all allegiances owed, should a king act unfairly or unjustly he becomes a tyrant, breaking the mutual contract. He was not alone in this.[88]

These intransigencies were further complicated by notions of reciprocal and mutual duties and ultimate accountability. It was on these matters that relationships of trust were fought. The Royalists 'maintayne[d] that the king [was] king by an inhaerent birth-right' with 'his kingly office an office upon trust'[89]; while Parliamentarians, in the words of Milton, held 'the power of Kings and Magistrates is nothing else, but what is only derivative, transferr'd and committed to them in trust from the People, to the common good of them all'.[90] Such expressions of trust were repeatedly tossed back and forth in the political theatre of Charles I's trial. The king freely acknowledged that his power, which came from God, was held in trust for the welfare of his people, but he argued that he had done nothing to violate or forfeit that trust.[91] In turn, the Army Remonstrance stated 'no king be hereafter admitted, but upon the election of, and as upon trust from the people'; the king was a trustee for the people 'by and for whom he was instructed'.[92] Expressed as a legal instrument,[93] disagreement existed between the parties in this relationship of trust and their accountability, with no common ground between opposing advocates.

The effects were experienced first-hand, as political control continually changed throughout this turbulent century.[94] Yet while Aylmer argues that without such oppositional ideology the English Revolution is ultimately unintelligible,[95] contemporary literature often paints a less polarized picture. Therefore, rather than interpreting the ensuing political 'ping-pong' as a victory of one theory over another, it should be construed as tensions and ambivalences within a body of widely shared beliefs. Irrespective of the oppositional stances taken, underlying notions of honour, order and loyalty (or trust in the law) remained constant throughout. Used in common discourse, daily interactions and practices, as well as a legal instrument, the term 'trust' was also taken a step further by some contemporary political theorists. However, its multiple uses often obfuscate its meaning and intent.

Not usually considered a Hobbesian concept, trust is more commonly associated with Locke. Nevertheless, Hobbes made reference to trust,[96] defining it by turn as 'an opinion of the veracity of the man' or as a passion of the mind.[97] Writing in a period of crisis for monarchical absolutism, national identity and religion, of increasing political rights and engagement but also of an emerging nation, Hobbes saw the protection provided by a regime, together with the internal cohesion it created, as paramount for social order. Fearful of political disintegration into anarchy and the increasingly radical ideas in circulation, he theorized the need for 'artificial' structures of authority and trust to ensure a regime's legitimacy.[98] Without legitimacy, and the obligations it creates, there can only be mutual hostility and deep distrust, as seventeenth-century England bore witness. Such a state of nature pits every person against every other person in a perpetual state of war. For Hobbes, therefore, opposing even the most oppressive government was 'scarce sensible, in respect of the miseries, and horrible calamities that accompany a Civill Warre'.[99]

Hobbes argued that men were not to be trusted in the state of nature, which led him to advocate an authoritarian system of government.[100] This is not to say that trust is absent in his work. However, it was the child, not the parent, of a benign commonwealth, which could only be established by overcoming the mutual fear endemic in the state of nature.[101] A sovereign's legitimacy ('given power') is, therefore, predicated on their good use of common coercive powers.[102] Trusted by his subjects, as a 'signe of opinion of his virtue and power',[103] to protect property and life, to ensure the rule of law and punish those who flout it; without it there is no incentive to cease fighting.[104] Trust can, therefore, be considered 'the key concept connecting the dimensions of [Hobbes's] theory'.[105]

In contrast to Hobbes, trust has always been seen as central to Locke's theory, defining it as 'the bond of society'.[106] Trust was both a virtue and a causal explanation, sustaining society. It increased the tolerance for uncertainty, while trustworthiness meant keeping agreements, promises and oaths, in fear of God's wrath.[107] For Locke, trust played a crucial role in each stage of political society: creation, maintenance and dissolution. First, in coming together for the mutual preservation of property,[108] like-minded individuals must 'quit their natural power and resign it up into the hands of the community'.[109] To be able to do this they must trust in the community's ability to safeguard both their lives and their property and subject offenders to retribution. It is clear, with Locke's distrust of monarchy,[110] that the act of joining civil society required tremendous trust since in doing so individuals invited new risk.[111] A calculation had to be made: security and benefit versus insecurity and loss. It underscored that risk was 'the very essence of trust'.[112] With this approach, 'Locke's work captured, in a nuanced way, the shifting power relations and asymmetries that characterise all trusting relationships'.[113]

Second, to maintain the legitimacy of such a binding compact,[114] with its horizontal networks of mutual obligations and benefit and its vertical bonds captured in the language of a legal trust, civil society required both continual consent and equality for all.[115] This was particularly true with the law as society requires a certain level of predictability to function. Thus for Locke, citizenship was a 'personal challenge', while political participation was a duty and a right; it was also a burden not a pleasure or privilege.[116] Although committed to the rule of law, Locke advocated strongly for good governance,[117] highlighting that the 'power to act according to discretion for the public good, without prescription of law, and sometimes even against it', was demonstrable proof of trust. Using such a 'prerogative' reinforced the duality of Locke's trust/risk,[118] endorsing its practical use while simultaneously acknowledging it was open to abuse.[119] In Locke's third stage, if and when a government falls short of its duties, 'trust must necessarily be forfeited',[120] as it both legitimizes and symbolizes political power.[121] Locke focused on the breakdown of trust, on sensory knowledge in judging, or predicting tyranny, and on the necessity of political agency. He stressed that it required constant vigilance, intellectual work and the ability to calculate risk. However, by focusing attention on the seat of power, rather than the relationship between citizens, he downplayed the idea that trust can be a partnership of equals. He required 'thinking' subjects with a thirst for knowledge to continually inform the practice of political trust. Locke's theory 'combines a radically individualist conception of both the human significance and the rationality of political agency, with a wholly unalienated conception of its social context'[122]; he thus set an extremely high bar.

It is clear that 'idioms of trust and ideas of accountability' filled literature and political thought in this 'age of strife and genius', but equally important in gaining a complete picture of a society in transition, 'were vernacular traditions around "trust"'.[123]

While these political and philosophical debates continued, the populace tried to survive in what could be considered a fractured and fragile world. Despite this, society continued to function by relying upon the adhesion to existing forms of behaviour, rituals, tradition and unifying shared values. Honour was deemed to be of great importance.[124] It brought status, respect and prestige. Without it, an individual was subordinate in society, making patronage and political positions impossible. It was 'so near a neighbour unto man's life, that he is ever accounted cruel to himself, that is careless of his Reputation for dishonour is more to be feared than death, and honour more to be desired than life'.[125] Referred to in popular ballads, literature and plays,[126] it was a vital concept, not only in all social relationships but also political ones. Dishonour was castigated through 'shaming' practices and the newly emerging 'scandal sheets'.[127] Similarly, the imposition and enforcement of, often localized, moral codes, helped to preserve order and defend a community's cohesion.

The maintenance of these shared values proved essential in the face of potentially anarchic volatility, ensuring that society remained 'surprisingly stable'. Despite political experimentation, after the Restoration, England was still Anglican, aristocratic and monarchical.[128] The years of conflict had taken their toll on families, communities and loyalties; however, social relationships were still ones of deference rather than class enmity, reinforced by cooperative practices and communal notions of order.[129] Meanwhile widespread participation

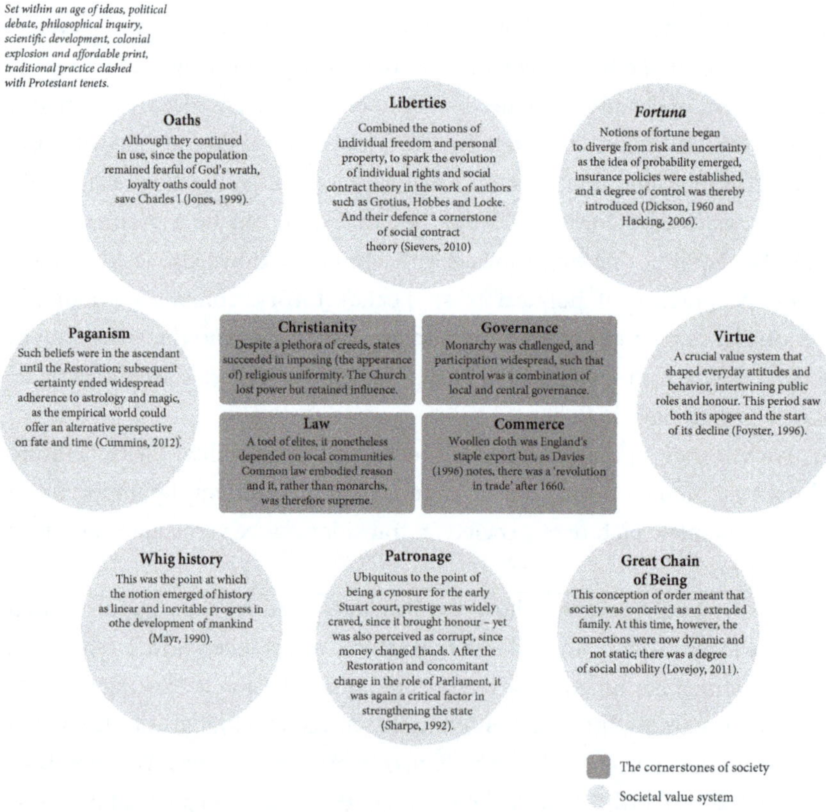

Set within an age of ideas, political debate, philosophical inquiry, scientific development, colonial explosion and affordable print, traditional practice clashed with Protestant tenets.

Oaths
Although they continued in use, since the population remained fearful of God's wrath, loyalty oaths could not save Charles I (Jones, 1999).

Liberties
Combined the notions of individual freedom and personal property, to spark the evolution of individual rights and social contract theory in the work of authors such as Grotius, Hobbes and Locke. And their defence a cornerstone of social contract theory (Sievers, 2010)

Fortuna
Notions of fortune began to diverge from risk and uncertainty as the idea of probability emerged, insurance policies were established, and a degree of control was thereby introduced (Dickson, 1960 and Hacking, 2006).

Paganism
Such beliefs were in the ascendant until the Restoration; subsequent certainty ended widespread adherence to astrology and magic, as the empirical world could offer an alternative perspective on fate and time (Cummins, 2012).

Christianity
Despite a plethora of creeds, states succeeded in imposing (the appearance of) religious uniformity. The Church lost power but retained influence.

Governance
Monarchy was challenged, and participation widespread, such that control was a combination of local and central governance.

Virtue
A crucial value system that shaped everyday attitudes and behavior, intertwining public roles and honour. This period saw both its apogee and the start of its decline (Foyster, 1996).

Law
A tool of elites, it nonetheless depended on local communities. Common law embodied reason and it, rather than monarchs, was therefore supreme.

Commerce
Woollen cloth was England's staple export but, as Davies (1996) notes, there was a 'revolution in trade' after 1660.

Whig history
This was the point at which the notion emerged of history as linear and inevitable progress in othe development of mankind (Mayr, 1990).

Patronage
Ubiquitous to the point of being a cynosure for the early Stuart court, prestige was widely craved, since it brought honour – yet was also perceived as corrupt, since money changed hands. After the Restoration and concomitant change in the role of Parliament, it was again a critical factor in strengthening the state (Sharpe, 1992).

Great Chain of Being
This conception of order meant that society was conceived as an extended family. At this time, however, the connections were now dynamic and not static; there was a degree of social mobility (Lovejoy, 2011).

The cornerstones of society

Societal value system

Figure 16 The evolving framework of trust in seventeenth-century England.

in adaptive and responsive local community governance[130] provided both a mouthpiece for the 'middling sort'[131] in communities and an 'escape valve' for the tensions and frustrations both within communities and between the regions and central government. These were two-way processes,[132] none more so than in the provision of Poor Law relief and the prosecution and punishment of crime. Both provided opportunities for localized and selective enforcement.[133]

In combination, shared values and communal practices strengthened social bonds, neighbourliness and community spirit in the face of increasing migration and mobility,[134] conflicting allegiances[135] and a growing sense of individualism.[136] Within this milieu Whiggish[137] and conservative notions continually, often violently, clashed. Emphasizing the rise of constitutional government, personal freedoms and scientific progress, Whiggism presented history as an inevitable linear progression of mankind.[138] In contrast, conservatism sought to preserve the status quo; it emphasized stability and continuity. Whiggism dominated British politics after 1688 for the next eighty years, with perhaps its most controversial legacy being its interpretation of history.[139] Against this backdrop, the framework of trust underpinning society inevitably evolved. No longer inextricably intertwined, it was now required to support increasingly diverse, often overlapping and simultaneously conflicting connections and allegiances. It adapted to both the lack of uniformity of religious beliefs and differing notions of loyalty to the Crown and State. Individual components of the framework were no longer all-encompassing. An overview of this framework is presented in **Figure 16**.

In this age of affordable print, where belief in magic and astrology was widespread, and lawbreakers became the first celebrities,[140] revolution and trust were portrayed by influential contemporary political theorists as interconnected rational calculations. Yet, on a practical and vernacular level, it was the 'trust' in tradition, custom and community which maintained social order in this period of uncertainty. In combination, throughout this period, conservative shared values, belief in the law and widespread participation in local community governance repeatedly restored English equilibrium, thus bringing 'revolution' full circle.[141]

France in the eighteenth century

Divided into three estates, eighteenth-century French society comprised 'those who prayed' (the clergy), 'those who fought' (the nobility) and 'those who toiled' (the *bourgeoise* and peasants).[142] Defined retrospectively, the *Ancien Regime* ('old regime') was monarchic and aristocratic. Rigidly hierarchical, power was centralized in this all-encompassing social and political system. When the term 'revolution' first appeared in English print in 1794, it was typically used pejoratively: 'Automatically freighted with associations of both traditionalism and senescence. It conjured up a society so encrusted with anachronisms that only a shock of great violence could free the living organism within.'[143] In this 'Age of Reason' and 'Enlightenment', France remained staunchly Catholic, with the Crown vigorously imposing religious uniformity on a populace more superstitious than devoted.[144] Meanwhile, firmly under Bourbon rule, the nobility were effectively neutered by an extremely elaborate system of court etiquette.[145]

Culturally hegemonic,[146]France was both a linguist patchwork and a country of varying local privileges, historic difference and administrative incoherence.[147] Its population was estimated at 28 million in 1789, 95 per cent of whom lived on the land under a seigneurial system,[148] although an urban population was growing.[149] French peasants remained largely illiterate.[150] However, 'education, literacy and learning' were gradually provided to 'rich and poor alike'.[151] Reading became the fashion, books the leading media of the day although secular rather than religious as the French Church did not encourage the reading of scripture.[152] Men gathered in coffee houses to read and discuss the newspapers, reading rooms offered access to periodicals, while salons and newly formed societies explored intellectual issues. Enlightened ideas of science, rationality and commerce slowly came to replace superstition and prejudices, while 'rational men of goodwill [sought] society's reform' and to 'cultivate the virtues of simplicity, kindness, rationality and hard work'.[153]

The French Revolution was a 'momentous public event'. This was the 'age of conversation'[154]; 'evidenced not only by the multitude of arguments for and against, but also simply the greatest proliferation of periodicals and pamphlets in history'.[155] Together with religious influence (vernacular bibles, charities, and schooling), the French Revolution, rather than its subsequent vision of mass education, did more to stimulate a dramatic increase in literacy by fostering one of the largest and broadest debates in literary and cultural history.[156] This was a revolution, as Chartier argues, made by books; not for what they said but for how they were read.[157] Changes in eighteenth-century reading practices and sociability were without doubt contributory factors in the 'success' of the French Revolution.

During this period '"revolution" as the disorder of events [and] expression of the instability of all things human, began to give way to "Revolution" as a dynamic transformational process, an expression of the historical rhythm of the progress of the human mind'.[158] With it the French Revolution became the classic prototype for revolution. True revolution no longer followed conventional stages in a repetitive cycle but marked new milestones in history's unique journey; it was linear and progressive.

Even prior to the revolutionary events of 1789, the term 'revolution' and its use were already somewhat mixed in the long eighteenth-century literature, having gained wider currency and new meaning with the constitutional upheavals of 1688–9 in England.[159] The 'Glorious Revolution' referred to as the 'Great', the 'Wonderful' and the 'Happy' Revolution, and such terminology, celebrated the absence not only of civil war but also of social upheaval from below.[160] Retaining its cyclical conception the word continued to 'suggest restoration; the return to a previous state of affairs, far more often than rebellion, the change to something new – a cyclical rather than progressive theory of history'.[161] But it had demonstrated a developmental aspect. As early as 1634, Duc De Rohan argued that 'whatever it is that cause[s] the circular revolution of the things of this world, also causes the basic principle of good government to change'.[162] 'Following the events of 1688/9, "Revolution" quickly became the accepted term … for the overthrow of a tyrannical ruler, followed by a new constitutional regime, guaranteeing specific rights for the people'.[163] What followed was recognized as a new epoch, a new order, a better base on which to stand,[164] while the Huguenots, in exile, capitalized on the '*Révolution d'Angleterre*', exalting its importance as a true return while simultaneously highlighting the dawning of a new era.[165] Thus, rather than simply recursive, the change could be regarded as unique and irrevocable. Such political terminology was then revived in discussions, for and against, the American Revolution (1765–83), as contemporary historians regarded its development as inevitable, creating a polity that was without historical parallel.[166]

In response, the vast literature on revolutions was produced in the eighteenth century, increasing through its use, in a variety of socio-cultural contexts.[167] 'In so doing, [these] writers ultimately drained all historical specificity from the notion'.[168] For instance, Defoe describes how 'Revolution in Trade, brought a Revolution in the very Nature of Things'.[169] Stothard meanwhile outlines the 'very extraordinary revolutions … in the habits of this kingdom'.[170] Whereas Addison observed 'a very great revolution that has happened in this article of good-breeding [manners]'.[171] The term was invoked generously and indiscriminately in 'the century of revolution'.[172] Eighteenth-century writers proclaimed 'everything is revolution in this world', adding further layers to the widespread perceptions of this powerful notion. Although all agreed that revolution was inevitable with no dynamic of its own, it gradually became apparent that there was no definitive meaning but a number of increasingly banal interpretations.[173] In particular, in a growing genre of French historiography, 'revolution' lacked any specificity although at its core was a threat: a fear of the disorder caused: it contrasted revolution against the stability of absolutist French monarchy. Ascribed with no moral inferences, the revolution was seen as an outcome, only possible to describe once it had taken place: 'objects of analysis not objectives of will'.[174] So 'far from being an unfamiliar term in 1789' it had long been associated with change and disorder.[175] Furetiere, in 1690, having given 'revolution' its astronomical meaning, added 'also used of extraordinary changes that occur in the world', while the Academie later defined it as 'change which occurs in public affairs, in the things of this world', but more succinctly Richelet's dictionary of 1680 listed 'revolution' as 'trouble, disorder and change'.[176]

However, the sheer magnitude and impact, action and experience, of the French Revolution came before its far-reaching and long-lasting cultural conception in terms of language and understanding.[177] It was greeted with widespread enthusiasm, with, for example, Fox, the opposition Whig leader, exclaiming 'how much the greatest event that has happened in the history of the world, and how much the best'.[178] Such a spectacle initially dumbfounded its contemporaries, as 'never before was such an inevitable event so unforeseen'.[179] Coleridge spoke of 'France in wrath her gigantic limbs upreared'.[180] Burke meanwhile was struck by its theatricality 'what spectators and what actors!' he wrote, 'England, gazing with astonishment at a French struggle for liberty, not knowing whether to blame or to applaud'.[181] Only a small minority ever joined Jacobin Clubs.[182] However, 'once the French set out in 1789 to make the world anew' everyone was affected by revolutionary change.[183] It extended its reach into everything: the law, religion, even the map of France, recreating time and space. In so doing it profoundly altered the notion of revolution. In part, this was because this 'great talking machine'[184] created an explosion of new words and new vocabularies with notions of left and right being drawn from the Assembly seating and the emergence of words such as aristocrat (1789) *sans culottes* (1790) capitalist, regime, *émigré* (1792), *guillotine* (1793), terrorism (1795) and *tricolore* (1797). The alteration occurred, however, principally because of the perceived revolutionary nature of the events themselves. It quickly became regarded as a watershed event in modern European history as it swept away the structures of the absolute monarchy perfected by Louis XIV, replacing them with a parliamentary system based on electoral politics. It replaced the traditional social order, based on hierarchy and privilege, with one based on modern principles of freedom and equality. A long and violent process, on an unprecedented scale, it was perceived as a fundamental transformation.

Designed to remove all reference to Christian and feudal past, the dramatic changes that the 'Revolution' implemented were many and varied. Perhaps the boldest was the adoption of a revolutionary calendar in 1793. Amid nostalgia for the ancient Roman Republic it looked to nature for inspiration, dividing time into multiples of ten.[185] The scope of its ambition was astounding. It created a rupture in time, lifting the Revolution out of the existing historical timeline, as revolutionary history began anew: its 'goal [was] to create a new collective memory for the nascent French Republic'.[186] Mirroring the recent metrication of space, the currency was also decimalized and redesigned.[187] The system of weights was also reorganized and systematized. It was estimated that before the Revolution, over 60,000 different measures of weight were used in France.[188] These changes had the combined effect of introducing notions of universality, of shared experience, and equality while simultaneously uniting a once disparate kingdom into a nation. Previously each social order had laid claim to different origins, systems and understanding which reflected divine order and reaffirmed the hierarchical pyramid of social relations. In a similar vein and in a concerted attempt to change old habits, 1,400 streets in Paris were renamed together with 6,000 towns, chess pieces, playing cards, crockery and furniture. As part of this exercise to destroy the old symbols of royal despotism, revolutionaries renamed themselves: no longer Louis they called themselves Brutus or Spartacus. Meanwhile, in order to create a new civic order to replace the old, their children were named after martyrs ('Marat'), conceptions ('Tyrannicide') and events ('Civilization-Jemappes-Republique').[189] They were also drawn from nature ('Radish', 'Celery', 'Rhubarb').[190]

This historical experience shaped the very concept of revolution in a rich dialectic interchange between consciousness, language, the new regime and its many spectators, as Burke and Paine argued, and an established circle of British and American supporters debated.[191] The French sought to redefine revolution anew.[192] With France being seen as its inventor, the term was subsequently recognized as having acquired its distinctively modern meaning.[193] Its first effect was to discredit the notion that revolution might restore previous social order. Revolution was no longer a recurrent cycle or the reversion to a previous state, but created something radically new: a new system of society, a new civilization, a new world. 'What were formerly called revolutions, were little more than a change of persons, or an alteration of local circumstances. They rose and fell like things, of course, and had nothing in their existence or their fate that could influence beyond the spot that produced them.'[194] In quick succession both the English and American models of revolution were dismissed,[195] for the 'French nation [was] not made to receive examples but to set them'.[196] Even so, secular supporters, on the sidelines of the French Revolution, quickly foresaw the threat of regression and petition of past cyclical patterns.[197]

Burke was 'the first English writer [for whom] the word carrie[d] the new sense of a large violent upheaval from below that brings about a restructuring of society'; however, competition rapidly developed to frame the public's understanding of the events they were experiencing first-hand.[198] Political narratives were spun, inventing, imposing and enforcing new symbolism, political practices, language, and even dress codes to create citizens out of slaves.[199] Exhilarating and traumatic, these events profoundly touched upon individual and collective identity. As Foucault has argued, it 'is actually a very important factor in struggle … If one controls people's memory, one controls their dynamism … It is vital to have possession of this memory, to control it, administer it, tell it what it must contain'.[200] At its very creation, after the Bastille fell and during the October Days, a new conception of revolution emerged as a direct consequence of the deliberate reordering and recombining of its existing meaning.[201] This was vividly demonstrated in the pages of the popular revolutionary journal *Revolutions de Paris*, which transformed over time from giving simple day-by-day accounts to defining these momentous events in chronological order. This stood in stark contrast to pre-revolutionary journals which conceived of revolution as a crisis. It went from 'a revolution' to 'the astonishing revolution' to 'this revolution forever memorable in the annals of our history' to, finally, this 'French Revolution'. It was now a 'lived experience, with its own dynamic and its own chronology, an unfolding drama for which the journal offered its own compelling script'.[202] Juxtaposing the misery of life pre-revolution with the liberty and Enlightenment that came after, the revolutionary press and others sought, as those of the *Ancien Régime* had done, to frame and control the public's understanding of these events.[203] They did this by creating a unique cultural conception of the French Revolution using a newly emerging 'Enlightened' political language, associating it with the glories of Roman antiquity society and citizenship, and rewritten stories from French folklore.

In this veritable 'age of revolutions, in which everything may be looked for', early historians sought to write a supportive and noble version of the history of the French Revolution.[204] It contributed to the realization of its ideals using their language of revolution which was an intellectual creation.[205] Their 'ethical' intervention 'made' history, shaping the collective historical consciousness of later generations.[206] Portrayed as unprecedented, man-made, a rupture with the past, it first challenged and eventually established a new order radically different from the preceding one. Seen as 'an act of universal significance, imbued with meaning for all mankind … a moral obligation, inscribed in the logic of human history', it established the classic pattern of revolution.[207] As Guerin remarked, the French Revolution was 'the mother of the revolution of the present and the future'.[208] It was 'the master theme of the epoch'.[209] For early nineteenth-century historians, writing a history of the French Revolution was both a declaration of political faith and a political act in itself.

Against such a backdrop it is somewhat ironic that the eighteenth century is well known for its distrust of language and *Ars rhetorica*.[210] According to many, language was subject to much abuse.[211] In multi-lingual France it was a clear sign of regional diversity, privilege, and disunity.[212] Not of immediate concern, the notion that a single language would unite the nation became a crucial goal of the new regime. It would strengthen social cohesion, after the chaos, and convey the messages of the Revolution, completely eradicating the past.[213] Requiring a great deal of 'trust' and the conscious actions of its patriotic citizens, language was increasingly politicized in the late eighteenth century. In this 'Age of Enlightenment' trust was bonded with reason. By trusting in 'the power of logic rather than by belief in a *deus ex machina*' there was a widely held belief that nature could be conquered, and social problems solved.[214] Notions of liberty, order and trust became inextricably entwined in theorizing notions of progressive functioning society. De Tocqueville assumes 'freedom presupposes order and that freedom is itself the source of order … and only in free societies can people develop trusting co-operative relationships' – he argues, 'living in freedom is a condition of trust'.[215] As a result, by the eighteenth century the language of civil society was really the language of trust.

There remains a perception that trust is a modern conception.[216] Emerging linguistically in French in the sixteenth century, this 'modern' idea was highlighted linguistically in the difference between *confiance* and confidence.[217] With this growing awareness, philosophers wrestled with the question of how to promote trust and trustworthiness in a world of distrust, where self-interest was often more profitable. Considered essential, modern conceptions of trust were first articulated in early modern European political theory (as discussed earlier in the chapter). Locke, for one, not only described it as *societatis vinculum* (the bond of society) but also indispensable in language, as it 'makes words work'.[218] In this enlightened age many early theorists argued for man to trust in reason, positing that 'in a reliable social order ... people [would] find it rational to trust one another' thus ensuring continuity and stability.[219] However, trust and trustworthiness proved increasingly problematic for those philosophers who desired to place them on a rational foundation.

In France, it fell to Montesquieu and de Tocqueville who regarded trust as crucial components of social order, uniting notions of individualism, liberty and equality.[220] Vague on detail and abstract in nature, it was within their nuanced visions of civil society that the social norms and trust necessary for people to work together were fostered. The Enlightenment camps contained a variety of political views.[221] However, 'most of the *philosophes* preferred to put their trust in enlightened despots (such as Frederick II (the Great), Peter I (the Great), Catherine II (the Great), Maria Theresa, Joseph II, and Leopold II), rather than radical democrats, to deliver a new tolerant order embodying "truth, happiness and virtue".[222] For 'in all of France there were not ten of us who were republicans before 1789'.[223] Rousseau, however, while expressing a similar sentiment, suggested replacing the existing tyrannical systems (social, political and religious) with a 'new contract, a spontaneous act of mutual trust among free and politically equal persons which will create a collective body, "*une personne publique*", whose general will has the force of natural law'.[224] With his 'societies of perfect creatures',[225] sovereign over themselves, Rousseau 'imagines epistemic security as the basis and necessary condition for fidelity, trust and constancy'.[226] A 'man of the people', he became the unofficial ideologue of the Revolution in 1790.[227]

Through Rousseau's writing, individuals learnt to question their own situation, to be made aware of, appreciate, and effectively use their 'natural rights' and liberties. In his novel *Emile*, he stated 'you trust in the present order of society without thinking that this order is subject to inevitable revolutions ... We are approaching a state of crisis and the age of revolutions'.[228] These philosophers 'taught [many] to find [their] condition wretched, or in any case, unjust and illogical'.[229] Arguing the king did not rule in their interests but for his own, they emphasized the *Ancien Régime*'s betrayal of its people's trust. By this breach of trust, this broken contract, the king forfeits his power and his people reclaim it. Trust simultaneously became a '*call to arms*' for change and the *civic virtue* necessary for civil society, as social revolution became a 'trust' revolution.

By separating society 'produced by our wants' from government and 'by our wickedness', Enlightenment theorists, such as Paine, counterpoised this notion of civil society with those of antiquity.[230] They envisaged it as separate from, and running in parallel to, government, being an ethical compact of sociability and cooperation.[231] Civil society was seen as voluntary, its conception a stark contrast to the 'necessary evil' of government.[232] It utilized a different notion of trust, one less rational, more moral and emotional. A pro-French Revolution propagandist, Paine's ideas of equality were particularly influential in early revolutionary France where 'association envisaged a robust democracy, based on conflict in marked contrast to the assured American consensus'.[233] It mirrored eighteenth-century French understanding of sociability and friendship, experienced first-hand in the salons, clubs, and clandestine Masonic Lodges.[234] It implicitly relied upon trust before, during and after the French Revolution; 'the mutual dependence and reciprocal interest which man has upon man, and all the parts of a civilised community upon each other, to create that great chain of connection which hold it together.'[235]

Although contemporary political theorists make few explicit references to trust,[236] it is not unsurprising that as the French Revolution progressed, literature in the eighteenth century showed a marked increase in the use of *confiance*, the French term denoting confidence, or trust, and, in financial discourses, 'credit'.[237]

Ever since Burke first suggested that the thoughts of the Enlightenment played a central role in the French Revolution, it has arguably been portrayed as '"a revolution of ideas" before it was "a revolution in fact"'.[238] Yet very little is known about the influence of these key writers on either the different stages of revolution or their influence on certain key actors. In contrast to the English and American Revolutions, there was a veritable cauldron of competing and conflicting ideas.[239] Moreover, these emerged at different stages of the revolution – almost creating micro revolutions in their own right – such that the intellectual underpinning of 1789 was far more complex than the revolutionary slogan of '*liberté, égalité, fraternité*'. Regarded as 'the men who prepared for Revolution, rather than those who made it', these ideologues of the late eighteenth century arguably provided the world with its first meaning and haunting experience of political ideology. However, it was just one component amongst the many that produced this revolution which was 'confused, turbulent and irrational like everything that men accomplish by collective action'.[240]

This philosophical backdrop, which reached into all social levels, produced 'an ardent passion for thought, for embodying ideas in deeds, and for proposing universal laws'.[241]Shaping what was thought, presented and promoted in an unprecedented way, it accounts for the long-lasting international influence of the French Revolution. On a practical level, pre-revolutionary France has been described as carrying a legacy of general distrust, caused in part by the anonymity and lack of trust that characterized life in court and by the divisive 'divide and rule' politics of the Bourbon kings.[242] Interpreted by some as lacking community, de Tocqueville, writing after 1789, described the social isolation of the social classes before 1789: 'It was no easy task bringing together fellow citizens who had lived for many centuries aloof from, or even hostile to, each other ... Indeed, even today, though class distinctions are no more, the jealousies and antipathies they caused have not died out.'[243]

Yet there are many examples of networks of trust operating within pre-revolution French society, some of which continued into the new regime; others were redrawn while yet others were reimagined. Take, for example, the rural credit market. Credit and/or loans were often used by peasants in the *seigneurie* within a closed circle, before the establishment of proper banking systems.[244] The relative familiarity of the lender and debtor, their social and geographical proximity, the high rate of inter-marriage and their shared goals, created a strong network which ensured the continued operation and success of this often informal system.[245] In the early eighteenth century the system was underpinned by communal self-regulation (through lost access to credit, tarnished reputation and even exclusion) rather than legal recourse. But this was to change even before the Revolution. It slowly grew throughout the century, in number and value (e.g. from 131 contracts totalling 23,667 livres in 1733–9, to 472 contracts totalling 177,926 livres in 1780–9, in la Seigneurie de Delle).[246] The system was transformed by new investors with their different goals, an increasingly challenging environment (poor crop yields, demographic pressures and inflation), and changes in the judicial system.[247] With it trust migrated from one-to-one relationships supported by the local community, to the judicial system and notaries. Eighteenth-century French peasants had a 'strong, almost blind, confidence in legal documents', while notaries were respected for their expertise; sought out as business confidants, they symbolized legal authority.[248] Despite traditional historiography's opinion of local justice as slow, costly and biased, sustained by self-interest and privilege, the rural judiciary had a good reputation.[249] Deeds, by this time, had all but replaced informal notes, reducing perceptions of risk and uncertainty. As increasingly complex economic relationships and networks developed, trust necessarily transferred to institutions with the authority and power to enforce contracts. Records show that this move actually extended co-operation.

Money was another useful weather vane of trust in eighteenth-century French society, for money is a social convention based on trust. This despite French banking setbacks and the monarchy changing the value of supposedly 'secure' gold and silver coins; while small coins held no intrinsic value and much of what was in circulation was worn and indistinguishable, people trusted in the continuity of the system.[250] In an economy reliant on continuous circulation of credit this was crucial. By the late eighteenth century, horrendously short of money,[251] the economy of the *Ancien Régime* creaking and operating hand to mouth, was nevertheless functioning. But, in 1789 in the chaos of revolution, money and credit, the crucial lubricants of day-to-day socio-economic transactions, evaporated. The *Ancien Régime*'s response was twofold. First, they seized control of Church lands as collateral; and second, with patriotic confidence, they issued innovative *assignats* (a paper instrument) which they believed were worthy of confidence and resistant to forgery. They immediately traded 10–20 per cent below face value, necessitating the printing of ever-larger amounts which in turn caused a collapse in their value. Burke succinctly explained the situation in 1791, by stating 'the utter destruction of *assignats*, and … the restoration of order, [were] one and the same'.[252] It was not until after 'the terror and the death of Robespierre, that France solved its problems by going to war'.[253] The monetary experiments of the new revolutionary regime had the effect of compounding insecurity and creating situations of distrust. It both affected and reflected the course of the Revolution in France.

A 'judicial society', the law was central to the governance of the *Ancien Régime*.[254] It operated in unison with networks of patronage, clientage and other informal channels of influence conferring legitimacy. As such, it should be understood primarily as a cultural system. Flexible and adaptive, it was shaped by and in turn shaped local communities. Traditionally regarded as slow, inefficient and venal, 'it provided the principal linguistic, cultural, and procedural framework through which individuals and corporations articulated, contested and resolved disputes over the allocation of resources, status, authority, and power'.[255] This complex, overlapping and often convoluted legal system supported a wide variety of local, regional, and national authorities that collectively constituted the institutions of governance. In so doing it emphasized the 'all-pervasive legalism' of the *Ancien Régime*.[256] Widely used by noble and peasant alike, there was nonetheless no definitive legal code; instead there was a variety of concepts, languages, and procedures 'by which culture and community [were] established, maintained and transformed'.[257] It was a system of compromise reliant upon shared values, oaths, and notions of honour.[258] De Tocqueville would later describe this frame of reference as 'the last rampart of national liberty' under the *Ancien Régime*.[259]

The revolutionaries sought to wipe away the various overlapping legal codes and replace them with one unified legal system. However, while some historians have emphasized the benefits and enthusiasm for the Revolution *juges de paix,* highlighting speed, accessibility and low cost, others, including Crubaugh, have simultaneously remarked on the value and general appreciation which rural communities placed on the *Ancien Régime*'s local court system.[260] They highlight the judges' flexibility and discretion, their ability to mediate and arbitrate to the mutual satisfaction of those involved and their understanding of local needs. The system allowed the centre to maintain authority in the regions.[261] Studies highlight not only that officers of the various courts received the same training but also that the seigneurial courts were increasingly used as a conduit to publicize and enforce royal edicts, leading to the argument that, by the eighteenth century, in essence there was one system of justice: that of the king.[262]

A powerful presence, the Catholic Church in France had a distinct national identity. Although it was once a strong uniting force, by the eighteenth century differences in belief and practices were clear to see, between regions, urban and rural, elites and peasants, and even between men and women. Facing growing criticism, tension within and challenged by 'enlightened unbelief', the Church was in disarray. This raises the question: Would so many have challenged the divine right of kings and divine social order if the Church had been strong in eighteenth-century France? And yet the Church was still recognized for its promotion of moral and social order, being praised for creating a sense of community and for its provision of social welfare and education. However, it was condemned for its power and influence. Intolerant and mired in scandal, it was resented for its wealth and privileges. In contrast to the institution, local parish priests were usually highly respected religious leaders and moral guardians; they were trusted village notables.[263] Seeking reform, even before the Revolution, they sought 'new signs of trust from the episcopate'[264] and, finding none, they became increasingly politicized, prompting them to support the Third Estate in 1789.[265] Religion rapidly became 'one of the most contentious issues of the Revolution and the government's treatment of it was one of the major causes for popular discontent; even counterrevolution',[266] while the public oath of loyalty became a 'referendum on whether one's first loyalties were to Catholicism [God] or to the Revolution'.[267] Catholicism was systematically 'squeezed' out of the Republic. New ceremonies and festivals were introduced to commemorate revolutionary martyrs, events, and symbols, together with a new calendar which removed all reference to saints' days. They were purposefully created to fashion new republican traditions while reinforcing the narrative of the Revolution. A sustained, yet controversial, policy of de-Christianization did not end its practice. Instead, private masses continued, executed priests became Christian martyrs and their old churches became pilgrimage sites.[268] Rather than exploit the Church's ability to create and maintain a sense of community and stability, its independence was challenged. Without the clergy's collaboration, the outcome of the Revolution was significantly impacted, as trust and loyalties were divided, weakening both.[269] And yet it is the resilience rather than the failures of the Church in the eighteenth century that is striking in the end.[270]

These interactions, relationships and networks of trust overlapped each other and were often re-established and re-enforced in newly emerging forms of sociability and friendship which stood 'in stark contrast to traditional sociability anchored in family, guild, court and Church, the new social universe, possessed a signal characteristic: men and some women met as individuals'.[271] Within this changing social environment, having violently toppled the established regime and instituted radical institutional change, the question arises: How can individuals trust everyday social interactions? In turn, how can a functioning society be created, maintained and sustained, when the pillars of society, the traditional networks of trust and the cultural landscape which inscribes such meaning into these interactions, are overturned? 'Friendship was one way to imagine a solution to the problem of an atomized and suspicious society'.[272] When combined with shared values (such as equality and virtuous citizen patriotism) and vivid, affecting communication, the very sociability of the age enabled some networks of trust to survive, some to evolve and for others to emerge.[273] This combination was nothing new and could be seen in the pre-revolutionary French salons, as it was in English coffee houses. These literary public spaces, which sat at the very 'heart of philosophic community', became part of the political realm as a result of the Revolution.[274] 'A whole world of social arrangements and attitudes supported the existence of the French salons: an idle aristocracy, an ambitious middle class, an active intellectual life, the social density of a major urban centre, sociable traditions, and a certain aristocrat feminism'.[275] These 'theatres of conversation and exchange' offered a glimpse, for some, of equality for the sharing and debating of new ideas.[276] The company was 'carefully selected', often creating a 'homogenous unity'.[277] The world of salons did not disappear in 1789 but was soon replaced.[278] Salons reflected the early days of the Revolution; however, by 1790 a new model was taking centre stage, the political club.[279]

Revolutionaries differed from the *Ancien Régime* in that, rather than the bonds of patronage in a rigid social hierarchy or the restrictions and rules of the salon, they prized voluntary emotional ties, though political friendship was 'suspect'. Despite the perceived differences, the mechanism of friendship which underpinned both remained the same. It was, in a large part, the complex interconnections between friends in the political arena that facilitated, stabilized and legitimized new political practices,[280] forging bonds of trust and allowing its citizens to unite after the chaos of revolution and the trauma of such widespread violence.[281] To create the 'new' civil society that they envisioned, the revolutionaries had already reached into some traditional networks of trust (such as the network of Masonic Lodges)[282] while simultaneously adapting the traditions of 'general' sociability, inspiring them with their 'revolutionary' notions of honour, patriotism, and the virtuous citizen.[283] This creation of a 'civil society' was of primary concern, as theorists amongst the revolutionaries posited that the equality and individualism, fostered with their hard-won democracy, could convince men that they needed nothing from nor owed anything to their neighbours, and thus, without civil society, they would isolate themselves from the community. In the wake of the king's repeated betrayal of trust and the fragility of the Republic, decisive and purposeful actions were taken.[284] Trust was purposefully re-personalized, moralized, and quickly institutionalized by the new regime.

First, they arguably created the long-lasting *social imaginary* of the self-interested individual (a moral and politically corrupting force) for all to fear and despise.[285] By creating a counterpoint they could unite the citizenry in rooting out such corruption which divided society. This later contributed to 'The Terror' – as the revolution continued, standards of political and personal purity and virtue were raised ever higher.[286] It used Rousseau's language but distorted his ideas as those in power sought to show their legitimacy by quashing any appearance of dissent or opposition. It was a betrayal of the 'few' to unite the many, and it was marked by mass executions of 'enemies of the revolution'. Estimates of the death toll ranged from 16,594 up to 25,000.[287] This was linked to the notion of *fraternité* (brotherhood). Citizens were bound together through a combination of an idealized vision of society (free and equal), a newly emerging sense of patriotism and concern for their fellow man. This was reflected in the 'impulse to give patriotic gifts which grew out of the experience of revolution … [as] givers sought to re-establish trust in society'.[288] *Fraternité* offered a pragmatic and reassuring expression of solidarity, the most abstract and idealist of the revolutionaries' notions: it was more often referenced in the earlier days of the Revolution. Then, despite the clergy's support of the Third Estate, the revolutionaries sought to replace religion with a secular interpretation; promoted and celebrated, it was cloaked in revolutionary myth and symbolism.[289] Its festivals took centre stage, simultaneously celebrations and lessons; they were essential to understanding the new revolutionary value system and reuniting society.[290]

This was all underpinned by an unprecedented propaganda campaign which combined trusted imagery with rededicated past glories and traditional folklore; it rewrote history with a 'revolutionary' narrative. And so, 'from the outset, the ideal Jacobin was a man of independence, courage and heroism, who stood firm against the egoist "vampires" and "parasites," and considered only the public good – in short, a man of virtue'.[291] Trusting the 'personal' and practical, relationships were built and sustained on shared *morals*, experiences, and expectations of behaviour, while social cohesion was maintained by shaping collective intentions and actions through new political practice, rituals and festivals.[292] For example, patriotic giving became a litmus test for loyalty as stinginess 'smelled' of treason while state pensions (1792–3) required proof of *contributions patriotique*. Similarly, the grain law (August 1789) began with gushing fraternalism, reminding citizens of their 'duty', providing 'reciprocal aid' to their brothers, but quickly threatened anyone interfering with free-market forces with the capital crime of *lèse-nation* (treason). In this way the French Revolution was a 'revolution' in political culture, as political participation, mobilization, ritual and organization took on new meaning. Perhaps its most revealing legacy is 'its linguisticality', its structure and status its most 'disclosive' feature.[293]

Regarded by many as the 'political event that cuts French National history in two',[294] the French Revolution is reflected and reinforced by the historiographies of the two – the *Ancien Régime* and the 'new order'.[295] Its 'myth', built by contemporary historians, revolutionary politicians, pamphleted propaganda, authors and poets, quickly created a solid reality, becoming the foundation stone of 'modern' France.[296] This narrative, however, largely ignores the structural continuities and ongoing continuing administrative centralization, highlighted by de Tocqueville, that survived the rupture of 1789.[297] The revolution, therefore, accelerated and completed the work of the reforming monarchy. It emerged out of the old regime despite the protestations of its leaders. It was, therefore, *not* a new start but a culmination of an old process.

Regardless, the French Revolution is portrayed as a progressive rupture, a fundamental departure which first challenged the existing order before establishing a new radically different one, synonymous with modernity. Intensely emotional, it made heroes of individuals in its quest for the perfectibility of *man*. 'Differing from other revolutions in being not merely national, it aimed at benefiting all humanity'.[298] Its long-term impact and influence have been profound. The archetypal revolution, it defines the very meaning of the word. Although betrayal sat at its centre, a recurring theme throughout this revolutionary period was trust, which eventually prevailed. Purposefully re-personalized and moralized, it was quickly institutionalized by the new regime. It drew heavily on the emerging sociability and friendship of the age. Not simply rational transactions, trust and revolution in eighteenth-century France were emotional and personal.

Interlude

Bridging the revolutionary centuries

The notion of *modern* revolution and trust

Marking a paradigm shift, the French Revolution established the modern meaning of revolution that has dominated the long nineteenth and short twentieth centuries. 'Beginning in 1789, the obsession with origins ... came to be centred precisely on the Revolutionary break ... 1789 became the birth date, the year zero, of a new world'.[1] With it, revolution denoted the sudden and violent overthrow of an existing regime. It simultaneously encompassed a wider and more general meaning of any process of radical and fundamental change. The French Revolution violently intersected history. With narratives of rupture heralding the arrival of a new 'utopia', disrupting people's sense of time by restarting at year zero, the disjunction between the present and the past created a new historical awareness. Publically reimaged, appropriated and preserved, the past became the counterfoil to the narrative of modernity and progress. It remains the archetypal revolution, defining the very meaning of the word and colouring our collective imaginations.[2]

However, while the nineteenth century was the 'age of the revolutionary' and revolutionary theory,[3] modern revolution did not come of age until the twentieth century.[4] It played witness not only to the Russian and Chinese but also to the Vietnamese, Cambodian and Cuban revolutions.[5] For all their differences and nuances, in this 'century of revolution', there remains the distinctive and visible common thread of 'rupture', of a new start. In the same perceived vein of the French, each revolution is perceived to catapult society forward along a linear path of development. It thus mirrored the European Enlightenment vision of unlimited material progress, of positivist and historical materialism; science, technology, logic and reason became the driving forces behind societal advancement. Adopted by the Marxist/Leninist revolutionary movements,[6] who 'self-consciously proclaim[ed] themselves the architects of the only real revolution since the French Revolution', this notion of revolution became a mantle for post-colonial anti-imperialistic struggles.[7] It was 'the triumphant product of ineluctable historical forces'.[8] As such, revolution sat at the heart of the State and society, reshaping the global political landscape and reordering daily life in the twentieth century, 'influencing flows reciprocally from the centre to the periphery and back again'.[9]

Revolution ran in parallel to the emergence and uneven development of the modern State, in which 'societies were undergoing a painful transition from local, traditional, relatively immobile societies to mass modern ones', where cultural and national homogenization figured prominently.[10] In a patchy process the State took over many of the functions traditionally performed by social organizations and individuals: educational practices, linguistic policies, postal and telephonic systems, health, and welfare. This increased dependency on, and extended the functions of, the State. Limited by constitutional boundaries these increasingly centralized forms of governance drew extensively from newly emerging theories of organization derived from industrial studies and practices at the beginning of the twentieth century.[11] Over time, states became a fusion of economic-industrial statism, military-bureaucratic statism and welfare statism.[12] Dominated by modern large-scale hierarchical organizations, these top-down authoritarian structures were increasingly popular as they could ensure control and maintain discipline. These structures had the capacity to penetrate society and to implement logistically political decisions, thus creating a quasi 'infrastructural power'.[13] Unified by a rising sense of nationalism, emphasized through shared symbolism and national identity, these bureaucratic mechanisms of state shaped and directed collective action throughout society.[14]

One outcome of these structural changes was to transform the relationship between citizens and the State. While citizens were tied to the State, through a combination of ever more inclusive and egalitarian forms of citizenship, a newly emerging sense of nationalism and a concern for their fellow citizens, the State needed to demonstrate its authority by maintaining order and unity while delivering a self-sustaining economy. An increasingly contractual relationship, it was underpinned by trust. However, the nature of that trust had evolved from the institutionalized, re-personalized, emotional and moralized trust experienced during the French Revolution. It had adapted to circumstance and became a reflection of the society of the day. In practical terms, across Europe, political/institutional trust, having subsumed traditional networks of trust (of patronage, of kinship friendship, ethnicity and affiliations) into the bureaucratic structures of state, operated as a belief in 'government reliability', with associated expectations, rather than a deep 'trust' in government.[15] In this environment, the concept of 'good citizenship' referred more to obedient subjecthood than to active day-to-day involvement. States, in turn, sought to ensure obedience through a variable synthesis of influence and force, a mixture of persuasion and coercion, implicit and explicit, varying between democratic and authoritarian regimes.[16]

In response, to successfully 'overthrow' the State and institute root-and-branch reforms, twentieth-century revolutionary groups needed to mirror the structures of the state they operated in, and in so doing they purposefully became inflated reflections of what they sought to destroy.[17] Organized along military lines (orderly, structured and rigid), Lenin's approach became a template for those who followed. It was a vital step, he vehemently argued, to create the monolithic unity and strength required to bring about social and political revolution, as operating with one mind and will called for total obedience and submission.[18] Revolutionaries created centralist, vertical, hierarchical and secretive command-and-control structures, with rigidly controlled and compartmentalized lines of communication, directly modelled on the State, to challenge and ultimately replace the State.[19] In step with 'scientific socialism'[20] these structures reflected the modern and progressive industrial thinking of the time,[21] with an emphasis on heavy industry, of a single-party State, and the all-encompassing use of propaganda to control and propel the State forward. Over time 'Lenin, Stalin and others reshaped communism into a nationalist and statist form of authoritarian socialism'.[22] Such models of 'socialism-from-above' were fictional and idealized in Edward Bellamy's novel *Looking Backward*, which portrayed a bureaucratic socialist utopia.[23] As with the State, these models relied upon the same notion of institutional trust (a combination of reliance, expectation, acquiescence and loyalty) but to 'succeed', the revolutionary movement went further.

Absolute trust in the State became the defining feature of communism replacing the Russians' required trust in their Tsar. Revered and feted as 'their father', the Romanov dynasty lasted three centuries.[24] They operated a reinforced tripartite system by which Russians submitted 'to [the Tsar's] supreme will, not only out of fear' of the military 'but also for the sake of conscience, as ordained by God' as taught by the Church.[25] To maintain control of Russia's vast territories, this tripartite system was underpinned by extensive networks of trust. Described as a 'presence society', it operated a localized system of *krugovaia poruka* (joint responsibility).[26] 'As a result Russians have tended to direct their trust towards persons rather than institutions or laws, which they usually regard with suspicion amounting to distrust'.[27] With the Revolution, required trust was transformed into absolute trust in the new State (and its leader).[28] Shaped, in part, by both the legacy of joint responsibility and the mutual dependency and mutual trust created 'in the trenches' of the early revolutionary fight, it was also the intended outcome of the near total dismantling of traditional networks of trust and destruction of everyday routines and reputations. In subtle contrast to the French Revolution, the new State overturned the past, disrupted the predictable and destroyed traditional symbols of authority and trust.[29] It simultaneously created prophetical narratives of absolute good versus absolute evil,[30] of comrades and enemies,[31] which left no room for doubt or dissent. Breaking down the traditional nexus of trust was intentional; for it was to be replaced by a single relationship with the communist apparatus. This is the continuing legacy of communism.

This deftly dovetailed with the revolutionary movement's need for total obedience, as it had under the Tsar.[32] Each system required ideological and practical measures to enforce its authority and control. The Tsar used the Church as the spokesperson for Russian autocracy while the military was its iron fist,[33] its power supported and strengthened by a systematic programme of censorship, counter-revolutionary espionage and police activity. In the early twentieth century the dysfunctional Tsarist autocratic regime, based on a largely peasant economy, 'collided violently with the political forces of the modern world'. Out of the chaos a new revolutionary communist totalitarian state, repressive and closed, emerged, a product and a reflection of its past.[34] Obedience was once again the overriding priority, deemed necessary to maintain control in the new State, and so 'to achieve their ends, the planners create[d] power – power over men wielded by other men – of a magnitude never before known'.[35] In this environment all other forms of trust became luxuries no one could afford, least of the all the party elite, in this 'land of maximum distrust'.[36] Although many within the revolutionary movement acknowledged that leading a party to success in a hostile world required maximum distrust, vigilance, and ruthlessness, it created divisions which then led to cyclical purges.[37] It ensured widespread social obedience through a combination of terror, mass murder and disappearance, the censoring of communications and extensive use of propaganda. Learning from the past, it surpassed it. In spite of the complete lack of justice and almost complete absence of a civil society, in this environment of officially inspired distrust, absolute trust in the Communist State was resolute.[38]

The Western concept of modern revolution, unchanged for two centuries, enjoyed a new lease of life as the precedent of the Russian Revolution became a model for newly decolonized Africa, Asia, and the Middle East. There were many similarities among this generation of revolutionaries: they each sought to replicate, and then replace, the State and its impersonal networks of trust. They also shared a similar rhetoric of new beginnings but, in fact, each struggle was shaped by this legacy, as well as the unique history of those taking part.[39]

Since 1989, 'the biggest year in world history since 1945', the practice and outcome of revolution have markedly changed.[40] Although the modern revolutionary model still remains the paradigm, it increasingly lacks the ability to explain and capture the processes and diverging outcomes that emerged with the collapse of the Soviet Union, the break-up of Yugoslavia, the Taliban insurgency, Islamic State, and the Arab Spring.

A new revolutionary paradigm?

Twenty-first-century revolutionary situations

It remains to consider the contemporary world, which has experienced another shift in the concepts of trust and revolution. Numerous facets of identity characterize the 'Networked Age'[1] and the era of 'New Capitalism'.[2] Tensions have developed in the ensuing fluidity within society and disconnection with place: there is both a strengthening and weakening of the command-and-control capacities of centralized states.[3] This questions the future of revolution.

While there have been no classical revolutions in the twenty-first century in the West, there has certainly been much potential – consider the headline-grabbing protests of global social movements, such as Occupy.[4] Despite their stated intention to bring about progressive social change through the reinvention of politics, their impact to date has been limited[5]: such movements have been more concerned with freedom of expression, active participation, and ethical and moral values than revolution *per se*. They are a response to the growing size of the state, the 'bureaucratization of modern society',[6] the backlash against globalization and the failed promises of New Capitalism.[7] Insofar as they qualify as revolutionary incidents, the focus has been more on the idea itself: large-scale involvement in social change and the spirit of resistance, which provide a space for the politically marginalized and those hopeful of together creating a new utopia. From this perspective, the *idea* of revolution is an end in itself.

In stark contrast are the aims of revolutionary Islamic fundamentalists, which constitute a more far-reaching incarnation of revolution. The idea of *thawrah alamiyyah* (complete and comprehensive world revolution)[8] goes beyond even its secular, Marxist[9] equivalent in that there is no debate about its global ambition.[10] Working beyond the confines of a state to create a new global caliphate governed by Sharia law, this breed of revolutionary seeks to reshape the social structure and to redraw the world order. With an uncompromising *Weltanschauung*, it is reminiscent of past religious wars – and we have seen in earlier chapters that this has profound implications for trust.

Described as the prototype for twenty-first-century conflict, the Arab Spring falls between these two extremes.[11] 'On one side are the government thugs firing bullets … [and] on the other side are young protesters firing "tweets".[12] An analogy can be drawn with Flower Power in the 1960s and early 1970s.

With a rallying cry of *Ash-sha'ab yurid isqat an-nizam*! ('The people want the fall of the regime'), the long-standing dictators of Tunisia, Egypt and Libya were quickly toppled and the Syrian regime's position remains precarious.[13] 'The timing of the popular revolts – so sudden and almost simultaneous – suggests that the similarities these autocracies shared … were sufficient to explain the wave of revolutions'.[14] In an historical moment, the paradigm of authoritarian resilience dominant in previous decades was unexpectedly overturned.[15]

Five years later, the media mourn 'a season that began in hope but ended in desolation' as 'possibility has largely given way to gloom and pessimism'.[16]References to counter-revolution are commonplace in this 'Islamist Winter'.[17] Meanwhile, events on the ground have created an air of uncertainty, through increasing militarization and the Islamization of political relationships.

Labelling such events as revolutions makes a normative statement about their preconditions, participants, processes, and outcomes. Although usually referred to by name or date,[18] this is why the use of the term 'revolution' is debated in the literature: many prefer uprising, upheaval, revolt, riot, or insurrection.[19] Indeed, the distinctiveness of the events has led some scholars to invent new terms altogether. Bayat, for example, argues for the term 'refolution' to describe a process of 'revolutions which aim to push for reforms in, and through, the institutions of existing regimes'.[20] When measured against the classic revolutionary ideal – the French Revolution – the Arab Spring uprisings are found wanting.

Although alike in many respects, the diversity between countries throughout the Middle East and North Africa is striking, with 'different political and cultural landscapes crisscrossed with ethnic, religious and economic divisions'.[21] Each country's experience of the Arab Spring was unique, emphasized by their differing trajectories and outcomes. Tunisia has revised its constitution to be the most progressive in the region, yet did so within the confines of its previous state structures. On the other hand, Egypt has come full circle with its military once again in power. Meanwhile, Libya and Syria are being torn apart by civil wars and battles with the Islamic State. This ongoing political turmoil has displaced and disillusioned many: the Syrian conflict alone has created the largest refugee crisis of the twenty-first century.[22]

The events of the Arab Spring have yet to run their course, but from the outset exhibited divergent narratives and competing claims; they simply do not neatly fit into the long-held conceptual framework of revolution dominated by Western academic theories.[23] It raises the question: do these twenty-first-century revolutions represent something quite new or an echo of past models? Indeed, are they a reflection of a past unfinished?[24] They certainly do not exist in a vacuum and must be interpreted contextually.

The wider contemporary context

This section highlights three features of the contemporary period. First, it is a time of transition. Second, it is the Digital Age. Third, a new relationship is emerging between networks of personal and impersonal trust.

First, it is a time of transition. 'We are now living in a new, fast-evolving multipolar world economy in which some developing countries are emerging as economic powers, others are moving towards becoming additional poles of growth, and some are struggling to attain their potential within this new system'.[25] These changes are the outcome of large-scale globalization, understood as a new phase of internationalization and characterized by instantaneous connectivity in information and finance.

States are fast losing their pre-eminence as a consequence: the international order is increasingly being challenged by *transnational* networks, *supranational* unions and *global* corporations. Equally, national identity and parochial values continue to be 'eroded by the impact of global cultural industries and multinational media'.[26] Moreover, there has been a marked reaction against both trends. This backlash is reflected in the Brexit vote, Trump's inauguration and the popularity of the far right across Europe. Recent studies suggest that there is not a one-way cultural tide from America, or even the West, but an uneven exchange where ideas, values and identities are cherry-picked. This is not the American century.

Second, the Digital Age has led to a series of extremes: the order of the State versus the disorder of personal networks; the globalization of the economy versus the fragmentation of society; the increased connectivity of people versus the atomization of urban communities. All of these phenomena are underpinned by competing forms and networks of trust.[27] Each has the potential to unite or divide and, furthermore, the turbulent politics that results from their conflict, challenges the status quo.[28]

This dense digital mediascape impacts everything we do: 'the matrix is everywhere'[29] or, as countless Hollywood screenwriters have it, we are never 'off the grid'. The new mediascape is defined by the unprecedented speed, range, volume, and variety of things that can be done with the information. With this evolution in communication technology and its applications, many academics are investigating the networked form, 'a pattern common to all life'.[30] Their focus is on the emergence of apparently casually formed, yet cohesive networked communities, whose aim is social and/or political change. As Lash points out, these information and communication structures are replacing traditional social hierarchies.[31]

We are connected not just through the sharing of ideas but, perhaps more significantly, through the idea of sharing, which the introduction of digital communications technology has popularized.[32] It has empowered people to participate actively and offers the potential for a new global hegemony based on people, rather than State power. Where Anderson's concept of nations was one of 'imagined communities',[33] we now talk about 'virtual communities'. Both link terrain, frame thinking and shape identity, yet the latter is increasingly fluid, since it facilitates the co-existence of multiple identities – such as European, British, English, Pakistani, and Londoner.[34]

Social graphs are increasingly self-generated collections of individuals connected by personal trust and shared community. Although digital resources are increasingly available to all, access and distribution remain uneven. Given the way they organize, revolutionaries are best placed to embrace digital media; by contrast, regimes face structural handicaps, although they are quickly catching up. In a world that is becoming increasingly interconnected, (1) being heard through all the noise, (2) capturing attention, and (3) retaining interest and enthusiasm have made Lewis's AIDA model relevant once more.[35]

Third, the period is marked by movement *between* impersonal and personal trust and also by a dynamic *within* both impersonal trust (towards expectation and reliance) and personal trust (between 'weak' and 'strong' ties).[36] This is coming about because the two developments just outlined – the transitional and digital nature of the age – have a profound effect on the State, the polity, and therefore debates on revolution in the West.[37]

The State has, to varying degrees, become an important component of solidarity and identity in Western nations; it is 'an instrument of generalised trust'[38] that increases the confidence of citizens while reducing risk and uncertainty. Furthermore, the modern State has trampled 'the closely knit and cliquish local bodies which had made collective provision in the past and replaced them with overarching, more impersonal institutions on a city-wide or even national scale'.[39] Yet a structure well suited to a fiscal-military state of the eighteenth century is no longer fit for purpose in the twenty-first century.[40] The addition of 'low' as well as 'high' politics to its responsibilities has meant that the nature of trust inevitably evolved as citizens became confident that (1) bureaucracy delivers reliability, consistency, and universality, and (2) checks and balances reduce uncertainty and risk.

How, then, can some interpret the State as 'hollowed-out' and irrelevant?[41] Challenges have come from (1) international organizations that fulfil the role of the State and (2) global corporations that exert greater influence on the individual. The first is the most potent, an outdated intermediary authority in an ever more internationalized system; a better alternative to the State has still to be found. The State retains a vital position as the pillar of the 'international', since the latter cannot be contemplated without the intergovernmental, given the conjunction of State and nation. The two challengers have added to, rather than displaced, layers in a rigid organizational hierarchy, increasing the potential for tension and conflict in this complex artificial landscape.[42]

Set against this structural legacy is the individual, for whom personal relationships, interactivity and networks are remarkably complex and fluid. The latter are built, sustained, broken and reconstructed with personal trust – such that the process creates connections that transcend politically and territorially defined spaces.[43] We are increasingly familiar with the other, sharing ideas and forming communities of like-minded individuals that now stretch around the world. The mobility and connectivity of these networks typify the spirit of our age, while the communities that result have become an important feature of the global political landscape.[44] Empowered by digital technology, which reconceptualizes time and space,[45] the State faces a pincer movement, intentional or otherwise, from these networks. The effect is compounded by the permeability of the State in liberal democracies. Furthermore, it continues to produce multiple levels of overlapping authority and uncertain competitive allegiances, which in turn challenge notions of legitimacy in a constantly shifting landscape. Each is underpinned by different forms of trust: personal versus impersonal, weak versus strong, calculative, versus co-operative.

Contemporary notions of trust

Long acknowledged by academics as a complex interpersonal and organizational construct, trust has only recently become a major topic of study.[46] Each discipline theorizes, approaches and measures personal and impersonal trust differently: to illustrate, as disposition, expectation, intention, and/or behaviour. This has produced multiple definitions and sub-categories. The various definitions nonetheless share two features. First, they are discussed in reference to society. Second, trust involves cognitive, affective, and behavioural components – the qualitative and quantitative mix of which changes, to reflect the situation and individuals.[47] It weighs risk and reward, an individual's propensity to trust, and experience of this specific relationship. In addition, temporality (an evaluation of the current circumstances within the wider environment) and emotion (linked to an individual's perception of the world) were helpful dimensions in the earlier, historical chapters of the present work.

Although drawing on relationships of personal trust, this discussion concentrates on the relationships of impersonal trust between a citizen, the State and its institutions. In contrast to the personal trust evidenced between citizens of the *polis*, impersonal trust is the motif of modern states. Cultural theorists argue that the latter is learned, and that interpersonal trust is projected onto the system.[48] Institutional scholars[49] posit that it stems from the 'perceived legitimacy, technical competence, and ability to perform assigned duties efficiently' of the State.[50] The latter is supported by a defined, transparent and accessible legal framework.

Modern states first developed concrete, rather than abstract, relationships of impersonal trust with specific institutions – such as the police, the central bank, the National Health Service (NHS) – that went on to cohere into a mutually supportive web of impersonal trust. The consequence is that states can survive critical failure on individual dimensions – such as the banking crisis of 2008, the National Security Agency (NSA) spying case and the Westminster expenses scandal – since the overall relationship is a function of the whole rather than the parts. This is why states can survive the loss of trust, in particular individuals, or even a dramatic fall, in recorded levels of impersonal trust.

The contemporary notion of trust is thus radically different to what went before. Always the difference between survival and annihilation, it was soon also recognized as vital for prosperity yet is now acknowledged as a crucial ingredient for social cohesion in a diverse populace, economic development in a flat world and good governance in a demanding polity.[51]

As a consequence, levels of trust are now constantly measured and surveyed in an attempt to better understand how it is created, maintained, and rebuilt.[52] When taken at face value, these results reinforce the simplistic, binary view that low trust equals revolution. This is a correlation of some concern, as trust in most Western governments and institutions is already low and continues to fall.[53] This suggests that revolution is a real possibility yet, even at the height of the so-called revolutionary protests experienced in these countries, revolution was a figure of speech rather than a plan of action. Protestors only interpreted the world, in various ways; the point, however, was not to change it.[54] A minor puzzle has emerged as the result of a recent change in the relationship between citizen and State: on the one hand, governments are experiencing low levels of trust while, on the other, they are criticized for the dependency of individuals on government.[55] In expanding the rights of citizens, the growth of the Welfare State has blurred the boundary between the public and private. This increasing reliance on the State has a profound and counter-intuitive implication for impersonal trust: rather than invest more time and effort in the relationship, we instead fall back on rules and sanctions, checks and balances, laws and bureaucracy. With no room for uncertainty or risk, we simply rely on them to work. It has led to the expectation of *no* risk rather than *low* risk. The result is an even weaker form of impersonal trust: *non-betrayal*. When mistakes come to light or an institution fails, this is met not with a growing sense of unease, caution and distrust, but the more destructive notion of betrayal.

The absence of value judgements or an emotional component within this weak form of impersonal trust means that fewer institutions can differentiate themselves and thereby sustain goodwill. This is reminiscent of concerns over (1) the decline in social capital in Western states[56] and (2) the need to create social capital *ex nihilo* in the former communist states during the 1990s.[57]

In response, modern 'industrial nations are being forced to redefine and articulate new collective values and aspirations' to ensure and sustain social cohesion,[58] by shifting the notion of trust (from a passive, impersonal role to an active, re-personalized one) that underpins concepts of authority and legitimacy from compliance to co-operation.[59] With it – as Tyler as well as Jackson and Gau argue – the once-dominant instrumentalist-based models of governance are evolving into motive or legitimacy-based models. The modern State desires to replicate, and thereby benefit from, the co-operative relationships that develop between individuals in groups, communities and organizations. The reasoning is that societal objectives can be better achieved with a co-operative model built on values rather than an instrumentalist model based on self-interest.[60] Confidence, judgement, behaviour and character replace risk, vulnerability, rationality, rules, and sanctions.

Trust and obligation together deliver legitimacy under the consent-based model. As Jackson and Gau explain, obligation is the reaction to current authority while trust enables future action.[61] The latter explains and motivates the behavioural shift required. It offers three important advantages: (1) it encourages citizenry to pro-actively participate, such that an individual is more vested in the process and outcome; (2) it enables both State and society to adapt more quickly to a rapidly changing situation than if they were built on more rigid values (although values are changeable, it is a longer and slower process); and (3) it increases the discretion of the state, since authority has the latitude to act within mutually agreed parameters. These models aim to 'transfer' the benefits of personal trust to impersonal relationships of trust – that is, to re-personalize them. This also offers the potential for more flexible forms of authority.

Although many Western regimes see the benefit of such a shift, this is not universal and, indeed, can be divisive – some embrace a participatory model, popular within global social movements, while others seek not only to limit the reach of the State but to reduce individual reliance upon it. It also has the effect of shifting emphasis within 'trust' away from notions of competency towards those of character, together with feelings of betrayal when trust is seen as misplaced. This mixed approach raises two concerns: (1) it muddies the waters about what constitutes trust, and (2) regimes can abuse the discretion they are given.[62]

In this transitional period, trust has taken centre stage.[63] Although supported by a growing multi-disciplinary corpus of literature and research, the precise nature of trust remains elusive nonetheless. Widely understood to aid collaboration, bond communities and boost economic growth, trust is a day-to-day coping mechanism that simplifies the complexities of life. Trust is presented 'as an irreducible and multidimensional social reality' – inherent, functional and fluid in each and every one of our social interactions.[64] It is marked in this period not just by movement *between* impersonal and personal trust, but also by the dynamics *within* impersonal trust (towards expectation and reliance, on the one hand, and by re-personalization and discretion, on the other) and personal trust (between 'weak' and 'strong' ties).

The previous twentieth-century approach where revolutionaries sought to replicate State structures and networks of impersonal trust is no longer possible in this increasingly fluid and complicated environment. It is changing the nature of revolution.

Contemporary notions of revolution

The collapse of the Soviet Union signalled the end of the classic modern revolution: a template for all-encompassing social and political revolution was replaced, almost immediately, by a model of 'reforming non-violent revolution'.[65]

Described as almost carnivalesque,[66] it produced examples of so-called corrective, conservative, negotiated revolutions or transitional democratic reforms – stretching their boundaries and conflating both concepts.[67] Once again, it was the event rather than the process that took precedence in the discourse on revolution. By focusing on the replacement of despotic political regimes as the revolutionary event, the extant systems of governance were left intact, with the notion of revolution diluted. A decade later, politicians and academics went so far as to consider 'revolution' defunct.[68]

Recent happenings in Europe and beyond shattered this illusion: the notion of, and the potential for, revolution re-emerged in the era of globalization and New Capitalism. This is simultaneously a reflection of, and response to, the fragmentation and divisions within post-modern society.[69] Revolution is not the clearly defined *event* of antiquity, but a *process* operating within a widening spectrum. At one pole, religious fundamentalism has replaced communism as the basis for action; at the other, revolution remains an intellectual pursuit.

In its desire to understand and interpret, the West again relies on rules, categories, and labels; its goal is to predict, control and impede. Academics analyse and compare the Arab Spring to exemplars of revolutionary success and failure using Western-centric historical templates. The media, reporting an 'Arab Awakening', widely proclaimed the events as a new form of revolution or people power: the 'Leaderless Facebook Revolution'.[70]

This notion – that revolutions in communication technology would produce radical social and political transformations, too – was commonplace before the internet but has since mushroomed.[71] It embraces the point made by Castells: technological change threatens political hegemony by 'the reprogramming of communication networks, so becoming able to convey messages that introduced new values to the minds of people and inspire hope for political change'.[72] The establishment of Al-Jazeera, the satellite TV network, in 1996 and growing internet penetration were the forerunners of hope for rapid change. However, the immediate expectation of digitally connected revolution burst with the dot-com bubble. The unprecedented success of Egyptian bloggers in 2005–7 briefly reignited optimism before regimes cracked down.[73] The failure to bring about change meant that fatigue soon set in.[74] Facebook followed[75] but it was soon derided.[76] Dreams of a Twitter revolution took over, first in Moldova and then in Iran.[77] Shirky declared 'this is it, the big one. This is the first revolution that has been catapulted onto a global stage and transformed by social media'.[78] At best, these were spectator-driven Twitter revolutions; at worst, they risked the lives of the protestors for no change, as authoritarian regimes used these very tools to track them down and silence them. Then events in Tunisia and Egypt began to unfold.[79]

Heralded as a new revolutionary paradigm, these events did not just comprise, but were seen through the lens of, social media. They played directly into a Western technologically deterministic viewpoint.[80] This linear way of thinking divides human history into inevitable stages of social evolution and development, where the 'new' continually replaces the 'old' to eventually produce a technological utopia. In this account, technology not only enabled, but altered, the meaning of revolution. It was built on simplistic representations of 'Arabs' as passive and backwards, lacking the vitality for change and missing the spirit of initiative – in short, incapable of democratic transformation without the help of the West and its technology.[81] It was thus no surprise that the Western media, soaking up 'a heady brew of social media activism, scarce official pronouncements and revolutionary romanticism', quickly shaped an account that privileged digital.[82] Uprisings were given a 'palatable face' to Western audiences: the 'plausible result' of citizens using social media and digital mobile technologies.[83] Caught up in the bewildering speed of the revolutionary moment, 'the medium became the message' 'that shaped and controlled the scale and form of human association and action'.[84] In such a scenario, social media was a proxy for community and widespread popular empowerment.[85]

This relates to a wider debate about the potential of social media to create a new kind of politics that supports a two-way, citizen-centric society.[86] Governmental structures reassert themselves, such that outcomes are unstable, inconsistent and unsustainable. Most instances fail, but some reach the 'tipping point'.[87] These few demonstrate the potential for, and risks of, large-scale mobilization without formal organization, infrastructure and leadership. Such a twenty-first-century interpretation of events can account for disruptive change in a region without the normal trappings of revolutionary change.

The initial interpretation of the Middle East and North Africa (MENA) revolutions as leaderless and technology driven is misplaced. What matters is the sheer variety of outcomes, which profoundly affects our understanding of both revolution and reform. Debates reopened around their causes, trajectories, and consequences. Regarded as revolutions by those on the ground, they are challenging both definitional constraints and Western theoretical hegemony.[88]

At the same time, the use and misuse of the term are widespread. Widely adopted, and a buzzword in marketing, 'revolution' has become commonplace. Its 'symbolic resonance' is so overstated as to make the term, in many instances, meaningless – a reflection perhaps of the twenty-first century's wide but thin communication that omits context, history, or culture.[89] What effect will this have in the longer term? Language not only shapes thought and action but, through social interaction and community, plays a central role in the process of 'making meaning'.[90] This process plays out in a constant feedback loop across society.

Despite the continual stretching of its boundaries and little or no definitional clarity, the term 'revolution' has retained its strong emotive power and 'call to action'.[91] Words persist, as Tarrow argues, because they not only capture what a culture and society already know but can adapt to new contingencies.[92] 'Revolution' is a case in point and while that continues its durability is assured. It embodies so much – and while many may struggle to clearly define or differentiate 'revolution' from associated terms[93] – they know it when they see, feel and experience it.[94] Acknowledging the power of words is a legacy of the French Revolution and thereafter it became a crucial component in revolutionary strategy: the use of the term became 'an ideational battle' in and of itself and 'a source of social and political fracture'.[95] Each interpretation is shaped in part by embracing or reacting against the political narratives of regime elites or revolutionaries, of past victors and losers. The importance of an adaptable official narrative to communicate foundational stories, forms of identity, notions of unity and the meaning of revolution itself should not be underestimated. For 'no political leader or elite, even in authoritarian states, rules solely through the threat of coercive violence'.[96]

With the memory, interpretation and reinterpretation of revolution adding layers of meaning onto the term within a constellation of shared understanding, the concept carries ever more connotations and expectations[97] – in turn being shaped by and shaping society.[98] Inevitably a reflection of the societies from which it emerges, the inherent fluidity in the notion of revolution nonetheless enables people, whether involved or a bystander, to draw their own conclusions. The meaning of revolution for any individual reflects a moment in time that links the past, present and future: it is the combination of that person's knowledge, memory and experiences together with those of the wider society – including its religion, culture, norms, traditions and, particularly, its unique revolutionary history and system of governance.

Ideas, thoughts and images bounce around so freely in the Digital Age – interpreted by their recipient, repackaged, and recirculated instantaneously – that it is reasonable to ask whether the 'foreshortened, simple and telegraphic' messages already so popular and ubiquitous can 'employ the subtlety of language that can inspire collective trust that will endure beyond the protest movement'.[99] Are we not already witnessing a conflation of terms which ultimately conceal and camouflage what is taking place? Revolution remains the pinnacle of contentious political action, the epitome of ultimate social and political discontent. It conflicts with a citizen's trust in the legitimacy and authority of government, institutions, and the State. Evolving alongside trust, this transition marks the start of the next paradigm in revolution and related terms: multiple and diverging trajectories of meaning. We must wait to see which of these terms will survive, what they will embody and which will become obsolete.

10

Conclusion

There is undoubtedly an awareness in the literature that trust and revolution are linked, which makes it especially surprising that there has been no study examining their connection. Setting out to fill this gap, the present work explores the relationship and interaction between the concepts of trust and revolution. The book has a long historical sweep in order to address the diversity of revolutionary situations and investigate whether a new paradigm is emerging. It concludes that trust is a new lens through which to interpret revolution, with the typology of trust set out here offering an additional tool for analysis.

Although trust is ever present in one form or another, over time it retreats into the background until called upon, only to reappear at times of uncertainty. Whether defined as a significant constitutional adjustment or a radical socio-political transformation, revolution requires change and therefore inherently involves risk and insecurity – which drive the need for trust. Underpinning every interaction, trust is a vital component in the creation of memory through the fragmentation, reordering or stopping of time; the formation of values and adoption of social norms; and the manipulation of narratives in revolutionary situations. The cornerstone of all communication, trust continues to have a pivotal role in the concept of revolution.

With the exception of the Roman Empire's conversion to Christianity, revolution was circumscribed in antiquity: although 'there were major alterations in the nature of the "State" including changes in the extent of popular participation, [the] social character of the leadership remained the same, regardless of changes in personnel'.[1] Relationships of trust were personal and its networks interconnected, complementary, and mutually reinforcing. They created a framework that wove individuals together into society. This framework was not static, but ensured continuity rather than the ruptures we have since come to associate with revolution. Firmly set in individuals' day-to-day lives, revolutions were not ventures into the future.

Revolutions in the city-states of *quattrocento* Italy were the visible manifestation of a growing tension between two relationships of trust: commercial versus mutual. Revolution performed a vital social function: it rebalanced and restored equilibrium in society. Fifty years later, the overlapping spatial, social and economic networks of trust, which defined an individual's identity, inverted and brought about revolution. Communal and procedural trust was replaced with a relationship with the State.

In Tudor England, trust became a matter of loyalty – to God or to King. It was simultaneously cause and effect, influence and threat, recruiter and pacifier as citizens were actively taught to trust. Top-down and bottom-up, religious-political revolution created a variety of outcomes. One hundred years later, revolution and trust in England were portrayed by contemporary political theorists as interconnected rational reckonings. Yet, on a practical and vernacular level, it was *trust* in tradition, custom and community – not a calculus – which maintained social order in this period of uncertainty. Shared conservative values, belief in the law and widespread participation in local government again and again restored English equilibrium, thus bringing revolution full circle.[2]

It was only with the French Revolution that the concept took on its modern meaning of progressive rupture. Revolution cut through the process of laborious change, violently leap-frogging the years hitherto needed for reform. Yet, despite its grand ambitions, heroic connotations and romanticized imagery, revolution was still circumscribed, and its outcome constrained, by context and history. While betrayal lay at the heart of Robespierre's France, trust was a recurring theme throughout this revolutionary period that ultimately prevailed. Intentionally re-personalized and moralized, drawing heavily on the emerging sociability and friendship of the age, it was quickly institutionalized by the new regime. Trust and revolution in eighteenth-century France were emotional and subjective, not rational and objective.

An ever-evolving unifying framework of trust delimited political revolutionary possibilities. Thus, when viewed through a wide sweep of history, it is a notion of continuity rather than change that emerges. The revolutions with the most significant and far-reaching impact were very different. First, the conversion of the Roman Empire reinforced the unifying framework with the commonality of faith; second, the Reformation divided it, resulting in centuries of conflict and tension.

Today, the notion of revolution sits on a loosely defined sliding scale with no limits. Taking direct aim at political and social transformation, this dynamic process goes beyond the boundaries of the State. Played out on the international stage, it is influenced by, and influences, its global audience in multiple and diverging ways. No longer simply circular nor linear, twenty-first-century revolution has the potential to be winding and repetitive, disruptive and chaotic – underpinned by an explosion in personal networks of trust, which not only interconnect and mutually reinforce, but also bisect, dissect and compete over time. Often technologically empowered, these networks of trust have demonstrated that they are capable of challenging the relationships between citizen and State in an increasing number of areas. Together they have come to define the quickly shifting focus and activity which ebb and flow within the revolutionary process. These rapid and exponentially emerging networks of re-personalised trust have already demonstrated an ability to underpin an environment of unstable and unsustainable 'turbulent politics',[3] and with the slightest trigger they have proven their capacity to morph into unpredictable revolution. This is set to continue.

Returning to the principal exercise with which this study began – namely the exploration of trust in the evolving concept of revolution – three dominant themes emerge in the twenty-first century.

First, the evolving nature of trust has significantly affected the concept of revolution. From the communal in Antiquity; to the collective and collaborative in medieval England; to the overlapping spatial, social and economic network of trust of Renaissance Florence; to the rational calculation of seventeenth-century England, each change in the nature of trust has also shaped the notion of revolution. The nature of trust reflects the tension created by the movement *between* impersonal and personal trust, but also the dynamics *within* both impersonal trust and personal trust. The redrawing and reshaping of relationships offer a powerful insight into the diverging trajectories of contemporary revolutions.

Second, networks of personal and impersonal trust have increased exponentially, many driven by advances in digital technology, to produce a dizzying array of weak and strong ties. They mirror the growing complexity of society, along with the expanding role and reach of the State in an increasingly interconnected and globalized world. With the development of the modern State, the two types of relationships of trust – personal and impersonal – separated and increasingly diverged. Impersonal trust, unlike its personal counterpart, is predominantly one-way, interpreted as rational and legal, and bound by rights and duties. Such impersonal relationships came to rely not on trust but on expectation, reliability, confidence, and objective application of the law. As reducing uncertainty has become an ever-greater priority, governments have systematically removed all emotion and morality from impersonal trust. Creating an expectation of *non-betrayal*, it has weakened the networks of impersonal trust that underpin a state. Such states may become less resilient, unable to overcome adversity or govern in uncertain or high-risk situations.

This trend is mirrored in the declining trust in governments and their institutions. Raising levels of trust has become a priority and led to a move away from instrumentalist-based models of governance towards motive or legitimacy-based models. The aim is to transform the relationship between citizen and State, re-personalizing the impersonal through the replication of co-operative relationships. Confidence, judgement, behaviour, and character replace risk, vulnerability, rationality, rules, and sanctions. Consider China's plans to implement a social credit system, the Social Credit Score, by 2020.[4] A citizen's score will derive from monitoring their social behaviour, and will become the basis of that person's trustworthiness, which would also be publicly ranked. It will affect their eligibility for jobs, mortgages, travel visas and schools for their children. In many ways it resembles a chilling episode from *Black Mirror*. In stark contrast, in the West, a sense of government betrayal has not only become commonplace as the counterpoint to relationships of non-betrayal: it is also a response to what Bennett notes is the personalization and changing style of participation in contemporary Western politics.[5]

Third, while division has long been supported by trust, it is now exacerbated by growing individualism and the fragmentation of a once unifying framework of trust. Together with the growth of trust networks which not only interconnect and overlap but bisect and dissect, it has led to the creation of an increasingly uneven landscape where competition and conflict can flourish. Consider, for example, how Brexit has divided the UK, the migrant crisis has split the European Union and the inauguration of President Trump has polarized global opinion – all set within a landscape where trust in the media has hit an all-time low.

Limitations and implications for the future

Any book has its limitations, which must be noted. First, because of its great sweep of history, trust is not mapped in detail throughout the revolutionary stages of the illustrative examples used; that is for another day. Second, contemporary events go beyond the present work's focus on Western Europe; future studies in trust and revolution would benefit greatly from transnational collaboration.

While arguing that trust offers a novel means through which to interpret revolution – in particular, explaining its diverging trajectories and its typology – it has its challenges as an additional tool of analysis. These range across the lack of relevant historical sources to draw upon, its multiple and varied definitions, the difficulty seeing and capturing the meaning of the term 'trust', and the lack of detailed comparative cultural studies on which to draw. Trust remains an under-researched field of study which lacks its own history. Despite these issues, it promises to open up new areas for research and subsequent debate. It should be seen as an exciting opportunity in the study of revolution. For implicit within both the meaning of the term 'revolution' and its practice, trust, as a tool of analysis, has the benefit of mirroring the contextual specificity of every revolution. As a new lens, with which to interpret revolution, trust will have its critics. Yet, as recent events have highlighted, the classical concept and theories of revolution have been found wanting, underlining the need for a new approach. Perhaps by acknowledging that changes in trust produce the most far-reaching revolutions, a more ambitious theory of revolution may emerge.

The book should, however, sound a note of caution to governments and policy makers who see 'trust' as a solution for all their troubles. First, I question whether they actually mean trust or non-betrayal – and, indeed, which they set out to achieve by means of the much-vaunted panacea of transparency. Second, while it is a stated goal of Western governments to increase trust, they face an increasingly atomized citizenry (referred to by Upshaw as *narcissistic individuality*)[6] and, without a unifying set of core shared values to underpin a universal framework of trust, it is important to remember that trust has the same potential to divide as it has to unite.

Notes

Chapter 1

1   The term comes from Beer (1982).
2   Seldon (2010) argues that this is the 'worst crisis' of trust in Britain, while half the countries which Edelman (2016) surveyed have fallen into the 'distruster' category (meaning that fewer than half of respondents trust institutions).
3   Cf. Putnam (2000).
4   Bolt (2012), p. 259.
5   Cf. Foucault (1972).
6   McMahon (2013).
7   Braudel (1982), p. viii.
8   Braudel (1996), p. 20.
9   McGlade (2006), p. 78.
10 Braudel (1996), pp. 1242–43.
11 Compare critique of Lovejoy's (2011) unit-ideas.
12 Grote (2015), p. 8.
13 Koselleck (2003), pp. 12–13.
14 Grote (2015), p. 8.
15 Gordon (2012), p. 1.
16 Syrjämäki (2011), p. 18.
17 Saussure (1983) outlined two different yet complementary viewpoints.
18 Cf. Armitage (2012), p. 7.
19 Armitage (2012), Collingwood (2013).
20 Koselleck (1985), Neustadt and May (1986).
21 Armitage (2012), pp. 6–7.
22 Skinner (1969).
23 Bevir (2011), p. 14.
24 Dorschel (2010), p. 43.
25 Gordon (2012), p. 3.
26 As Vanheste notes on this somewhat 'idealist' approach, he accepts ideas as constitutive elements of human history, contradicting social-scientific positivism in historiography (2007), pp. 9–10.
27 A view held across a wide scholarly spectrum: within personality research – Rotter (1971), behavioural research – Axelrod (1984), and within social psychology – Lewis and Weigert (1985a).

28 Recognizable to all but meaning different things to different people, the concept of trust is similarly too complex to be accurately described in a single word. However, the search for one unambiguous all-encompassing definition continues. As Krzanic (2013) argues, this reductive approach seems incongruous in an age when we have multiple terms to describe the coffee we are drinking. By separating out trust through the use of adjectival qualification, one can better map out, understand and analyse one's trust relationships.

29 Williamson (1993), p. 453.

30 McKnight and Chervany (1996), p. 17.

31 For example: Lewis and Weigert (1985b) who define trust through its component parts, acknowledging that all are present in each and every instance of trust but to varying degrees; Zucker (1986), whose typology includes process, characteristics and institutional-based trust; and Shapiro *et al.* (1992) who advocate deterrence, knowledge and identification-based trust. Some academics, such as Barber (1983), Bromiley and Cummings (1995), and Mishra (1986), define types of trust based on disposition, situation and intent.

32 Kee and Knox (1970), Lewis and Weigert (1985a).

33 Doney *et al.* (1998), p. 603.

34 McKnight and Chervany (1996).

35 Mayer *et al.* (1995), p. 711, Pennanen (2009), p. 28.

36 'Understood either as a mere accumulation, an additive and unstructured collection of many individual people, or as an object existing beyond individuals' incapable of further explanation'. Elias (2001), p. vii.

37 Lee (2007), Draper (2013).

38 Hermanson (2012), p. 1. Hanks (2012) notes the role of knitting in politics, as both medium and message, while artists such as Auerbach and Schwandtner suggest repositioning knitting as a political tool.

39 Dickens (2004).

Chapter 2

1 'A partnership of the free', a polis, or a political entity 'of citizens' who form 'a system of government' amongst themselves. Aristotle, 1279a.21 and 1276b.1–2.

2 Pocock (1972), p. 119.

3 See Halliday (1999).

4 Colombo (2008), p. 1.

5 Thucydides writes of the revolution in Corcyra that 'words had to change their ordinary meaning' (2000), ch. 9, 10.33.

6 Herodotus 3.44, Thucydides 2.27.

7 Thucydides 6.17.

8   Ibid., 1.115.
9   This image of the mob has been cultivated by chroniclers Polybius (2010) and
    Tacitus (2007) as well as by contemporary historians Scullard (2013) and Dickinson
    (1963). Rather than seeing them as the reactions of an irrational and uncontrollable
    mob, these actions should be understood as their only outlet to voice grievances
    while defending justice and legitimate government, from which they were excluded.
    Africa (1974), Parenti (2007).
10 Aristotle illustrated Book 5 with examples of revolution from democracies (Cos,
    Rhodes and Cyme), oligarchies (Massili, Istros and Heraclea) and aristocracies
    (Sparta and Thurii). He stated that 'when political and economic powers are
    separated, and combined with the desire for "justice," revolutionary change ensues'.
11 Inequalities, in this context, should be viewed as incongruity between wealth and
    political privilege – described as 'equality proportionate to desert'. Aristotle (2000)
    V, 1, revisited centuries later in the Pareto-Davis Theory.
12 Aristotle (2000).
13 Shear (2011).
14 Considered an aspect of Western civilization (Zarrow 1997), ancient citizenship is
    often argued, although vigorously disputed, to be a simpler form when compared to
    modern citizenship. See Burchell (2003), Ober (1996b).
15 For example, in Sparta, 7–30-year-old males ate, trained and slept communally,
    developing and maintaining their sense of unity and social cohesion. With a strict
    moral code and sense of duty, Spartans endured extreme hardships to become full
    citizens.
16 Hosking (2005a).
17 Hosking (2002), p. 8, Johnstone (2011).
18 Aristotle (2000), Cicero (2013).
19 Taubman (2009).
20 A doctrine of royal and political legitimacy, described by Shakespeare in Richard
    II, 4.1. In Christian teaching it had the effect of delegitimizing revolts or rebellions
    against the monarchy. They constituted a sacrilegious act. See Bodin (1992) for a
    contemporaneous argument on sovereignty and Burgess (1992) for more recent
    discussions.
21 Contemporary historians use the term retrospectively. See Sizer (2008).
22 Heater (2004), pp. 15–17.
23 Failure and bankruptcy (kings reneging on their debts) were said to have more dire
    consequences than military defeats.
24 The social divide increased significantly and, with it, demands on the peasants
    to pay ever-increasing taxes. Inflation, war and the effects of the Black Death
    (fixing wages) not only exacerbated the situation but more often than not led
    to the peasants seeking legal solutions rather than rising up. Hilton (1985), pp.
    127–33.

25 Silva-Vigier (1992), pp. 192–93, Froissart (1967), p. 225 and Walsingham (1869), p. 169 respectively.

26 Referred to as Wat Tyler's Rebellion or the Great Rising, these events have subsequently been described as a 'passing episode' (Postan 1975, p. 172) and 'a bloody affair, fired by revolutionary zeal that threatened for a few brief days to overturn the social order of England' (Dunn 2004).

27 The Dutch peasant revolts (1323–8), the Cabochien revolt (1413), the rebellion of the Remences (1462 and 1485), the Ciompi revolt (1378). See TeBrake (1993), Freedman (2013) and Sizer (2008) respectively.

28 Chroniclers provided biased coverage, while stressing that rebels were disobedient and illegitimate, undermining their cause to great effect. Crane (1992), p. 208.

29 The Ancient Greek definition of revolution is tied to the notion of betrayal, more specifically of political betrayal against king or polis.

30 Neither Froissart (1967) nor Knighton (1995) in their contemporary descriptions of 1381 used the term 'revolution', while Walsingham (2003) focused on the terror of social unrest.

31 Breay (2011), Worcester (2010).

32 Linebaugh (2008).

33 Leca (1994), p. 161.

34 French for 'rebirth', the term 'renaissance' was first used in the early nineteenth century. Although contested (Caferro 2011), it refers to the fourteenth to sixteenth centuries. It marks the rediscovery of rational thought and civilization, so well exemplified in antiquity.

35 Bacon (1620), by detailing his inductive reasoning for exploring causality, introduced a 'new method' for the sciences.

36 Such as Galileo's Observations (1610) and Laws of Falling Bodies (1638), Napier's Logarithms (1614), Hooke's Discovery of the Cell (1665), Harvey's Theory of Blood (1628), Romer's Measurement of the Speed of Light (1676) and Newton's Law of Motion (1687).

37 By 1500 *c.* 20 million books were being produced, by 1600 *c.* 150–200 million. Febvre and Martin (1997). It was vital to the process of democratizing knowledge and helping to raise literacy rates, while establishing communities of scientists, standardizing and recording knowledge, and demonstrating the advantages of mass production. It was also an important factor in the shift from Latin to the vernacular. Briggs and Burke (2010).

38 Melville (1992), ch.45.

39 'Revolution' is used in four of his plays with no overtly political meaning attached.

40 Shakespeare's Sonnet 594.

41 Chaucer employed the word for the circular motion of the stars, speaking of 'hevenish revolucioun', using the phrase 'Thrugh change and revolucioun' in his translation of *Le Roman de la Rose*.

42 Villani (2011), vol. 4.

43 Nardi (2012).

44 Varchi (2012), ch.2.

45 Certainly for Machiavelli (2007), political change represented an individual's self-interest and desire for power, seizing the opportunity and using violence, when necessary, to succeed. Twentieth-century examples include the caudillos and juntas of South and Central America (Fossum 1967). Also described as a 'regular, recurrent, normal part of the Latin American political process' (Silvert 1961). For generations it was regarded 'as the province of domineering military tyrants' (Smith 2004, p. 7).

46 Machiavelli uses the phrase '*tante rivoluzioni d'Italia*' (Italy's many revolutions) but it is understood in a general sense, referring to innovations or changes in art rather than in its political sense (2007, 26).

47 Kaplan argues that '[Machiavelli] emancipated politics from theology and moral philosophy. He … anticipated what was later called the scientific spirit to discover only what really happens' (2005, Lecture 7).

48 Ascham (1648).

49 A new system of political order, of sovereign states, was introduced across most of Europe as a result of this large diplomatic congress and the signing of the Treaties of Westphalia which ended the Thirty Years' War. It simplified the map of Europe – although according to Strayer (2011), Britain, as well as France, had looked like sovereign states since around 1300. Contemporaneously, different influential notions of sovereignty emerged. For a detailed insight see Croxton (2013).

50 Micklethwait and Wooldridge (2014).

51 Hobbes (2004), ch.18.

52 It was most clearly manifested in England in the reign of James I (VI Scotland). 'The State of Monarchy is the supremest thing upon earth: for Kings are not only God's lieutenants upon earth, and sit upon God's throne, but even by God himself, they are called Gods.' Transcribed from James I, Works (1616), pp. 528–31.

53 Such rights have been enshrined in the laws of state: Magna Carta (1215), Golden Bull (1222), the American Declaration of Independence (1776), the French Constitution (1793), together with the Universal Declaration of Human Rights (1948).

54 Hobbes (2004), ch.21, para.21.

55 Initially published anonymously in 1689 but dated 1690 according to the conventions of the day. Locke (1988).

56 Ibid., Book 2, 122.

57 Kiefer and Munitz (1970), p. 327.

58 John Hampden (1653–96) coined the term 'Glorious Revolution' in testimony before a House of Lords committee in 1689. Cited in Schwoerer (2004, p. 3), Jardine (2008) and Vallance (2007), who are an academic minority in arguing that 1688 was an invasion, rather than a revolution. Not only called revolutions in their own day but, in anticipation, there appears in the Clarke Papers (1655), 'Hee (Sir

Hasilrige) was very jealous of the intended revolution of the government to his Majestyie's advantage', quoted in Hatto (1949, p. 505).

59 'Revolution' says Collingwood, 'was borrowed towards the end of the seventeenth century by the vocabulary of politics from the vocabulary of literary criticism' (2013), p. 199. It was a reversal of fortune. Evelyn's diary entry for 2 December 1688 describes a scene of total chaos 'it looks like revolution' (2004).

60 Clarendon (2009).

61 Excerpt from the High Court of Justice sentence on Charles I, 27 January 1649. It was not until the early nineteenth century that these events were seriously termed as revolution, by Guizot (2010) drawing comparisons with the French Revolution. The Great Rebellion was rechristened as a revolution after the French beheaded their monarch.

62 Hatto comments 'that whereas the makers of earlier revolutions had lagged behind events in their thoughts, up-to-date revolutionaries seemed to be one, if not three or four steps ahead' (1949), p. 507.

63 Arendt (2006), p. 31.

64 Lawson (2005), p. 4.

65 Kumar (2001).

66 Watson (1998), p. 37.

67 The period's literary utopias included Bacon's *New Atlantis*, Campanella's *The City of the Sun*, More's *Utopia*, Andreae's *Christianopolis* and Neville's *Isle of Pines*. Many were totalitarian and austere, abnegating the individual in favour of the collective.

68 The controversy began with Burke's 1790 publication, to which Paine responded in 1791. Fundamentally opposed, Paine saw its sanctity, while Burke argued against its barbarism.

69 Feared throughout history, mobs are believed to drive individuals 'insane', turning them from rational beings into emotional creatures and so 'when one with honeyed words but evil mind persuades the mob great woes befall the state', Euripides, *Orestes* I, 907. These mobs are either described as feminine in nature – suggestible, excitable and emotionally irrational – by psychologists such as Freud (2012) and Le Bon (2009), or they are presented as 'unthinking masses' (Kant 2009, p. 3) by writers such as Orwell (2000), Huxley (2007) and Wells (2005). Even in the twentieth century they are portrayed as slaves to their passions, out of control, ineffectual, and stereotyped as 'crazy'. Violent anger has been the paradigm emotion in politics, the central charge against mobs for 2500 years (Jasper 2013).

70 For example, the Nika Riots which left more than 30,000 dead and destroyed over half of Constantinople (532 CE); the Salt Riot in Moscow (1648), painted by Lissner; and the Réveillon Riots in Paris (1789), where artisans ransacked a wallpaper factory and seventy-one were killed clashing with troops.

71 Shakespeare's *The Life and Death of Julius Caesar*, Act 3, Scene 2.

72 It was not until Le Bon (2009), Tarde (2009) and Freud (2012) in the nineteenth century that the psychology of crowds and their actions were studied and began to be understood in any depth.

73 Orwell highlights this association, writing 'fear of the mob is a superstitious fear. It is based on the idea that there is some mysterious, fundamental difference between rich and poor, as though they were two different races, like Negroes and white men. But in reality there is no such difference' (1986, 22 p. 127.)

74 Although used earlier by Blanqui in 1837 and Briavoinne in 1839, and implicit in the writings of Blake (1970, p. 136), Hardy (2010, p. 192) and Wordsworth (2004, p. 144), the term 'industrial revolution' was first made fashionable by Toynbee (the English economic historian) through his lecture series of 1884.

75 Griffin (n.d.), p. 1.

76 Hobsbawn (2010b), Mokyr (1993).

77 McClosky (2010), Allen (2009).

78 Including Proudhon, Fourier, Owen, Blanqui, Kropotkin, Bakunin, Blanc, Hess, Marx and Engels.

79 Marx and Engels (1975), vol. 9, p. 212.

80 The European political landscape became increasingly fragmented as distance increased, not only between the political right and left but within the political left too, as irreconcilable differences split movements into more radical groupings.

81 Green, Hobhouse and Hobson posited that the only way to improve the position of the poor was for a strong (welfare-centric) interventionist state to co-ordinate collective action. In Germany leftist liberals, such as Brentano and von Schulze-Gavernitz, established trade unions to improve conditions. Strongly opposed to the Welfare State, which they called 'State Socialism', they sought representative government. In France Fouill and Durkheim (solidarists) posited that individuals owed a debt to society and argued the role of the State was one of co-ordination rather than management. See Richardson (2001) and Feuchtwanger (1985). Anarchist schools of thought range from complete collectivism to extreme individualism; compare Ostergaard (2002, p. 14) and Kropotkin (2008). Graeber separates the two as follows: Marxism is often theory-heavy analytical discourse about revolutionary strategy, whereas anarchism is an ethical discourse about revolutionary process (2009, p. 211).

82 Although anarchists and Marxists agree on the long-term desirability of a stateless society, their individual conceptions differ. For Marx and Engels, the State withers and dies in a higher phase of communism (Engels 1947, part 3, ch.2), while Godwin (1992) initially advocated 'government of the simplest construction' but gradually came to consider that 'government by its very nature counteracts the improvement of the original mind'. Bakunin (2007) rejects a socialist state as an immense cemetery that limits individual freedom, while Kropotkin (2008, p. 117) advocates a society based on voluntary associations, and Proudhon (1979) argues

for a society in which power radiates from the bottom upwards along federal or regional lines.

83 Machiavelli (2013) uses the republic as a political model while Rousseau (1998) refers to the democratic model of Sparta.

84 Thinkers include Constant (1988) and his notion of the Liberty of the Moderns.

85 Kroeber (1996), p. 23.

86 Marx defines the working class as individuals who physically earn a wage but do not own the means of production.

87 Yoder (1926), p. 433.

88 Small, Adams, Sorokin, Ross, Martin, Dewe, Edwards and Spargo seem to consider revolution as a purely political phenomenon. Bodin (1955), pp. 406–07.

89 Le Bon (2007), p. 25.

90 Ellwood (2012), pp. 20–21.

91 Finney (2009), pp. 35–37.

92 Hyndman (2012), pp. 11–12.

93 Foran (2003) calculated that there were thirty-one revolutions in the twentieth century.

94 Described by Mao as 'not a dinner party ... it cannot be so refined ... so temperate ... and magnanimous. A revolution is an insurrection, an act of violence by which one class overthrows another' (Tse-Tung 1972, pp. 11–12). Lenin describes them as 'the masses ... [who] have no other road of salvation except the revolutionary overthrow of their governments' (1970a, vol. 21).

95 Marx and Engels (1975), vol. 5, p. 53.

96 These techniques and tactics are about authoritarian centralism and hierarchical control over the process of enforced revolutionary change. Moving Marx's inevitability of proletarian change forward, they give history a shove.

97 Prolific political theoreticians and philosophers, they wrote pamphlets, articles and books, simultaneously corresponding with comrades, allies and friends worldwide. See Lenin's (1970a) and Mao Tse-Tung's collected works (2012).

98 Extracted from A and E's biography series (2005), Vladimir Lenin: Voice of Revolution.

99 Cheek (2010), p. 6. His greatest legacy was three-phase warfare. Tse-Tung (1961).

100 Lenin formed the Communist International to spread communism worldwide, while a worldwide Islamic caliphate is the stated aim of many Islamic extremists – such as Hizb ut-Tahrir and factions within the Muslim Brotherhood. Rosecrance (1986) notes self-preservation while Palmer, Brinton and Godechot all studied the causes of revolutionary waves.

101 Their very existence, for Marx, signalled the possibility of world revolution, while for Luxemburg, 'The most precious thing ... is the proletariat's spiritual growth ... an inviolable guarantee of its further progress' (Cliff 1985, p. 5).

102 As witnessed in Latin America, South East Asia and Africa in the second half of the twentieth century.

103 Lawson (2005), p. 474.

104 Although the collapse of the USSR in 1991, together with over 30 years of increasing commercialization in China, has been heralded as a victory for free market forces and capitalism, the legacy of Marx remains. For many, he remains a formidable intellectual, a principal architect of modern social sciences, his writings an evocative doctrine and the principal intellectual source for radical political movements; see Calhoun (2012b, pp. 23–24), Berlin (1967, p. 139), Allan (2010, p. 68), Singer (1980, p. 1) and O'Laughlin (1975). While Marxism still speaks to a wide audience (and anarchist movements), its primary aim remains the abolition of social inequalities and the liberation of the working classes through political and, if necessary, revolutionary action, appealing to a world increasingly divided between the haves and have-nots. For discussions on contemporary approaches to Marxism in social movements, see Williams and Satgar (2013), Barker *et al.* (2013).

105 For technological determinists such as McLuhan (1964) and Anderson (2012), these 'revolutionary' changes drive social change, shaping its structural and cultural values.

106 Portrayed as the overthrow of repressive puritanism, the sexual revolution is credited with a plethora of attitudinal and behavioural changes. The notion that these were 'revolutionary' changes has, however, been increasingly challenged by Smith (1990), Niemi *et al.* (1989).

107 Brought about in part by Bernach's 1949 manifesto for the 'creative revolution', Teitelman (2011) outlines the misuse of the term in general, drawing specific attention to the many instances of overuse in advertising, and reiterated in a list of the 100 most overused marketing buzz words.

108 Lenin, Mao, Napoleon and countless others have revisited and reshaped history in much the same way, and for similar reasons, as the pigs rewrote history in Orwell's (2000) *Animal Farm.*

109 Although varied, the definitions tend to overlap in a number of areas: violent by definition, dramatic in intent and consequence, the result of a popular groundswell of support from the deprived, discontented and disenfranchised against a regime, perceived to be either illegitimate, autocratic or totalitarian, and they are all 'rooted in the basic assumption that true revolutions are likely to take place in modernising societies though still largely peasant and traditional' (Dix 1991, p. 228).

110 Appearing frequently in the Quran, jihadi (جهادي in Arabic) refers to resistance or struggle – it is used 164 times according to Natan (2011). A religious duty, contested amongst Muslim scholars, its meaning can be interpreted spiritually, physically (with a military meaning – a 'holy war') or as a struggle to create and maintain a good society. Steffen (2007), Ghamidi (2010).

111 For example, the Muslim Brotherhood, founded in 1928 by Hassan al-Banna, to combat what he saw as the degrading effects of foreign influence and a secular way of life. His most potent notion was that Islam offers the opportunity to create a new world order. They set up 'separate' political parties in several countries (including Hamas in the Gaza strip/West Bank, the Islamic Action Front in Jordan and the Freedom and Justice Party in Egypt). Wickham (2013).

112 Adib-Moghaddam (2013), p. 63.

113 The Pahlavi dynasty was overthrown. The revolution followed demonstrations and civil unrest which began in 1977, before intensifying in 1978, with paralysing strikes across the country. Fleeing the country, a regency government invited the Ayatollah Khomeini out of exile. After some street fighting, those loyal to the Shah were overwhelmed. With the rebels assuming power on 11 February, Iranians voted in a national referendum to approve a new constitution. Kurzman (2004) and Abrahamian (2009); also see Goldstone (2001).

114 Benard (1986), p. 18.

115 Skocpol (1979), p. 240, Amuzegar (1991), p. 9 respectively.

116 Refers to the peaceful transfer of power to non-communist governments in Poland, Hungary, Czechoslovakia, Bulgaria and Albania and the reunification of Germany between 1989 and 1992.

117 Referring to events in Georgia (2003), Ukraine (2004) and Moldova (2009), resulting in regime change. Auer (2009).

118 Although Auer (2009) theorizes that the 'Velvet Revolutions' refuted the integral nature of violence in revolution, his definition of violence refers to insurgent or terrorist tactics, mass confrontation between the state's instruments of power, the people and civil war, excluding the forms of violence encountered when the very foundations of a society are changed.

119 Schell (2003), p. 186.

120 'There were no demands to replace democracy with a fundamentally new and different form of government' with the Ukrainian (Orange) revolution, 'rather, Ukrainians protested in order to guarantee the rules and institutions of democracy' (McFaul 2006, pp. 190–91); see also Auer (2009) and Lawson (2005).

121 'first used by Foreign Policy Magazine and then adopted by journalists and activists in the USA as a way to brand the revolution' (Haschke 2011).

122 Kroeber (1996), pp. 21–40.

123 Dix (1991), p. 231.

124 Berman (2003), p. 11.

125 Although these actions have sometimes brought about the removal of government figureheads, the machinery and corruption inherent within these long-instituted autocratic regimes remains. At best they may ultimately conform to a two-stage revolutionary theory; at worst the power vacuum created leads to longer-term conflict.

126   An ongoing debate: Gerges (2012, 2013) posits that the Arab Spring has weakened
        Jihadism while Scheuer (2011) argues that its limitations and failures have
        strengthened the Jihadi Spring. Often overlooked, Gartenstein-Ross and Vassefi
        (2012) seek to add the Jihadis' perspective on the Arab Spring into this debate. It
        has often been overlooked.

127   Duderija (2011) and Kepel (2006) locate neo-traditionalist *Salafis* against the
        broader Islamic tradition – antecedents, including Sayyid Qutb, who developed
        the 'intellectual underpinnings' of the ideology.

128   While Bin Laden (2005) spoke of a caliphate it was a distant aspiration. The
        Islamic State, Al Shabaab and Boko Hare seek to create Islamic states. Caris and
        Reynolds (2014), Vidino *et al.* (2010) and Onuoho (2014) respectively.

129   'In Qutb's view, Islam is a universal system offering the only true freedom:
        freedom from governance by other men, man-made doctrines or "low association
        based on race and colour, regional and national interests". Its utopian goal is a
        global theocracy. Kissinger (2014), p. 1.

130   Each Russian leader had their own interpretation – see Trotsky (1906) and Stalin
        (1924) – of the role, timing and implications involved. Relationships post-
        revolution were regulated and they were still separate nation states.

131   Buchan (2013), Adib-Moghaddam (2013).

132   Although Marxist theory argues that world revolution would lead to world
        communism and, later still, stateless communism, it was less a reality than an
        utopian ideal requiring education and a change in nature.

133   It appears sixty-two times in the Quran, its meaning changeable and ever-
        evolving. Bearman *et al.* (2013).

134   Garwin (2014), p. 185. There is a long and often-disputed history of the
        caliphates, beginning with the first two caliphs of Islam Abu Bakr (632–4) and
        Umar ibn al Khattab (634–4) and ending in 1924 with the Ottoman Caliphate
        (refer to Esposito 2004). A reflection of the Sunni/Shia split, it highlights the
        elusive ideal of a unified ummah.

135   Binding individuals with society, Allah is entrusting them to establish a peaceful
        society with a just social order.

136   Compare Fukuyama's 1989 statement with Ledwith (2013). More recently,
        Fukuyama (2005) has qualified his earlier argument highlighting the need for
        state-building to solve the issue of failed and weak states, replicate Western liberal
        democracy, and ensure political order.

137   Clarity ensures universal grounding while clear definitions are essential for
        research purposes. See Goertz (2005) and Collier and Levitsky (1997).

138   This development goes against Mao's definition of a revolution and also the terms
        used by Lenin. Cheek (2010), p. 6.

Chapter 3

1   Ayto (1990).

2   Compare Luhmann (1979) and Giddens (2009); see also Dasgupta (1988), and
    Casson and Della Giusta (2006); also Hardin (1996) and O'Neill (2002a); also
    Hosking (2014) and Pagden (1990); also Cook *et al.* (2005) and (2001); and also
    Erikson (1963), Vygotsky *et al.* (1978) respectively.

3   Various studies, including those by Branzei *et al.* (2007) and Yamagishi *et al.* (1998),
    have compared the levels of trust and the 'propensity to trust' in different cultures
    and countries.

4   Compare Hardin (1996) and Uslaner (2002).

5   Lewis and Weigert (1985b), p. 968.

6   Hardin (2004), Mayer *et al.* (1995).

7   Lewicki and Bunker (1995), p. 135.

8   White (1992), p. 174.

9   Rotter (1980) and Shapiro (1987) respectively.

10 A small group, including McKnight and Chervany (1996) and Tiryakian (1968),
    has sought to classify and categorize the multiple definitions in use, representing
    trust as a broad but coherent set of constructs.

11 Compare Shapiro (1987) and Uslaner (2008).

12 Marsh (1994), p. 20.

13 Lahno (2001), Barber (1983) and Luhmann (1979) share this 3D view of trust.

14 Although Batson, Shaw and Oleson noted in the early 1990s that 'affect, mood,
    and emotion are used interchangeably' (1992, p. 295), interest in differentiating
    them only began in the twenty-first century – with Carruthers (2000) developing
    a deeper understanding of these notions and Seigworth's (2010) compendium of
    affect theory writings.

15 'Affect' is innate, unconscious, a moment of unformed and unstructured potential,
    while emotions and feelings are learnt, experienced and stored to recall later.
    Tomkins (1995), p. 54.

16 McDermott (2000), p. 40.

17 Such as Baier (1995), Gambetta (1988), Hardin (1992) and Sztompka (1997).

18 Coleman (1990), p. 99.

19 Referring to three components of attitude (the affective, conative and cognitive).
    These feelings, behaviours and beliefs or knowledge which a person has about
    a person or object shape one's attitude and in turn one's responses. Hogg and
    Vaughan (2005) and Simpson (2012).

20 Baier (1995), p. 99.

21 See Jones (1996) and Lahno (2001).

22 Although trusting a doctor in this scenario, on a personal and professional level, is separate, it can overlap and/or conflict.

23 O'Neill (2002b), p. 14.

24 Holton (1994), p. 5.

25 Jones (1996), p. 4.

26 Holton (1994), p. 67.

27 Hardin (2004).

28 Zsolnai (2005), pp. 268–69.

29 Michel (2011), p. 7.

30 Hollis (1998), pp. 10–14.

31 Ruzicka and Wheeler (2010).

32 Mercer (2005), p. 95.

33 For Kierkegaard it is more a 'leap into faith', necessary to accept Christianity. The phrase is usually taken to mean believing or trusting in something without robust and supportable empirical evidence (1992, pp. 263–66).

34 Although Coleman (1990) and Dasgupta (1988) have used Game Theory, the Prisoner's Dilemma and the Assurance Game for some time, this approach is criticized, not only for assuming individuals are rational decision makers seeking to maximize their utility/value, but also for conflating co-operation and reciprocity with trust. Beset with problems of context and oversimplification, these experiments provide trust research with empirical data. However, their wider value is limited by the difficulties surrounding the measure of trust (Kydd 2005). Trust is more than simply calculating odds, or cost–benefit analysis, and these experiments tell us little about the richness and nuances of trust.

35 Henrich *et al*'s (2010) research focuses on family (in Tsimane) and on the notion that trust is a gift with a cost attached (in Gnaut).

36 Wheeler (2007), p. 6.

37 Osgood's (1962) conception of graduated reciprocation in tension reduction and Kydd's (2005) model of costly signalling.

38 Wheeler (2012).

39 Lachowski (2004), Rotfeld (2008).

40 Wheeler (2010).

41 A dispute over Pakistani-occupied Indian army lookout posts in Kashmir, May–July 1999.

42 Mercer (2005), p. 95.

43 Michel (2011), p. 11.

44 Lahno (2001), pp. 172–73.

45 An emotion is the genuine or feigned display of a feeling (a personal, autobiographical sensation), an internal state broadcast to the world, or a contrivance in order to fulfil social expectations. Although infants display

emotions, they have no biographical or language skills to experience feelings – their emotions are direct expressions of affect (Berk 2012).

46 Spinoza (1996), Deleuze and Guattari (1987).

47 Holton (1994), p. 63, Ruzicka and Wheeler (2010), p. 71.

48 Phronesis is understood, by Aristotle (2009b), to be a type of wisdom. Referred to as practical wisdom (and the process of good decision-making) or prudence, combining rational thought with experience, practical knowledge and decorum, it is concerned with the context and specifics of a situation. It is referred to by Flyvbjerg as 'practical knowledge and practical ethics' (2001), pp. 56–57.

49 MacIntyre (2007).

50 It is the ability to make good decisions and deliver on them. See Aristotle (2009b).

51 Michel (2011), p. 17.

52 Such checks and balances, norms, procedures, regulations, routine and institutionalization required by rationalists in a more functional approach to trust, the very need of which highlights a lack of trust.

53 Lagerspetz (1998), pp. 38–39.

54 Lahno (2001), p. 172.

55 Baier (1995), p. 110.

56 Lahno (2001), pp. 172–73.

57 Haidt (2001).

58 Buss (2001), Ketelaar and Clore (1997); while Scherer suggests 'that emotions can be assessed as to whether, in particular situations, they are adaptive (functional), based on well-grounded inference from available information … considered as reasonable by others' (2011), p. 330.

59 de Sousa (1988), Kahneman and Tversky (1982).

60 Lahno (2001), p. 177.

61 Heidegger (1962).

62 Goodwin (2008), pp. 45–46.

63 Michel (2011), p. 40.

64 Trust is seen as a dependent variable (Coleman (1990)), an independent variable (Luhmann in Gambetta (1988)), or a process (Khodyakov (2007)).

65 See Khodyahov's description of trust as a two-way process (2007) p. 125.

66 Solomon and Flores (2003), p. 15.

67 Within sociology, functionalism, symbolic interactionism and conflict theory, whether implicitly or explicitly, draw on the concepts of trust and distrust to understand the social processes that underpin social actions, social structure and functions. Functionalists' macro-perspective – Parsons (1967), Merton (1996) and Huntington (1973) – emphasizes the pre-eminence of an orderly social world over its constituent parts, often with biological analogies, while socialization of the individual into society is achieved through the internalization of norms and

values. This requires trust. On the other hand, symbolic interactionists – Blumer
in Lee (1969), pp. 219–88; and Mead (1969) – with their focus on the micro, see
'... humans as active, creative participants who construct their social world and are
not passive conforming objects of socialisation' and therefore focus on cohesive
systems and a 'more changeable continually re-adjusting social process'. Hunter
and McClelland in Ferguson (2012), p. 36. Garfinkel's 1967 trust experiments
specifically question how individuals who interact can create the illusion of a
shared social order. In marked contrast, conflict theorists – Mills (1956), Engels and
Marx (1969) and Collins (1975) – emphasize domination, power and manipulation
in maintaining social order, highlighting the interaction of the concepts of trust
and distrust. Change is seen as rapid and disorganized.
68 Khodyakov (2007) p. 126.
69 It cannot be conceived as a finite and bounded set of things and events (in the classical
    sense of *a universitas rerum* or *aggregatio corporum*). Luhmann (1982) p. 232.
70 Lewis and Weigert (1985b) p. 968.
71 Luhmann (1979) pp. 22 and 81.
72 Pixley (1999).
73 Luhmann (1995) p. 158.
74 Ibid., p. 158.
75 Ibid.
76 Here, rationality does not refer to the decisions concerning action, but the
    meaningfulness of the action taken. Luhmann (1979), p. 88.
77 Ibid., p. 10.
78 Ibid., pp. 10 and 25.
79 The majority-held view is that trust is either a dependent – Coleman (1990),
    Levi (1998) and Yamagishi (2001) – or independent variable – Putnam (2000),
    Putnam *et al.* (1993), Gambetta (1988) and Luhmann (1988), with the exception of
    Nooteboom and Six (2003), Mollering (2005) and Khodyahov (2007) who regard it
    as a process.
80 The majority-held view is that trust is either a dependent (Coleman 1990, Levi
    1998) or independent variable (Gambetta 1988, Luhmann 1988), with the
    exception of Möllering (2005) and Khodyakov (2007) who regard it as a process.
81 Khodyakov (2007), p. 125.
82 Solomon and Flores (2003), p. 15.
83 Within sociology, functionalism, symbolic interactionism and conflict theory,
    whether implicitly or explicitly, draw on the concepts of trust and distrust to
    understand the social processes that underpin social actions, social structure and
    functions. The functionalist's macro-perspective (Merton (1996) and Huntington
    (1973)) emphasizes the pre-eminence of an orderly social world over its constituent
    parts, often with biological analogies, while socialization of the individual into
    society is achieved through the internalization of norms and values – which

requires trust. On the other hand, the symbolic interactionists, Blumer (1969) and Mead (1969), place their focus on the micro. Garfinkel's 1963 trust experiments specifically question how individuals who interact can create the illusion of a shared social order. In marked contrast the conflict theorists, Mills (1956) and Collins (1975), emphasize domination, power and manipulation in maintaining social order, highlighting the interaction of the concepts of trust and distrust. Change is seen as rapid and disorganized.

84 Solomon and Flores (2003).

85 Luhmann (1988).

86 Khodyakov (2007), p. 126.

87 First cowry shells then base metal coins (*c.* 600–300 BCE) and leather banknotes (118 BCE), followed by paper currency (*c.* 960 CE). Although China was the first to develop a monetary system (*c.* 1200 BCE), it differed from the later European one. I have summarized the European development to illustrate my discussions on trust. Davies (2010) and Ederer (1964).

88 Hosking (2014), p. 81.

89 A commodity of exchange, a measure of value, a medium of circulation, money is a tool: fungible, calculable, flexible, convenient, divisible, portable and interchangeable in a way that bartering is not (Greco 2001). Whereas the first banking system originated around 3000 BCE in Babylonia, temples and palaces were used to store valuables (Davies 2010).

90 Borges (1999), p. 244.

91 Dostoevsky (2004), iv.

92 Ashmolean Museum exhibition label.

93 O'Sullivan (2003) refers to 'commodity money': the commodity constitutes money; it has value in and of itself. It began with cattle but was primarily gold, silver or salt.

94 Quickly gaining a monopoly, heads of state had the means to fund, and the power to control, the value of money (Davies 2010, Challis 1992). An exceedingly visual way to legitimize their position, it also enabled them to validate the coinage. When Athelstan united England in the tenth century, he introduced the first 'national' coin, decreeing where and how these standard weight coins, which bore his name and profile, could be minted (Foot 2011, pp. 155–56).

95 Herodotus noted that the Lydians were the first to use gold and silver coins and to establish permanent retail shops, which he criticized as 'blatant commercialisation' (2012), p. 94.

96 'Their nominal value was coincident with their metallic value', although that value could differ by location (Jevons 1876).

97 The Cappadocian rulers who first introduced the notion of government (or State) guaranteed the weight and purity of its money in 22 BCE. See Davies (2010) for a detailed history of money.

98   Hosking (2014), p. 83.

99   During the second Punic War, and under both Nero's and Constantine's rule, coins were debased. As their value fell, people lost confidence, demanding more in compensation, and consequently prices rose, leading to rapid inflation.

100 Abandoned in 440 CE, as Rome fell to the Visigoths, a banking system did not return until the need arose with the Crusades (1095–1270). Similarly, coins were not minted again until *c.* 561 (Davies 2010, pp. 107–11). An international banking system was subsequently created by the Knights Templar (Martin 2005) but by 1307 the French king, deeply in debt to the order and feeling his position, power and status were challenged, moved swiftly and violently against the order. The secrecy surrounding the order had exacerbated the situation, undermining people's trust in it (Barber 2006).

101 Davies (2010), ch.3.

102 Greif (1997), p. 4. Moore (1985) concentrated on disputes within the system, viewing it as archaic and barbaric rather than practical and functional – a relic of the past that hindered, rather than advanced, trade.

103 Greif (2006), p. 222.

104 Banking, in the modern sense, is traceable to medieval/early Renaissance Italy. Originally 'merchant banks' were set up by Italian grain merchants. Ferguson (2012).

105 France reneged on her debts in 1648/1661, England in 1672, Denmark in 1660 and Spain at various times.

106 First used in the Italian city-states to augment the money supply, these, in so doing, actively augmented social trust. Economic solidarity enabled public loans to be floated – initially they were obligatory but with their growing success quickly became voluntary, and they secured the growth and defence of these city-states. Pezzolo (2005).

107 Compare John Law and the Mississippi Trading Company, which caused the collapse of La Banque Royale in 1720. This financial instability was one of the causes of the French Revolution. Adams (2012).

108 Roseveare (1991), pp. 61–63.

109 Mahoney (2001) highlights how differences in the quality of cross-country legal systems can explain, to an extent, the variations in financial development and economic growth, whereas the 'revolution' in tax collection, 1689–97, increased the British government's revenues substantially, which spread to Europe and America. Fukuyama (2011), ch.27.

110 Brewer (1990) applied the term to Britain, differing from Dickson's (1993) view that success was funded by the national debt, backed by parliament and supported by regular taxation, arguing that only *c.* 30–40 per cent of national debt funded Britain's military campaigns. In 1688 national debt was £1m, by 1698 £15m, by

1750 £78m, by 1770 £131m, by 1790 £244m, by 1801 £456m, and by 1815 £745m. In 1819 it stood at £844m. (Extracted from UK public spending statistics.)

111 The British Royal Navy became the most powerful navy in the world, from the end of the seventeenth century into the twentieth century, thanks, in part, to superior financing, while other powers did not have access to such finance. Rodger's (2005) and Sussman and Yafeh's (2004) writings show a direct correlation between the cost of public debt and the size of the British navy – the risk and uncertainty of war, as one would expect, increased the cost of capital.

112 Daunton (2007), p. 6.

113 Coffee houses were 'places where people gathered to drink coffee, learn the news of the day, and perhaps to meet with other local residents and discuss matters of mutual concern' (Cowan 2005, p. 79).

114 Williams (2009).

115 Huygens published on the subject in 1657.

116 Property insurance dates back to the Great Fire of London (1666) while the first insurance company was established in 1681. Raynes (1948).

117 Early regulations were replaced with a rule book when the first regulated exchange was introduced in 1801. Michie (1999).

118 First developed in China (ninth to fifteenth centuries), it differed from the European system in that it quickly rescinded the redemption promise (it was not underpinned by gold or other assets of value). Before Europe moved to fiat money, China suffered multiple currency debasements and temporarily abandoned paper money in *c.* 1455. Davies (2010), pp. 181, 183.

119 The Bank of Sweden was the first chartered bank in Europe to issue paper banknotes (1661), although goldsmiths' deposit notes had been used for some time as guarantee of payment/proof of funds. Geisst (2006).

120 Bearing the promise 'pay the bearer', it is still in use and legally binding.

121 These paper notes were lighter, reducing the need to check the fineness of commodity monies, which had been time-consuming and bore the risk of fraud. They also reduced the need for strongholds and watchmen. Jevons (1876), ch.16.

122 This notion of trust in, and between, individuals operating a monetary system is also seen in the Hawala system, an informal value transfer system developed in medieval times but still in operation today. See Ballard (2010) for discussion on Hawala scandals and their long-term effects.

123 'In London I have on occasion signed an underwriting agreement for £2,000,000 … without any more than a verbal agreement noted on a piece of paper', Beddington-Behrens remarked in his 1963 memoirs. 'In this small circle we all know and trust each other and every man's word is his bond. While this standard remains, the city will always hold its own.' Quoted in Kynaston (2002), p. 203.

124 Keynes (2011).

125 Drawing from diverse sources, including Shakespeare and Goethe, Marx (1844) was the first to highlight that money was more than a token and method of exchange – it had a life of its own, becoming a symbol of wealth.

126 Lanchester (2012).

127 Fraudulent banknotes, breaches in bank security, failures in regulation.

128 Canetti argues that losing trust in money in Germany, 1922–23, was a significant factor against the Jews (1978), p. 189 (Reichsbanknotes were referred to as Jewish confetti), quoted in Fergusson (1975), p. 106.

129 Keynes (1920), p. 235.

130 The Roman Empire endured repeated debasement – supporting constant warfare, the shortage of precious metals, emperors' overspend and its growing trade deficit in the West, contributing to the ultimate collapse of both Roman Empires. Davies (2010).

131 In response to the Treaty of Versailles' (signed 28 June 1919) war reparations, the Weimar government ran the printing presses. The result was that, in 1922, a loaf of bread cost 163 marks, by September 1923, 1,500,000 marks; and, at its peak in November 1923, 200,000,000,000 marks; bringing with it financial ruin, starvation and death. The hyperinflation experienced destroyed an already fragile government, tainted by revolutionary intent and plagued by infighting. With a new German chancellor, Gustav Stresemann, the 1924 Dawes Plan, and a $200 million American loan, Germany was able to recover. Fergusson (2010).

132 Hanke and Kwok (2009).

133 Golembiewski and McConkie (1975).

134 Shapiro (1987), Deutsch (1973).

135 Gellner (1988), p. 142.

136 Hetherington (1998), Mishler and Rose (2001).

137 Giddens (1984), p. 83.

138 Brown and Uslaner (2002).

139 Barber (1983), Giddens (1984) and Luhmann (1988).

140 Bachmann and Inkpen (2011).

141 'Every kind of peaceful co-operation among men is primarily based on mutual trust and only secondarily on institutions', as Einstein (1950) succinctly puts it.

142 Khodyakov (2007), p. 123. For instance, Levi (1998) defines trust as only existing between individuals, yet individuals and institutions can be trustworthy.

143 Examples include politicians' expenses, bribery and sex scandals, the NSA spying debacle, the 'sexing-up' of the Iraqi WMD dossier, together with the institutionalized racism, sexism and corruption still prevalent in many police forces around the world.

144 Citrin (1974), p. 974.

145 For example, during the banking crisis of 2007–8, trust in bankers plummeted yet societies remained reliant on the banking system. Losing trust in the underlying system would create chaos, similar to the panic of 1930. See Wicker (1996).

146 The distinction lies not in the form but in the degree of governance. See Lippmann (1963), p. 24.

147 Communitarians such as MacIntyre (2007) and Taylor (1992).

148 With a strong caveat, the citizens of a 'new' state/regime retain their past experiences of institutional trust/distrust. Consider post-communist Europe and the former USSR which were based on fear, control and corruption. Hosking (2014). These citizens are generally more distrustful of the state, its institutions, and each other. Shlapentokh (1989).

149 See Inglehart (1997) and for critique Foley and Edwards (1999).

150 Hetherington (1998).

151 Mishler and Rose (2001), pp. 8–9.

152 'Institutions by definition are the more enduring features of social life.' Giddens goes on listing – institutional orders, modes of discourse, political institutions, economic institutions and legal institutions (1984), p. 24 and p. 31 respectively.

153 Eatwell (1997) and Almond and Verba (1989) discuss the ever-expanding role of government (Britain and Europe).

154 Treated as a metaphor for political participation. It is 'a theatre in modern societies in which political participation is enacted through the medium of talk' (Fraser (1990), p. 57) and 'a realm of social life in which public opinion can be formed' (Asen (1999), p. 115). 'The opposite of, and complementary to, the public sphere. It is the social realm of home and family.' The private sphere was traditionally a woman's 'rightful or proper' place, while the public sphere was the domain of men. See Habermas (1992), Heidegger (1962), and Deleuze and Guattari (1994).

155 In Britain, a modern welfare system began with the Old Age Pension Act (1908), National Insurance Act (1911), Employment Act (1934) and National Health Service (1948), with overall government spending increasing from 9.4 per cent of GDP around 1870 to 43 per cent in 1996 (in France from 12.6 per cent to 55 per cent and in Germany from 10 per cent to 49.1 per cent respectively). Tanzi and Schuknecht (2000), p. 6.

156 Belloc (2007), pp. 95–113. Iain MacLeod MP coined the term, referring to 'nanny state' in his column in *The Spectator* (1965), to describe an interfering/ overbearing state that sought to make decisions for its citizens. See Eatwell (1997) and Almond and Verba (1989).

157 Citrin (1974) and Putnam (2000) have charted the extraordinary collapse of political trust, sometimes referred to as 'trust'.

158 Mulgan (2008), p. 227.

159 For example, they are conflated by, amongst others, Williams and Luhmann.

160 See Williams (1988).

161 Aristotle (2009b) defines a virtue as a character trait, not a passion or faculty.

162 Machiavelli, however, writes that leaders should trust wisely and cautiously yet, to ensure their leadership continues unchallenged, they should be perceived as being trustworthy by the wider populace (2007), ch.17. Christie and Geis (1970) first recognized Machiavellianism as a personality trait in leadership, creating an instrument to measure it, yet, as noted by Gunnthorsdottir *et al.*, it is a more useful measure of reciprocity than trusting behaviour (2002), p. 20.

163 See Gambetta's work (1993) investigating the effects of trust within southern Italian villages and the Mafia.

164 Hardin (2004).

165 Hardin (1996), pp. 28–29.

166 Luhmann (1988).

167 Solomon and Flores (1997), p. 53.

168 Festinger's (1957) theory posits that inconsistency between internal beliefs and external information gives rise to psychological discomfort. Chou (2012) and Sher and Lee (2009) have linked it to trust in online retail scenarios.

169 Rotter (1980), Worchel (1979).

170 Jones (1996), p. 7.

171 McKnight and Chervany (2001), p. 42.

172 Barber (1983), p. 166.

173 Lewicki *et al.* (1998), pp. 438–58.

174 Sztompka describes democracy as 'a paradoxical mechanism' (1997), p. 16.

175 'It is the essence of democracy that we *not* trust and *not* have faith in our leaders. Democracy is a system built on distrust … At the heart of all procedural democracy is the idea that we must watch leaders closely, question them sharply and demand to see the documents.' (Parenti (1998), p. 26). Distrust plays a functional role in institutions of democracy. Hart (1978).

176 Bentham asked 'whom should I be wary of, if not the government who wield great power' (quoted in Blind (2007), p. 3) since, as it was later reported, 'power tends to corrupt and absolute power corrupts absolutely. Great men are almost always bad men' (Dalberg-Acton (1907), p. 504). Despite the checks and balances in place in many democracies, the system is nonetheless criticized by the likes of Plato (1992), Machiavelli (2007), Friedman (2002) and Madison (1787) as they rely on the political abilities and understanding of the populace.

177 See Pauley (1997) for an insight into fascism and its policies of indoctrination.

178 Freedman's description better captures the ironic balance of trust and verification (2009), p. 4.

179 On reliance, see Baier (1995) p. 98. On vulnerability, see Lahno (2001) p. 171.

180 A recognizable postal system was in place already in the twelfth century, but the Royal Mail was only set up in 1516. In 1635 Charles I opened it to the public. Use of the postal service became commonplace, yet it only became an offence

to intentionally open or delay the post with the Postal Services Act of 2000. Campbell-Smith (2012).

181 Baier (1995) p. 99.
182 Wright (2010) p. 617. Betrayal is defined as exposing an individual to threat/danger, disclosing a deep confidence/secret or breaking a promise/being disloyal.
183 Lahno (2001) p. 177, and Lewis and Weigert (1985b) p. 971, respectively.
184 Axelrod (1984).
185 Cook *et al.* (2005).
186 The conviction that the earth was flat was promoted in the Victorian Age by such authors as J. W. Draper, A. D. White and W. Irving against an ideological backdrop that struggled with evolution, despite evidence to the contrary. Russell (1997), p. 1.
187 While there are many different definitions of ideology, the consensus is that an ideology is a system of ideas. See Converse (2006), Herbert McClosky (1964) and Mullins in Wilcox (1974).
188 Jost, Ledgerwood and Hardin (2008). Abstract; 'It is mainly in discourse that ideologies are transmitted and meanings and values are learned and taught [...] which in turn also influences how we acquire, learn or change ideologies.' Nahrkhalaji (2007), p. 1.
189 Researchers have found that trust prospers in more homogenous settings where an identification-based trust can flourish – see Kramer and Wei in Tyler *et al.* (1999) and Lewicki and Bunker in Kramer and Tyler (1996) – as shared memberships (when relevant) can reduce individual distinctions and simplify the trusting process. Turner (1987).
190 Solomon and Flores (2003), p. 51.
191 Rousseau *et al.* (1998), p. 395.

Chapter 4

1 'Historically, power has been...' and 'violence; these'.
2 Tilly (2006), p. 159.
3 Goodwin (2001), p. 9.
4 Tilly (2006), Huntington (1973).
5 Arendt (1972).
6 Orwell (2000) part 3, ch.3.
7 Mannheim (1950), p. 46.
8 Foucault (1980b), vol. 1, pp. 92–96.
9 The *sine qua non* of the modern State, as Weber posits, is the monopoly over the legal use of violence, simultaneously constraining and enabling its large-scale use.

Power can, therefore, be exerted by the State through the use of force or violence. Arendt (1965) and Foucault (1977) provide alternative viewpoints.

10 Wartenberg (1990), p. 9.

11 Hosking (2002), p. 6.

12 Diderot (1963), p. 35.

13 Including Bonoma (1976) and McKnight and Chervany (2001). Hosking (2014), p. 25.

14 See Citrin (1974) and Keele (2005) for trust and authority and Möllering (2005) and Das and Teng (1998) for trust and control.

15 Bierstedt (1950), p. 730.

16 Essentially a contentious concept (Lukes (2005b)), this claim is itself contested. Haugaard (2010).

17 Denegri-Knott *et al.* (2006), p. 951.

18 'Consensual or utopian theorists emphasise power-to and its integrational function. Conflict or rationalist theorists highlight power-over and its coercive nature.' Ng and Bradac (1993).

19 'To substitute violence for power can bring victory, but the price is very high.' Arendt (1965), pp. 53–54.

20 Pittacus (650–570 BCE) quoted by Krieger (2002), p. 228.

21 Dahl (1957), p. 201.

22 Weber (2013).

23 As 'every social act is an exercise of power, every social relationship is a power equation, and every social group or system an organisation of power' (Hawley 1963, p. 422). A 'dynamic process, not a static possession that pervades all areas of social life' (Olsen and Marger 1993, p. 1).

24 Hunjan and Pettit (2011), p. 5.

25 Weber (2009a), ch.7.

26 Lips (1991).

27 Foucault saw power as '…a complex strategic situation in a given social setting', involving both constraints and enablers (1980), p. 56. See Lukes (2005) and Gaventa (2003).

28 For example: Julius Caesar had power to compel, his wife had influence to persuade, while the senate had authority derived from the consent to govern. Coleman (2013) and Dahrendorf (1959).

29 For example: when the American colonists questioned British legitimacy, authority was lost; however, power was maintained by force. Similarly, while the Bush administration and European Union had power, their influence in the Middle East was limited, beyond their area of operations.

30 Manz and Gioia (1983), p. 459.

31 Lawler (1976), p. 1248.

32 Tannenbaum (1962), p. 239.

33 Taking power and control as one, Nye (2004) contrasts the notions of 'hard' and 'soft' power, while 'smart' power refers to a combination of the two (Pallaver 2011). It is much debated: Hyman (1987), Ferguson (2012) and Katzenstein (1996).

34 Fiske (1993), p. 624.

35 Weber (2013).

36 Rahim (1989), p. 545.

37 Keltner *et al.* (2003), p. 265.

38 Stereotypically, power was thought to be authority, command and control; it is now recognized as one facet of power. Grimes (1978), p. 724.

39 Weber (2013), p. 53. Weber has three types of authority: traditional, charismatic and legal-rational, while Bocheński (1974) recognizes only two: epistemic and deontic authority. Weber (2009b), p. 324.

40 Buckley (1967), p. 186.

41 Cicero, III, 28.

42 Sennett (1980), p. 18.

43 From the prevailing philosophical standpoint, 'practical' authority consists of the right to rule such that subjects are obligated to obey (Raz 1990), although Ladenson (1980) argues that subjects are under no obligation to obey.

44 Cole (2001), if left unchecked dictatorial authority can develop.

45 Dahrendorf (1959), p. 166.

46 Grimes (1978), pp. 724–25.

47 Barnard (1948), p. 161.

48 Properties include: invested in position, voluntary, requiring subordinates' suspension of judgement, it can only arise in a collective context. Blau and Scott (1962).

49 Gamson (1968).

50 Persuasion, propaganda, brainwashing, leadership, peer pressure and marketing are all forms of social influence.

51 Deutsch and Gerard (1955).

52 In Kelman's (1958) typology, normative influence leads to public compliance, informational influence to private acceptance.

53 Latané's (1981) social impact theory highlights strength, immediacy and numbers. Cialdini's (2009) Weapons of Influence defines six factors affecting the strength of social influence: reciprocity, commitment and consistency, social proof, authority, liking and scarcity.

54 Milgram's 1963 obedience experiments focused on unanimity.

55 Frager's (1970) experiments demonstrated that Japan's collectivist culture resulted in a higher propensity to conform but, when alienated, Japanese students were more susceptible to anti-conformity. Also Milgram (1961) Norway versus France.

56   Gamson (1968).

57   Bush (2011) and Bacharach and Lawler (1980).

58   Eisenstadt (1995) and Bachmann (2001).

59   Belaya *et al.* (2009).

60   Trust is seen positively, but power and control are not always legitimate. Contrast Luhmann (1979) with Giddens (1984).

61   Maslow (1943) and Siegel (2010).

62   Foucault (1980b).

63   Wartenberg (1990), p. 9.

64   Luhmann (1979) and Giddens (1984).

65   Control is a process that regulates, influences and/or determines behaviour. There are two main approaches: (1) formal or behavioural control and (2) informal or social control.

66   Costa and Bijlsma-Frankema (2007).

67   Consensus – Das and Teng (1998) and Bijlsma-Frankema and van de Bunt (2003). There are many contradictory interpretations of how trust and control relate. Anderson and Narus (1990) and Zaheer and Venkatraman (1995).

68   Bachmann (2001), p. v.

69   Dekker (2004) described trust as a social control, and it was viewed as an alternative control mechanism by Gulati (1995), while Tomkins (2001) argues that trust is a reason not to use controls.

70   Conceptualizing trust and control as opposites, inversely related, low trust requires formal control while high trust requires less formal control. Dekker (2004). A view summarized succinctly as 'trust but verify' or 'trust is good but control is better'. Child (2005).

71   As supplementary – Nooteboom (2002). As mutually reinforcing, Inkpen and Currall (1997).

72   Costa and Bijlsma-Frankema (2007) and Möllering (2005).

73   Das and Teng (1998). Dualism, 'the condition or state of being dual or consisting of two parts', for example: man–nature, good–evil, heads–tails on a coin.

74   Das and Teng (2001), p. 276.

75   Möllering has elaborated on his meaning of 'duality' through examples. First, 'to be human a body needs a soul and a soul needs a body', and second, 'a coin needs to have a head side in order to have a tail side and vice versa' (2005), p. 284.

76   Ibid., p. 283.

77   Providing an example, he refers to the Lindner/Lafontaine book deal.

78   Generalized trust is no longer tied to an individual but expected of all concerned (Rothstein and Stolle 2008) and gains a control-like quality as individuals become embedded within it: 'trust is a quintessentially social reality that penetrates not

only individual psyches but also the whole institutional fabric of society'. Lewis and Weigert (1985b), p. 982.

79 Grey and Garsten (2001), p. 233.

80 Sydow and Windeler (2003), p. 75.

81 Siegel (2010).

82 As a driver one has control, but a passenger cedes control.

83 Kriesberg (1992), p. 57.

84 Öberg and Svensson (2010).

85 Hardin (2004).

86 Cook *et al.* (2005) question whether you need to be powerful to be trusted, or whether power drives out trust. Arguably power's inequalities create 'fertile ground for distrust' either 'block[ing] the possibility of trust' or 'imped[ing] the development of trust'. Cook *et al.* (2005), pp. 40–42.

87 Naude and Buttle (2000).

88 Kumar *et al.* (1998).

89 Critical analysts reject the notion of a relationship between power and trust, arguing that trust is simply a particularly sophisticated tool with which to exert power (Bachmann 2001, p. 339) while Nooteboom and Six (2003) describe power/ trust as 'opposites' and 'alternatives'.

90 Belaya *et al.* (2008), p. 3.

91 Bachmann (2001) suggests that exercising power can reduce uncertainty and, therefore, facilitates a leap of faith, while the existence of trust may ease the exertion of power. Ireland and Webb (2007).

92 Oskarsson *et al.* (2009a) highlight that power does not drive out trust; on the contrary, trust increases as power increases. Cook *et al.* (2005) argue that these concepts should be considered simultaneously in any theory of social relations.

93 Bachmann (2001), p. 357.

94 The traditional notion: the more power held the less trust required, while extreme disparities in power can either negate the need for trust or on occasion prevent much-needed trust (North and Weingast 1995). Turner (2005), however, argues that asymmetries of power are not incompatible with trust.

95 Bachmann (2001).

96 Ibid., p. 350.

97 Turner (2005), p. 19.

98 Ibid., p. 15.

99 Alvarez *et al.* (2003) and Lane and Bachmann (1997).

100 Huber *et al.* (2011).

101 Huber and Hurni (2014) used French and Raven's five types of power, dividing trust into two: inter-personal and inter-organizational trust.

102 Ibid., p. 12.

Chapter 5

1 First settled in the fourth millennium, it was mostly ruled by mythical kings. Harding (2007), Gantz (1993). One 'polis' amongst many, each a unique city-state with its own identity, traditions, laws and alliances (>1,000 in the sixth century), Plato described them as being 'like frogs (or ants) about a pond'. Dominated by its ranked citizen classes, it was remarkably diverse. Greek or foreign – all had their defined roles.

2 Aristotle highlighted the inferiority of women, 'based on faulty notions of biology', and slaves, arguing 'some people were by nature bound to be slaves, their souls lacked the rational part that should rule in a human being'. Martin (2000), 15.14, Ober (2009).

3 Siedentop (2014).

4 Underlined why citizens so feared the 'mob': ruled by passions, their actions were without reason, a trait they naturally lacked.

5 Arguably Herodotus and Thucydides represent the Greeks as practical, reasoned political thinkers. Describing at length their thoughts, decisions and actions to enable their readers to understand why they acted as they did within the overall narrative, careful observation and rational prudent assessment run through their texts. See Marincola's (2001) survey of recent literature on both.

6 Widely regarded in modern literature as a 'revolution', debate raged amongst Ancient Greek writers (Goldhill and Osborne (2006), p. 10). Herodotus (6.131.1) regards Cleisthenes's reforms as a revolutionary moment, while Aristotle argues Solon is the crucial figure (1273b36–1274a21). Thucydides does not distinguish between the expulsion of Hippias and the establishment of a new constitution, whereas the council and assembly are the heart of a democratic city for Aristophanes.

7 Ober (1998), p. 19. Herodotus was the first to use the term *demokratia*; although descriptions of democracy were used by major playwrights of the age, the word does not appear (Clarke and Foweraker (2003), p. 200). See Ober (2007) and Sealey (1975) for its origins.

8 For Thompson and Davis the Athenian riots 'read as a collective act of political self-definition', a physical 'manifestation of having come to be "one-mind"' (Ober (1998), p. 50).

9 Aristotle refers to a number of *metastaseis* (revolutions) which the Athenian Constitution (AC) underwent (Ion, Theseus, Draco and Solon) 'from which the beginnings of *demokratia* occurred', noting Cleisthenes's changes were 'more populist than Solon's' (41.2).

10 Numbers of citizens now '…varied between 30,000 and 50,000 out of a total population of around 250,000 to 300,000. There were perhaps 80,000 slaves… Adult male citizens were probably no more than 30% of the total adult population'. Thorley (1996), p. 74.

11 Martin (2000), p. 94.

12 The Macedonians suppressed democracy in 322 BCE although its institutions were later revived.

13 Socrates (philosopher), Herodotus, Thucydides (historians), Aeschylus, Sophocles, Euripides (playwrights) and Hippocrates (physician) all lived and worked in fifth-century BCE Athens.

14 Goldhill and Osborne (2006), p. 10.

15 The earliest recorded use of the word 'revolution' with the meaning of 'great change' dates to *c.* 1450 (OED), while it did not take on the meaning of 'complete overthrow of the established government' until 1600. Harper (2010).

16 Herodotus, 6.131.1.

17 Hansen (1991), Lanni and Vermeule (2013) – see both Aristotle's account which focuses primarily on legal and constitutional matters (Polity of the Athenians 29–32) and Thucydides, 8.67 (Rhodes (1993) pp. 362–415), for a comparison of the two.

18 The people acted spontaneously and independently of any political leader to expel the Spartans – a response, in part, to their occupation and to Isagoras disbanding the governing council, expelling 700 families. Herodotus, 5.72.

19 Aristotle, *Athenaion Politeia* (AP). Initially exiled in 510 BCE for supporting the citizenry – whether this was a matter of expediency rather than a true calling is a matter of some debate (Finley (1977), p. 76, Ober (2009), p. 69) – Cleisthenes was invited to return after the Spartans' expulsion. Aristophanes' *Lysistrata* replays this event.

20 Aristotle states, 'Cleisthenes enacted other new laws in his bid for popular support, among them the law of ostracism.' AP 22.1.

21 Johnstone (2011) notes systems of impersonal trust were often 're-personalized' relationships or supplemented personal trust.

22 Humiliated in 508 BCE, the Spartans and their allies attacked Athens in 506 BCE, but they were soundly defeated by its citizen-soldiers. Blunsom (2013), p. 92 and Herodotus, 5.75.

23 Embedded within honour was the notion always to be first (competition was central to Greek life), superior to the others (Homer, *Iliad*, 6 208), and the pursuit/recognition of honour was a constant goal of the elite. Gallant (1991).

24 There is a strong case for arguing that democracy was a major reason for Athens's extraordinary record of military success – increasing numbers and introducing new ideas, it funded the army and navy, and simultaneously reduced the risk of cultural militarism by rigorously debating war. Pritchard (2015).

25 'Reform designed to break the power of the aristocratic families, by replacing regional loyalties (and factionalism) with pan-Athenian solidarity...preventing the rise of another tyrant.' Blackwell (2003), p. 4.

26 Regarded as a god, *Pistis*, representing trust, honesty, reliability and good faith, is said to have fled back to heaven after escaping from Pandora's box (Theognis, Fragment 1.1135), while the myth of Eros and Psyche represents distrust and betrayal.

27 Herodotus 3.8, 4.172.e, 4.70, 1.74.6.

28 Herodotus, IX 92; Herman (2002); and Foster and Lateiner (2012), pp. 160–62. Note that Herodotus refers to three types of 'oaths'. Specifically, they identified thirteen references to πιστά (*pistis*) – an oath-like pledge or assurance. Unlike oaths (*horkoi*) they do not invoke the gods to bear witness.

29 Describing how the Scyths made oaths by mixing the blood of oath takers with wine before drinking it, and how the Lydias and Medes sealed oaths by cutting their arm and licking the blood of the other, amongst others. Herodotus (1998).

30 Thucydides I, 120, 5.

31 Referred to as *arete*, this notion of excellence was ultimately bound up with the notion of the fulfilment of purpose or function: the act of living up to one's full potential. Aristotle, NE, II vi 15, Hawhee (2002), Jaeger and Highet (1986).

32 The concept of order and unity, of concord, being of one mind together, the Greeks viewed *homonoia* as an absence of factional fighting in their city-states (Mauriac (1949), p. 106). Traditionally it did not apply outside Greek culture, as outsiders were 'barbarians'.

33 Vernant (1984), p. 90.

34 A description applied by Johnstone (2011) and Szendi (2014), p. 2.

35 Pericles' funeral oration (Thucydides ascribes to Cleon) illustrates the focus of trust on the individual (character and reputation). Calling for trust only where it is merited, Cleon's point is that many whom the Athenians trust, at home as well as abroad, are nothing short of traitors (Thucydides, 2.37). Aristotle (Rhetoric) similarly warns against relying on character alone, especially as the main means of persuasion.

36 Antiphon, Speeches, 6.10, '...at today's trial, when they are prosecuting for prosecution to the charge before the court, they are seeking to achieve my downfall with a tissue of lies calculated to bring my public life into disrepute...the prosecutor who refuses to confine himself to the charge before the court...does not so much deserve to be believed as to be disbelieved'.
Isocrates, Speeches 13.5–6, '...what is most ridiculous of all is that they distrust those from whom they are to get this money – they distrust, that is to say, the very men to whom they are about to deliver the science of just dealing – and they require that the fees advanced by their students be entrusted for safe keeping to those who have never been under their instruction, being well advised as to their security, but doing the opposite of what they preach...nothing prevents...from being dishonourable in the matter of contracts. But men who inculcate virtue and sobriety – is it not absurd if they do not trust in their own students before all others?'

37 Demosthenes 56.2.

38 'Civic friendship is constituted according to utility' (Aristotle, EE, 1242a6-
    8). Aristotle, Thucydides and Plato all place trust within a framework of civic
    friendship. Johnstone (2011).

39 Aristotle, NE, VIII.13.

40 Johnstone (2011) explores the systems and practices of 'trust' in Ancient Greek
    society using everyday activities, such as haggling, measuring, keeping track,
    valuing, collaborating, apportioning liability, deciding, as a frame of reference.

41 Defined here as having a reputation worthy of respect and admiration in a group of
    equal peers, honour is of central importance to family and society, as illustrated in
    Homer's *Iliad* and Sophocles' *Antigone*.

42 Gallant (1991), Eisenstadt and Roniger (1984).

43 'Greek recognition of the supremacy of the law…was something the Greeks were
    proud of.' (Guthrie (1969), p. 69). This is illustrated by Herodotus, who comments
    that Demaratus, in Xerxes' court, said '…[the Greeks] are free, but not entirely free.
    For they have a master, and that master is Law, whom they fear even more than
    your subjects do. Whatever this master commands, they do.' (1998), p. 450.

44 Siedentop (2014).

45 Although unknowable, Maine (1861) argued that the first unit of organization was
    the patriarchal family, while Engels (1884) and Morgan (1877) posited that the first
    domestic institution in history was the clan.

46 Bodel and Olyan (2012).

47 The hearth, the heart of the family, was the origin for property rights, held in 'trust'
    by the eldest male heir, with rules of succession.

48 Only the family could worship at their hearth. A new bride who was an 'outsider'
    had to be brought across the threshold into her husband's house, and welcomed
    into the family after first renouncing her family gods. (Llewellyn-Jones (2003),
    p. 173). Similarly, an adopted son was required to make a ritual transition to join
    his new family. (Buxton (2013), p. 203).

49 de Coulanges (1874), p. 42.

50 Ibid., p. 42.

51 Siedentop (2014), p. 21.

52 For example, a debtor lost control of his labour, not his property and, later, those
    ostracized retained ownership of their property. Siedentop (2014).

53 Homer's historical epics, the *Iliad* and the *Odyssey*, attempted to encapsulate a code
    of conduct, based on notions of loyalty and honour within customs of hospitality
    and reciprocity in a partially fictionalized self-image, to create a Greek 'identity'.

54 Aristotle, 1259b1.

55 Deeply connected with everyday life, there was no separation between the public
    and the domestic, the political and the social spheres: a citizen's destiny was
    united with that of the community as a whole and therefore each citizen had to be

active within it. Aristotle famously stated, '...to take no part in the running of the community's affairs is to be either a beast or a god!'

56 These magistrates whose '...appointment to the supreme offices of state went by birth and wealth, and they were had for life, and afterwards for a term of ten years', presided over both the Boule (council) and ecclesia (assembly). The number of Archons changed over time. AC 3.1.

57 This aristocratic council exercised an ill-defined authority, a 'guardianship', by functioning as the High Court of Appeal.

58 By replacing the prevailing system (oral laws and blood feuds) with a written code of law, Draco became the first legislator of Athens. Dynneson (2008), p. 8.

59 de Coulanges highlights the intermingling of government and religion, describing how the practices of divination were used to make key decisions (war!). Similarly marriages, assemblies or justice were not administered on 'unlucky' days (1874), p. 217.

60 For example, an attempted coup by Cyclon. Herodotus Hist 5.71.

61 Explosive population growth, scarcity of arable land, displacement of people and famine exacerbated by crop failures together put increasing pressure on communities, while power struggles amongst the aristocracy repeatedly drew them into conflict as soldiers.

62 Aristotle, P, 2, 1274b, Plutarch, Sol. 17.1 and Aristotle, AP, 4. Socrates and Epicurus were hoplites (citizen-soldiers) who could afford bronze armour and weapons. Gat (2008), Krentz (2002).

63 Plutarch, Sol. 17.7.

64 In a period of normative discourse, Solon's speeches did not have the language of later moral philosophers. Ober (2005b), p. 445.

65 Aristotle, AP, 9.1.

66 Ibid., 7.3.

67 Out of Athens's citizenry, 400 would be chosen to form the Boule based on wealth, not birth, weakening the aristocracy's monopoly of power, meanwhile, democratic juries, an assembly, a council, and officials selected by lots, not votes.

68 Goldhill and Osborne (2006), p. 13.

69 Bellamy (2014), p. 4 – a public life was expected, with society constantly watching and scrutinising behaviour.

70 In 561 BCE, appearing in the Agora (the heart of the city) with a self-inflicted wound, he appealed to the citizenry to protect him. Given his reputation as a hero and 'friend of the people', the assembly granted him fifty bodyguards. Peisistratus used these men to seize the Acropolis and proclaim himself ruler. Aristotle, AC, part 13, Herodotus, Hist, 1.59 and Plutarch, Sol 185.

71 Carrying no ethical censure, the original Greek term merely referred to anyone, good or bad, who obtained executive power in a polis by unconventional means. A tyrant was later defined by Plato and Aristotle, as '...one who rules without law,

looks to his own advantage rather than that of his subjects, and uses extreme and cruel tactics' – against his own people as well as others, reflecting experiences endured under military dictators in the late fifth and fourth centuries BCE.

72 Under Peisistratus' rule, confiscated lands were redistributed; land policies contributed to an effective agricultural system; the uniform silver currency which was issued helped trade; a reliable water supply was provided; roads were built; an efficient and extensive travelling judiciary was instituted; a peaceful foreign policy was pursued, and the arts flourished – Athens benefited and prospered. Thucydides 6.54.6.

73 Herodotus 5.62, Thucydides 6.59.4.

74 Herodotus describes how '…the men from the plain and the men by the sea' were engaged in stasis before Peisistratus' coup '…with the aim of obtaining a tyranny', and he discusses the strife between Cleisthenes and Isagoras. Lintott (2014), pp. 75–76.
'Death thus raged in every shape, and as usually happens at such times, there was no length to which violence did not go, sons were killed by their fathers, and suppliants were dragged from the altar or slain upon it. So bloody was the march of the revolution and the impression which it made…the whole Hellenic world was convulsed.' Thucydides, The Peloponnesian War, 3.81–82. He went on to discuss many other examples in his works.

75 Plato believed that a constant, firmly entrenched code of beliefs could prevent revolution. Aristotle elaborated, concluding that if a culture's basic value system is tenuous (or radically altered), the society will be vulnerable to revolution.

76 When Peisistratus seized power, he banished many aristocrats who opposed him, seized land and distributed it to his supporters.

77 'Words had to change their ordinary meaning and to take those which were now given them. Reckless audacity came to be considered the courage of a loyal ally, prudent hesitation, specious cowardice… Frantic violence became the attribute of manliness, cautious plotting, a justifiable means of self-defence. The advocate of extreme measures was always trustworthy, his opponent a man to be suspected.' Thucydides, The Peloponnesian War, 3.82.

78 Aristophanes' Lysistrata, Euripides' Hecuba, and Sophocles' Oedipus Tyrannos.

79 Stasis originally meant rivalry among the powerful, its meaning changed in the fifth century BCE. Defined by Thucydides as a set of symptoms indicating an internal disturbance in both individuals and states, he provides two accounts: the Plague of Athens (2.47–58) and the effect of the Peloponnesian Wars (3.82–83), Orwin (1988), p. 832 (also compare Plato, Republic, 545a–569c, Aristotle, Politics, 1301a19–1321b3). By the fourth century, stasis came to represent political conflict, a sign of a deeply unhealthy city or deviant political process (Kalimtzis (2000), pp. 6–12), described by Plato as the natural consequence of injustice (Republic, V.470c-d).

80 While Cleisthenes is '...a highly skilled interpreter of statements made in a revolutionary context and of revolutionary action itself' rather than '...the authoritative leader of the revolution', Ober recognizes it was '...Athenian mass action [that] created new political facts' (1996b), p. 52, yet without an embedded framework of trust, this would have failed.

81 As Ober suggests: 'We are all Athenians in this together, we all take part in decisions, and we are all bound to support mutually agreed upon solutions. Active dissent is unacceptable, but he who accepts decisions that are not in his favour remains part of the group' (2009), p. 74.

82 Just as governance and religion were intermingled, so the social and political were intertwined in Ancient Greece.

83 A vicious struggle began when Peithias (a pro-Athenian civic leader) was charged with 'enslaving Corcyra to Athens'. Acquitted, he charged his accusers but they took up arms, killing sixty. In the ensuing chaos the citizenry enlisted the help of slaves, while the oligarchs hired mercenaries. In the disorder and panic '...the Corcyraeans were engaged in butchering those of their fellow-citizens... the crime imputed was that of attempting to put down the democracy [yet] some were slain for private hatred, others by their debtors'. Thucydides, 3.69–3.85.

84 Thucydides, 3.84.2.

85 Socrates (Book 7) summarizes the failures of four types of government: Timocrats neglect their social/civic responsibilities, oligarchs exploit the masses, democrats unjustly expropriate the elites' resources, while wretched tyrants please only themselves.

86 This kyklos (cycle) was first elaborated on in Plato's *Republic* (chs 8–9). In Aristotle's version, set out in *Politics*, the cycle begins with monarchy and ends with anarchy, while Polybius' later version, in *Histories VI*, rotates through three basic and three degenerate forms of government. Accompanied by violence, turmoil and chaos, such cycling was viewed by all as harmful.

87 Ober (1996a, 1996b), Brock (2013).

88 Aristotle, AP, ch. 21.

89 Walker (1926) quoted in Goldhill and Osborne (2006), p. 17.

90 Morgan (1990), p. 148. Similarly, Solon sought the advice of the oracle, who told him, 'Seat yourself now amidships, for you are the pilot of Athens. Grasp the helm fast in your hands, you have many allies in your city'. Refusing the opportunity to become a revolutionary tyrant, Solon and Athens were justly honoured. Fontenrose (1981).

91 Aristotle, AP, ch. 21.

92 Estimates vary but around 30,000 adult male citizens were entitled to vote in the assembly. Numbers fell during the Peloponnesian War. Compare Rothchild (2007) and Ober and Vanderpool (1993).

93 Jealousies were not forgotten but given alternative outlets as Athens flourished. They resurfaced when citizenship was refused to non-Athenians who fought with Thrasybulus. Wolpert (2001).

94 Contrast the Russian system of *krugovaia poruka* (circular surety), understood as 'joint responsibility'. Hosking (2004), p. 70.

95 Johnstone's (2011) anthropological archaeology of the practices of 'trust' in Ancient Greece is written almost without mentioning the word pistis.

96 'Courage true to the party' changed its values during stasis from constructive to destructive. Price (2001), pp. 41–42.

97 Siedentop (2014), p. 22, Scott (2016).

98 This was reflected in the change in focus, over time, from the acropolis (the defensive citadel) to the agora (the meeting place and centre of spiritual, ascetic and political life). Shear (2007).

99 Plato, *Statesman*, 305e. Depicted as idealized versions of themselves, classical art presented the Athenians as uniformly beautiful with a well-drilled sense of community and a powerful sense of their own identity. Public works were statements of political togetherness and Athenian self-confidence; they represented the communal identity of the city-state to one and all. Sooke (2015), Scott (2016).

100 Walsh posits that this metaphor persists in our present-day discussions of the 'social fabric' of society, emphasizing the interrelated, overlapping nature of social relationships based on trust as well as the fragility of such relationships (2012), p. 43.

101 There are no contemporary accounts of Rome's transition to a republic. This period requires bold reconstruction from scraps of pottery and fragments of stone inscriptions. However, by the first century BCE there is a lot of competing evidence to contend with. Constantly being rewritten, first by the Romans themselves, Rome's history is a work in progress.

102 Scott (2016), on the Roman obsession with the gods and their moods, while Rome's structures and rituals can be traced back to King Numa Pompilius (who reigned 715–673 BCE).

103 Compare Sallust's discussions: he longed for *concordia cum certamine* while Cicero dreamt of *otium cum dignitate*, whereas Livy describes the 'moral community' of the republic – noted by Kapust (2011), p. 6.

104 Coined by Tertullian (2005) in the third century BCE, it pejoratively referred to those in his native Carthage who aped Roman culture. It became the shorthand for Roman identity and self-image.

105 A sacred city with a manifest destiny: refer to Virgil's (2014) reimagining of Rome's history, where religion and politics were inseparable and divination was used for every important decision, while decisions were only legal if made on consecrated ground. Regulating religious life, the post of Pontifex Maximus,

'the bridge' between the people and the gods, was a powerful political authority. Montefiore (2013b).

106   As Cicero noted '…We Romans, however, outstrip every people and nation in our piety, sense of religious scruple and our awareness that everything is controlled by the power of the gods'. Temples were built and dedicated following military successes, while victorious generals (dressed as Jupiter) were honoured with victory parades to the forum.

107   Woolf (1994), p. 120, in Virgil's *Aeneid* the celebrated 'foreign' Trojan hero is folded into Rome's founding legend. Virgil (2014).

108   Aristotle, Book IV 1295a–1297a.

109   Polybius (2010).

110   'Revolution' demarcates the end of the Roman Kingdom (753 BCE), the Roman Republic (509 BCE), and the beginning of the Roman Empire (27 BCE). However, unlike the Greeks, the '…Romans did not formulate well-constructed theories either of revolt or good governance, except at the level of ethics'. (Woolf (2002), p. 43). 'Rome's political system may have been uncodified and complex, but there was an architecture of institutions, processes, rules and principles which supported the community that was the *res publica* (the public affair).' Swithinbank (2012), p. 103.

111   The Jewish Revolt (66–70 CE), the slave revolts of 133 and 73 BCE, the town of Tarquini and the Hernici tribal revolts (307 BCE): while threatening peace and stability, such actions were rationalized with ethnic stereotyping (Tacitus (2007), Dio (1914)), plugging the 'gaps in Rome's systematic understanding of revolt patterns'. Woolf (2002), p. 43.

112   Livy's retelling of Lucretia's rape and its effects – people voted to depose the king and banish the royal family. (1.57.6–58).

113   494 BCE was referred to as the *secessio plebis*, a plebeian (commoners') campaign for economic and political rights, and the first recorded strike. The second *secessio plebis* was in 449 BCE, while 287 BCE saw a later threat to secede, which resulted in a new law, Lex Hortensia. It ended the 'conflict of the orders'. (Livy (2006), p. 122) The constitution combined elements of democracy, aristocracy and monarchy in the forms of legislative assemblies, the senate and term-limited consuls. In 494 BCE the plebeians won the right to elect their own officials, while changes in 449 BCE ensured acts of the plebeian council became law, and in 287 BCE the Hortensian Law was passed. Abbott (1901) pp. 28, 51, 52. Comparable to the Greeks, these early revolutions were notable for improving the well-being of the community as a whole. Romans put the republic and its security ahead of personal considerations. Cowell (1962), p. 213.

114   The title of Syme's (1939) influential study.

115   Syme describes how the success of Octavianus's revolution lay in his ability to masquerade his authority as part of the greater republican ideals, and while the

constitution remained intact, control of its institutions lay in the hands of the few (1963).

116 The Roman notion of morality was dictated by what those governing deemed to be right or wrong. Aristotle, Book V 1302a34.

117 Siedentop (2014), p. 54.

118 It combined different elements of other systems of governance – the burgeoning Greek democracy and Spartan aristocracy.

119 An historical legend, there are no contemporary sources, but Livy (1, 57–60) and Dionysius (I–IV) note the rape and its impact.

120 This stood in stark contrast to the Greeks' notion of a community. Scott (2016).

121 A commission of ten men was appointed (455 BCE) to codify the law, binding on both parties, that magistrates would enforce impartially. It formed the centrepiece of Rome's constitution and the core of the *mos maiorum* (custom of the ancestors). Livy III 34.

122 From the dual power of its two elected consuls to the compromise needed to establish both the senate and *plebian* assembly (it could not debate, only vote to accept/reject motions), as described by Cicero 239–41, Polybius 132–5, Byrd (1995) and Lintott (1999).

123 Compare the Foedus Cassianum (493–358 BCE) of the Latin city-states (Dionysius I, Cornell (1995)) with the voluntary Delian League under Athens. It quickly suffered from defections, arrears of tributes and vessels, and failure of service, as described by Thucydides (I.99).

124 Madden (2008).

125 Meyer (2004) – business and law, Barlow (1978) – financial systems. Berger's definition of *bona fides*, 1968 p. 374.

126 Cicero, in *De Officiis*, describes *fides* as a fundamental virtue, referring to it in relation to a man of good conscious duty towards others (3.22), the greatest duty is to serve the state (1.72) and reliability of one's words as the foundation of justice (1.23). However, this idealistic work represents a view of what should be, rather than what was.

127 Perley (2012) highlights the importance of *fides* in personal relationships and international relations.

128 Virtue (*virtus*) is defined here as 'acting like a man', rather than the virtue described by Aristotle which was rediscovered in the medieval period and fused with Christianity by Thomas Aquinas. Derived from *vir*, meaning 'man', it carries connotations of valour, manliness, excellence, courage, character and worth. McDonnell (2006).

129 Perley (2012), p. 16.

130 Cicero, *De Officiis* 1, 40.

131 Ibid., 1, 23.

132 Wood (1998), p. 146.

133 Although Polybius (20, 9–10) is best known for the notion that Greeks and Romans held sharply divergent understandings of trust, Gruen (1982) argues they are quite compatible in diplomacy.

134 Weltecke (2008), pp. 388–89.

135 'The fount of the Auspices on which the relationship of the city with the gods rested', it dominated Rome. Beard *et al.* (1998), p. 59.

136 With Rome's decisive victory in the Latin Wars (341–338 BCE), territories were annexed or given satellite status. Cornell (1995).

137 In contrast, the 'gift' of citizenship was a rare event in Ancient Greece. Passion is one example. Davies (1971), pp. 428–29.

138 Contemporary questions raised (the senatorial debates of Caesar's genocide in Gaul) and court records (the trial of the governor Gaius Verres) highlight the consideration given to the nature of Rome's governorship of conquered and incorporated territories.

139 Debated amongst Romans (Tacitus: 'They make a desert and call it peace'), as it is today. Mattingly (2011), also see Monty Python, *Life of Brian*, 'What have the Romans ever done for us?'

140 From a sacred village to a holy city filled with a multi-national pantheon of deities. Montefiore (2013b).

141 Beard (2015), ch.9.

142 In changing his name, he evocated the favour of the gods, recalled the auspices that founded Rome and reaffirmed the link to his murdered uncle, who was declared a god by the senate. Contemporary Romans and historians have puzzled over Octavius' transformation.

143 Res Gestae states gifts of over 100 million sesterces were made in the Capitol, while he restored street corner shrines to lares and penates, emphasizing the link between state, neighbourhood and family. Davies and Swain (2010), p. 320. In 12 BCE Augustus took the role of Pontifex Maximus (Horace, *Odes* 4.5.29–36).

144 He revived old Roman values and the nationalistic ideals of the Roman populous. Appearing to put Rome first, he stopped corruption and self-interest, re-sanctifying Rome, restoring the gods' favour.

145 Dissent within the Senate between the Optimates and Populares, and within the Plebeian Assembly, the need for, and obstruction to, land reforms, together with an evolving economy from land-based to money-based, led to growing tension and confrontation.

146 Beard (2015).

147 Stocks (2015). It was '…used by Vespasian and his sons…terms to cement the new regime by anchoring it to an Augustan past and by demonstrating that Rome was now on a good-faith footing after an extreme period of civil strife'.

148 Attested to in Ennius' verses and Cato's oratory (Cicero, *De Officiis* 3.104), examples can be found in works by Livy and Polybius.

149 Gruen (1982), Perley (2012) and Barry (2005).

150 Hamberg (1945) established this link.

151 Morgan (2015b), p. 84, Mattingly (1948), p. 4 and De Blois (1976), p. 101. Peoples benefiting from Rome's *fides* are included on Augustus' funeral inscription (Cooley 2009), while thirteen inscriptions to patrons/non-patrons are referenced by Forbis (1996), p. 63.

152 Characters in Plautus' *Captivi* appeal to the goddess *fides*. Franko (1995), p. 155, Virgil's *Aeneid* (2014) demonstrate the effects of a lack of trust.

153 Radboud University's conference Fides in Roman (Flavian) literature.

154 Theorizing *fides*, in surviving republican prose combines profound and sincere frankness, honesty and candour in all public affairs as a matter of honour; conspicuous fidelity to inherited fundamentals of all kinds; and the perceived capacity to act effectively with regards to all honourable commitments. Barry (2005), pp. 21–22.

155 Caesar wrote *Bellum Civile* to justify his actions to a politically astute audience. Barry (2005).

156 Compared to the Greeks and Carthaginians.

157 Regulus' negotiations with the Spartans (Cicero, 3, 99–100) and Camillus' handling of the siege of Falerii. (Livy, 5.28.1).

158 In *Captivi* Plautus explored the idea of reputation, while Caesar used his book to enhance his reputation and win over the Senate.

159 Bernstein highlights Domitian's preference for coins displaying *fides*. (2008), p. 156.

160 Beginning with Diocletian (284 CE), this despotic phase ended with the Western Empire (476 CE) and autocratic-absolutism in the East.

161 de Wilde (2011), p. 466.

162 Trusted by its allies to defend their security, not to oppress or violate their rights, no one wished to destroy it. Madden (2008).

163 Sharply divided, only 5 per cent belonged to the senatorial, equestrian and Decurion classes – they ruled, while others followed.

164 After Octavius, standing professional armies were no longer loyal to local generals/political elites but dedicated to the emperor's will – renewing their voluntary oath of allegiance annually. Foulkes (2005).

165 In contrast, while Todd posits that politics and law in Athens were indistinguishable, they were more at ease merging them (1993), p. 29.

166 Sallust (86–c. 35 BCE) looked negatively upon the expansion of citizenship, with all its rights, privileges and duties, arguing that it caused internal dissension, disputes with Rome's Italian allies, slave revolts and riots.

167 The use of *fides* by playwrights Plautus and Catullus implied that the audience implicitly understood the concept. Perley (2012), pp. 7–19.

168 Livy (2012) and Virgil (2014) address traditional Roman values/social norms, separating moral and immoral behaviour.

169 It controlled over one fifth of the earth's population (>25 nations today). Won by force, it relied on co-operation to govern, encouraging the conquered to partake in the glory and wealth of Rome. Some civilizations were honoured by Rome, which incorporated them within the Empire. These were the lucky ones, who benefited from an efficient legal system and stable administration. For others, it meant slavery and destruction.

170 Johnston (2007), pp. 98–111.

171 Siedentop (2014), p. 53.

172 'There were two exceptions. No cult would be authorised which was…"hostile" to the state, nor any which was itself exclusive of all others.' Hughes (1948), p. 157.

173 Livy, regarding the Baccanals (2012), states it was due to the fact that '…there was nothing wicked, nothing flagitious, that had not been practised among them', while Pliny (1991) wrote of the Druids, '…it is beyond calculation how great is the debt owed to the Romans, who swept away the monstrous rites, in which to kill a man was the highest religious duty and for him to be eaten a passport to health', whereas Suetonis (2004) comments more ambiguously that it was '…because the Jews at Rome caused continuous disturbances at the instigation of Chrestus that he [Claudius] expelled them from the city'. Hughes argues that the general tolerance shown to other religions did not extend to those seen as hostile to the 'state', claiming exclusive rights to religious beliefs and practice (1948), ch.6.

174 Paraphrasing Tertullian, '…the blood of martyrs is the seed of the Christian Church' (1890), p. 143, implying that the martyrs' willingness to sacrifice their lives led to the religious conversion of others. Salisbury (2004), Frend (2008).

175 The Christian message of moral equality (no distinction in the eyes of God) was diffused by St Paul. Yet ideas of hierarchy and inequality remained central to Roman civilization and, indeed, Church structure, incorporating the Ancients' natural order of things.
    Kahan characterizes Christian charity as being '…different in kind from the generosity praised in the classical tradition', for, while '…absorb[ing] those Greco-Roman attitudes towards money that complemented its own…never before had any god been conceived of as poor' (2010), pp. 42, 44. Contrast this with the views of Seneca, the Cynics and Socrates. Perrotta (2004), p. 44.

176 Siedentop (2014).

177 Promulgated by Judaism's story of creation, it spread through Christianity. Richet (2007).

178 Cahill (2010).

179 Weltecke (2008), p. 389.

180 The notion of morality embedded within the concept of *fides* had changed: no longer a collection of principles dictated by the Empire and its political elite,

it embodied Christian teachings and values (such as humility, charity and equality).

181 Latourette described Diocletian's abdication in 305 CE, '...none of the contestants [for emperor] could avoid the religious issue, and each had his own policy' (1937), p. 155.

182 Pax deorum – the 'peace of the gods'. Jones (1978), p. 250.

183 Santangelo (2013), p. 16.

184 Cicero, http://searchworks.stanford.edu/view/7600020, 2 February 2014.

185 Lactantius (1984) and Eusebius (1964) provide contemporary accounts. There is little doubt about his 'conversion'; debate revolves around his motivation. Jones (1978), p. 73, Flick (1959), p. 117.

186 Eusebius (1964) notes that these were Licinius' pro-Christian policies. They '... marked a revolution in the relation of the Church to the Empire, for each made a conquest of the other'. Flick (1959), p. 293.

187 Blair (2007), p. 102.

188 Controversy still surrounds the events at Milan. Latourette (1937), pp. 18–160.

189 Flick (1959), p. 119.

190 Frend (1984), p. 505.

191 Ibid., p. 212.

192 Pragmatic philosophy dictated the 'good life' (Belliotti 2009) for Romans, until Christianity taught that life on earth was temporary, merely a preparation for one's eternal life. It required a 'religiously' moral life.

Chapter 6

1 'Feudalism' was first used in a French legal treaty (1614); it has no commonly accepted definition. Compare Ganshof (1952) and Bloch's (1961) definitions. Manoralism is an essential element of feudalism, originating in the Roman villas of the late Roman Empire; these bipartite estates (see Verhulst) '...emerged out of the social, political, and agrarian conditions specific to several regions of the early Middle Ages'. McCormick (2001), p. 7.

2 Still contested, '...there is now widespread agreement that of all the medieval European actors it is monarchy that was the immediate predecessor of the contemporary state'. Glenn (2013), p. 32 and Sueur (2007), p. 23.

3 In England, Magna Carta (1215) attempted to limit the powers of the monarch while confirming the rights and privileges of free men. It created an assembly to grant taxes and lay the foundations for a parliament and legal system. Starkey (2015).

4 Loyn (1989).

5   Pennington (1992).

6   Duby's (1978) totalizing argument provides an explanation for all the elements
    associated with the medieval period. A dominant theory for many years, it has
    become increasingly controversial. Compare West (2013) and Barthelemy and
    White (1996) for contrasting positions.

7   Moore (2000), p. 2 and Southern (1953), p. 15, respectively.

8   Note that a similar feudal system existed in China under the Zhou Dynasty
    (eleventh century to 256 BCE) while feudalism in Japan began in 1192 CE and
    ended in the nineteenth century.

9   Anderson (1996), p. 128, reiterates the same thesis as Marx and Engels (1975), ch.8.

10 Moore (2000), pp. 2–3 and p. 6 respectively.

11 Barthelemy and White's theory (1996) is legal and anthropological in nature; see
    the Annales School.

12 The Hundred Years' War (1337–1453) left a legacy of rapid military evolution
    and strong nationalistic sentiment, while recovery of the lost lands in France long
    remained a wishful national aspiration. Allmand (1988).

13 This schism caused a split within the Roman Catholic Church. Political rather than
    theological, it was resolved by the Council of Constance (1414–18). Smith (1970).
    Scotus and Ockham objected to the application of reason to faith, arguing that
    reason operates independently of faith and that it allowed science to be separated
    from theology and philosophy. Davies (1996), pp. 433–34.

14 Hudson (1988) and Fudge (2010), respectively.

15 Using modern economic concepts, Lopez (1976) explains that it is an
    underdeveloped economic system which gave birth to Europe's commercial
    revolution. It '...set the stage for modern Europe's exploration and colonisation
    of the world, and its institutional and political development on the path toward
    modern growth'. Cantoni and Yuchtman (2014), p. 823.

16 Freeman (2013) TeBrake (1993) and Sizer (2008).

17 For example, with Alfonso X's *siete partidas* laws (mid-thirteenth-century Castile),
    the king was responsible, not just to God but to the people, who were to watch over
    him, and for preventing damage to the kingdom, and for resisting those who ill
    advised him.

18 The best example, the *Leges Anglorum Londoniis collectae* refers to 'by common
    counsel' while free men are '...as if sworn brothers for the utility of the kingdom',
    presented as accepted law and supported by a weight of ancient precedent.

19 Langland (1999).

20 Valente (2003) stressed the legitimacy of rebellion by outlining the right of feudal
    defiance (*diffidato*), together with customary distinctions in Roman law between
    kingship and tyranny.

21 Altamira (1917), pp. 227–43, Madden (1930), pp. 167–69 and Holt (1972), pp. 128–30.

22   Valente (2003).

23   Contemporary chroniclers (eleventh and twelfth centuries) divided society
     into *oratores*: those who pray (clergy), *bellatores*: those who fight (nobility) and
     laborares: those who work – with all three participating in government.

24   In Germany (1336–1525) there were over 60 incidences of militant peasant unrest.
     Blickle and Catt (1979).

25   Lantschner (2009), p. 290.

26   Neither Froissart (1967) nor Knighton (1995), in their contemporary descriptions
     of the events of 1381, used the term 'revolution', while Walsingham's commentary
     focused on the terror of the social unrest (2003), section 4, part 3. Instead
     Froissart's Chronicles include 55 references to 'revolt', 215 of 'rebellion', 10 of
     'uprising' and 3 of 'insurrection'.

27   Spencer (2013), p. 12.

28   Ibid., p. 94.

29   Sizer (2008), p. 57.

30   Freedman (1998), pp. 171–88.

31   Sizer (2008), p. 61.

32   A reference to the specific late-medieval forms of history-writing. Much research
     has been conducted into studying how official chronicles proposed proto-national
     ideologies and spread monarchic/dynastic propaganda – the untruthfulness of
     historiographical works.

33   Zagorin notes, 'It was not until the end of the nineteenth and twentieth centuries,
     however, that revolution became one of the supreme and central preoccupations of
     historiography' (1973), p. 24.

34   Lewis (2013).

35   Valente (2003).

36   Brown (2011), p. 2.

37   Sizer (2008).

38   Oaths in the middle ages can be divided into four major categories: for testimony/
     proof in a trial; of fidelity; of peace or for a Landfriede; and coronations.

39   In England alone, from the thirteenth to fifteenth centuries, ten kings faced serious
     rebellion, eight of whom were captured, deposed and/or murdered.

40   Inherited from the Romans, the goddess represented life's capriciousness, bringing
     both good and bad luck. Arya (2002). Three mental attitudes to *fortuna* persisted:
     as an independent ruling power for pagans; as the attitude of compromise and
     power-sharing illustrated by Boethius; and, within Christian belief, as a servant of
     God. Patch (1927).

41   Fortune was becoming increasingly tied to reconciling the moral/religious world
     with the ever-expanding importance of the mercantile world. Lehtonen (1995),
     p. 73. This required ever more creativity, 'understanding and explanations' from

scholastics, due to the complexity of the secular system of commerce and politics. Sizer (2008).

42   Medieval England was tri-lingual with Middle English, Anglo-Norman and Latin in use. Writers made choices, sometimes explaining them (Speculum Vitae), but often used more than one in the same document. Haines (2010) and Yeager (2010) explore Gower, a medieval tri-lingual poet, and the use and applications of these three.

43   For example, the widespread use of the phrase '*Fides servanda est*' (trust is preserved) – meaning that, in the execution of treaty or contract, each party must act in good faith towards the other.

44   Weijers' (1977) work on *fides* and related words in Medieval Latin.

45   Turold's Song of Roland (*c.* 1115), de Troyes's Lancelot (*c.* 1175), Monmouth's Arthurian legend (1136). Reemtsma notes how poetry explores 'different ways in which social trust is articulated – bound by personal rights and obligations' (2012), p. 43.

46   Reynolds (2007), p. 3.

47   Augustine's teaching contributed to the medieval orthodoxy that God intended there to be social inequality on earth, rationalizing the realities of actual social, economic and political inequality, while concurrently justifying the aristocracy and offering solace to the peasantry. Freedman (1999), Siedentop (2014).

48   Beneficial, as Henry I's doctor said, 'A king is like a fire: if you are too close, you burn, if you are too far away, you freeze'.

49   Failure to fulfil lordly (or kingly) obligations justified renouncement of homage and fealty, known as *diffidato* (defiance). Kern (1948), pp. 121–22. Strickland (1994) questions its legitimacy; however, the Fouke romance (*c.* 1260–80) confirms its widespread acceptance as legitimate and heroic.

50   A 'feudal pyramid' in strict order. Thomas (2008), pp. 71–72.

51   As per Tilly's description of pre-modern revolts, before the thirteenth century they were typically 'localised, uncoordinated, dependent on the normal rhythms of congregations like marketing, church-going or harvesting' (1972), p. 199. They centred on unfulfilled feudal responsibilities, competing claims of authority, the Church's materialism and excessive demands/taxes for the Crusades.

52   An important theme in medieval public life, expressed in art and literature, the beliefs and procedures of burial were complex, often requiring the mutual support of the wider community. Daniell (1997).

53   Carpenter (2015).

54   Members of the community would walk the boundaries of the parish, usually led by the priest and church officials, to share the knowledge of where they lay and to pray for protection and blessings for their lands.

55   In addition, Ayton and Price (1998) posit that war was a major engine of early state development, requiring ever higher taxes to fund military campaigns, in order to protect the realm from attack.

56 It is widely accepted that the Masonic fraternity emerged from the stonemasons' guilds during the Middle Ages; however, early Masonic texts such as the *Regius* poem (1390–1425) trace the craft history back to Euclid in Egypt. Speth (1889), vol. 1, pp. vi–vii.

57 Reynolds (1984), pp. 77–78.

58 Explains why the formal name of the Drapers' Company remains the 'Brethren and Sisters of the Fraternity of the Blessed Virgin Mary', the Guild of Tailors is the Fraternity of St John the Baptist, the Goldsmiths Company is the Fraternity of St Dunstan. Pooley (1947), pp. 8–12.

59 Thrupp writes, '…in addition to the regulations governing their craft, guilds were benevolent and religious societies with rules covering provisions for mutual aid, the arbitration of disputes, and the procuring of spiritual benefits' (1989), p. 19.

60 Should 'trust' be broken, penalties were harsh. Mielke (2005) outlines the issues of trust in Italian city-states during the period.

61 Byrne (2004), p. 479.

62 Reynolds (1984), p. 152.

63 The secular and the religious were reluctant to outlaw or excommunicate. This was only applied to the most obstinate and persistent offenders, when the normal legal processes had failed. Oakley (1923), p. 163.

64 As outlined in King Aethelred's laws (VI, 7), used to draw a line between acceptable and unacceptable social behaviour.

65 Excluded from the wergild system, they accounted for 10 per cent of the population detailed in the Domesday Book. (Pelteret (1985), p. 122) – integral, yet excluded from society's basic privileges.

66 Brady (2013) argues that the medieval poem 'The Fortunes of Men' depicts the culpability of human society, which is fundamentally accountable for these deaths, occurring in isolation, brought about by expulsion from society.

67 Riddiford (2008).

68 Rigby (2008), for example, drawn directly from medieval literature.

69 Reynolds (1984), p. 332.

70 Siedentop (2014).

71 References to risk, related to *fortuna* not trade, were first seen centuries later in Battaglia's Dictionary and Du Cange's Glossary, in reference to the medieval period.

72 Watts (2009).

73 Ho (2003).

74 Davies and Fouracre (1986), pp. 14–22, 113.

75 Roman law was first resurrected in Bologna in the eleventh century. Its doctrines provided medieval jurists with a sophisticated model for contracts, procedural rules, family law, testaments and a strong monarchical constitutional system. Pennington (1992), p. 334.

76   Although determining cases and deciding culpability typically relied on 'oath-takers', biased accounts were more often the result of prejudice than perjury, as the fear of facing God's wrath was deep and genuine. Stern (2004), p. 621.

77   'They were the record and statement of *villein* status, servile dues, and labour obligations that the insurgents sought to eradicate' (Emery (1996), p. 15). Burning these records was a symbolic gesture, a way of securing their future. Barker (2014), ch.16.

78   Neville notes that Scottish medieval 'records are redolent of the language of friendship' and 'quite consciously imbued them with the multi-layered meaning of friendship' (2010 p. 191), while Alfonso X's *Siete Partidas* includes an entire title on friendship (in Book IV). Contemporary documents are now used to analyse and track such friendships. Knobbe *et al.* (2014).

79   Scorpo (2014).

80   Harriss (1993), p. 37.

81   White (1933).

82   Embodying major changes: to recruitment, organization and foot soldiers' pay in the rapidly expanding armies of the day. Keen (1999), p. 148.

83   Notably coincided with thirty widespread conflicts between nobles and the king between 1215 and 1415. Valente (2003).

84   Younger sons deprived of landed inheritance had to find their place in society – as knights, the new urban elite or serving in the rapidly developing ecclesiastical or secular administrative bureaucracies. Moore (2000).

85   Under the influence of Cluny monks in the twelfth century, a social and ethical dimension is added to the profession, giving moral impetus to the Crusades. They espoused theories of the 'just' war, creating the 'knights of Christ' (*miles Christi*). Medieval literature provided guides, glorifying and critiquing a knight's behaviour. Saladin, Godfrey of Bouillon, William Marshal and Bertrand du Guesclin all demonstrated knightly behaviour. They differed from mercenaries, bands of paid foot soldiers, noted for their lawlessness – they quickly fell from favour in the thirteenth century. Mallett (1999).

86   Although nobles wanted to feel that they voluntarily pledged their oath of allegiance, they were bound by custom and the wider community. Reynolds (2012), IX, pp. 92–93.

87   Examples include the Peasants' Revolt (1381) and the Jack Cade Rebellion (1450).

88   Drawn from Roman law, it dominated the fourteenth century, but never prevailed in England. Post (1964), pp. 310–32.

89   Compare John Salisbury's (1259) *Policraticus*, together with other 'mirrors of princes' literature, such as Marsilius' (1324) *Defensor pacis*, in which he calls for an elected monarch, and Ockham in his defence of secular states against clerical pretensions.

90 Reinforced by the '...assumption that good order required good government, and that good and lawful government meant consultation and collective judgement in accordance with [accepted] custom, as well as on the due obedience of subordinates to those placed over them'. Reynolds (2012), XVI, p. 16.

91 First recorded in the late eleventh century, medieval communes took many forms and varied widely in organization and make-up from real city-states, based on partial democracy in parts of Italy, to free cities independent of local nobility in Germany.

92 Seen as violent and often guilty of sin. See Sizer (2008), p. 220, the fear of 'the mob'.

93 Greif (2006) outlines the history and development of guilds, although he presents opposing views as to the influence of merchant guilds on economic growth.

94 Carpenter (2000) and Reynolds (2012).

95 From urban rebellions in Ghent and Bruges (1280), the Ciompi Revolt (1378–82), to the Harelle and Maillotins Revolts (1382).

96 While they were not granted full sovereignty, they were given immunity from many royal and feudal impositions. They were also exempted from feudal service and royal taxes, except those agreed in advance.

97 Such oaths bound the citizens of a commune to respect each other's liberties, to defend, protect and assist while promoting their common interests. For example, a twelfth-century Flemish charter prescribed 'let each help the other like a brother'.

98 Siedentop (2014), p. 272.

99 Kuran (2005) notes that medieval Islamic cities were never founded as autonomous legal entities.

100 Berman (1983), pp. 357–403. Arguably these charters, later, became one source of modern social contract theory.

101 The sense of equality, however, should not be overstated: individuals within the communes were differentiated by wealth, power and status. The poor, unskilled, most immigrants and women were excluded from the guilds and houses, while every merchant and artisan acknowledged that they were still socially inferior, submissive to royalty/nobility and prevented from holding key roles in public life.

102 Reynolds (2012), XVI, p. 12.

103 Guenee (1981), p. 76. Alternative forms of governance, explicitly oligarchy and democracy, were only considered after the re-emergence of Aristotle's Politics in the mid-thirteenth century.

104 Reynolds (2012), IX, p. 92.

105 Arrighi (2007) has stated that rebellions were as prevalent then as industrial strikes post-1945.

106 The Mapping History (University of Oregon) Project traces the shifting pattern of urban and rural unrest throughout Western Europe (1300–1800).
107 Dumolyn and Haemers (2005).
108 Goodman (1995), pp. 260–61.
109 Walshingham, II 1–4, translation in Dobson (2008), p. 243.
110 Froissart (1967).
111 Barker's (2014) book explores the lives of the individuals involved using tax records, court proceedings and other source documentation.
112 Although John Ball's sermons promoted equality among all, irrespective of social class, Walshingham attributed the demand for the abolition of the *villein* to Wat Tyler. This revolutionary demand, which would have transformed English medieval society, sat alongside the 1381 rebels' more concrete demands, including the abolition of the unjust poll tax.
113 Knighton, translated in Dobson (2008), p. 184.
114 Petrarch, in the 1330s, was the first to suggest that European culture had stagnated since the fall of Rome, underlining Renaissance scholars' belief that they lived in a new age (Mommsen, 1942). Bruni and Biondo later divided history into Ancient, Medieval and Modern (Rudolph (2006), p. 4), while the term 'Middle Ages' was first recorded in 1604. Albrow (1997), p. 205.
115 Refer to the virulently anti-Catholicism, Lutheran ecclesiastical history of the Magdeburg centuries.
116 Such as Pre-Raphaelite paintings, including Waterhouse's Rainsblood, Millais' Ophelia, Rossetti's The Blue Closet. Also see Pugin and Viollet-le-Duc's revival and restoration of Gothic architecture, William Blake's poetry (1908), Walter Scott's *Ivanhoe*, together with translations of medieval nationalistic stories into the vernacular (*The Lay of Cid, The Song of Roland, Beowulf*) and the designs, work and ideas of William Morris.
117 Moore (2000), p. 172.
118 Lopez (1976), Ayton and Price (1998), Grant (1996) and LePan (1996), respectively. There is continuing disagreement but nevertheless a general agreement that transformative change took place during this period.

Chapter 7

1   Michelet (1855), 7, pp. ii–iii.
2   From the frequent 'revolutions' endured by the Florentines, to the Dutch Revolt against Spain (1560s), then later the English Revolution (1640s) and the Glorious Revolution (1688–9). Goldstone (2014).
3   Melve (2006), p. 243.

4   Duhem quoted in Lindberg (1990), p. 14 (The Continuity Thesis).

5   Hobson (2004), Ghazanfar (2000).

6   Castiglione's (1528) *The Courtier* was a definitive account of Renaissance courtier.

7   Burckhardt (1944), pp. 81–82.

8   Elite, educated, honourable and dynamic, such men celebrated life. Heller (2015), p. 24.

9   Gardner *et al.* (1970), pp. 450–56.

10 Heller (2015), pp. 3–4.

11 Brucker (2008), p. 26.

12 Rosser (2011), p. 1.

13 Burke (1998).

14 Compare Starn, who argues 'rather than a period with definitive beginnings and endings and consistent content in between, [it is] a network of diverse, sometimes converging, sometimes conflicting cultures, not a single, time-bound culture' (1998), pp. 122–24.

15 Referring to the 'rebirth' of classical Greek/Roman humanism, it was preceded by the Carolingian (ninth-century), the Ottonian (tenth-century) and the twelfth-century renaissance of the High Middle Ages.

16 Caferro (2011) synthesizes the major debates.

17 Burckhardt (1944) envisions Renaissance Italy as the birthplace of modern individualism, political calculation, science and scepticism: a vision of modernity, but a dark and haunted one.

18 Bruni (1442), Vasari (1550).

19 Manetti (1452), quoted in Gelder (1961).

20 Described by de Saxoferrato (1313–57) as '*civitas se superioerum non recognoscens*' (independent of feudal subjugation), sovereignty was its distinguishing feature. Epstein (1999), p. 2.

21 Najemy (2004), p. 4.

22 Jurdjevic (2004), p. 602.

23 However, our understanding of these early communes is coloured by the 'ex post facto elaborations of subsequent centuries, when jurists, chroniclers, and local historians fabricated the ideological foundations of their town's civic identity in order to reinforce community cohesion'. Muir (1999), p. 380, contrasted with Lansing (1991).

24 Honour resulted in tireless vendettas: 'Men do injury through either fear or hate … such injury produces more fear, fear seeks for defence, for defence partisans are obtained, from partisans arises parties in states, from parties their ruin.' Machiavelli (2007), ch.7.

25 Brucker (1999), p. 27.

26 Banfield's (1958) theory.

27   The Albizzi family first held sway after the Revolt of the Ciompi (1378), followed by the Medicis.

28   To be a citizen of Florence, eligible for voting required guild membership and permanent residence: it was open to abuse.

29   In Venice various laws were enacted to reduce factional alliances (prohibiting insignias, limiting numbers of dinner guests and godparents). Ruggiero (1978).

30   Often founding families of urban communes, patricians became a defined class of governing elites. Lists were maintained – the most famous, *Libro d'Oro*, is still published privately today. See www.collegio-araldico.it/librodoro.html.

31   The Venetians were particularly effective in imbuing loyalty into those excluded. Mackenney (1987) and Davis (2009).

32   Weissman (1982) surveyed the prevalence of distrustful Florentine social relations.

33   Najemy (1982) and Dowlen (2008) detail electoral strategies involving chance.

34   Compare Della Mirandola (1996), who glorifies humanity and man's reason, with Shakespeare's *Hamlet* (2001) and Montaigne (1992).

35   Jurdjevic (2004).

36   Najemy (1982) highlights changes to the rules for eligibility, nomination and voting during the period.

37   Padgett (2001) has modelled Florentine republicanism.

38   Milner (2011), p. 42.

39   A negative notion of freedom (absence of domination or mastery), it differs from the Ancient Greeks. Skinner (1998).

40   Machiavelli (2007).

41   King (1986), p. 92.

42   Ricciardelli (2012).

43   The cradle of humanism (Najemy (2004), p. 31), the ideology formulated for its Florentine citizenry exalted the civic virtue of participation in public affairs, the concept of an 'active life', as opposed to the contemplative life of ascetics and scholars. Bloom (2004), p. 27. A pervasive mode of culture, it placed man at the centre. Critical of the Church but not Christianity, humanist mentality stood midway between medieval supernaturalism and modern scientific/critical attitudes. Kreis (2012).

44   Hyde (1972), Villani (2011) and Machiavelli (2007).

45   Compagni (1986), p. 22, Dante (1975) and Patrizi in Ricciardelli (2012).

46   Confraternities aimed to ensure their members' personal salvation through charitable work and devotional activities. Affluent landowners, they justifiably concerned themselves with secular and sacred issues. Weissman (1982).

47   Painted by Lorenzetti *c*. 1338–40.

48   Applying a nineteenth-century conception, they regard the 1378 Ciompi Revolt as a failed revolution.

49 Cohn (1980), p. 152.

50 Brucker (1968), p. 356.

51 Bruni (2007), p. 9.

52 Braccioloni (1715), p. 78.

53 Machiavelli (1990).

54 Winter (2012).

55 Atkinson (2011) considers communication and the relationship between sound and space.

56 Najemy (1982) argues that they shifted from partnership, institutionalized in guilds, to clientage, institutionalized in republicanism.

57 Padgett and McLean (2006), p. 4.

58 Ibid., p. 2.

59 Compare with the Ottoman Empire: the Church put certain limits on economic growth, imposing trade restrictions, enforcing boycotts and banning usury. Chalana (2012).

60 Mueller (1997).

61 De Roover (1944), p. 381.

62 Bills of exchange/credit were structured to circumvent the usury ban, enabling trade and wealth to grow exponentially.

63 De Roover (1944), p. 381.

64 Manucci's double-entry bookkeeping. Geoffrey (1977).

65 Padgett (2001).

66 Padgett and McLean (2006), p. 2.

67 Court (2008), pp. 77–79.

68 Malfeasance and bankruptcy were publicized, reputations destroyed. Goldthwaite (1982), pp. 23–24.

69 This public fund (est.1425) provided suitable dowry to Florentine brides.

70 Marks (1960), p. 127.

71 Moulakis (1998), p. 66.

72 In 1400 the population was around 60,000. Goldthwaite (1982), p. 33.

73 Butchers on Florence's Ponte Vecchio or goldsmiths on Rome's Via del Pellegrino.

74 Burke (2014), p. 223.

75 Still celebrated, *Il Palio di Siena* riders represent their city wards.

76 Muir (1999), p. 391.

77 Together with the guilds who 'lavished funds on Florence's major buildings and launched a campaign of patronage that marked the beginning of what we call the Renaissance'. Hollingsworth (1994), p. 19.

78 McLean (2007).

79 'Humanists and artists played key roles in the creation of images for their patrons, producing impressive propaganda designed to boost their patrons' prestige'. Hollingsworth (1994), p. 12.

80 Although women were patrons (arts), their position was often trivialized in an unequivocally patriarchal society. King (1998).

81 Hibbert (2003), p. 61.

82 In addition to guild/ward membership and the influence of patronage.

83 Cicero's *De Officiis* was a source of inspiration; it notes that formality promoted social stability. Burke (2013).

84 Saint cults offered divine sanction and legitimacy; they helped to create identity and maintain order. Solum links St John the Baptist and Florence with the notions of peace and civic freedom (2015), p. 87.

85 The number of itinerant notaries (in Roman law) multiplied (8/1,000 in Florence in 1427). They were steadily employed as everyone valued written records. Muir (1999).

86 'For since unanimity pleases God and since through bad manners the relations between men are not conserved, unanimity is damaged, and [God] is offended.' Barberino, quoted in Trexler (1991), p. 91.

87 Elias (1982).

88 Burke (2013, 2014).

89 Muir (1999), p. 382.

90 Self-consciously generating and preserving the city's identity, they understood the power of idealizing and memorializing their city. Najemy (2004) p. 5, Dante (1975), Villani (2011), Bruni (2005) and Machiavelli (2007).

91 Muir (1999), p. 395.

92 Trebizond praised Venice for inventing the most elaborate and complex election procedures (1997), pp. 129–33. They combined monarchy, aristocracy and democracy to best advantage. King (1986).

93 The 'republic transformed into its own political antithesis', Baker (2009), p. 446.

94 In 1434 the Medicis secured electoral control. Rubinstein (1966).

95 Giuliano de' Medici's assassination (1478) exposed the complexity and ambivalence of Florentine friendship, its meaning largely drawn from Cicero's *de Amictia*. Kent (2000). As Machiavelli generalized, men 'are ungrateful, fickle, liars, and deceivers … while you treat them well, they are yours … but when you are in danger they turn away' (2007), ch.6.

96 A similar allegory used to decorate a float in Rome in 1513. Minio-Paluello (2009), p. 2.

97 Desperate for protection from Charles VIII's invading army, the city turned against Piero. Refused entry to the Signoria he tried force, but the great bell summoned the citizens to the piazza; losing control he was exiled. Atkinson (2011) emphasizes the value of bells to community formation, concord, rebellion, memory and movement.

98 Landucci (1927), pp. 94, 110.

99 While Machiavelli (2007, 2013) believed Savonarola to be a hypocrite, he argued for Florence to retain some of the institutions and more inclusive government style initiated by him.

100 Strathern (2003), pp. 223–28.

101 Phillips (2014) for extracts of Parenti's translated chronicle.

102 Ibid., p. 225.

103 An earlier unsuccessful coup led to five executions. Political executions occurred more frequently thereafter, mapping the changing political culture of the city: republic to principality. Baker (2009), p. 445.

104 Strathern (2003), pp. 266–68.

105 The restoration of the Consiglio Maggiore and exile of the Medicis are usually referred to as a revolution, whereas the introduction of a new constitution, which replaced the Signoria with a hereditary monarchy and two new councils – the Duecento (200) and the *Quarantotto* (48) – five years later, is not.

106 Liberty was 'no less engraved in men's hearts than it [was] written on [the] walls and banners' (Guicciardini (1994), p. 16), yet by the end of the century it was losing credibility. Brown (2011), p. 225.

107 Compare Guicciardini (1994) and Machiavelli (2007 and 2013).

108 Baker (2013), p. 232.

109 It became a 'court society' under Francesco I (1541–87).

110 Baker (2013), pp. 228–30.

111 Rinuccini (1978).

112 Images of the *marzoco* (heraldic lion) and a beautiful woman, 'the flower of flowers', bearing an olive or laurel branch, were used on banners, insignia and coins, while Hercules and David were used on the communal seal and as painted images and statues.

113 Hornqvist (2000).

114 Liberty usually meant political independence from an overlord, while its recipients were communities rather than individuals, but by the fifteenth century it also came to mean a republican constitution that guaranteed freedom of speech and equality under the law (*aequa libertas*). See Bruni (1428), Nanni Strozzi's funeral oration and Rinuccini's (1479) Dialogue.

115 The Medicis's appropriation of Florentina *Libertas* includes Donatello's statue of David, Landino's Commentary on Dante and Pollaiuolo's painting of Hercules. Brown (2000).

116 Renowned as a republican, *Pater Patriae* (father of the fatherland) and engraved on his tomb, it was twice deleted. McKillop (1992), pp. 248–49.

117 Rinuccini (1978).

118 Split into three: the Lutheran (1517–55), Calvinist (1555–1618), and Thirty Years' War (1618–48).

119 'Germany' refers to a linguistic rather than a political region under the Holy Roman emperor's control, divided into secular and religious territories, numerous duchies, counties, principalities, imperial and free cities, bishoprics and archbishoprics, comprising all of central Europe.

120 A nineteenth-century 'invention' tied to the unification of Germany (1870–1), as represented by Ranke and Ritter. Brady (1995), p. 2.

121 Pelikan (1990), p. 90.

122 Dickens (2005) offers a Whig-Protestant approach, in contrast to the revisionist position of Haigh (1993) and Scarisbrick (1991).

123 Holt (2002).

124 Bleiker (2000), p. 66.

125 What had started as a protest movement, challenging the ancient gods, triggering violence and discord, became the dominant religion of the empire and feudal Europe (an instrument of unity and political stability at national and international levels), but as Protestantism emerged, discord and violence returned.

126 Hus, Waldo, Wycliffe, Flora and Savonarola tried, while the papacy also tried instituting reform – with varied success.

127 Foxe wrote, 'I suppose, that either the pope must abolish printing, or must seek a new world … [he] must abolish knowledge and printing, or printing at length will root him out' (1837), p. 720.

128 Smith (1920), p. 700.

129 Comprising four basic strands: Lutheran, Calvinist, Anglican and Anabaptist, more emerged.

130 Religion combines epistemic, existential, salvific, affective, social and cultural, trust-generating elements. Hosking (2014), p. 80.

131 Political elites used it to avoid high papal taxes and seize valuable church lands.

132 Holborn (1965), p. 91.

133 Machiavelli argued that a prince should take advantage of the situation, for 'it is better to try *fortuna* while she is still favourable than to try nothing and allow her surely to destroy you' (1965), p. 122.

134 Religious conversion, for some (the Huguenots), was used to gain more authority and independence. Mentzer and Spicer (2002).

135 Scarisbrick (1991), p. 135.

136 Arguably, instead of historians' black or white portrayal, Henry's changes 'suggest that ideology was central and that the dissolution in intention and in consequences was much more than a smash-and-grab raid'. Bernard (2011), p. 409.

137 Including tithes and crusading taxes, though 'Peter's Pence' was only levied in England and the Scandinavian countries.

138 The Church owned half of Germany, a fifth of France (although valued at three quarters of its wealth), while English monasteries owned 2 million prime acres, a sixth of all England. Varickayil (1980), p. 16.

139 In 1529 Henry VIII began separating the Church from Rome, completing it in 1537. However, religious changes proceeded cautiously and conservatively. On his death in 1547, Edward VI, a true protestant, became king. In 1553 Mary I, a devout and vengeful Catholic, became queen. Protestants faced five years of

persecution before Elizabeth I was crowned in 1558. Favouring pragmatism in religious matters, she sought a policy of toleration in the face of constant Catholic (and papal) plots and the Armada.

140 Rosendale (2001) and Shagan (2003).

141 Haigh (1993), pp. 279–81.

142 View held by Cranmer, Tyndale and Foxe, and posited by Dickens (1991).

143 Rosendale (2001), p. 1142. Also held by Gardiner, Bonner and 'revisionist' historians Scarisbrick (1991) and Haigh (1993).

144 By 1521, 300,000 copies had sold. Holborn (1965), p. 137.

145 He later said, 'I would never have thought that such a storm would rise from Rome over one simple little scrap of paper.'

146 An assembly of the Holy Roman Empire.

147 Durant (1957), p. 363.

148 The majority of local rulers in Germany (2,000 out of 2,500) were knights, who controlled less than 250 square miles of land. Holborn (1965), p. 39.

149 The German Peasants' Revolt was Europe's largest uprising prior to the French Revolution of 1789. Hunt (2007).

150 Hunt (2007), p. 174.

151 Justifying such action, Luther described the peasants as 'faithless, perjured, disobedient, rebellious, murderers, robbers, and blasphemers, whom even a heathen ruler has the right and authority to punish' and stated, 'anyone who is killed fighting on the side of the rulers may be a true martyr in the eyes of God.' (1970), pp. 122–23.

152 'Though protesting [he] eventually tolerated the extension of political authority into religious affairs. The "territorial church" in which the territorial ruler acted as the highest bishop, became the normal type of the visible Lutheran church.' Holborn (1965), p. 187.

153 To its religious monopoly, economic and socio-political power and dominance over every stage of life.

154 Ecclesiastical or structural reconfiguration, religious orders, spiritual movements and political dimensions.

155 Bleiker (2000), pp. 68–69.

156 With increasing persecution, Luther and Calvin abandoned their strict doctrine of non-resistance to tyranny, arguing it was both moral and legal to oppose a tyrant ruler. Skinner (1978), pp. 16–19.

157 Carroll (1993), p. 47.

158 Bleiker (2000), p. 70.

159 'It had started as a Religious War, it ended as a Political War, it resulted in the deaths of 10,000,000 to 20,000,000.' Halley (1939), p. 418. Despite which, it hardly changed the denominational split across the empire. Cantoni (2009), p. 8.

160 Referring to Berman *et al.*'s (2008) counter-insurgency model.

161 North and West Germany, Switzerland, Holland, Britain and Scandinavia.

162 Protestants privileged the word of God, not his image, and so they focused on literacy and education for all.

163 Compare Byzantine iconoclasm, the Taliban at Bamiyan, and the Islamic State at Nimrud and Palmyra.

164 Beginning in *c.* 1600, such art was largely funded by papal and Spanish New World wealth.

165 Burrell (2013), p. 235.

166 Rookmaaker (2002), p. 171.

167 Hunt (2007).

168 Durant (1957), p. 5.

169 Schwiebert (1948), p. 3.

170 Underwood (1957), p. 149.

171 Weidenkopf (2015).

172 Bodensieck (1965), p. 2010.

173 Schwiebert (1950), p. 8.

174 Luther (1957), p. 5.

175 Daniel-Rops (1961), p. 297.

176 Ibid., p. 297.

177 Caused by the gospel, the subsequent secular revolt was the 'fruit of [his] gospel'. Peters (1970), p. 3.

178 'I have begun no rioting and rebelling, but so far as I was able, I have helped the worldly rulers, even those who persecuted the Gospel and me, to defend their authority and honour.' Luther, XVI, p. 58.

179 All social relationships: agricultural, trade and commercial, and all guilds and convivial fraternities were religious in nature and integral components of the Church system.

180 Through church bells, mass, the liturgical calendar.

181 Shagan (2003), p. 10.

182 Ibid., p. 1.

183 Covington's (2003) work focuses on persecution in Tudor England.

184 The Church's Papal Bull (1555), expelling Jews from Spain (Stow 1977), Luther's infamous *On the Jews and Their Lies* (Paras 2008), and secular leaders' convenient scapegoating of Jewish communities throughout history.

185 A familiar dynamic: the next generation is more radical, the previous one looks moderate in comparison.

186 'What gave the radicals their coherence as the Reformation's "left-wing" was the rejection of a hierarchical conception of politics in which legitimate authority, whether secular or ecclesiastical, devolved from the top down. Instead, the radical's vision of politics was rooted in notions of local autonomy

and community control which also implied egalitarianism.' Baylor (1994), p. xvi.

187 With no doctrinal consensus, hyper-pluralism emerged. Breakaway groups advocated great purity of worship and doctrine, while often practising 'revolutionary' lifestyles. Caryl Churchill's recent play, *Light Shining in Buckinghamshire*, shows how the Levellers, Diggers and Rants all played a vital role in the Putney Debates (1647).

188 Consider the threat 'the maid of Kent' posed to Henry.

189 Seligman (1997), p. 138.

190 Flemings, Walloons and Huguenots emigrated to the New World after the Vassy massacre (1562) – 1,200 Huguenots killed; the St Bartholomew Massacre (1572) – 8,000 killed; and the Wars of Religion (1562–98); while the 'great migration' of English puritans (1620–40) resulted from a lack of religious freedom within the Protestant church. Baird (1885), Betlock (2003) respectively.

191 Hutson (1998).

192 Wolffe (2013), p. 212.

193 Morris (2004).

194 Church wardens, constables, jurymen and poor relief wardens. Kesselring (2005).

195 Dixon (2015) argues that Protestants so disliked the emotionalism of Catholic piety, such as the 'howling and barbarous outcries' (referencing Stanihurst (1547–1618)) at funerals, that 'excessive tears' were banished in Cranmer's *Book of Common Prayer*. See Southwell's pamphlet, *Marie Magdalens funeral teares* (1822), describing the literature of tears in England.

196 Luther (1957), p. 329.

197 Replacing Catholicism's ambiguous attitude to family life (God came first), although equal (reading/studying), women were cast firmly in a domestic role, subordinate to husbands/fathers.

198 Since 1468, bishops' secular service to the Crown outweighed their papal allegiance. Drawn from the aristocracy/gentry, they were typically ambitious, experienced administrators rather than devoted theologians (Rosenthal, 1970), content to go along with Henry VIII's reforms. In comparison, church records reveal a disinclination at parish level. Dickens (1991), pp. 42–43.

199 Montgomery (1995), Sweden, and Gordon (2002), Switzerland.

200 Were reliant on a properly functioning church, based on an idealized notion of social and political harmony. Duffy (2005).

201 'The English [for example] had retained the older *cantus firmus* techniques and favoured extremely florid polyphony, full of dynamic rhythms and ornamental melody.' Arnold (1983), p. 629.

202 There were marked regional differences, with outward conformity concealing a range of responses: York was conservative (Pilgrimage of Grace, Mass under Mary), Bristol neutral, while Norwich witnessed a 'quiet reformation'.

203 Doctors Layton, Leigh and London collated evidence of vice and corruption as
     they worked to produce the *Valor Ecclesiasticus* (1535), a detailed record of church
     wealth and relics.

204 Burnet (1679), Strype (1709).

205 'The truly astonishing feature ... is that a manifestly unpopular and unwanted
     policy was imposed so successfully and with so little disturbance.' Rex (2006), p. 25.

206 Divorcing England from the Pope, the Act of Supremacy of 1534 made Henry
     Supreme Head of the Church in England.

207 When 'one adult man in fifty was in religious orders.' Bernard (2011), p. 390.

208 A symbol of defiance, Becket's tomb was destroyed, his bones scattered and all
     mention of his name obliterated.

209 King's Lynn had over seventy religious guilds in the 1500s, Bodmin had over
     forty, while the York cycle included forty-eight pageants. Davidson (2007).

210 This 'cult of the living in serve of the dead' played a vital role in memory
     and obligation within society, and destroying this connection had profound
     consequences. Marshall (2002).

211 The Tate estimated that over 90 per cent of all English art was destroyed in this
     period, while the Bodleian was left without a single book.

212 Similarly, Marian writers Bullingham (1554) and Standish (1556) wrote of the
     betrayal of those who strayed from the 'True Path'.

213 Top-down – propaganda, pamphlets, preaching and the law – was used on a scale
     previously unknown. Cooper (2003).

214 Engagement made this an increasingly nuanced two-way dialogue on ideas of
     obedience, authority, succession and supremacy.

215 Wall (2000).

216 Slack (1984) pp. 1–15.

217 The Merlinic prognostications that suffused the Pilgrimage of Grace (1536).

218 Kesselring (2005), p. 8.

219 Dobin describes how Merlin served as 'official crown prophet' (1990), p. 51.

220 Jansen (1991), p. 154.

221 Walsham (1999), p. 169.

222 In general, ignorance and fear, both of the unknown and religious conflict, when
     combined with false conceptions of causality and cessation, resulted in many
     trusting in superstition, magic and chance, reflective of the widespread notion of
     risk in the period.

223 Pollock (2013), p. 65.

224 Combining chivalric, humanist, classical, legal and ecclesiological concepts.

225 It united the disparate legal strands (Roman, customary, medieval Christian law),
     leaving its mark on every aspect of Western law, to create a common Western
     tradition, and gave rise to the first highly organized 'modern' State (the papacy).
     Ewald (2005).

226 Berman (2009).

227 Arguing for the 'divine right', Luther and Calvin called for ungodly kings to be held to account. Sommerville (1986).

228 Cooper (2003).

229 Best summed up in the 1571 anonymous collection of legal essays.

230 Crompton (1587), Gardiner (1535).

231 Mayer (2000), p. 22.

232 Reflected in Shakespeare's Hamlet. Lavery (2005).

233 de Castro condemned such action and Renard warned that such 'cruel enforcement' could 'cause a revolt'. Waller (2006), p. 102.

234 Hunt (2007).

235 'A difficult crime to condone or forgive. Its necessary condition is a prior relationship of intimacy and trust.' Marshall (2008), p. 77.

236 Gray (2012), p. 18.

237 Imposed with oaths: the Royal Supremacy (1534), renewed in 1559, Edward VI's coronation oath, James I's Oath of Allegiance, the Oath of Abjuration under the Commonwealth and the Test Oath (1678).

238 Gray (2010), p. 731.

239 Ibid., p. 115.

240 Morice (1590) and Fuller (1607) contributed to this argument.

241 Rubenfeld (2005), p. 34.

242 Elton's (1953) revisionist argument posits the changes in government introduced by Henry VIII which ushered in a modern bureaucratic legal state. Starkey (1986) and Coleman (1986) have each challenged his argument.

243 Dickens (1991), Haigh (1993), Scarisbrick (1991) and Shagan (2003).

244 With official texts, legislation and decrees, and through pamphlets and fantastical histories linking England to a mythical past.

245 Drawing on Miller's (2008) discussion on the history of rhetoric and trust in texts.

246 Hazlett (2003).

247 There were few protestant preachers in England before the death of Edward VI. Haigh (1993), p. 19.

248 Ibid., p. 31.

249 One hundred years later this theory of resistance became a reality, directly challenging the divine right of kings in 1638. Hunt (2007).

250 While the Catholic Church Christianized traditions, subtly altering their meaning to create a unified and orderly community, Protestants' purification removed communal traditions. Religion was now individual and internal.

251 Hunt (2007) and Naphy (2007).

252 Bryce (2012) outlines the meaning and significance of the empire's/emperor's existence.

253 Croxton (2013).

254 'For Henry, obedience was paramount, as important as faith in Lutheranism or
       the real presence in Catholicism.' Rex (1996), p. 894.

Chapter 8

1   Distinct until the 1707 Acts of Union.
2   Greenblatt (2006).
3   Lambert (2014).
4   Between 1639 and 1651, 200,000 lost their lives. Mortimer (2012).
5   Radical ideas on religion and society proliferate: 'Levellers for a democratic
     republic, Diggers for a communist society, many others for religious and sexual
     freedom.' Hill (1991).
6   85 per cent lived on the land. Lambert (2014).
7   4.2 million in 1600 to 5.5 million by 1660. Sommerville (1986).
8   Including the sale of Church lands, the practice of enclosures, harvest failures and
     rural crises.
9   Its population doubled between 1600 and 1700 to 500,000, despite disease, war and
     high mortality. See the Old Bailey proceedings (1647–1913), *A Population History*
     www.oldbaileyonline.org/static/Population-history-of-london.jsp, 2 May 2016.
10   Hindle (2002). Sometimes interpreted as a cultural conflict between the elite and
     the popular.
11   At the local level, Laudianism emphasized the maintenance of traditional social
     values: ministers cheered at local games, drank ale, led rogation processions and
     presided over bucolic festivals (gaining favour under James I, it became the regime's
     religion under Charles I). Meanwhile Puritanism led to the withdrawal of the parish
     elite from communal sociability (games, festivals, the alehouse) and the imposition
     of 'godly' behaviour through court prosecutions (for drunkenness and vagrancy).
12   Sharpe (1993), p. ix.
13   Images were crucial, as the *Mercurius Civicus* found to its cost when it temporarily
     dropped them. Plomer (1905), p. 190.
14   'Despite the significant amount of paper in circulation most news was still spread
     by word of mouth.' Bastos *et al.* (2012), p. 5.
15   Standage (2013), p. 107.
16   These new forms of communication helped to create a vibrant news culture. Cust
     (1986), Levy (1982). They include epideictic, forensic and deliberative genres, as
     well as literary techniques and theories. Schneck (2012), p. 10.
17   De Krey (1985) and Harris (1993).
18   In 1673 T. Player wrote to J. Williamson, 'the common people talke anything, for
     every carman and porter is now a statesman, and indeed the coffee-houses are

good for nothing else'. Christie (1874), pp. 67–68. They fed the elite's desire to court popular support and manipulate public perceptions. Lake (2007), Cust (2002), Cogswell (2002).

19 In London's Cornhill parish (1640s) one in sixteen men were officeholders, elsewhere it was even higher. Hindle (2002).

20 Peacey (2013), p. 402.

21 Hopper (2013), p. 15.

22 Ibid., p. 17.

23 Clarke (2015), EP 30.

24 Although not meeting Habermas's three criteria (reason, inclusiveness and non-instrumentality), the 1640s saw the rapid development of informed popular debate. Building on the Tudors' political communications, the 'public sphere' began in 1694–5. This period witnessed 'the emergence of something approaching a shared national culture of news and comment'. Habermas (1992), p. 31.

25 Davies (1625) and Fuller (1642), respectively.

26 Peacey (2013), pp. 2, 6.

27 Raymond (2013), p. 109.

28 Charles I paid a heavy price for not having a newspaper to present official views. His was just one almost silent voice in a cacophony of noise. In sharp contrast, Charles II's government set up *The London Gazette* (1665) as the official journal of record.

29 It functioned to 'gratify and whet the public appetite for news'. Frank (1961), p. 18.

30 Magliocco (2014) and Cressy (1980).

31 Fox (1997), pp. 61–62.

32 Contemporary practices provide a nuanced picture of seventeenth-century readers' relationship to print. Peacey (2013), p. 123.

33 Raymond (1998), p. 133.

34 Adamson (2009), p. 3.

35 MacGillivray (2012).

36 Lloyd (1668) and Rushworth (1649).

37 Clarendon (2009).

38 Guizot (2010).

39 For 'he who controls the present, controls the past. He who controls the past, controls the future'. Orwell (1949), Book 1.

40 Popper (2012), p. 473.

41 Repeated references made in the Clarke Papers of 1655.

42 'What to a ruler looks like a rebellion against their authority may be a civil war to the insurgents who aim to overturn that authority. If the rebel succeeds, one way to mark the triumph of their cause is to rebrand civil war a revolution.' Armitage (2009), p. 5.

43 OED cites that its astronomical meaning was in use by 1390, and by 1450 it also referred to 'great change or alteration in affairs or in some particular thing'.

44 Snow (1962), p. 167.

45 Cotgrave (1611) defined revolution as 'a full compassing, rounding, turning backe to its first place, or point, the accomplishment of a circular course'; Cockeram (1623) as 'a winding or turning about'; and Blout (1656) as 'a cycle of the sun'.

46 Jackson Literary Studies module – Department of English and Comparative Literary Studies, Warwick University.

47 In *Paradise Lost* (1688) and *Hamlet* (1604), revolution equates to the ebb and flow of life, to restoration, a return.

48 The Dutch and French civil wars and the Neapolitan Revolt 1647–8.

49 Collingwood (2013), p. 199.

50 Snow (1962), p. 169.

51 Peacey and Villani ('Observations from Europe') in Hessayon and Finnegan (2013).

52 Clarendon's (2009) 'giddy revolutions', 'fully compassing', Howell (1661), Ascham (1648).

53 An anonymous 1644 parliamentary tract describes how 'revolutions of time' brought 'revolutions of fortune' while, as Howell notes in a letter in 1646, 'the strangest revolutions' suggested 'the perpetual rotations of Fortune'. Published in Howell (1655).

54 The King's success is 'a just subject for wonderment' attributable 'principally to God Almightie' (Howell 1643, p. 42), while the Restoration is 'the sole glory' of God (Heath 1663, p. 37), 'such a prodigious act of Providence as [God] hath scare vouchsafe to any nation, since he led his own chosen people through the Red Sea'. Clarendon (2009), VI, p. 143.

55 Heath (1663) considered any power shift a revolution. He recounts England's 'amazing revolutions' from 1637 onward.

56 Harrington (1992), Temple (1814) and Locke (1988).

57 'Radical' only became a political concept associated with reform in the eighteenth century.

58 Hessayon and Finnegan (2013), p. 25.

59 Hynes (2013), p. 206.

60 Dunn (1997), Laslett (1988) on Locke. Compare Tuck (1989), Skinner (2008) on Hobbes.

61 Mirrored in wider cultural forms and discourse appropriated for diverging and opposing purposes: to support or contest royal power. Sharpe (1993). Lucan's *Pharsalia* is used to both defend absolutism and advocate republican values.

62 He primarily uses the term for geometry and natural philosophy but it also appears in his dialogue. Hobbes (2014).

63 Rogers (1998), p. 2.

64 Ibid., p. 204.

65 If 'the common people were...diligently instructed in the true principles of their duty', peace would follow, otherwise, 'all the states of Christendom' will suffer 'fits of rebellion, as long as the world lasteth'. Hobbes (2014), pp. 70–71.

66 Schwoerer (2004), p. 547.

67 A physicist's term, Hobbes has been described as a motionalist. Herbert (2003), p. 91.

68 Locke (1988).

69 Temple (1693) makes the same point, highlighting that the English quickly abandoned the extreme Cromwellian experiments after his death. In 1672, similarly, the Dutch returned to the House of Orange. Israel (1995).

70 There was a perceivable shift during the period, from discourse emanating from political authorities to text about power, authority and legitimacy. Peacey (2013).

71 It has been claimed, and recently reaffirmed, that Locke, in particular, had considerable influence on the American revolutionaries and the writing of the American Declaration of Independence. And although influential in France, in the early 1700s this waned, as the French came to view the English as conservative.

72 As Browne (1642) argues, these 'lying and scandalous pamphlets fly about the city in every corner, and prove vendible ware, whereas solid and learned men's works are nothing regarded'.

73 Locke (1988), ch.5, Hobbes and Tuck (1996).

74 Anderson (2003), p. 52.

75 Weil (1986).

76 Anderson (2003), p. 52.

77 Locke (1988), pp. 78, 121.

78 'From Middle English came "confidence" and "safety", to which was added, by the fifteenth century, a sense of expectation for the future.' Hoffer (1990), p. 29.

79 (a) The grantor transfers in 'trust' to (b) the trustee, for the benefit of (c) creating a fiduciary obligation. Nenner (2009), p. 866.

80 Cromartie (2006), p. 1, McElligott and Smith (2007), p. 12.

81 Appelbaum (2010), Hill (1991).

82 Sheppard (2003), pp. 195–200.

83 Coke (1826), p. 19.

84 Its value contested by historians, after much debate and pamphlet controversy, by 1650 all men aged eighteen and over were required to take an oath of loyalty to the new republic. Burgess (2009), Tubbs (2015).

85 Bagshaw (1660), p. 36.

86 Cleveland (1689).

87 Buchanan (2004).

88 See Beza (1574), du Plessi-Mornay (1648) and Althusius (1614).

89 Strangeways quoted in Rapin de Thoyras (1733) vol. 2, p. 564.

90 Milton (1649), p. 11.

91 Howell (1816), 4, 1003, Lockyer (1959), p. 95.

92 Muddiman (1928), p. 79, Lockyer (1959), p. 85.

93 Trust as a legal instrument was first recorded in England in the twelfth century; however, the concept itself is much older – *fideicommissum* was a well-developed concept in Roman law.

94 From monarchy to the first commonwealth, to a protectorate, a commonwealth, a return to monarchy and, finally, to constitutional monarchy.

95 Aylmer (1986).

96 It is noteworthy that 'trust' is used as a coherent and systematic concept only in the English texts. In the Latin version of Leviathan it is only mentioned as '*fidere*' in ch.10, p. 27 and is then not referred to again in the remaining text.

97 Hobbes (2004), p. 48 and (1999), p. 53.

98 Legitimacy depends on its ability to protect those who consented to obey its rules and obligations, not on how it came to power.

99 Hobbes (2004), p. 137.

100 As 'we are all grasping egotists with no sense of morality and restraint'. Wolff (2006).

101 Hobbes (2004), p. 85, p. 187, p. 286, Weil (1986), and see Gauthier (1969).

102 Baumgold (2013) interprets this relationship as one of mutual trust.

103 Hobbes (2004), p. 98.

104 Refer to Neal's (1988) interpretation of the reply to the fool.

105 Baumgold (2013), p. 839.

106 Locke (1954), p. 212.

107 Dunn (1984) analyses Locke's 'trust' as a legal arrangement, a strategic social and political practice, a passion analogous to faith.

108 Locke (1980), p. 66.

109 Ibid., p. 46.

110 Questioning whether a monarch could/should be trusted to act in his citizens' best interests, he sought to set constitutional limits, and he argued the right to rebel.

111 As Locke states, they can be 'so foolish that they take care to avoid what mischiefs can be done them by polecats and foxes, but are content, nay, think it safety, to be devoured by lions' (1980), p. 50.

112 Baier (1995), p. 196.

113 Nacol (2011), p. 580.

114 Interestingly, Locke uses the word 'trust' a lot more often than 'contract'. Laslett (1988), p. 114.

115 Locke (1976), p. 148.

116 Laslett (1988), p. 122.

117 By providing examples of the absurdity of the law. Locke (1980), p. 77 and pp. 81–82.

118 Fatovic (2004), p. 296.

119 Nacol (2011), p. 581.

120 Ibid., p. 78.

121 'established, by consent...according to the trust put in'. Locke (1980), ch.4, section 22.

122 Dunn (1984), p. 299.

123 Grayling (2015) argues that in this period mankind experienced 'the greatest ever change in ... mental outlook', a powerful legacy for later generations. Maloy (2008), p. 37.

124 Even criminals. Willis (2015), Spraggs (2001).

125 Markham (1625), p. 1.

126 In particular, dishonour within a marriage. Etherege (1667–8), Dryden (1671) and Wycherley (1675).

127 Such as *charivari* and skimmingtons. Coward (2003) and Kent (1983).

128 Clark (2000), p. 7.

129 Such as rogation, boundary walks, wakes, village sports, festivals and carnivals. Ingram (1984).

130 Herrup (1987), Roberts (1988), Goldie (2001), Braddick (2000), Hindle (2002).

131 Roberts (1988), p. 167.

132 Tanner 71 f, 142 in Sharpe (1992).

133 Herrup (1985).

134 Cornwall (1967), Spufford (1970).

135 Coward (2003).

136 While MacFarlane claims the English were rampant individualists by the thirteenth century ((1979), p. 163), England's reputation as the historical *locus classicus* of individualism only developed in the seventeenth century. Mascuch (2013).

137 Hickeringill (1682).

138 de Thoyras (1723), Hume (1751–61), Macaulay (1848).

139 Coined by Butterfield in 1931, 'Whiggism' is used to criticize any teleological, hero-based, trans-historical narrative. Mayr (1990).

140 Spraggs (2001).

141 In reference to a 'cultural pendulum', after Huygens's clock (1656), highlighting the dramatic swings between Cavalier and Roundhead, religious lifestyles, respectable and plebeian culture in seventeenth-century English society. Wrightson (2013).

142 The clergy were <1 per cent of the population, they owned or controlled between 5 and 10 per cent of the land, they were exempt from tax. The nobility comprised 0.5 per cent of the population, they were exempt from tax, and the rest accounted for >95 per cent of the population and paid taxes.

143 As Schama (1990), p. 184, noted. Yet for Tallyrand-Perrigord, it denoted a certain nostalgia, while de Tocqueville argued against such a defining narrative, highlighting continuities pre/post revolution. It was established in the fifteenth century.

144 Woloch (1982), p. 282.

145 Vividly depicted in the 1996 film *Ridicule*; it captures the court atmosphere on the brink of revolution.

146 Scott and Simms (2007).

147 While a standardized form of French was developing, only half the population spoke it. Latin was the administrative language.

148 Derived from medieval feudalism, the seigneurial system was almost entirely economic. The payment of these dues became a major grievance in the late eighteenth century. Markoff (1986).

149 Paris grew to 650,000 by 1790. Rusnock (2002).

150 In 1686 *c.* 29 per cent of men and 14 per cent of women were literate, rising to 47 per cent and 27 per cent respectively, between 1786 and 1790. Melton (2001), pp. 80–81.

151 Kurtz (1994), p. 2.

152 The first vernacular bible was only published, in parts, between 1667 and 1693. Bell (2001), p. 85.

153 Lieven (1993).

154 Craveri (2006).

155 In France they increased from an estimated 12 in 1780 to over 500 between 1789 and 1792. Crafton (1997), p. 43.

156 Graff (1987), p. 267.

157 Chartier (1991).

158 Baker (1990), p. 212.

159 Taking the phrase used by many British historians to cover a more natural historical period (1660–1830).

160 Welwood (1689), Beverley (1689), Crouch (1693), Steele (1713), Gale (1713), Hertzler (1987), and Pickard (1761), respectively. Arguably neither glorious nor a revolution, historians still remain divided on the issue (see Speck (1989) and Pincus (2014)). Regardless, contemporary commentators referred to it as a revolution. Quotations are drawn from Gale's seventeenth- and eighteenth-century Nichols Newspapers Collection: www.gale.com/uk/c/17th-and-18th-century-nichols-newspapers-collection. Also see Corfield (2013).

161 Ward (1972).

162 Quoted in Hobson (1999), p. 78.

163 Corfield (2013), p. 7.

164 Hume (1983), vol. 6, p. 531, and Millar, Molesworth and Bolingbroke, all cited in Pincus (2014), p. 12.

165 Absolutists, such as Orleans, countered this argument by decapitalizing and de-singularizing it, reducing it to a long series of vicissitudes. Baker (1990), p. 207.

166 Gordon (1788), Ramsay (1789).

167 In contrast, see Goulemot's (1967) work comparing the use of the term in various translations of Machiavelli's *Discorsi* over time.

168 Furet and Ozouf (1989), p. 808.

169 Defoe (1728), p. 36.

170 Stothard (1786), p. 83.

171 Addison (1711).

172 In voltaire's (1953) letters to d'Alembert dated 16 September 1772 (1953) and Feraud (1787–8).

173 Including works by René Aubert de Vertot, Gabriel de Massaic and Pierre-Joseph d'Orléans.

174 Furet and Ozouf (1989), p. 808.

175 Baker (1990), p. 204.

176 Furetière (1690), Richelet (1680), and Académie (1717) quoted in Baker (1990), p. 205, respectively.

177 Represents a powerful example of 'consciousness determin[ing] language'. Cf. Deutscher (2011) and Spirkin (1983).

178 Fox quoted by Godwin in Avery (2014), p. 19.

179 de Tocqueville (2012), p. 33.

180 Coleridge's (1798) 'France: An Ode'.

181 Burke's letter to Lord Charlemont, 9 August 1789 (1967), vol. VI, 10.

182 Founded in Brittany in 1789, it grew into a nationwide republican movement with *c.* 500,000 members. Brinton (2011), p. xix.

183 Baker (1990), p. 203.

184 Hunt (1981), p. 318.

185 Shaw (2011).

186 A somewhat contradictory situation has subsequently arisen; while the notion of revolution has subsumed ideas of rupture and of revolutionary time, the revolutionary calendar has not survived. Perovic (2012).

187 Introduced in 1795, the metric system was to be 'for all people for all time' (the quotation comes from Concorcet's proposals accepted by the French Assembly on 30 March 1791 – see Concorcet, 2012), while the franc, replacing the *livre tournois*, established decimalization of the French currency. Allen (2009), p. 111.

188 Frey and Frey (2004), p. 44.

189 The name foreign minister Pierre-Henri Lebrun gave his daughter. Darnton (1989), unpublished.

190 Sutherland (2008).

191 In over 300 pamphlets. Brown (2013).

192 Macleod (2013) captures the British fascination with the French Revolution, highlighting its limited understanding, the influence of domestic political debate and the widespread fluctuations of opinion as these events developed.

193 Hunt and Censer (2001) and Furet and Ozouf (1989).

194 Paine (1984), p. 144.

195 As Mourier (1789) noted, 'a scornful eye [was cast] on the Constitution of England, whereas not a year ago we spoke enviously of English liberty', quoted

in Mason and Rizzo (1998), ch.18. 'It was more complete, more entire than that of America, and of confequence was attended with greater convulfions in the interior of the nation'. Condorcet quoted in Smollett (1795), p. 539.

196 Saint-Etienne quoted in Rosenthal (1882), p. 208.

197 volney (1792).

198 Paulson (1983).

199 The *tricolore* cockade, liberty cap, Marianne and La Marseillaise. Hunt and Censer (2001).

200 Foucault (1975), pp. 25–26.

201 Retat (1985).

202 Baker (1990), p. 219.

203 See Moreau (in Baker, 1990, ch.3) for an insight into the pre-revolutionary regime's attempts to control French history, archivally and symbolically.

204 Paine (1791), p. 84. See Carlyle (1837), Mignet (1824), de Tocqueville (1856) and Michelet (1855).

205 In the books published, some, such as Burke, were critical while others (Abbé Barruel 1798), presented conspiracy theories.

206 Hughes-Warrington (2013), p. 89, argues 'histories are written and revised around the clock'.

207 Baker (1990), p. 203.

208 Guerin quoted in Cobban (1977), p. 11.

209 From Shelley's letter to Byron dated 6 September 1816.

210 Skinner (2002).

211 For an example of abuse, see Goulemot (1967) on the word 'revolution'.

212 Bell (2009), p. 171.

213 Sahlins (1989).

214 Meecham and Sheldon (2013), p. 9.

215 Misztal (1996), pp. 28–29.

216 For discussion, see Misztal (1996), Luhmann (2012) and Seligman (1997).

217 Seligman (1997), p. 31.

218 Dawson (2007), p. 287.

219 Hollis (1998), p. 4.

220 Montesquieu (1989), de Tocqueville (2012).

221 Israel (2009) demonstrated it was riven by conflict: reformist versus radical variants.

222 Perry, Chase and Jacob (2015), p. 442, and O'Hagan (2003), p. 213.

223 Desmouslins cited in Peyre (1949).

224 Sambrook (2014), p. 111.

225 Rousseau (1856), p. 167.

226 Dick (2015).

227 Burke, E (2013), p. 48.

228 Rousseau (1979).

229 Peyre (1949), p. 73.

230 Paine (1776). See Ehrenberg's (1999) history of the idea of civil society.

231 Carothers (1999).

232 Paine (1776).

233 Anheier and Toepler (2009), p. 440.

234 Horowitz (2014) and Craveri (2006).

235 Paine (1984).

236 For example, Paine in *The Rights of Man* (1984) only uses the word nine times.

237 Meanwhile, an alternative term, *croyance,* meaning belief, faith and trust, remained fairly consistent, perhaps a reflection of its primary use in religious matter. This separation of uses removes the element of faith from more general use of the term 'trust'.

238 Kelly (2014).

239 Recent scholarship has not only challenged the notion of the stereotypical view of the eighteenth century as an 'Age of Reason', but also the idea that there were Enlightenment and Counter-Enlightenment movements at all. Schmidt (2003).

240 These include an absolutist monarchy, inequitable tax burdens, growing government debt, feudal privileges, poverty, industrial growth, the emergence of a middle class, and external influences. Of the causes listed, many remain contested while the historical controversies surrounding them continue. Hanson (2009), Peyre (1949).

241 Peyre (1949), p. 71.

242 Delers (2015), p. 113.

243 de Tocqueville (2012), p. 107.

244 Fontaine (2001), Dermineur (2015). The development of banking in France lagged behind other European countries, reflecting France's precarious agricultural economy, church influence and its perception as a venture, not an economic enterprise. Walker *et al.* (1896).

245 Informal system of charity, solidarity and cooperation (Binmore 2006) in this precapitalist 'moral economy'. Fontaine (2001), Thompson (1971).

246 Dermineur (2015).

247 Fontaine (2001) highlights how administrators, merchants and officials from the seigneurial hierarchy became investors. They wished to make a profit and create a network of obliges (obligations).

248 Dermineur (2015), p. 494.

249 Crubaugh (2001), Oates (1980).

250 The South Sea Bubble and Laws' banking failure in 1720 discredited bank enterprises in France, but did not undermine the monetary or local credit systems. Davies (2010), Plessis (2003) and Sprang (2015).

251 Fiscal mismanagement is one reason given for the French Revolution.

252 Burke (1984), p. 332.
253 King (2013), p. 156.
254 Bell (1992), p. 933.
255 Breen (2007), p. 13, also Baker (1990), pp. 4–5.
256 Parker (1980), p. 19.
257 White, cited in Crook (1995), p. 26.
258 Oaths were not taken lightly in eighteenth-century France (Neely 2008), and continued to play an important public role before, during and after the Revolution. Examples include the King taking the Coronation Oath in 1775, revolutionaries taking the Tennis Court and Fete de la Federation oaths in 1789 and 1790 respectively, and priests taking the Ecclesiastical Oath in 1791. (Tackett 1986). 'Honour and shame the motor elements of social interaction'. Peristany (1965), Introduction.
259 de Tocqueville (1998), pp. 176–77.
260 Crubaugh (2001).
261 Hayhoe (2008).
262 Schneider (2008) and Follain (2001).
263 The image of bon cure as overseer of education and charity and adviser to local government, with links to royal administration and the outside world. McManners (1969), Hutt (1957).
264 Aston (1992), p. 135.
265 Tackett's (1977) work traces this politicization and its consequences.
266 Kalthoff (2015), p. 5.
267 Jones (1999), p. 247. Varying by region, *c.* 48 per cent swore the oath.
268 Six per cent of all those executed were clergy; they suffered disproportionately. See Desan (1990).
269 Alloway (2007), Kalthoff (2015).
270 Napoleon signed the Concordat in 1801, restoring most of the Church's civil status.
271 Jacob quoted in Stanley (2012), p. 80.
272 Horowitz (2014), p. 67.
273 Notions of patriotism (*patrie*) pre-date the Revolution by *c.* 40 years, emerging, in part, from the aristocracy's desire to reinvent and regenerate themselves. Love of France replaced hereditary privilege. Campbell (2007), Bell (2009).
274 Goodman (1989), pp. 339, 280. Kale is alone in arguing for their ongoing relevance to 1848 (2005), p. 9. Noting the differences, Calhoun (2012) compared the roles of coffee houses and salons in shaping the public sphere in this period.
275 It maintained the ideals of *sociabilité* and *politesse*. Lilti (2009).
276 Habermas (1992), p. 30.
277 Clergue (1971), p. 23.
278 Kale (2005), p. 9.
279 Lilti (2009).

280 Linton (2015) argues that the mechanisms were the same: expressions of friendship, particularly new-found ones, came with implicit expectations of future usefulness and partiality.

281 Horowitz (2014).

282 Loiselle (2014).

283 Parallels were drawn with the Ancients' ideal of the citizen-soldier. Schama (1990), ch.1.

284 'Spoil[ing] communication, creat[ing] distrust and suspicion, mak[ing] agreements unenforceable, undermin[ing] transition, reduc[ing] solidarity, discredit[ing] leadership.' Schelling (1984), p. 211.

285 Maza uses this term to describe the manner in which people conceived of their world (2003), p. 4. He offers the notion of the French bourgeoisie as an imaginary counterfoil for the revolutionaries to rally against. While they may have been a myth, they were an economic and social reality.

286 Hampson (1988).

287 Linton (2011) and Greer (1935), respectively.

288 Conceived of as (1) the price for receiving freedom and rights, (2) civic sacrifice, patriotic giving was institutionalized in 1789. Initially a voluntary 25 per cent of income was requested, but that quickly became obligatory. Walton (2013).

289 Germani, Leith and Swales (1998).

290 Requiring the festival to be reimagined and relived as a series of events across time demanded virtually impossible tricks of memory. Ozouf and Sheridan (1991).

291 Linton (2015).

292 Walton (2013).

293 Hunt (1984), p. 22.

294 Furet (1981), p. 400.

295 Adams *et al.* (2005), p. 2.

296 Cobban (1977).

297 For example, the role of enduring religious beliefs, the continuation in political attitudes and discourse, both in Adams *et al.* (2005) and the emergence of a public sphere. Censer (1994) and Maza (1993).

298 Aulard cited in Tilly (1922), p. 115.

Interlude

1 Furet (1981), p. 2.

2 Spielvogel (2014).

3 Pilbeam (2001).

4   Dunn argues '...as far as sheer destructive power is concerned, capacity for
     upheaval, the twentieth century has been the great century of revolution' (1972), p.
     22.
5   Despite being a Western historical invention, revolution was rarely seen in the
     West in the twentieth century. Instead, European revolutionary models were used
     by Western-educated intellectuals, such as Mao, Castro and Ho Chi Minh, to bring
     revolution to the Third World. Fanon (1967), with some irony, challenged the
     legacy and Westernization of Third World revolutions.
6   The Minister of Justice (1917–18), described by Tolstoy (1966) and Steinberg as a
     slavish imitation of the French, copying even the speech and gestures of the French
     Jacobins.
7   Contested, it had a marked effect on the model of revolution. Donald and Rees
     (2001), p. 3.
8   Brenton (2016), p. 1.
9   Kumar (2001), p. 187, and Arendt (1965).
10   Uneven in nature, the emergence of the modern State saw the sedimentation of
     political rule into State structures, the territorialization of politics, the spread of the
     interstate order, the development of forms of accountability within certain states
     while, simultaneously, there was a denial of such accountability to others through
     colonialism, empires and war. Held *et al.* (1999), and Jasinski (2011), p. 128.
11   Mehta and Yadav (2014) and Rahman (2012) outline Taylor (1911) and Fayol's
     (1949) pioneering work in industrial management thought.
12   The result of 'modern industrial enterprise' (refer to Chandler's *The Visible Hand*).
     This fusion fostered two world wars. Cerny (2009), p. 18.
13   Mann (1984), p. 189.
14   Breuilly (1993).
15   Hardin (1992 and 2004), Cook *et al.* (2005).
16   Compare the Russian authoritarian state with Japanese and German models, and
     with European democracies.
17   'Models you are to imitate and at the same time rivals you are to combat.' Harris
     (1828), p. 208.
18   1920s Comintern publications increasingly mirrored the professional military
     manuals of their opposition. Kumar (2001), p. 180. Critiqued by Luxemburg (1904
     and 1922) and summarized by Luban (2012), Le Blanc (2012).
19   Acknowledging that unique sets of historical circumstances demanded
     correspondingly unique applications of this structured revolutionary approach,
     which would diverge from the Soviet approach.
20   Scoville argues that the Taylor System was vital to the success of the Revolution
     (2001, p. 625).
21   Wren and Bedeian (2004) explore the reality of Lenin's Taylor System.
22   Cerny (2010), p. 45.

23 A view Draper (1966) contrasted with the purer, more Marxist, version of socialism: socialism-from-below. Young (1988).

24 Pipes described this as 'patrimonial monarchy', arguing that subjects were in effect slaves ((1977), pp. 64–79). Hosking refers to it as a form of patronage ((2012), pp. 43–44), and Eisenstadt and Roniger as a relationship of domination supplemented by mutual trust ((1984), pp. 48–49).

25 From Codes of Laws of the Russian Empire quoted in Shanin (1985), p. 1.

26 Referring to Russia's semi-feudal society where the recognizable 'big man' at the top acts as both patron and protector, linked through kinship to the Tsar at the apex of the system. Baberowski (1999), also see Hosking (2012) and Malfliet and Scharpé (2003).

27 Hosking (2012), p. 44, also see Orlovsky (1983), Ransel (1988).

28 It may explain why Lenin and Stalin are still regarded as two of Russia's 'best' leaders. Refer to the Levada Center poll www.rt.com/politics/brezhnev-stalin-gorbachev-soviet-638/, 5 May 2016.

29 The new state '…murdered the Tsar…undermined the Church and weakened the family, it overturned property relationships and transformed the educational system…institutional bulwarks of habitual trust were enfeebled or eliminated, making routine activities more unpredictable.' Hosking (2014), p. 13.

30 'At school they said: "Look how [the enemies] won't let us live under Communism – look how they blow up factories, derail trams, and kill people – all this done by enemies of the people." They beat this into our heads so often that we stopped thinking for ourselves. We saw "enemies" everywhere', recalled a worker in Figes (2007), p. 274.

31 'He who is not with us is against us' became a popular refrain (Kaellis 2012, p. 65). Such polarization quickly isolated so-called enemies, borne out by Trotsky's exile and subsequent demonization.

32 Total obedience in Russia is nothing new – consider life under Ivan the Terrible and refer to Brenton (2016), p. 292.

33 'The visible broadsword, complementing the hidden dagger of the Okhrana (secret police)', as one historian describes it (Hosking 2014).

34 Beer (2016), prologue. It often relied upon the enduring, once localized, communities of joint responsibility, nationalizing, systematizing and bureaucratizing them into the institutions of state.

35 Hayek (1945), p. 107.

36 Hosking (2014), ch.1.

37 As noted in Bukharin's letters to Stalin before his execution on 15 March 1938. Getty and Naumov (1999), pp. 556–60.

38 For example, the fate of Iuliia Piatnitskaia, outlined in her diary (1996), depicts how officially inspired distrust could become contagious, while co-existing alongside total trust.

39 Brenton (2016), pp. 291–92.

40 Garton Ash (2009).

Chapter 9

1   Compare the 'culture of real virtuality' (Castells 2000b) and the 'notion of technological de-differentiation'. (Lash 2002).

2   The Western capitalist model after the 2008 financial collapse.

3   As a metaphor, notions of fluidity are drawn from different ideas: from Bauman's (2000) Liquid Modernity, implying a rootlessness to all forms of social construction in an increasingly disorganised and complex world, to Castells' (2000a) changing structural and organizational environment, to Melucci's (1996) notion of a 'nomadic' subject, as summarized by Sutherland (2013), pp. 3–4.

4   Sexton (2012).

5   Social theorists have long studied revolution within the field of 'contentious politics', starting with social psychological theories of group/mass action before branching off into three approaches: structural (Offe (1985) and Tarrow (1994)); rational choice (McAdam (1982), McCarthy and Zald (1977)); and cultural (Thompson (1966), Anderson (1990)). Each approaches their study from a different perspective on theorists of revolution, focusing a different lens on the origin, social base, organization and dynamics of the movement. They often stress agency, rather than outcome. The result is quite different terminology and a disjunction between the fields of study. A cross-disciplinary approach may well prove more insightful. (McAdam, Tarrow and Tilly (1997)).

6   Inglehart and Siemienska (1988), pp. 440–57.

7   Sennett (2006) describes how corporations become more diffuse and decentred under 'New Capitalism', in contrast with Weber's (2009) 'iron cage' bureaucracy.

8   Sayyid Qutb quoted in Tibi (2012), p. 145.

9   The objective was to achieve world socialism and then stateless communism. Bukharin (1933).

10 Contrast, on the one hand, the different vision of, and methods for creating, a global caliphate as exemplified by Bin Laden (2005) and the Islamic State and, on the other, successive interpretations of 'international' communism by Russian leaders. Mawdudi (1995), quoted in Jackson (2014), p. 144.

11 First seen in Packer's 'Dreaming of Democracy' (2003), an intense debate surrounds the label 'Arab Spring', due to the orientalist connotations and its notion of being a spectacle for the West. Zevallos (2012).

12 Kristof (2009).

13 Khalidi (2011) and Challand (2011).

14 Anderson (2011), p. 3.

15 Heydemann (2007).

16 Cockburn (2016) and Falk (2015), respectively.

17 Jones (2013) and Phillips (2012).

18 The Jasmin Revolution in Tunisia, the January 25 Revolution and June 30 Revolution in Egypt.
19 Coomb (2011), pp. 138–39.
20 Bayat (2013), p. 53.
21 Hirst (2012), pp. 1–2.
22 13.5 million Syrians needed assistance, 6.6 million were internally displaced and 4.8 million have fled, according to the UN. www.unocha.org/syria, 4 July 2016.
23 See Goldstone's useful classifications (2001, 1980 and 1982).
24 Anderson (2011), p. 2.
25 Patrick (2010).
26 Kirby (2000), pp. 407–08.
27 Around 63 per cent of the world population is mobile phone users; 40 per cent have an internet connection: nearly 3.5 billion as at 29 July 2016. Extracted from Statista's mobile phone user penetration as a percentage of the population worldwide from 2013 to 2019 (www.statista.com/statistics/470018/, 22 October 2016) and Internet Live Stats' statistics report (www.internetlivestats.com/internet-users/, 24 October 2016).
28 Lukacs (2013), p. 1.
29 Castells (2004), pp. 1–73.
30 Capra (2002), p. 9.
31 Lash (2002), p. 28.
32 Referred to as the 'Access' or 'Sharing Economy'. Rifkin (2000).
33 Anderson (2006).
34 Steiner's 'On the Internet, nobody knows you're a dog', *The New Yorker*, 5 July 1993.
35 Lewis's AIDA (Awareness, Interest, Desire, Action) model is the best known of the hierarchy of effects models, all of which imply that consumers move through a series of stages when they make purchase decisions.
36 Granovetter's strong and weak ties (1973). Compare Putnam's 'thick and thin trust' (2000) and refer to the Gladwell versus Shirky debate in 2010–11.
37 Clavin (2011). See Vincent (2013) for an overview of whether political science is sufficiently state-centric.
38 Hosking (2014), p. 174.
39 Ibid., p. 175.
40 The West has '…inherited a nineteenth-century bureaucracy which for all its modifications and refinements remains ill-suited to the task of translating political wishes into practical reality'. (Hennessey, cited in Bevir and Rhodes (2003), p. 150).
41 Lagendijk *et al.* (2009) argue it has neither retreated nor been hollowed out, but is disorientated.
42 Sur (1997), p. 422.

43 Beckert *et al.* (2006), p. 1459. Their list is not comprehensive, but includes religious sects, trade diasporas, craft associations, patron–client ties, credit networks, kinship groups and mutual aid societies.

44 Crack (2008), p. 137.

45 'Mediat[ing] time and space', 'problematising the multi-layered significance of how they are experienced'. Tsatsou (2009), p. 11.

46 Duck (1997).

47 McKnight and Chervany (1996), Barber (1983) and Luhmann (1979) share this 3-D view of trust.

48 Coleman (1990), Dasgupta (1988).

49 Mishler and Rose (2001).

50 Khodyakov (2007), p. 123.

51 While sharing these notions, they are interpreted and applied differently around the world – a reflection of multiple factors including history, culture and religion.

52 For example, Edelman Group has measured trust in business, media, NGOs and government for sixteen years. Their 2016 report is available at www.edelman.com/insights/intellectual-property/2016-edelman-trust-barometer/, 15 October 2016, while World Value Survey, a worldwide network of social scientists which explores people's personal and cultural beliefs, how they change over time, and what social and political impact they have, also measures trust. http://www.worldvaluessurvey.org/wvs.jsp, 15 October 2016.

53 Edelman's 2014 Trust Barometer noted that, among the general population, trust in government was below 50 per cent in twenty-two of the twenty-seven countries surveyed, with strikingly low levels in Western Europe – particularly in Spain (14 per cent), Italy (18 per cent) and France (20 per cent).

54 With apologies to Marx (1998).

55 Eatwell (1997) and Almond and Verba (1989).

56 Citrin (1974) and Craig (1996) have charted the extraordinary collapse of trust.

57 Putnam (2000).

58 Misztal (1996), p. 4.

59 Trust, in influential definitions, is assumed to be an integral element of legitimacy. Tyler (2006).

60 Tyler (2016).

61 Jackson and Gau (2016).

62 Uslaner (2018).

63 Widely acknowledged in the social sciences as a period of transition, it is variously referred to under the headings of post-modernity, post-industrial society and global society.

64 Lewis and Weigert (1985b), p. 968.

65 See Auer (2009).

66 Schell (2003), p. 186. For Burke (1984), it draws on Bakhtin's use of the term to depict the temporary reversal of power in the same way that medieval carnivals mocked the 'normal rules' of order and morality.

67 Auer (2009), Lawson (2005).

68 Snyder (1999). As Goodwin argued, near universal access to the ballot box negated the need for revolutionaries (2001), p. 8.

69 Selbin (2001), Foran (2003).

70 Ross (2011). By contrast, Tugal (2013) has used recent events in Egypt to discredit the concept.

71 The fifth 'communications revolution'. Kovarik (2011).

72 Castells (2009), p. 284.

73 Isherwood (2008) notes that blogging led to the conviction of two police officers for torture of a minibus driver in 2007, while el-Nawawy and Khamis (2013) point out that reporting on sexual harassment led to the introduction of draft legislation in 2010.

74 Loewenstein (2008), Herrera (2014).

75 'Regarded as the new way out that "might work better" than political parties for organising social action' (Hofheinz 2011, p. 1419), it boosted support for, and participation in, the 6th April Movement, a Facebook group which encouraged support for strikes in Egypt between 2003 and 2010. However, they received little or no coverage outside the country.

76 It was characterized by Faris as 'engendering extraordinary low levels of commitment' when a call to strike on Mubarak's eightieth birthday went unanswered (2010), p. 130.

77 Morozov coined events in Moldova a 'Twitter revolution', but quickly became disillusioned. Contrast Morozov (2009a) with (2009b and 2011).

78 Shirky (2009).

79 Hofheinz (2011), p. 1420. Such online communities of trusted friends united by shared values quickly gained fame in 2011.

80 This is a reductionist theory that seeks to show technology as the key mover in history and social change. Kunz (2006), p. 2. It is challenged by Friedman (2002) who sets out a dystopian account. Graff also argues that there are 'variable paths to societal change' (1987), p. 35.

81 Said (2003) makes reference to such constructs.

82 Hermida (2010). Facing the continuous deadlines of the 24-hour news cycle and reliant on social media for information not tainted by the regime, the Western media readily embrace this viewpoint. See Burns (2010) and Hirst (2012) in reference to such 'ambient journalism'.

83 Smith (1994), p. 11 and Tovey (2011) refer to the fraudulent blog, *A Gay Girl in Damascus*, which had credibility because it matched liberal Western perceptions of the Middle East.

84 McLuhan (1964), p. 23.

85	Mosco (2004), p. 25.

86	Margetts *et al.* (2016).

87	Gladwell (2000).

88	In the case of the Arab Spring, this not only sits uncomfortably with traditional Middle Eastern thinking in general, but reinforces a widespread suspicion of foreign models.

89	Tarrow (2013).

90	Boroditsky (2011). Although still contested, an increasing body of empirical evidence has accrued which supports the Sapir-Whorf hypothesis: language shapes thought even at the most fundamental level of human experience (Vygotsky *et al.* 1978). As Moulene argues, 'society is spoken by individuals and with all the words they have learnt by living and doing' (2015), p. 119.

91	This well-known marketing phrase captures the intrinsic nature of 'revolution' to induce action.

92	Tarrow (2013).

93	'What does revolution mean to you?', *The New Statesman*, 31 October 2013.

94	First used in 1964 by Justice Potter Stewart to describe his threshold test for obscenity in *Jacobellis v. Ohio*. (378 U.S. 184, 1964).

95	Rennick (2013), p. 2.

96	Brand (2014), p. 5.

97	'The tradition of all dead…weighs like a nightmare on the brains of the living.' Marx (1852).

98	As noted in sociolinguistics and the sociology of language.

99	Tarrow (2013), p. 209.

Conclusion

1	Finley (1986), p. 50.

2	Wrightson (2013).

3	Margetts *et al.* (2016).

4	Refer to discussions in *The Wall Street Journal* www.wsj.com/articles/chinas-new-tool-for-social-control-a-credit-rating-for-everything-1480351590, *Wired* www.wired.co.uk/article/chinese-government-social-credit-score-privacy-invasion, and *The Washington Post* www.washingtonpost.com/world/asia_pacific/chinas-plan-to-organize-its-whole-society-around-big-data-a-rating-for-everyone/2016/10/20/1cd0dd9c-9516-11e6-ae9d-0030ac1899cd_story.html?utm_term=.dba43fcc054c.

5	Bennett (2012).

6	Upshaw (2005).

Bibliography

A and E Home Video Biography (2005), *Biography Series – Vladimir Lenin: Voice of Revolution*.

Abbott, F. F. (1901), *A History and Description of Roman Political Institutions*. (Boston: Ginn; London: Athenaeum Press)

Abrahamian, E. (2009), 'Mass Protests in the Islamic Revolution, 1977–79', in A. Roberts and T. Garton Ash (eds) *Civil Resistance and Power Politics: The Experience of Non-Violent Action from Gandhi to the Present*. (Oxford and New York: Princeton University Press), pp. 162–78.

Achcar, G. (2016), *Morbid Symptoms*. (London: Saqi Books)

Adams, C. *et al.* (eds) (2005), *Visions and Revisions of Eighteenth-Century France*. (Penn State Press)

Adams, G. J. (2012), *Letters to John Law*. (Newton Page)

Adamson, J. S. A. (2009), *The English Civil War: Conflict and Contexts, 1640–49*. (Palgrave Macmillan)

Addison, J. (1711), 'Article of Good Breeding', *The Spectator*, vol. 119.

Adib-Moghaddam, A. (2013), *On the Arab Revolts and the Iranian Revolution: Power and Resistance Today*. (Bloomsbury Academic)

Africa, T. W. (1974), 'Urban Violence in Imperial Rome', *The Journal of Interdisciplinary History*, vol. 2, no. 1, pp. 3–21.

Albrow, M. (1997), *The Global Age: State and Society beyond Modernity*. (Stanford University Press)

Allan, K. (2010), *The Social Lens: An Invitation to Social and Sociological Theory*. (Sage Publications)

Allen, R. C. (2009), *The British Industrial Revolution in Global Perspective*. (Cambridge University Press)

Allmand, C. T. (1988), *The Hundred Years War: England and France at War c. 1300–c. 1450*. (Cambridge University Press)

Alloway, K. (2007), *The Limits of Dechristianization: Religion and Revolution in the District of Montpellier, 1789–99*. (Durham)

Almond, G. and Verba, S. (1989), *The Civic Culture: Political Attitudes and Democracy in Five Nations*. (London: Sage Publications)

Alston, R. (2015), *Rome's Revolution: Death of the Republic and Birth of the Empire*. (Oxford University Press)

Altamira, R. (1917), 'Magna Carta and Spanish Medieval Juriprudence', in *Magna Carta Commemoration Essays* (The Lawbook Exchange, Ltd), pp. 227–43.

Althusius, J. (1614), *Politica*. F. S. Carney (ed.) (Liberty Fund)

Alvarez, S. A. *et al.* (2003), 'Trust and Its Alternatives', *Human Resource Management*, vol. 42, no. 4, 393–404.

Amuzegar, J. (1991), *The Dynamics of the Iranian Revolution: The Pahlavis' Triumph and Tragedy*. (Albany, NY: State University of New York Press)

Anderson, B. (2006), *Imagined Communities: Reflections on the Origin and Spread of Nationalism*. Steven Seidman and Jeffrey C. Alexander (eds) (Verso)

Anderson, C. (2012), *Makers: The New Industrial Revolution*. (New York: Crown Business)

Anderson, C. (2003), 'Hobbes, Locke and Hume on Trust and the Education of the Passions', *The New England Journal of Political Science*, vol. 1, no. 1, 52–80.

Anderson, E. (1990), *Streetwise: Race, Class, and Change in an Urban Community*. (Chicago: University of Chicago Press)

Anderson, J. C. and Narus, J. A. (1990), 'A Model of Distributor Firm and Manufacturer Firm Working Partnerships', *Journal of Marketing*, vol. 54, 42–58.

Anderson, L. (2011), 'Demystifying the Arab Spring: Parsing the Differences between Tunisia, Egypt, and Libya', *Foreign Affairs*, vol. 90, no. 2, 2–7.

Anderson, P. (1996), *Passages from Antiquity to Feudalism*. (Verso)

Anheier, H. K. and Toepler, S. (eds) (2009), *International Encyclopaedia of Civil Society*. vol. 24. (Springer Science and Business Media)

Anon. (1644), *Britannia, Passionately and Historically, Remembering Her Misery and Happinesse in Former Ages, and Declaring Her Calamities, and Expectations*. (Printed according to order by, G.B. and R.W.)

Anon. (1571), *A Collection of the Lawes and Statutes of This Realme Concerning Liueries of Companies and Reteynours*. (Richardi Tottelli)

Antiphon (n.d.), *Speeches*. (Perseus Online, University of Chicago)

Appelbaum, R. (2010), *Literature and Utopian Politics in Seventeenth-Century England*. (Cambridge University Press)

Arendt, H. (2006), *On Revolution*. (Penguin Classics)

Arendt, H. (1972), *Crises of the Republic: Lying in Politics, Civil Disobedience on Violence, Thoughts on Politics, and Revolution*. (Harcourt Brace Jovanovich)

Arendt, H. (1965), *On Revolution*. (New York: The Viking Press)

Aristotle (2009a), *The Athenian Constitution*. F. G. Kenyon (ed.) (Merchant Books)

Aristotle (2009b), *The Nicomachean Ethics*. Revised Edition. L. Brown and D. Ross (eds) (Oxford: Oxford University Press)

Aristotle (2000), *Politics*. B. Jowett (ed.) (Dover Publications Inc.)

Armitage, D. (2012), 'What's the Big Idea? Intellectual History and the Longue Durée', *History of European Ideas*, vol. 38, November, 493–507.

Armitage, D. (2009), 'Ideas of Civil War in Seventeenth-Century England', *Annals of the Japanese Association for the Study of Puritanism*, vol. 4, 4–18.

Arnold, D. (1983), *The New Oxford Companion to Music, volume 1*. (Oxford University Press)

Arrighi, G. (2007), 'States, Markets, and Capitalism, East and West', *Positions*, vol. 15, no. 2, 251–84.

Arya, D. A. (2002), *The Goddess Fortuna in Imperial Rome: Cult, Art, Text*. (University of Texas)

Ascham, A. (1648), *A Discourse, Wherein Is Examined What Is Particularly Lawfull during the Confusions and Revolutions of Goverment*. (London)

Asen, R. (1999), 'Toward a Normative Conception of Difference in Public Deliberation', *Argumentation and Advocacy*, vol. 25, Winter, 115–29.

Aston, N. (1992), *The End of an Élite: The French Bishops and the Coming of the Revolution, 1786–1790*. (Oxford University Press)

Atkinson, N. (2011), 'They Rang the Bells at the Wrong Time'. Early Modern Communities online.

Auer, S. (2009), 'Violence and the End of Revolution after 1989'. *Thesis Eleven*. vol. 97, no. 1, 6–25.

Avery, J. (2014), *Progress, Poverty and Population: re-reading Condorcet, Godwin and Malthus*. (Routledge)

Axelrod, R. (1984), *The Evolution of Cooperation*. R. Axelrod (ed.) (New York: Basic Books)

Aylmer, G. E. (1986), *Rebellion or Revolution? England, 1640–1660*. (Oxford University Press)

Ayto, J. (1990), *Bloomsbury Dictionary of Word Origins*. (London: Bloomsbury)

Ayton, A. and Price, L. (1998), *The Medieval Military Revolution: State, Society and Military Change in Medieval and Early Modern Europe*. A. Ayton and L. Price (eds) (I.B. Tauris)

Baberowski, J. (1999), 'In Search of Clarity: Colonialism and Civilizing Mission in the Tsar's Empire and in the Soviet Union', *History of Eastern Europe*, vol. 47, 482–504.

Bacharach, S. B. and Lawler, E. J. (1980), *Power and Politics in Organizations*. (Jossey-Bass)

Bachmann, R. and Inkpen, A. C. (2011), 'Understanding Institutional-Based Trust Building Processes in Inter-Organizational Relationships', *Organization Studies*, vol. 32, no. 2, 281–301.

Bachmann, R. (2001), 'Trust and Control in Organizational Relations', *Organization Studies*, vol. 22, Special Issue, v–viii.

Bacon, F. (1620), The New Organon or True Directions Concerning the Interpretation of Nature. Available at www.constitution.org/bacon/nov_org.htm.

Bagshaw, E. (1660), *The Rights of the Crown of England, as It Is Established by Law*. (A.M.)

Baier, A. C. (1995), *Moral Prejudices: Essays on Ethics*. (Harvard University Press)

Baird, C. W. (1885), *History of the Huguenot Emigration to America*. (New York: Dodd, Mead and Company)

Baker, K. M. (1990), *Inventing the French Revolution: Essays on French Political Culture in the Eighteenth Century*. (Cambridge University Press)

Baker, N. S. (2013), *The Fruit of Liberty*. vol. 4. (Harvard University Press)

Baker, N. S. (2009), 'For Reasons of State: Political Executions, Republicanism, and the Medici in Florence, 1480–1560', *Renaissance Quarterly*, vol. 62, no. 2, 444–78.

Bakunin, M. (2007), *To the Comrades of the International Workingmen's Association of Locle and Chaux-De-Fonds. Marxist.org* online.

Ballard, R. (2010), *Hawala and Hundi: Vehicles for the Long-Distance Transmission of Value*. (University of Manchester, Centre for Applied South Asian Studies (CASAS))

Banfield, E. C. (1958), *The Moral Basis of a Backward Society*. (Free Press)

Barber, B. (1983), *The Logics and Limits of Trust*. (New Brunswick, NJ: Rutgers University Press)

Barber, M. (2006), *The Trial of the Templars*. Second Edition. (Cambridge: Cambridge University Press)

Barker, C. *et al.* (eds) (2013), *Marxism and Social Movements*. (Leiden, Holland: Brill)

Barker, J. (2014), *England, Arise: The People, the King and the Great Revolt of 1381*. (Little, Brown Book Group)

Barlow, C. T. (1978), *Bankers, Moneylenders, and Interest Rates in the Roman Republic*. (University of North)

Barnard, C. I. (1948), *The Functions of the Executive*. (Cambridge, MA: Harvard University Press)

Barruel, A. A. (1798), *Memoires pour Sevir a l'histoire du Jacobinisme*. (A Hambourg: Chez P. Fauche, Libraire)

Barry, J. M. (2005), *Fides in Julisus Caesar's Bellum Civile: A Study in Roman Political Ideology at the Close of the Republican Era*. (University of Maryland)

Barthelemy, D. and White, S. D. (1996), 'The "Feudal Revolution"', *Past and Present*, vol. 152, 196–223.

Barton, C. A. (1995), *The Sorrows of the Ancient Romans: The Gladiator and the Monster*. (Princeton: Princeton University Press)

Bastos, M. T. *et al.* (2012), 'Tweeting Political Dissent: Retweets as Pamphlets in #FreeIran, #FreeVenezuela, #Jan25, #SpanishRevolution and #OccupyWallSt', in Oxford University: *The Internet, Policy, and Politics Conference*, pp. 1–22.

Batson, C. D. *et al.* (1992), 'Differentiating Affect, Mood and Emotion: Toward Functionally Based Conceptual Distinctions. Emotion', in M. S. Clark (ed.), *Emotion: Emotion v. 13 (The Review of Personality and Social Psychology)* (Newbury Park, CA: Sage Publications), pp. 294–326.

Bauman, Z. (2000), *Liquid Modernity*. Zygmunt Bauman (ed.) vol. 30. (Polity Press)

Baumgold, D. (2013), '"Trust" in Hobbes's Political Thought', *Political Theory*, vol. 41, no. 6, 838–55.

Bayat, A. (2013), 'Revolution in Bad Times', *New Left Review*, vol. 80, March/ April, 47–60.

Baylor, M. G. (1994), *The Radical Reformation*. (Cambridge University Press)

Beard, M. (2015), *SPQR: A History of Ancient Rome*. (Profile Books)

Beard, M. *et al.* (1998), *Religions of Rome: A History (vol. 1)*. (Cambridge University Press)

Bearman, P. *et al.* (2013), *Umma.* (Brill)

Beckert, S. *et al.* (2006), 'AHR Conversation: On Transnational History', *The American Historical Review*, vol. 111, no. 5, 1441–64.

Beer, D. (2016), 'Prologue: The Bell of Uglich', in *The House of the Dead: Siberian Exile under the Tsars* (Allen Lane)

Beer, S. H. (1982), *Britain against Itself: The Political Contradictions of Collectivism.* (W.W. Norton and Company)

Belaya, V. and Hanf, J. H. (2009), 'Power Struggle in the Food Chain?', in *A Resilient European Food Industry and Food Chain in a Challenging World.* (Chania, Crete, Greece: Leibniz Institute), pp. 1–33.

Belaya, V. *et al.* (2008), 'Recognizing the Links between Power and Trust in Managing Supply Chain Relationships', in *12th Congress of the European Association of Agricultural Economists* (EAAE), pp. 1–4.

Bell, D. A. (1992), 'The "Public Sphere", "the State, and the World of Law in Eighteenth-Century France"', *French Historical Studies*, vol. 17, no. 4, 912–934.

Bell, D. A. (2001), 'Culture and Religion', in W. Doyle (ed.), *Old Regime France*, 1648–1788 (Oxford University Press), pp. 78–104.

Bell, D. A. (2009), *The Cult of the Nation in France: Inventing Nationalism, 1680–1800* (Harvard University Press)

Bellamy, R. (2014), 'Citizenship: Historical Development of', in J. Wright (ed.), *International Encyclopaedia of Social and Behavioural Sciences* (Elsevier), pp. 1–18.

Belliotti R. A. (2009), *Roman Philosophy and the Good Life.* (Lexington Books)

Belloc, H. (2007), *The Servile State.* (Cosimo Classics)

Benard, C. (1986), *'The Government of God': Iran's Islamic Republic.* Reprint. (Columbia University Press)

Bennett, W. L. (2012), 'The Personalization of Politics: Political Identity, Social Media, and Changing Patterns of Participation', *The Annals of the American Academy*, November, 20–39.

Berger, A. (1968), *Encyclopedic Dictionary of Roman Law, Volume 43.* (American Philosophical Society)

Berk, L. E. (2012), 'Emotional Development', in *Child Development* (Pearson), pp. 398–443.

Berlin, I. (1967), *Karl Marx: His Life and Environment.* (New York: Time Inc Book Division)

Berman, E. *et al.* (2008), 'Can Hearts and Minds Be Bought? The Economics of Counterinsurgency in Iraq', *Journal of Political Economy*, vol. 119, no. 4, 766–819.

Berman, S. (2003), 'Islamism, Revolution, and Civil Society', *Perspectives on Politics*, vol. 1, no. 2, 11–26.

Berman, H. J. (2009), *Law and Revolution II: The Impact of the Protestant Reformations on the Western Legal Tradition.* (Harvard University Press)

Berman, H. J. (1983), *Law and Revolution: The Formation of the Western Legal Tradition.* (Harvard University Press)

Bernard, G. W. (2011), 'The Dissolution of the Monasteries', *History*, vol. 96, no. 324, 390–409.

Bernstein (2008), *Complex Rituals: Games and Processions in Republican Rome.* (Blackwell Publishing Ltd)

Betlock, L. (2003), 'New England's Great Migration', *New England Ancestors*, vol. 4, no. 2, 22–24.

Beverley, T. (1689), *The Late Great Revolution in This Nation…to Be Duly Ascribed to the Supreme Spirit, Now about to Move in the Fulfilling All Prophecy….* (London)

Bevir, M. (2011), 'The Contextual Approach', in G. Klosko (ed.), *The Oxford Handbook of the History of Political Philosophy* (Oxford University Press), pp. 11–23.

Bevir, M. and Rhodes, R. A. W. (2003), *Interpreting British Governance.* (London: Routledge)

Beza, T. (1574), *De jure magistratuum (On the Rights of Magistrates).* P. S. Poole and H-L. Gonin (eds) Henry-Louis Gonin (trans.) (Geneva)

Bierstedt, R. (1950), 'An Analysis of Social Power', *American Sociological Review*, vol. 15, no. 6, 730–38.

Bijlsma-Frankema, K. M. and van de Bunt, G. G. (2003), 'Antecedents of Trust in Managers: A "Bottom up" Approach', *Personnel Review*, vol. 32, no. 5, 638–64.

Binmore, K. (2006), *The Origins of Fair Play.* ESRC through University College London, Working Paper no. 614.

Blackwell, C. W. (2003), *The Development of Athenian Democracy* (STOA Publications), pp. 6–7.

Blair, R. (2007), *The Great Omission: Amazing Ways the Church Muddles the Message: How to Get It Right and Tell It Right.* (CSS Publishing)

Blake, W. (1908), *The Poetical Works of William Blake.* J. Sampson (ed.) (London, New York: Oxford University Press)

Blake, W. (1970), *Songs of Innocence and of Experience: Shewing the Two Contrary States of the Human Soul.* New Edition. G. Keynes (ed.) (Oxford: Oxford University Press)

Blau, P. M. and Scott, W. R. (1962), *Formal Organizations.* (San Francisco, CA: Chandler)

Bleiker, R. (2000), *Popular Dissent, Human Agency and Global Politics.* (Cambridge University Press)

Blickle, P. and Catt, C. (1979), 'Peasant Revolts in the German Empire in the Late Middle Ages', *Social History*, vol. 4, no. 2, 223–39.

Blind, P. K. (2007), 'Building Trust in Government in the Twenty-First Century: Review of Literature and Emerging Issues', in *7th Global Forum on Reinventing Government* (Vienna, Austria: UNDESA), pp. 1–31.

Bloch, M. (1961), *Feudal Society, Volumes 1 and 2.* (University of Chicago Press)

Bloom, H. (2004), *The Italian Renaissance.* (Infobase Publishing)

Blout, T. (1656), *Glossographia.* (G. Olms)

Blumer, H. (1969), 'Collective Behavior', in A. M. Lee (ed.), *Principles of Sociology.* Third Edition. (New York: Barnes and Noble Books), pp. 219–88.

Blunsom, E. O. (2013), *The Past and Future Of Law*. (Xlibris Corporation)

Bocheński, J. M. (1974), 'An Analysis of Authority', in F. Adelman (ed.), *Authority* (The Hague: Martinus Nijhoff), pp. 56–85.

Bodel, J. and Olyan, S. M. (eds) (2012), *Household and Family Religion in Antiquity*. (John Wiley and Sons)

Bodensieck, J. (ed.) (1965), *The Encyclopaedia of the Lutheran Church, Volume 2*. (Augsburg Publishing House)

Bodin, J. (1955), *Six Books of the Commonwealth*. Abridged and Translated by M. J. Tooley (Blackwell)

Bodin, J. (1992), *Bodin: On Sovereignty*. (Cambridge University Press)

Bolt, N. (2012), *The Violent Image: Insurgent Propaganda and the New Revolutionaries*. (C Hurst and Co Publishers Ltd)

Bonoma, T. V. (1976), 'Conflict, Cooperation, and Trust in Three Power Systems', *Behavioural Science*, vol. 21, 499–514.

Borges, J. L. (1999), *Collected Fictions*. A. Hurley (ed.) (Penguin Books)

Boroditsky, L. (2011), 'How Language Shapes Thought', *Scientific American*, February, 63–65.

Borowski, M. (2015), 'Language and Its Influence on How We Understand Reality', *SKASE Journal of Theoretical Linguistics*, vol. 13, no. 2, 70–91.

Braccioloni, P. (1715), *Poggii Historia Florentina*. (Kessinger Legacy Publishing)

Braddick, M. J. (2000), *State Formation in Early Modern England, c. 1550–1700*. (Cambridge University Press)

Bradley, K. (1997), 'The Problem of Slavery in Classical Culture', *Classical Philology*, vol. 92, 273–82.

Brady, L. (2013), 'Death and the Landscape of the Fortunes of Men', *Neophilologus*, vol. 98, no. 2, 325–36.

Brady Jr., T. A. (1995), *Protestant Politics: Jacob Sturm (1489–1553) and the German Reformation*. (Studies in German Histories, Humanities Press International Inc.)

Brand, L. A. (2014), *Official Stories: Politics and National Narratives in Egypt and Algeria*. (Stanford University Press)

Branzei, O. *et al*. (2007), 'Culture-Contingent Signs of Trust in Emergent Relationships', *Organizational Behavior and Human Decision Processes*, vol. 104, no. 1, 61–82.

Braudel, F. (1996), *The Mediterranean and the Mediterranean World in the Age of Philip II: Volumes 1 and 2*. Second Edition. (University of California Press)

Braudel, F. (1982), 'Preface', in S. Matthews (ed.), *On History* (University of Chicago Press)

Breay, C. (2011), *Magna Carta: Manuscripts and Myths*. Second Edition. (London: The British Library Publishing Division)

Breen, M. P. (2007), *Law, City, and King: Legal Culture, Municipal Politics, and State Formation in Early Modern Dijon*. (University Rochester Press)

Brent, A. (1999), *The Imperial Cult and the Development of Church Order: Concepts and Images of Authority in Paganism and Early Christianity before the Age of Cyprian*. (Brill)

Brenton, T. (2016), *Historically Inevitable? Turning Points of the Russian Revolution*. T. Brenton (ed.) (Profile Books)

Breuilly, J. (1993), 'Nationalism and the State', in R. Michener (ed.), *Nationality, Patriotism, and Nationalism in Liberal Democratic Societies*. (St. Paul: Professors World Peace Academy), pp. 19–48.

Brewer, J. (1990), *The Sinews of Power: War, Money, and the English State, 1688–1783*. (Harvard University Press)

Briggs, A. and Burke, P. (2010), *Social History of the Media: From Gutenberg to the Internet*. Third Edition. (Polity Press)

Brinton, C. (2011), *The Jacobins: An Essay in the New History*. (Transaction Publishers)

Brock, R. (2013), *Greek Political Imagery from Homer to Aristotle*. (Bloomsbury Publishing)

Bromiley, P. and Cummings, L. L. (1995), 'Transactions Costs in Organizations with Trust', in R. Bies *et al.* (eds) *Research on Negotiations in Organizations* (Greenwich, CT: JAI Press), pp. 219–47.

Brown, A. (2011), 'De-Masking Renaissance Republicanism', in J. Hankins (ed.), *Medicean and Savonarolan Florence: The Interplay of Politics, Humanism, and Religion* (Brepols Publishers), pp. 225–46.

Brown, A. (2000), 'De-Masking Renaissance Republicanism', in J. Hankins (ed.), *Renaissance Civic Humanism: Reappraisals and Reflections* (Cambridge University Press), pp. 179–99.

Brown, M. and Uslaner, E. M. (2002), 'Inequality, Trust and Political Engagement', in *Annual Meeting of the American Political Science Association*. (Boston, MA: University of Maryland)

Brown, N. (2013), 'Edmund Burke v. Thomas Paine', *National Review*, December.

Brown, W. C. (2011), *Violence in Medieval Europe (The Medieval World)*. (Harlow: Longman)

Browne, E. (1642), *A Paradox Usefull for the Times*. (Oxford: Ann Arbor)

Brucker, G. (2008), 'The Course of Renaissance Events', in G. Ruggiero (ed.), *A Companion to the Worlds of the Renaissance*. (John Wiley and Sons), pp. 21–104.

Brucker, G. (1999), 'Civic Traditions in Premodern Italy', *The Journal of Interdisciplinary History*, vol. 29, no. 3 (Part 1), 357–77.

Brucker, G. A. (1968), 'The Ciompi Revolution', in N. Rubinstein (ed.), *Florentine Studies*. (London: Faber and Faber), pp. 314–56.

Bruni, L. (2007), *History of the Florentine People*. (Harvard University Press)

Bruni, L. (2005), *In Praise of Florence: The Panegyric of the City of Florence and an Introduction to Leonardo Bruni's Civil Humanism*. A. Scheepers (ed.) (Olive Press)

Brunt, P. A. (1965), '"Amicitia" in the Late Roman Republic', in *Proceedings of the Cambridge Philological Society (New Series)*. (Cambridge: Cambridge University Press), pp. 1–20.

Bryce, J. (2012), *The Holy Roman Empire*. (CreateSpace Independent Publishing Platform)

Buchan, J. (2013), *Days of God: The Revolution in Iran and Its Consequences*. (John Murray)

Buchanan, G. (2004) *De jure regni apud Scotos, or, A Dialogue, Concerning the Due Priviledge of Government, in the Kingdom of Scotland, betwixt George Buchanan and Thomas Maitland, by the Said George Buchanan.* (Oxford: Ann Arbor)

Buckley, W. F. (1967), *Sociology and Modern Systems Theory.* (Prentice-Hall)

Bukharin, N. I. (1933), 'The Theory of Proletarian Dictatorship and Scientific Communism', in *Marx's Teaching and Its Historical Importance. Marxist.org* online.

Bullingham, J. (1554), 'Preface', in *A Notable Oration, Made by John Venaeus, a Parisien, in the Defence of the Sacrament of the Aultare.* (London)

Burchell, D. (2003), 'Ancient Citizenship and Its Inheritors', in E. F. Isin and B. S. Turner (eds) *Handbook of Citizenship Studies*. First Edition. (Sage Publications), pp. 89–104.

Burckhardt, J. (1944), *The Civilization of the Renaissance.* L. Goldscheider (ed.) (Phaidon Press)

Burgess, G. (2009), 'Usurpation, Obligation and Obedience in the Thought of the Engagement Controversy', *The Historical Journal*, vol. 29, no. 3, 515.

Burgess, G. (1992), 'The Divine Right of Kings Reconsidered', *The English Historical Review*, vol. 107, no. 425, 837–61.

Burke, E. (2013), *Reflections on the Revolution in France.* (CreateSpace Independent Publishing Platform)

Burke, E. (1984), *Selected Letters of Edmund Burke.* H. C. Mansfield (ed.) (University of Chicago Press)

Burke, P. (2014), *The Italian Renaissance: Culture and Society in Italy.* (Princeton University Press)

Burke, P. (2013), *The Fortunes of the Courtier: The European Reception of Castiglione's Cortegiano.* (Polity Press)

Burke, P. (1998), *The European Renaissance: Centers and Peripheries.* vol. 2. (Wiley)

Burnet, G. (1679), *The History of the Reformation of the Church of England, Volume 1.* Printed for J. Churchill, 1715.

Burns, A. (2010), 'Oblique Strategies for Ambient Journalism', *Media/Culture Journal*, vol. 13, no. 2.

Burrell, G. (2013), *Styles of Organizing: The Will to Form.* (OUP Oxford)

Bush, T. (2011), 'Political Models', in *Theories of Educational Leadership and Management.* Fourth Edition. (Sage Publications), pp. 99–125.

Buss, D. M. (2001), 'Cognitive Biases and Emotional Wisdom in the Evolution of the Conflict between the Sexes', *American Psychologist Society*, vol. 10, no. 6, 219–23.

Buxton, R. (2013), *Myths and Tragedies in Their Ancient Greek Contexts.* (Oxford: Oxford University Press)

Byrd, R. (1995), *The Senate of the Roman Republic.* (US Government Printing Office)

Byrne, J. P. (2004), 'Social and Religious Aspects of Italian Guilds', in C. Kleinhenz (ed.) *Medieval Italy: An Encyclopedia.* (Routledge), p. 479.

Caferro, W. (2011), *Contesting the Renaissance*. (Chichester: Wiley-Blackwell)

Cahill, T. (2010), *The Gifts of the Jews: How a Tribe of Desert Nomads Changed the Way Everyone Thinks and Feels*. (Knopf Doubleday Publishing Group)

Cairns, A. (1993), *The Psychology and Ethics of Honour and Shame in Ancient Greek Literature*. (Oxford: Clarendon Press)

Calhoun, B. (2012a), 'Shaping the Public Sphere: English Coffeehouses and French Salons and the Age of the Enlightenment', *Colgate Academic Review*, vol. 3, no. Spring 2008, 75–99.

Calhoun, C. J. (2012b), *The Roots of Radicalism: Tradition, the Public Sphere, and Early Nineteenth-Century Social Movements*. (University of Chicago Press)

Campbell, P. R. (2007), 'The Language of Patriotism in France, 1750–1770', *e-France*, vol. I, 1750–1770.

Campbell-Smith, D. (2012) *Masters of the Post: The Authorised History of the Royal Mail* (Penguin)

Cantoni, D. (2009), *The Economic Effects of the Protestant Reformation: Testing the Weber Hypothesis in the German Lands*. Economics Working Papers from Department of Economics and Business, Universitat Pompeu Fabra.

Cantoni, D. and Yuchtman, N. (2014), 'Medieval Universities, Legal Institutions, and the Commercial Revolution', *The Quarterly Journal of Economics*, vol. 129, no. 2, 823–87.

Capra, F. (2002), *The Hidden Connections: Integrating the Biological, Cognitive, and Social Dimensions of Life into a Science of Substainability*. (Doubleday Books)

Caris, C. C. and Reynolds, S. (2014), *ISIS Governance in Syria*. (July)

Carlyle, T. (1837), *The French Revolution: A History*. (London: Chapman and Hall)

Carothers, T. (1999) 'Civil Society', *Foreign Policy* 117, pp. 18–29.

Carpenter, C. (2000), *The Formation of Urban Elites: Civic Officials in Late-Medieval York, 1476–1525*. (University of York)

Carpenter, D. A. (2015), 'The Decline of the Curial Sheriff in England 1194–1258', *English Historical Review*, vol. 91, no. 358, 1–32.

Carroll, J. (1993), *Humanism: The Wreck of Western Culture*. (Fontana)

Carruthers, P. (2000), *Phenomenal Consciousness: A Naturalistic Theory*. (Cambridge University Press)

Caskey, J. (2013), 'Medieval Patronage and Its Potentialities', in C. Hourihane (ed.), *Patronage: Power and Agency in Medieval Art*. (Penn State University Press)

Casson, M. and Della Giusta, M. (2006), 'The Economics of Trust', in R. Bachman and A. Zaheer (eds) *Handbook of Trust Research* (Edward Elgar Publishing), pp. 332–54.

Castells, M. (2009), *Communication Power*. (Oxford Univerity Press)

Castells, M. (2004), 'Informationalism, Networks, and the Network Society: A Blueprint', in Manuel Castells (ed.), *The Network Society: A Cross-Cultural Perspective* pp. 1–73.

Castells, M. (2000a), 'Materials for an Exploratory Theory of the Network Society', *British Journal of Sociology*, vol. 51, no. 1, 5–24.

Castells, M. (2000b), *The Information Age: Economy, Society and Culture Volume I: The Rise of the Network Society, Volume II: The Power of Identity, Volume III: End of Millennium*. (Blackwell)

Censer, J. R. (1994), *The French Press in the Age of Enlightenment*. (Routledge)

Cerny, P. G. (2009), 'Neoliberalization and Place: Deconstructing and Reconstructing Borders', in B. Arts *et al.* (eds) *The Disoriented State: Shifts in Governmentality, Territoriality and Governance*. (Springer Netherlands), pp. 12–40.

Cerny, P. G. (2010), *Rethinking World Politics: A Theory of Transnational Neopluralism*. (Oxford: Oxford University Press)

Chalana, A. (2012), *Commerce in Istanbul vs. Florence during the Renaissance*. Exploring Distances: An Alternate Reality. Available at: http://achalana.evolutionofinstruction. org/2012/03/10/commerce-in-istanbul-vs-florence-during-the-renaissance.

Challand, B. (2011), 'The Counter-Power of Civil Society and the Emergence', *Constellations*, vol. 18, no. 3, 271–83.

Challis, C. E. (1992), *A New History of the Royal Mint*. (Cambridge University Press)

Chandler, A. D. (1993), *The Visible Hand: The Managerial Revolution in American Business*. (Harvard University Press)

Chartier, R. (1991), *The Cultural Origins of the French Revolution*. (Duke University Press)

Cheek, T. (2010), *A Critical Introduction to Mao*. (Cambridge: Cambridge University Press)

Child, J. (2005), *Organization: Contemporary Principles and Practice*. (Wiley)

Chou, S. Y. (2012), 'Online Reviews and Pre-Purchase Cognitive Dissonance: A Theoretical Framework and Research Propositions', *Journal of Emerging Trends in Computing and Information Science*, vol. 3, no. 2, 199–204.

Christie, R. and Geis, F. L. (1970), *Studies in Machiavellianism (Social Psychology Monographs)*. (Academic Press Inc)

Christie, W. (1874), *Letters Addressed from London to Sir Joseph Williamson while plenipotentiary at the Congress of Cologne in the Years 1673 and 1674: Volume 2*. (Cornell University Library)

Churchill, C. (2015), *Light Shining in Buckinghamshire*. New Edition. (Nick Hern Books)

Cialdini, R. B. (2009), *Influence*. (HarperCollins)

Cicero, M. T. (n.d.), 'M. Tvlli Ciceronis de legibvs Libritres' (Outline of Cicero's proposed Constitution)', in *de Legibus (On the Laws)*. (Latin Library), p. 28.

Cicero, M. T. (2013), *How to Run a Country: An Ancient Guide for Modern Leaders*. P. Freeman (ed.) (Princeton, NJ: Princeton University Press)

Cicero, M. T. (1917), *The Orations of Marcus Tullius Cicero, vol. 2*. C. D. Yonge (ed.) (London: G. Bell and Sons)

Cicero, M. T. and Yonge, C. D. (1888), *Second Pleading of Cicero in the Gaius Verres Trial. (Actio Secunda)*

Citrin, J. (1974), 'Comment: The Political Relevance of Trust in Government', *The American Political Science Review*, vol. 68, no. 3, 973–88.

Clarendon, E. H. (2009), *The History of the Rebellion: A New Selection*. P. Seaward (ed.) (Oxford: Oxford University Press)

Clark, J. C. D. (2000), *English Society, 1660–1832: Religion, Ideology and Politics during the Ancien Régime*. (Cambridge University Press)

Clarke, P. B. and Foweraker, J. (2003), *Encyclopedia of Democratic Thought*. (Routledge)

Clarke, S. (2015), *The Elizabethan Pamphleteers Popular Moralistic Pamphlets 1580–1640*. (Bloomsbury Academic)

Clavin, P. (2011), 'Introduction: Conceptualising Internationalism between the World Wars', in D. Laqua (ed.), *Internationalism Reconfigured: Transnational Ideas and Movements between the World Wars* (I.B.Tauris), pp. 1–15.

Clergue, H. (1971), *The Salon: A Study of French Society and Personalities in the Eighteenth Century*. (New York, NY: B. Franklin)

Cleveland, J. (1689), *Majestas Intemerata: Or, the Immortality of the King*. (London: S.N.)

Cliff, T. (1985), 'Patterns of Mass Strike', *International Socialism*, vol. 2, no. 29, 3–61.

Cobban, A. (1977), *The Myth of the French Revolution*. (Arden Library)

Cockburn, P. (2016), 'The Arab Spring, Five Years On: A Season that Began in Hope, but Ended in Desolation', *The Independent*, 8 January.

Cockeram, H. (1930), *The English Dictionary of 1623*. (Huntington Press)

Cogswell, T. (2002), 'The People's Love', in T. Cogswell *et al.* (eds) *Politics, Religion and Popularity in Early Stuart Britain: Essays in Honour of Conrad Russell*. (Cambridge University Press), pp. 211–34.

Cohn, S. K. (1980), *The Laboring Classes in Renaissance Florence*. (Acad. Press)

Coke, E. (1826), *The Reports of Sir Edward Coke*. vol. 4. J. H. Thomas and J. F. Fraser (eds) (J. Butterworth and Son)

Cole, G. A. (2001), *Organisational Behaviour*. (Thomson Learning)

Coleman, C. (1986), *Revolution Reassessed: Revisions in the History of Tudor Government and Administration*. (Clarendon Press)

Coleman, J. A. (2013), 'Authority, Power, Leadership: Sociological Understandings', *New Theology Review*, vol. 10, no. 3, 31–44.

Coleman, J. S. (1990), *Foundations of Social Theory*. (Cambridge, MA: Balknap Press of Harvard University Press)

Coleridge, S. T. (1798), 'France: An Ode.' Available at: https://rpo.library.utoronto.ca/poems/france-ode.

Collier, D. and Levitsky, S. (1997), 'Democracy with Adjectives: Conceptual Innovation Comparative Research', *World Politics*, vol. 49.

Collingwood, R. G. (2013), *The New Leviathan or Man, Society, Civilisation and Barbarism*. Revised. D. Boucher (ed.) (Oxford: Clarendon Press)

Collingwood, R. G. (1994), *The Idea of History: With Lectures 1926–1928*. Revised Edition. J van der Dussen (ed.) (Oxford Paperbacks)

Collins, R. (1975), *Conflict Sociology: Toward an Explanatory Science*. (Academic Press Inc)

Colombo, E. (2008), *The Revolution: A Concept Dissolvable in Postmodernity*. Anarchist online.

Compagni, D. (1986), *Dino Compagni's Chronicle of Florence*. (University of Pennsylvania Press)

Concorcet, N. de (2012) *Political Writings*. Steven Lukes and Nadia Urbinati (eds) (Cambridge University Press)

Constant, B. (1988), 'The Liberty of the Ancients Compared with that of the Moderns', in B. Fontana (ed.), *The Political Writings of Benjamin Constant* (Cambridge: Cambridge University Press), pp. 309–28.

Converse, P. E. (2006) 'The Nature of Belief Systems in Mass Publics', *Critical Review*, vol. 18, no. 1–3, 1–74.

Cook, K. S. *et al.* (2005), *Cooperation without Trust?* (New York: Russell Sage Foundation)

Cook, K. S. (ed.) (2001), *Trust in Society*. (New York: Russell Sage Foundation)

Cooley, A. E. (2009), *Res Gestae Divi Augusti*. (Cambridge University Press)

Coombs, N. (2011), *What Is Revolution? [R x ']* Available at: https://speculativeheresy. files.wordpress.com/2011/02/what-is-revolution_-rx-nathancoombs.pdf.

Cooper, J. P. D. (2003), *Propaganda and the Tudor State: Political Culture in the Westcountry*. (Clarendon Press)

Corfield, P. J. (2013), 'Britain's Political, Cultural and Industrial Revolutions: As Seen by Eighteenth-Century Observers and Later Historians', in *International Society for Eighteenth-Century Studies Special Conference*. (Rotterdam: Erasmus University), pp. 1–24.

Cornell, T. J. (1995), *The Beginnings of Rome: Italy and Rome from the Bronze Age to the Punic Wars (c. 1000–264 BC)*. (Routledge)

Cornwall, J. (1967), 'Evidence of Population Mobility in the Seventeenth Century', *Historical Research*, vol. 40, no. 102, 143–52.

Costa, A. C. and Bijlsma-Frankema, K. (2007), 'Trust and Control Interrelations: New Perspectives on the Trust–Control Nexus', *Group and Organization Management*, vol. 32, no. 4, 392–406.

Cotgrave, R. (1611), *A Dictionarie of the French and English Tongues*. G. Lindahl (ed.) (London: Adam Islip)

Court, R. (2008), 'The Language of Trust: Reputation and the Spread and Maintenance of Social Norms in Sixteenth Century Genoese Trade', *RiMe*, vol. 1, no. 1, 77–95.

Covington, S. (2003), *The Trail of Martyrdom: Persecution and Resistance in Sixteenth-Century England*. vol. 30. (University of Notre Dame Press)

Cowan, B. (2005), *The Social Life of Coffee: The Emergence of the British Coffeehouse*. (New Haven and London: Yale University Press)

Coward, B. (2003), *The Stuart Age: England, 1603–1714*. (Longman)

Cowell, F. R. (1962), *The Revolutions of Ancient Rome*. (London: Thames and Hudson)

Crack, A. (2008), *Global Communication and Transnational Public Spheres*. (Palgrave Macmillan)

Crafton, L. P. (1997), *The French Revolution Debate in English Literature and Culture.* (Greenwood Publishing Group)

Craig, S. C. (1996), *Broken Contract? Changing Relationships between Americans and Their Government (Transforming American Politics).* (Westview Press)

Crane, S. (1992), 'The Writing Lesson of 1381', in B. A. Hanawalt (ed.), *Chaucer's England: Literature in Historical Context.* (Minneapolis: University of Minnesota Press), pp. 201–22.

Craveri, B. (2006), *The Age of Conversation.* T. Waugh (ed.) (NYRB Collections)

Cressy, D. (1980), *Literacy and the Social Order: Reading and Writing in Tudor and Stuart England.* (Cambridge University Press)

Cromartie, A. (2006), *The Constitutionalist Revolution: An Essay on the History of England, 1450–1642.* (Cambridge University Press)

Crompton, R. (1587), *A Short Declaration of the Ende of Traytors, and False Conspirators against the State.* (At London: Printed by I. Charlewood, for Thomas Gubbins, and Thomas Newman)

Crook, J. A. (1995), *Legal Advocacy in the Roman World.* (Duckworth)

Crouch, N. (1693), *The History of the House of Orange.* (Crouch)

Croxton, D. (2013), *Westphalia: The Last Christian Peace.* (Palgrave Macmillan)

Crubaugh, A. (2001), *Balancing the Scales of Justice: Local Courts and Rural Society in Southwest France, 1750–1800.* (Penn State Press)

Cust, R. (1986), 'News and Politics in Early Seventeenth-Century England', *Past and Present*, vol. 92, no. 112, 60–90.

Cust, R. (2002), 'Charles I and Popularity', in T. Cogswell *et al.* (eds) *Politics, Religion and Popularity in Early Stuart Britain: Essays in Honour of Conrad Russell.* (Cambridge University Press), pp. 235–58.

Dahl, A. R. (1957), 'The Concept of Power', *Behavioural Science*, vol. 2, no. 3, 201–15.

Dahrendorf, R. (1959), *Class and Class Conflict in Industrial Society.* (Stanford: Stanford University Press)

Dalberg-Acton, J. E. E. (1907), *Historical Essays and Studies.* J. H. Figgis and R. V. Laurence (eds) (London: Macmillan and Co.)

Daniell, C. (1997), *Death and Burial in Medieval England, 1066–1550.* (Psychology Press)

Daniel-Rops, H. (1961), *The Protestant Reformation.* (Dent)

Dante, A. (1975), *Divine Comedy: Inferno v.1: Wonders of the World.* (Harmondsworth: Penguin Classics)

Darnton, R. (1989), 'The Kiss of Lamourette', *The New York Times* (unpublished), 1–9.

Das, T. K. and Teng, B.-S. (2001), 'Trust, Control and Risk in Strategic Alliances: An Integrated Framework', *Organization Studies*, vol. 22, 251–83.

Das, T. K. and Teng, B.-S. (1998), 'Between Trust and Control: Developing Confidence in Partner Cooperation Alliances', *The Academy of Management Review*, vol. 23, no. 3, 491–512.

Dasgupta, P. (1988), 'Trust as a Commodity', in D. Gambetta (ed.), *Trust: Making and Breaking Cooperative Relations.* (Oxford: Oxford University Press), pp. 49–72.

Daunton, M. (2007), *Trusting Leviathan: The Politics of Taxation in Britain, 1799–1914*. (Cambridge University Press)

Davidson, C. (2007), *Festivals and Plays in Late Medieval Britain*. (Ashgate Publishing Ltd)

Davies, G. (2010), *History of Money: From Ancient Times to the Present Day*. (University of Wales Press)

Davies, J. (1625), *A Scourge for Paper-Persecutors, Or Papers Complaint, Compil'd in Ruthfull Rimes, against the Paper-Spoylers of These Times*. (London)

Davies, J. K. (1971), *Athenian Propertied Families, 600–300*. (Clarendon Press)

Davies, M. E. and Swain, H. (2010), *Aspects of Roman History 82BC AD14: A Source-Based Approach*. (Taylor and Francis)

Davies, N. (1996), *Europe: A History*. (Oxford University Press)

Davies, W. and Fouracre, P. (eds) (1986), *The Settlement of Disputes in Early Medieval Europe*. (Cambridge University Press)

Davis, R. C. (2009), *Shipbuilders of the Venetian Arsenal: Workers and Workplace in the Pre-Industrial City*. (JHU Press)

Dawson, H. (2007), *Locke, Language and Early-Modern Philosophy*. (Cambridge University Press)

De Blois, L. (1976), *The Policy of the Emperor Gallienus*. (Brill)

De Coulanges, F. (1874), *The Ancient City: A Study on the Religion, Laws and Institutions of Greece and Rome*.

De Krey, G. S. (1985), *A Fractured Society: The Politics of London in the First Age of Party, 1688–1715*. (Clarendon Press)

De Sousa, J. P. (1988), *The Rationality of Emotion*. (MIT Press)

De Wilde, M. (2011), 'Fides Publica in Ancient Rome and Its Reception by Grotius and Locke', *The Legal History Review*, vol. 79, no. 3, 455–87.

Defoe, D. (1728), *A Plan of the English Commerce: Being a Compleat Prospect of the Trade of This Nation, **as** Well the Home Trade as the Foreign. In Three Parts. Part I. Containing a View of the Present Magnitude of the English Trade… Part II. Containing an Answer to that Great and Important Question Now Depending, Whether Our Trade, and Especially Our Manufactures, Are in a Declining Condition, or No? Part III. Containing Several Proposals Entirely New, for Extending and Improving Our Trade…* (Great Britain: Charles Rivington)

Dekker, H. C. (2004), 'Control of Inter-Organizational Relationships: Evidence on Appropriation Concerns and Coordination Requirements', *Accounting, Organizations and Society*, vol. 29, 27–49.

Delers, O. (2015), *The Other Rise of the Novel in Eighteenth-Century French Fiction*. (University of Delaware Press)

Deleuze, G. and Guattari, F. (1994), *What Is Philosophy?* G. Birchill and H. Tomlinson (eds) (London: Verso Books)

Deleuze, G. and Guattari, F. (1987), *A Thousand Plateaus: Capitalism and Schizophrenia. Capitalism and Schizophrenia 2*. Brian Massumi (ed. and trans.) (Minnesota and London: University of Minnesota Press)

Della Mirandola, G. P. (1996), *Oration on the Dignity of Man*. (Regnery Publishing)

Denegri-Knott, J. *et al.* (2006), 'Mapping Consumer Power: An Integrative Framework for Marketing and Consumer Research', *European Journal of Marketing*, vol. 40, no. 9/10, 950–71.

Dermineur, E. (2015), 'Trust, Norms of Cooperation, and the Rural Credit Market in Eighteenth-Century France', *Journal of Interdisciplinary History*, vol. XLV, no. 4, 485–506.

Desan, S. (1990), *Reclaiming the Sacred: Lay Religion and Popular Politics in Revolutionary France*. (Cornell University Press)

Deutsch, M. (1973), *The Resolution of Conflict*. (New Haven, CT: Yale University Press)

Deutsch, M. and Gerard, H. B. (1955), 'A Study of Normative and Informational Social Influences upon Individual Judgment', *Journal of Abnormal and Social Psychology*, vol. 51, 629–36.

Deutscher, G. (2011), *Through the Language Glass: Why the World Looks Different in Other Languages*. (Arrow Books)

Dick, A. (2015), *Theory and Practice in the Eighteenth Century: Writing between Philosophy and Literature*. (Taylor and Francis)

Dickens, A. G. (2005), *The English Reformation*. (Pennsylvania State University Press)

Dickens, A. G. (1991), *The English Reformation*. (Pennsylvania State University Press)

Dickens, C. (2004), *A Tale of Two Cities*. Classics. (Barnes and Noble)

Dickinson, J. (1963), *Death of a Republic: Politics and Thought at Rome 59–44 B. C.* (Macmillan)

Dickson, P. G. M. (1993), *The Financial Revolution in England: A Study in the Development of Public Credit, 1688–1756*. (Gregg Revivals)

Dickson, P. G. M. (1960), *The Sun Insurance Office, 1710–1960: The History of Two and a Half Centuries of British Insurance*. (Oxford University Press)

Diderot, D. (1963), *Oeuvres politiques: Garnier classiques*. (Garnier)

Dio Cassius, C. (1914), *Dio's Roman History*. (W. Heinemann)

Dix, R. H. (1991), 'Eastern Europe's Implications for Revolutionary Theory', *Polity*, vol. 24, no. 2, 227–42.

Dixon, T. (2015), *Weeping Britannia Portrait of a Nation in Tears*. (Oxford University Press)

Dobin, H. (1990), *Merlin's Disciples: Prophecy, Poetry, and Power in Renaissance England*. (Stanford, CA: Stanford University Press)

Dobson, R. B. (2008), *The Peasants' Revolt of 1381*. (ACLS Humanities (E-Book))

Donald, M. and Rees, T. (2001), 'The Dynamics and Meaning of Revolution in Twentieth-Century Europe', in M. Donald and T. Rees (eds), *Reinterpreting Revolution in Twentieth-Century Europe* (Macmillan Press), pp. 1–18.

Doney, P. M. *et al.* (1998), 'Understanding the Influence of National Culture on the Development of Trust', *The Academy of Management Review*, vol. 23, no. 3, 601–20.

Dorschel, A. (2010), *Ideengeschichte*. (Gottingen: Vandenhoeck and Ruprecht)

Dostoevsky, F. M. (2004), *The House of the Dead*. (Dover Publications Inc)

Dowlen, O. (2008), *Sorted: Civic Lotteries and the Future of Public Participation*. (Mass LBP)

Draper, H. (1966), 'The Two Souls of Socialism', *New Politics*, vol. 5, no. 1, 57–84.

Draper, J. (2013), *Stitch and Structure: Design and Technique in Two and Three-Dimensional Textiles*. (Batsford Ltd)

Drayton, M. (1612), *Poly-Olbion*. (Lownes)

Duby, G. (1978), *The Early Growth of the European Economy: Warriors and Peasants from the Seventh to the Twelfth Century*. (Cornell University Press)

Duck, S. (1997), *The Handbook of Personal Relationships: Theory, Research and Interventions*. (New York, NY: Wiley)

Duderija, A. (2011), 'Neo-Traditional Salafi Qur'an-Sunna Hermeneutics and Its Interpretational Implications', *Religion Compass*, vol. 5, no. 7, 314–25.

Duffy, E. (2005), *The Stripping of the Altars: Traditional Religion in England, c.1400–c. 1580*. (Yale University Press)

Dumolyn, J. and Haemers, J. (2005), 'Patterns of Urban Rebellion in Medieval Flanders', *Journal of Medieval History*, vol. 31, no. 4, 369–93.

Dunn, A. (2004), *The Peasants' Revolt: England's Failed Revolution of 1381*. Second Revision. (Tempus)

Dunn, J. (1997), *Locke, Volume 1*. I. Harris (ed.) (E. Elgar Publishing)

Dunn, J. (1984), 'The Concept of "Trust" in the Politics of John Locke', in R. Rorty *et al.* (eds) *Philosophy in History: Essays in the Historiography of Philosophy*. (Cambridge University Press), pp. 279–302.

Dunn, J. (1972), *Modern Revolutions: An Introduction to the Analysis of a Political Phenomenon*. (Cambridge University Press)

du Plessi-Morney (1579) (attributed) *Vindicae Contra Tyrannos: A Defense of Liberty against Tyrants*. Available at: www.constitution.org/vct/vindiciae.htm.

Durant, W. (1957), *The Reformation: A History of European Civilization from Wyclif to Calvin, 1300–1564*. (Simon and Schuster)

Durkheim, E. (1984), *The Division of Labour in Society (Contemporary Social Theory)*. (Palgrave Macmillan)

Dynneson, T. L. (2008), *City-State Civism in Ancient Athens: Its Real and Ideal Expressions*. (Peter Lang)

Eatwell, R. (1997), *European Political Cultures*. (Routledge)

Edelman, R. (2016), *A Crisis of Trust: A Warning to Both Business and Government*. Edelman online.

Ederer, R. J. (1964), *The Evolution of Money*. (Public Affairs Press)

Ehrenberg, J. R. (1999), *Civil Society: The Critical History of an Idea*. (New York University Press)

Einstein, A. (1950), 'Albert Einstein Warns of Dangers in Nuclear Arms Race.' NBC News Broadcast, 12 February.

Eisenstadt, S. N. (1995), *Power, Trust, and Meaning: Essays in Sociological Theory and Analysis*. (University of Chicago Press)

Eisenstadt, S. N. and Roniger, L. (1984), *Patrons, Clients and Friends: Interpersonal Relations and the Structure of Trust in Society.* vol. 3. (Cambridge University Press)

Elias, N. (1982), *Power and Civility.* (Pantheon Books)

Elias, N. (2001), *The Society of Individuals.* Reissued Edition. (Continuum)

Ellwood, C. A. (2012), *Sociology and Modern Social Problems (Classic Reprint).* (Forgotten Books)

El-Nawawy, M. and Khamis, S. (2013), *Egyptian Revolution 2.0: Political Blogging, Civic Engagement, and Citizen Journalism.* (Palgrave Macmillan)

Elton, G. R. (1953), *Tudor Revolution in Government.* (Cambridge University Press)

Emery, A. (1996), *Greater Medieval Houses of England and Wales, 1300–1500: Volume 2, East Anglia, Central England and Wales.* (Cambridge University Press)

Engels, F. (1884), The Origin of the Family, Private Property and the State in K. Marx and F. Engels Selected Works, vol. 3. Available at: https://www.marxists.org/archive/marx/works/download/pdf/origin_family.pdf.

Engels, F. (1947), *Anti-Dühring: Herr Eugen Dühring's Revolution in Science.* Pls Burns (ed.) (Progress Publishers)

Engels, F. and Marx, K. (1969), *Manifesto of the Communist Party.* (Progress Publishers)

Epstein, S. R. (1999) *The rise and decline of Italian city-states. Economic History Working Papers* (51/99). Department of Economic History, London School of Economics and Political Science, London, UK.

Erikson, E. H. (1963), *Childhood and Society.* Second Edition. (W.W. Norton and Company)

Esposito, J. L. (2004), *The Islamic World: Past and Present.* (Oxford University Press)

Euripides (1995), *Orestes.* New Edition. (Oxford: Oxford University Press)

Euripides (1991), *Hecuba.* New Edition. (Oxford: Oxford University Press)

Eusebius (1964), *The Ecclesiastical History Volume II.* (London: Harvard University Press)

Evelyn, J. (2004), *The Diary of John Evelyn.* Guy De la Bédoyère (ed.) (Boydell Press)

Ewald, W. B. (2005), 'The Protestant Revolutions and Western Law', *Consitutional Commentary*, vol. 22, 181–96.

Falk, R. (2015), *Chaos and Counterrevolution: After the Arab Spring.* (Zed Books)

Fanon, F. (1967), *The Wretched of the Earth.* (Penguin)

Faris, D. (2010), 'Revolutions without Revolutionaries? Social Media Networks and Regime Response in Egypt', Ph.D thesis, University of Pennsylvania.

Fatovic, C. (2004), 'Constitutionalism and Contingency: Locke's Theory of Prerogative', *History of Political Thought*, vol. 25, no. 5, 276–97.

Fayol, H. (1949), *General and Industrial Management.* C. Storrs (ed.) (London: Sir Isaac Pitman and Sons)

Febvre, L. and Martin, H.-J. (1997), *The Coming of the Book: The Impact of Printing 1450–1800.* D. G. Nowell-Smith and D. Wootton (eds) (London: Verso Books)

Féraud, J.-F. (1787), *Dictionaire critique de la langue française.* (Marseille: J. Mossy)

Ferguson, N. (2012), *The Ascent of Money: A Financial History of the World.* (Penguin Group)

Fergusson, A. (1975), *When Money Dies: The Nightmare of the Weimar Collapse.* (London: William Kimber)

Fergusson, A. (2010), *When Money Dies: The Nightmare of Deficit Spending, Devaluation, and Hyperinflation in Weimar Germany.* (PublicAffairs)

Festinger, L. (1957), *A Theory of Cognitive Dissonance.* (Stanford University)

Feuchtwanger, E. J. (1985), *Democracy and Empire: Britain 1865–1914.* (London: Edward Arnold Publishers Ltd)

Figes, O. (2007), *The Whisperers: Private Life in Stalin's Russia.* First Edition. (Allen Lane)

Finley, M. I. (1986), 'Revolution in Antiquity', in R. Porter and M. Teich (eds) *Revolution in History.* (Cambridge University Press), pp. 47–60.

Finley, M. I. (1977), *The Ancient Greeks.* (Penguin)

Finney, R. L. (2009), *Causes and Cures for the Social Unrest.* (BiblioLife)

Fiske, S. T. (1993), 'Controlling Other People. The Impact of Power on Stereotyping', *The American Psychologist*, vol. 48, no. 6, 621–28.

Flick, A. C. (1959), *The Rise of the Medieval Church and Its Influence on the Civilisation of Western Europe from the First to the Thirteenth Century.* (New York: Burt Franklin)

Flyvbjerg, B. (2001), *Making Social Science Matter.* (Cambridge University Press)

Foley, M. W. and Edwards, B. (1999), 'Is It Time to Disinvest in Social Capital?', *Journal of Public Policy*, vol. 19, 171–73.

Follain, A. (2001), 'Justice seigneuriale, justice royale et régulation sociale du XVe au XVIIIe siècle: Rapport de synthèse', in A. Follain *et al.* (eds) *Administration et justice locales de la fin du Moyen Âge à la Révolution.* (Rennes: Presses universitaires de Rennes) pp. 9–58.

Fontaine, L. (2001), 'Antonio and Shylock: Credit and Trust in France, *c.* 1680–1780', *Economic History Review*, vol. 54, no. 1.

Fontenrose, J. (1981), *The Delphic Oracle: Its Responses and Operations with a Catalogue of Responses.* (University of California Press)

Foot, S. (2011), *Athelstan: The First King of England (English Monarchs Series).* (Yale University Press)

Foran, J. (ed.) (2003), *The Future of Revolutions.* (London: Zed Books)

Forbis, E. (1996), *Municipal Virtues in the Roman Empire: The Evidence of Italian Honorary Inscriptions.* (Walter de Gruyter)

Fossum, E. (1967), 'Factors Influencing the Occurrence of Military Coups d'Etat in Latin America', *Journal of Peace Research*, vol. 4, no. 3, 228–51.

Foster, E. and Lateiner, D. (2012), *Thucydides and Herodotus.* (Oxford University Press)

Foucault, M. (1980a), *The History of Sexuality: An Introduction, Volume 1.* (Vintage Books)

Foucault, M. (1980b), *Power/Knowledge: Selected Interviews and Other Writings, 1972–1977.* (Pantheon Books)

Foucault, M. (1977), *Discipline and Punish: The Birth of the Prison.* (Vintage Books)

Foucault, M. (1972), *The Archeology of Knowledge.* (Tavistock Publications)

Foucault, M. (1975), 'Film and Popular Memory: An Interview with Michel Foucault', *Radical Philosophy*, vol. 11, 25–26.

Foulkes, M. E. (2005), *Empire of Coercion: Rome, Its Ruler and His Soldiers.* (Durham University)

Fox, A. (1997), 'Rumour, News and Popular Political Opinion in Elizabethan and Early Stuart England', *Historical Journal*, vol. 40, 597–620.

Foxe, J. (1837), *The Acts and Monuments of John Foxe.* G. Townsend (ed.) (R. B. Seeley and W. Burnside)

Foxe, J. (1563), *Book of Martyrs.* (Forgotten Books)

Foxe, J. (1563), *Actes and Monuments (unabridged)* [online].

Foyster, E. A. (1996), *The Concept of Male Honour in Seventeenth-Century England.* (Durham)

Frager, R. (1970), 'Conformity and Anti-Conformity in Japan', *Journal of Personality and Social Psychology*, vol. 15, 203–10.

Frank, J. (1961), *The Beginnings of the English Newspaper, 1620–1660.* (Cambridge, MA: Harvard University Press)

Franko, G. F. (1995), 'Fides, Aetolia, and Plautus' Captivi', *Transactions of the American Philological Association*, vol. 125, no. 1995, 155–76.

Fraser, N. (1990), 'Rethinking the Public Sphere: A Contribution to the Critique of Actually Existing Democracy', *Social Text*, vol. 25, no. 26, 56–80.

Freedman, L. (2009), *Nuclear Disarmament: The Need for a New Theory.* (Sydney: Lowy Institute for International Policy)

Freedman, P. (2013), 'Peasant Servitude in Medieval Catalonia', *Catalan Historical Review*, vol. 6, 33–43.

Freedman, P. (1998), 'Peasant Anger in the Late Middle Ages', in B. H. Rosenwein (ed.), *Anger's Past: The Social Uses of an Emotion in the Middle Ages* (Ithaca, NY: Cornell University Press), pp. 171–88.

Freedman, P. H. (1999), *Images of the Medieval Peasant.* (Stanford University Press)

Frend, W. H. C. (2008), *Martyrdom and Persecution in the Early Church.* (James Clarke Company Ltd)

Frend, W. H. C. (1984), *The Rise of Christianity.* (Fortress Press)

Freud, S. (2012), *Group Psychology and the Analysis of the Ego.* (USA: Empire Books)

Frey, L. and Frey, M. (2004), *The French Revolution.* (Greenwood Publishing Group)

Friedman, M. (2002), *Capitalism and Freedom: Fortieth Anniversary Edition.* (University of Chicago Press)

Froissart, J. (1967), *The Chronicle of Froissart.* J. Bourchier (ed.) (New York: AMS Press Inc.)

Fudge, T. A. (2010), *Jan Hus: Religious Reform and Social Revolution in Bohemia.* (I.B.Tauris)

Fukuyama, F. (1995), *Trust: The Social Virtues and the Creation of Prosperity.* (London: Penguin Books)

Fukuyama, F. (2011), *The Origins of Political Order: From Prehuman Times to the French Revolution.* (Profile Books)

Fukuyama, F. (2005), *State Building: Governance and World Order in the Twenty-First Century.* (Profile Books)

Fukuyama, F. (2000), *Social Capital and Civil Society* (May 2013)

Fuller, G. E. *et al.* (2011), 'The Arab Revolution', *New Perspectives Quarterly*, vol. 28, no. 2, 39–41.

Fuller, N. (1607), *The Argument of Master Nicholas Fuller, in the Case of Thomas Lad, and Richard Maunsell, His Clients.* (London: William Jones' Secret Press)

Fuller, T. (1642), *The Holy State.* (R. Daniel)

Furet, F. (1981), *Interpreting the French Revolution.* (Cambridge University Press)

Furet, F. and Ozouf, M. (1989), *A Critical Dictionary of the French Revolution.* (Harvard University Press)

Furetière, A. (1690), *Dictionnaire universel, contenant généralement tous les mots françois tant vieux que modernes et les termes de toutes les sciences et des arts, Volume 3.* (Rotterdam: A. et R. Leers)

Gallagher, P. (2008), 'How the 14th-Century Lombard Banks Created the Dark Age', *Executive Intelligence Review. (Schilling Institute)*, vol. 35, no. 9, 28–32.

Gallant, T. W. (1991), *Risk and Survival in Ancient Greece: Reconstructing the Rural Domestic Economy.* (Stanford University Press)

Gambetta, D. (1993), *The Sicilian Mafia: The Business of Private Protection.* (Harvard University Press)

Gambetta, D. (1988), 'Can We Trust Trust?' in Diego Gambetta (ed.), *Trust: Making and Breaking Cooperative Relations* (Oxford: Blackwell) pp. 213–37.

Gamson, W. A. (1968), *Power and Discontent.* (Homewood, IL: Dorsey Press)

Ganshof, F. L. (1952), *Feudalism.* (Longmans, Green)

Gantz, T. (1993), *Early Greek Myth: A Guide to Literary and Artistic Sources.* (Johns Hopkins University Press)

Gardiner, S. (1535), *De vera obedientia.* (Lambrecht)

Gardner, H. *et al.* (1970), *Gardner's Art through the Ages.* (Harcourt, Brace and World)

Garfinkel, H. (1963), 'A Conception of, and Experiments with, "Trust" as a Condition for Stable Concerted Actions', in O. J. Harvey (ed.), *Motivation and Social Interaction* (New York: Ronald Press), pp. 187–238.

Gartenstein-Ross, D. and Vassefi, T. (2012), 'Perceptions of the "Arab Spring" within the Salafi-Jihadi Movement', *Studies in Conflict and Terrorism*, vol. 35, no. 12, 831–48.

Garton Ash, T. (2009), '1989 Changed the World. But Where Now for Europe?', *Guardian*, 4 November.

Garwin, R. L. (2014), 'Mitigation of Megaterrorism and Hybrid Threats', in R. Ragani (ed.), *International Seminars on Nuclear War and Planetary Emergencies 46th Session: The Role of Science in the Third Millennium* (World Scientific), pp. 165–206.

Gat, A. (2008), *War in Human Civilization.* (Oxford University Press)

Gauthier, D. P. (1969), *The Logic of Leviathan: The Moral and Political Theory of Thomas Hobbes.* (Clarendon Press)

Gaventa, J. (2003), *Power after Lukes : An Overview of Theories of Power since Lukes and Their Application to Development* (August)

Geisst, C. R. (2006), *Encyclopedia of American Business History (Facts on File Library of American History)*. (Facts on File Inc)

Gelder, H. A. E. (1961), *The Two Reformations in the 16th Century*. (Springer Netherlands)

Gellner, E. (1988), 'Trust, Cohesion, and the Social Order', in D. Gambetta (ed.), *Trust: Making and Breaking Cooperative Relations* (Wiley-Blackwell), pp. 142–57.

Geoffrey, L. A. (1977), 'The Coming of Age of Double Entry: The Giovanni Farolfi Ledger of 1299–1300', *Accounting Historians Journal*, vol. 4, no. 2, 79–95.

Gerges, F. A. (2013), *The New Middle East: Protest and Revolution in the Arab World*. (Cambridge University Press)

Gerges, F. A. (2012), 'Fawaz A. Gerges on How the Arab Spring Beat Al Qaeda'. *The Daily Beast*, 13 May, pp. 1–5.

Germani, I. *et al.* (1998), *Symbols, Myths and Images of the French Revolution: Essays in Honour of James A. Leith*. (University of Regina Press)

Getty, J. A. and Naumov, O. V. (1999), *The Road to Terror: Stalin and the Self-Destruction of the Bolsheviks, 1932–1939*. (New Haven, CT: Yale University Press)

Ghamidi, G. A. (2010), *Islam: A Comprehensive Introduction*. Fifth Edition. (Al-Mawrid)

Ghazanfar, S. M. (2000), 'The Economic Thought of Abu Hamid Al-Ghazali and St. Thomas Aquinas: Some Comparative Parallels and Links', *History of Political Economy*, vol. 32, no. 4, 857–88.

Giddens, A. (2009), *Sociology*. Sixth Edition. (Cambridge: Polity Press)

Giddens, A. (1991), *Modernity and Self-Identity: Self and Society in the Late Modern Age*. (Cambridge: Polity Press)

Giddens, A. (1991), *The Consequences of Modernity*. (Polity Press)

Giddens, A. (1984), *The Constitution of Society*. vol. 20. (Oxford, England: Polity Press)

Giddens, A. and Pierson, C. (1998), *Conversations with Anthony Giddens: Making Sense of Modernity*. vol. 90. (Stanford University Press)

Ginzburg, C. (1993), 'Microhistory, Two or Three Things that I Know about It', *Critical Inquiry*, vol. 20, no. 1, 10–35.

Gladwell, M. (2000), *The Tipping Point: How Little Things Can Make a Big Difference*. (Abacus)

Glenn, H. P. (2013), *The Cosmopolitan State*. (OUP Oxford)

Godwin, W. (1992), *Enquiry Concerning Political Justice*. (Oxford: Woodstock)

Goertz, G. (2005), *Social Science Concepts: A User's Guide*. (Princeton, NJ: Princeton University Press)

Goldhill, S. and Osborne, R. (eds) (2006), *Rethinking Revolutions through Ancient Greece*. (Cambridge University Press)

Goldie, M. (2001), 'The Unacknowledged Republic', in T. Harris (ed.), *The Politics of the Excluded, c. 1500–1850*. (Palgrave Macmillan)

Goldstone, J. A. (1980), 'Theories of Revolution: The Third Generation', *World Politics*, vol. 32, no. 3, 425–53.

Goldstone, J. A. (1982), 'The Comparative and Historical Study of Revolutions', *Annual Review of Sociology*, vol. 8, no. 1, 187–207.

Goldstone, J. A. (2014), 'Revolutions of the Renaissance and Reformation', in *Revolutions: A Very Short Introduction* (Oxford: Oxford University Press), pp. 52–60.

Goldstone, J. A. (2001), 'Towards a Fourth Generations of Revolutionary Theory', *Annual Review Political Science*, vol. 4, no. 1, 139–87.

Goldthwaite, R. A. (1982), *The Building of Renaissance Florence: An Economic and Social History*. (JHU Press)

Golembiewski, R. T. and McConkie, M. (1975), 'The Centrality of Interpersonal Trust in Group Processes', in G. L. Cooper (ed.), *Theories of Group Processes* (London: John Wiley and Sons.), pp. 131–85.

Goodman, E. (1995), *The Origins of the Western Legal Tradition: From Thales to the Tudors*. (Federation Press)

Goodman, D. (1989), 'Enlightenment Salons: The Convergence of Female and Philosophic Ambitions', *Eighteenth-Century Studies*, vol. 22, no. 3, 329–50.

Goodwin, C. J. (2008), 'Rationalist Responses to Empiricism', in *A History of Modern Psychology*. Third Edition. (John Wiley and Sons), pp. 45–46.

Goodwin, J. (2001), *No Other Way Out: States and Revolutionary Movements, 1945–1991*. (Cambridge: Cambridge University Press)

Goodwin, J. (2001), 'Is the Age of Revolution Over?' in J. Goodwin, *No Other Way Out: States and Revolutionary Movements, 1945–1991* (Cambridge University Press), pp. 293–306.

Gordon, B. (2002), *The Swiss Reformation*. (Manchester: Manchester University Press)

Gordon, P. E. (2012), 'What Is Intellectual History? A Frankly Partisan Introduction to a Frequently Misunderstood Field', *The Harvard Colloquium for Intellectual History* http://projects.iq.harvard.edu/harvardcolloquium/pages/what-intellectual-history.

Gordon, W. (1788), *The History of the Rise, Progress, and Establishment, of the Independence of the United States of America*. (Printed for Samuel Campbell, no. 124, Pearl-street, by John Woods)

Goto-Jones, C. (2008), *Re-Politicising the Kyoto School as Philosophy*. (London: Routledge)

Goulemot, J. M. (1967), 'Le mot "revolution" et la formation du concept de "revolution politique"', *Annales historiques de la Revolution francaise*, vol. 39, no. 190, 417–44.

Graeber, D. (2014), *Debt: The First 5,000 Years*. Reprinted Edition. (New York: Melville House Publishing)

Graeber, D. (2009), 'Direct Action, Anarchism, Direct Democracy: What Is Anarchism?', in *Direct Action: An Ethnography*. (Oakland, CA: AK Press), pp. 211–22.

Graeber, D. and Grubacic, A. (2004), *Anarchism, or the Revolutionary Movement of the Twenty-First Century*. Anarchist Library online.

Graff, H. J. (1987), *The Legacies of Literacy: Continuities and Contradictions in Western Culture and Society*. (Indiana University Press)

Granovetter, M. (1973), 'The Strength of Weak Ties', *American Journal of Sociology*, vol. 78, no. 6, 1360–80.

Grant, E. (1996), *The Foundations of Modern Science in the Middle Ages: Their Religious, Institutional and Intellectual Contexts*. (Cambridge University Press)

Gray, J. M. (2010), 'Vows, Oaths, and the Propagation of a Subversive Discourse', *Sixteenth Century Journal*, vol. 41, no. 3, 731–56.

Gray, J. M. (2012), *Oaths and the English Reformation*. (Cambridge University Press)

Grayling, A. C. (2015), *The Challenge of Things: Thinking through Troubled Times*. (Bloomsbury USA)

Greif, A. (2006), 'History Lessons: The Birth of Impersonal Exchange: The Community Responsibility System and Impartial Justice', *Journal of Economic Perspectives*, vol. 20, no. 2, 221–36.

Greif, A. (1997), *On the Social Foundations and Historical Development of Institutions that Facilitate Impersonal Exchange: From the Community Responsibility System to Individual Legal Responsibility in Pre-Modern Europe: Introduction*. Department of Economics, Stanford University research paper. Available at: ecsocman.hse.ru/data/944/768/1216/9712104.pdf.

Greco, T. H. (2001), *Money: Understanding and Creating Alternatives to Legal Tender*. (Chelsea Green Publishing Co)

Greenblatt, S. (2006), 'The Modern Foundations of Right', in *The Norton Anthology of English Literature: 16th and Early 17th Century*. Eighth Revision. (W.W. Norton and Company)

Greer, D. (1935), *The Incidence of the Terror during the French Revolution: A Statistical Interpretation*. (Harvard University Press)

Grey, C. and Garsten, C. (2001), 'Trust, Control and Post-Bureaucracy', *Organization Studies*, vol. 22, no. 2, 229–50.

Griffin, E. A. (n.d.), *The 'Industrial Revolution': Interpretations from 1830 to the Present*. (New York: Palgrave Macmillan)

Grimes, A. J. (1978), 'Authority, Power, Social Theoretical Synthesis', *The Academy of Management Review*, vol. 3, no. 4, 724–35.

Grote, G. (2013), *History of Greece: From the Time of Solon to 403 BC*. (Routledge)

Grote, M. (2015), *What Could the 'longue durée' Mean for the History of Modern Sciences?* Available at: https://halshs.archives-ouvertes.fr/halshs-01171257.

Gruen, E. S. (1982), 'Greek Pistis and Roman Fides', *Athenaeum*, vol. 60, 50–68.

Guenee, B. (1981), *States and Rulers in Later Medieval Europe*. (Basil Blackwell)

Guicciardini, F. (1994), *Guicciardini: Dialogue on the Government of Florence*. A. Brown (ed.) (Cambridge University Press)

Guizot, F. (2010), *History of the English Revolution of 1640, Commonly Called the Great Rebellion: From the Accession of Charles I to His Death*. Reproduction. (Nabu Press)

Gulati, R. (1995), 'Does Familiarity Breed Trust? The Implications of Repeated Ties for Contractual Choice in Alliances', *Academy of Management Journal*, vol. 38, 85–112.

Gunnthorsdottir, A. *et al.* (2002), 'Using the Machiavellianism Instrument to Predict Trustworthiness in a Bargaining Game', *Journal of Economic Psychology*, vol. 23, no. 1, 49–66.

Guthrie, W. K. C. (1969), *A History of Greek Philosophy: Volume 3, The Fifth Century Enlightenment*. (Cambridge University Press)

Habermas, J. (1992), *The Structural Transformation of the Public Sphere: Inquiry into a Category of Bourgeois Society*. New Edition. (Polity Press)

Hacking, I. (2006), *The Emergence of Probability: A Philosophical Study of Early Ideas about Probability, Induction and Statistical Inference*. (Cambridge University Press)

Haidt, J. (2001), 'The Emotional Dog and Its Rational Tail: A Social Intuitionist Approach to Moral Judgment', *Psychological Review*, vol. 108, no. 4, 814–34.

Haigh, C. (1993), *English Reformations: Religion, Politics, and Society under the Tudors*. (Clarendon Press)

Haines, J. (2010) *Medieval Song in Romance Languages*. (Cambridge University Press)

Halley, H. H. (1939), *Pocket Bible Handbook*. (Chicago, IL)

Halliday, F. (1999), *Revolutions and World Politics: The Rise and Fall of the Sixth Great Power*. (Palgrave Macmillan)

Hamberg, P. G. (1945), *Studies in Roman Imperial Art: With Special Reference to the State Reliefs of the Second Century*. (Almqvist and Wiksells boktryckeri aktiebolag)

Hampson, N. (1988), *Prelude to Terror: The Constituent Assembly and the Failure of Consensus, 1789–1791*. (B. Blackwell)

Hanke, S. H. and Kwok, A. K. F. (2009), 'On the Measurement of Zimbabwe's Hyperinflation', *Cato Journal*, vol. 29, no. 2, 353–64.

Hanks, M. (2012), *Knitting and Politics: Medium and Message*. (University of Gloucestershire)

Hansen, M. H. (1991), *Athenian Democracy in the Age of Demosthenes: Structure, Principles and Ideology*. (Blackwell, Oxford)

Hanson, P. R. (2009), *Contesting the French Revolution*. (John Wiley and Sons)

Hardin, R. (2004), *Trust and Trustworthiness*. (Russell Sage Foundation)

Hardin, R. (1996), 'Trustworthiness', *Ethics*, vol. 107, no. 1, 26–42.

Hardin, R. (1992), 'The Street-Level Epistemology of Trust', *Politics and Society*, vol. 21, no. 4, 505–29.

Harding, P. (2007), *The Story of Athens: The Fragments of the Local Chronicles of Attika*. (Taylor and Francis)

Hardy, T. (2010), *Poems of the Past and the Present*. (Kessinger Publishing)

Harper, D. (2010), 'Revolution', in the *Online Etymology Dictionary*.

Harrington, J. (1992), *Harrington: 'The Commonwealth of Oceana' and 'A System of Politics'*. J. G. A. Pocock (ed.) (Cambridge University Press)

Harris, T. (1993), *Politics Under the Later Stuarts: Party Conflict in a Divided Society, 1660–1715*. (Longman)

Harris, W. (1828), *The Oxford Encyclopædia: Or, Dictionary of Arts, Sciences, and General Literature*. (Bartlett and Hinton)

Harriss, G. (1993), 'Political Society and the Growth of Government in Late Medieval England', *Past and Present*, vol. 138, February, 28–57.

Hart, V. (1978), *Distrust and Democracy: Political Distrust in Britain and America*. (Cambridge: Cambridge University Press)

Haschke, P. (2011), *Yes, Mubarak Is Gone. But Now What?* UNAOC.

Hatto, A. (1949), '"Revolution": An Enquiry into the Usefulness of an Historical Term', *Mind*, vol. 58, no. 232, 495–517.

Haugaard, M. (2010), 'Power: A "Family Resemblance" Concept', *European Journal of Cultural Studies*, vol. 13, no. 4, 419–38.

Hauser, G. (1998), 'Vernacular Dialogue and the Rhetoricality of Public Opinion', *Communication Monographs*, vol. 65, no. 3, 83–107.

Hawhee, D. (2002), 'Agonism and Arete', *Philosophy and Rhetoric*, vol. 35, no. 3, 185–207.

Hawley, A. H. (1963), 'Community Power and Urban Renewal Success', *American Journal of Sociology*, vol. 68, 422–31.

Hay, C. *et al.* (eds) (2006), *The State: Theories and Issues*. (Basingstoke: Palgrave Macmillan)

Hayek, F. A. (1945), *The Road to Serfdom*. (London: George Routledge and Sons Ltd)

Hayhoe, J. (2008), *Enlightened Feudalism: Seigneurial Justice and Village Society in Eighteenth-Century Northern Burgundy*. (University Rochester Press)

Hazlett, I. (2003), *The Reformation in Britain and Ireland: An Introduction*. (Bloomsbury Academic)

Heater, D. B. (2004), *A Brief History of Citizenship*. (Edinburgh University Press)

Heath, J. (1663), *A Brief Chronicle of the Late Intestine War in the Three Kingdoms of England, Scotland and Ireland...* (W. Lee)

Heckel, D. (1991), 'Francis Bacon's New Science: Print and the Transformation of Rhetoric', in B. E. Gronbeck *et al.* (eds) *Media, Consciousness, and Culture: Explorations of Walter Ong's Thought: Explorations on Walter Ong's Thought* (Newbury Park, CA: Sage Publications), Chapter 4.

Heidegger, M. (1962), 'Being and Time (selection 03)', in *Being and Time* (Harper and Row), pp. 122–34.

Held, D. *et al.* (1999), *Global Transformations: Politics, Economics and Culture*. (Polity Press)

Heller, Á. (2015), *Renaissance Man*. (Taylor and Francis)

Henrich, J. *et al.* (2010), 'The Weirdest People in the World?', *The Behavioral and Brain Sciences*, vol. 33, no. 2–3, 61–83–135.

Herbert, G. B. (2003), *A Philosophical History of Rights*. (Transaction Publishers)

Herman, G. (2002), *Ritualised Friendship and the Greek City*. (Cambridge University Press)

Hermanson, T. (2012), 'Knitting as Dissent: Female Resistance in America since the Revolutionary War', in Textile Society of America (ed.), *Textile Society of America Symposium Proceedings* (Lincoln, NE: University of Nebraska), pp. 1–8.

Hermida, A. (2010), 'From TV to Twitter: How Ambient News Became Ambient Journalism', *Media/Culture Journal*, vol. 13, no. 2.

Herodotus, H. (2012), *Herodotus, vol. 1 (Classic Reprint)*. (Forgotten Books)

Herodotus (1998), *The Histories*. (Oxford University Press)

Herrera, L. (2014), *Wired Citizenship: Youth Learning and Activism in the Middle East*. (Routledge)

Herrera, L. (2012), 'Youth and Citizenship in the Digital Age: A View from Egypt', *Harvard Educational Review*, vol. 82, no. 3, 333–53.

Herrup, C. B. (1987), *The Common Peace: Participation and the Criminal Law in Seventeenth-Century England*. (Cambridge University Press)

Herrup, C. B. (1985), 'Law and Morality in Seventeenth-Century England', *Past and Present*, vol. 106, 102–23.

Hertzler, J. R. (1987), 'Who Dubbed It "The Glorious Revolution?"' *Albion: A quarterly Journal Concerned with British Studies*, vol. 19, no. 4, 579–585.

Hessayon, A. and Finnegan, D. (eds) (2013), *Varieties of Seventeenth- and Early Eighteenth-Century English Radicalism in Context*. (Ashgate Publishing Ltd)

Hetherington, K. (1998), *Expressions of Identity: Space, Performance, Politics*. M. Featherstone (ed.) (London: Sage Publications)

Hexter, J. H. (1979), *On Historians: Reappraisals of Some of the Makers of Modern History*. (Harvard University Press)

Heydemann, S. (2007), *Upgrading Authoritarianism in the Arab World, Analysis Paper* no.13 The Saban Center for Middle East Policy at the Brookings Institute.

Hibbert, C. (2003), *The House of Medici: Its Rise and Fall*. (New York: Harper Perennial)

Hickson, C. L. (2011), 'A Study Comparing the 1979 Iranian Revolution and the 2011 Egyptian Revolution in Regards to the Interconnection between Mainstream Media and Small Media and the Use and Change of Sources in News over Time', Ph.D thesis, University of Leeds.

Hickeringill, E. (1682), *The History of Whiggism, or the Whiggish-Plots, Principles, and Practices (Mining and Countermining the Tory Plots and Principles) in the Reign of... Charles I. During the Conduct of Affaires, under the Influence of...Buckingham, Laud and Strafford...* Available at: https://quod.lib.umich.edu/e/eebo/A70223.0001.001?rgn=main;view=fulltext.

Hill, C. (1991), *The World Turned Upside Down: Radical Ideas during the English Revolution*. (Penguin Books)

Hilton, R. H. (1985), *Class Conflict and the Crisis of Feudalism: Essays in Medieval Social History*. (London: The Hambledon Press)

Hindle, S. (2002), *The State and Social Change in Early Modern England, c. 1550–1640*. (Palgrave Macmillan)

Hirst, M. (2012), 'One Tweet Does Not a Revolution Make: Technological Determinism, Media and Social Change', *Global Media Journal*, vol. 12, no. 2, 1–29.

Ho, H. L. (2003), 'The Legitimacy of Medieval Proof', *Journal of Law and Religion*, vol. 19, no. 2, 259–98.

Hobbes, T. (2014), *Behemoth or the Long Parliament.* (University of Chicago Press)

Hobbes, T. (2004), *Leviathan.* Reissued. J. Popiel (ed.) (Oxford Paperbacks)

Hobbes, T. and Tuck, R. (1996), *Hobbes: Leviathan: Revised Student Edition.* (Cambridge University Press)

Hobbes, T. and Gaskin, J. C. A. (1999), *The Elements of Law, Natural and Politic: Part I, Human Nature, Part II, De Corpore Politico; with Three Lives.* (Oxford University Press)

Hobsbawn, E. (2010a), *The Age of Capital 1848–1875.* (London: Abacus)

Hobsbawn, E. (2010b), *The Age of Revolution 1789–1848.* (London: Abacus)

Hobson, C. Z. (1999), *The Chained Boy: Orc and Blake's Idea of Revolution.* (Associated University Press)

Hobson, J. M. (2004), *The Eastern Origins of Western Civilisation.* (Cambridge University Press)

Hoffer, P. C. (1990), *The Law's Conscience: Equitable Constitutionalism in America.* (University of North Carolina Press)

Hofheinz, A. (2011), 'Nextopia? Beyond Revolution 2.0', *International Journal of Communication*, vol. 5, 1417–34.

Hogg, M. A. and Vaughan, G. M. (2005), *Social Psychology.* (Prentice Hall)

Holborn, H. (1965), *A History of Modern Germany: The Reformation.* (Eyre and Spottiswoode)

Hölkeskamp, K.-J. and Heitmann-Gordon, H. (2010), *Reconstructing the Roman Republic: An Ancient Political Culture and Modern Research.* (Princeton University Press)

Hollingsworth, M. (1994), *Patronage in Renaissance Italy: From 1400 to the Early Sixteenth Century.* (Johns Hopkins University Press)

Hollis, M. (1998), *Trust within Reason.* (Cambridge: Cambridge University Press)

Holston, J. and Appadurai, A. (2003), 'Cities and Citizenship', in N. Brenner *et al.* (eds) *State/Space: A Reader.* (Blackwell Publishing), pp. 296–308.

Holt, J. C. (1972), *Magna Carta and the Idea of Liberty.* (Wiley)

Holt, M. P. (2002), *Renaissance and Reformation France, 1500–1648.* (Oxford University Press)

Holton, R. (1994), 'Deciding to Trust, Coming to Believe', *Australasian Journal of Philosophy*, vol. 72, no. 1, 63–76.

Hopper, A. (2013), 'Propoganda Parliment versus the King in the 1640s', *West Midlands History*, vol. 1, no. 3, 15–17.

Hornqvist, M. (2000), 'Two Myths of Civic Humanism', in J. Hankins (ed.), *Renaissance Civic Humanism: Reappraisals and Reflections* (Cambridge University Press), pp. 105–42.

Horowitz, S. (2014), *Friendship and Politics in Post-Revolutionary France.* (Penn State Press)

Hosking, G. (2014), *Trust: A History.* (Oxford: Oxford University Press)

Hosking, G. (2012), 'Structures of Trust: Britain and Russia Compared', in M. Sasaki and R. M. Marsh (eds) *Trust: Comparative Perspectives.* (Brill), pp. 31–68.

Hosking, G. (2005a), 'Ancient Greece', in *Epochs of European History: Antiquity to Renaissance* (Recorded Books), lecture 3.

Hosking, G. (2005b), *The Modern Scholar: Epochs of European Civilization: Antiquity to Renaissance [Unabridged]*. (Recorded Books)

Hosking, G. (2004), 'Forms of Social Solidarity in Russia and the Soviet Union', in A. Markov (ed.), *Trust and Democratic Transition in Post-Communist Europe*. (New York: Oxford University Press), pp. 64–79.

Hosking, G. (2002), 'Why We Need a History of Trust', *Reviews in History*, vol. 287.

Howell, J. (1655), *Epistolae Ho-Elianae. Familiar Letters Domestic and Forren: Divided into Sundry Sections, Partly Historicall, Politicall, Philosophicall, Volume 1*. vol. 9. (Moseley)

Howell, J. (1643), *The True Informer, Who…* (Lichfield)

Howell, J. (1661), *Twelve Several Treatises, of the Late Revolutions in These Three Kingdomes: Deducing the Causes Thereof from Their Originals*. (J. Grismond, and are to be sold by the book-sellers in London and Westminster)

Howell, T. B. (1816), *A Complete Collection of State Trials and Proceedings for High Treason and Other Crimes and Misdemeanors from the Earliest Period to the Year 1783: With Notes and Other Illustrations, Volume 4*. (T. C. Hansard for Longman, Hurst, Rees, Orme, and Brown)

Huber, T. L. *et al.* (2013), 'A Process Model of Complementarity and Substitution of Contractual and Relational Governance in IS Outsourcing', *Journal of Management Information Systems*, vol. 30, no. 3, 81–114.

Huber, T. *et al.* (2011), 'Substitutes or Complements? A Framework for Investigating the Dynamic Interplay of IS Outsourcing Governance', in *ICIS 2011 Proceedings* (Shanghai, China: ICIS)

Huber, T. and Hurni, T. (2014), 'The Interplay of Power and Trust in Platform Ecosystems of the Enterprise Application Software Industry', in Tel Aviv, Israel: *Twenty Second European Conference on Information Systems*, pp. 1–15.

Hudson, A. (1988), *The Premature Reformation: Wycliffite Texts and Lollard History*. (Clarendon Press)

Hughes, P. (1948), *History of the Church: Volume 1: The World in Which the Church Was Founded*. (A and C Black)

Hughes-Warrington, M. (2013), *Revisionist Histories*. (Routledge)

Hume, D. (1754–61), *History of England*, 6 vols (Printed for A Millar [1757–62])

Hume, D. (1983), *The History of England from the Invasion of Julius Caesar to the Revolution in 1688 (vol. 6)*. W. S. Todd (ed.) (Indianapolis: Liberty Fund)

Hunjan, R. and Pettit, J. (2011), *Power: A Practical Guide for Facilitating Social Change*. Democracy and Civil Society Programme. Available at: www.participatorymethods. org/sites/participatorymethods.org/files/Power-A-Practical-Guide-for-Facilitating-Social-Change_0.pdf.

Hunt, L. (1981), 'François Furet, Penser la Revolution française', *History and Theory*, vol. 20, 313–23.

Hunt, L. (1980), 'Engraving the Republic: Prints and Propaganda in the French Revolution', *History Today*, vol. 30, no. 10, 11–17.

Hunt, L. and Censer, J. R. (2001), *Liberty, Equality, Fraternity: Exploring the French Revolution.* (Penn State Press)

Hunt, L. *et al.* (2010), *The Making of the West, Peoples and Cultures, A Concise History, Volume I: To 1974.* (Boston and New York: Bedford/St Martin's)

Hunt, L. A. (1984), *Politics, Culture, and Class in the French Revolution.* (University of California Press)

Hunt, T. (2007), *Protestant Revolution.* BBC 4, 3 episodes.

Hunter, C. and McClelland, K. (2012) 'Theoretical Perspectives in Sociology', in S. J. Ferguson (ed.), *Mapping the Social Landscape: Readings in Sociology*, Seventh Edition (McGraw-Hill Humanities/Social Sciences/Languages)

Huntington, S. P. (1973), *Political Order in Changing Societies.* (Yale University Press)

Hutson, J. H. (1998), *Religion and the Founding of the American Republic. America as a Religious Refuge: The Seventeenth Century, Part 1.* Available at: www.loc. gov/exhibits/religion/rel01.html.

Hutt, M. G. (1957), 'The Cures and the Third Estate', *Journal of Ecclesiastical History*, vol. 8, 74–92.

Huxley, A. (2007), *Brave New World.* (Random House)

Hyde, J. K. (1972), 'Contemporary Views of Faction and Civil Strife in Thirteenth and Fourteenth Century Italy', in L. Martines (ed.), *Violence and Civil Disorder in Italian Cities, 1200–1500.* (University of California Press), pp. 296–302.

Hyman, R. (1987), 'Strategy or Structure? Capital, Labour and Control', *Work Employment and Society*, vol. 1, no. 1, 25–55.

Hyndman, H. M. (2012), *The Evolution of Revolution.* (Forgotten Books)

Hynes, S. (2013), 'Mapping Friendship and Dissent', in D. Finnegan and A. Hessayon (eds) *Varieties of Seventeenth- and Early Eighteenth-Century English Radicalism in Context.* (Routledge), pp. 205–20.

Inglehart, R. (1997), *Modernization and Postmodernization: Cultural, Economic, and Political Change in 43 Societies.* (Princeton University Press)

Inglehart, R. and Siemienska, R. (1988), 'Political Values and Dissatisfaction in Poland and the West: A Comparative Analysis', *Government and Opposition*, vol. 24, 440–57.

Ingram, R. E. (1984), 'Toward an Information Processing Analysis of Depression', *Cognitive Therapy and Research* 8, 443–78.

Inkpen, A. C. and Currall, S. C. (1997), 'International Joint Venture Trust: An Empirical Examination', in P. W. Beamish and J. P. Killing (eds) *Cooperative Strategies: North American Perspectives.* (San Francisco, CA: New Lexington Press), pp. 308–34.

Ireland, R. D. and Webb, J. W. (2007), 'A Multi-Theoretic Perspective on Trust and Power in Strategic Supply Chains', *Journal of Operations Management*, vol. 25, no. 2, 482–97.

Isherwood, T. (2008), 'A New Direction or More of the Same? Political Blogging in Egypt', *Arab Media and Society*, September, 1–17. https://www.arabmediasociety. com/a-new-direction-or-more-of-the-same/.

Isocrates (1929), 'Areopagiticus', in *Discourses*. (Harvard University Press)

Israel, J. (2009), *A Revolution of the Mind: Radical Enlightenment and the Intellectual Origins of Modern Democracy*. (Princeton University Press)

Israel, J. (1995), '1672: Year of Disaster', in *The Dutch Republic: Its Rise, Greatness and Fall, 1477–1806* (Oxford University Press), pp. 796–806.

Jackson, R. (2014), 'Jihad and Just War Theory', in *What Is Islamic Philosophy?*. (Routledge), pp.130–48.

Jackson, J. and Gau, J. M. (2016), 'Carving up Concepts? Differentiating between Trust and Legitimacy in Public Attitudes towards Legal Authority', in E. Shockley *et al.* (eds), *Interdisciplinary Perspectives on Trust: Towards Theoretical and Methodological Integration* (New York: Springer), pp. 1–19.

Jaegar, W. and Highet, G. (1986), *Paideia: The Ideals of Greek Culture, in Three Volumes*. (Oxford University Press)

Jansen, S. L. (1991), *Political Protest and Prophecy under Henry VIII*. (Boydell Press)

Jardine, L. (2008), *Going Dutch: How England Plundered Holland's Glory*. (Hammersmith: Harper Press)

Jasinski, M. (2011), *Social Trust, Anarchy, and International Conflict*. (Springer)

Jasper, J. M. (2013), 'Democracy and Emotion', Public Lecture at London School of Economics, recorded on 29 January.

Jevons, W. S. (1876), *Money and the Mechanism of Exchange*. (New York: D. Appleton and Co.)

Johnson, S. A. M. (1755), *A Dictionary of the English Language* (London: Printed by W. Strahan for For J. and P. Knapton; T. and T. Longman; C. Hitch and L. Hawes; A. Millar; and R. and J. Dodsley)

Johnston, S. I. (ed.) (2007), *Ancient Religions*. (Cambridge, MA, and London: Belknap Press of Harvard University Press)

Johnstone, S. (2011), *A History of Trust in Ancient Greece*. First Edition. (Chicago, IL: University of Chicago Press)

Jones, A. H. M. (1978), *Constantine and the Conversion of Europe*. (The English Universities Press Limited)

Jones, K. (1996), 'Trust as an Affective Attitude', *Ethics*, vol. 107, no. 1, 4–25.

Jones, D. M. (1999), *Conscience and Allegiance in Seventeenth Century England: The Political Significance of Oaths and Engagements*. (University of Rochester Press)

Jones, S. (2013), 'The Mirage of the Arab Spring: Deal with the Region You Have, Not the Region You Want', *Foreign Policy*, vol. January/February.

Jost, J. T., Ledgerwood, A. and Hardin, C. T. (2008) 'Shared Reality, System Justification, and the Relation- al Basis of Ideological Beliefs', *Social and Personality Psychology Compass*, vol. 2, no. 1, 171–86.

Jurdjevic, M. (2004), 'Trust in Renaissance Electoral Politics', *The Journal of Interdisciplinary History*, vol. 17, no. 3, 587–612.

Juris, J. S. (2005), 'The New Digital Media and Activist Networking within Anti-Corporate Globalization Movements', *The Annals of the American Academy of Political and Social Science*, vol. 597, no. 1, 189–208.

Kaellis, E. (2012), *Purge.* (Lulu.com)

Kaeuper, R. W. (2000), *Violence in Medieval Society.* (Boydell and Brewer Ltd)

Kahan, A. S. (2010), *Mind vs. Money: The War between Intellectuals and Capitalism.* (New Brunswick, NJ: Transaction Press)

Kahneman, D. and Tversky, A. (1982), *Judgment under Uncertainty: Heuristics and Biases.* (Cambridge University Press)

Kale, S. D. (2005), *French Salons: High Society and Political Sociability from the Old Regime to the Revolution of 1848.* (Johns Hopkins University Press)

Kalimtzis, K. (2000), *Aristotle on Political Enmity and Disease: An Inquiry into Stasis.* vol. 2. (Suny Press)

Kalthoff, M. (2015), *Faith and Terror: Religion in the French Revolution.* (University of Colorado)

Kant, I. (2009), *An Answer to the Question: 'What Is Enlightenment?'.* (Penguin)

Kaplan, J. (2005), *Political Theory: The Classic Texts and Their Continuing Relevance.* (The Modern Scholar)

Kapust, D. J. (2011), *Republicanism, Rhetoric, and Roman Political Thought: Sallust, Livy, and Tacitus.* (Cambridge University Press)

Katz, M. N. (2000), *Revolution: International Dimensions.* First Revision. (Washington, DC: CQ Press)

Katzenstein, P. J. (1996), 'Introduction: Alternative Perspectives on National Security', in P. J. Katzenstein (ed.), *The Culture of National Security: Norms and Identity in World Politics* (Columbia University Press), pp. 1–27.

Keddie, N. R. (1983), 'Iranian Revolutions in Comparative Perspective', *The American Historical Review*, vol. 88, no. 3, 579–98.

Kee, H. W. and Knox, R. E. (1970), 'Conceptual and Methodological Considerations in the Study of Trust and Suspicion', *The Journal of Conflict Resolution*, vol. 14, no. 3, 357–66.

Keele, L. (2005), 'Southern Political Science Association: The Authorities Really Do Matter: Party Control and Trust in Government', *The Journal of Politics*, vol. 67, no. 3, 873–86.

Keen, M. (1999), *Medieval Warfare: A History.* (OUP Oxford)

Kelly, D. (2014), '*Revolutionary Ideas*', *by Jonathan Israel. Financial Times* online.

Kelman, H. (1958), 'Compliance, Identification, and Internalization: Three Processes of Attitude Change', *Journal of Conflict Resolution*, vol. 1, 51–60.

Keltner, D. *et al.* (2003), 'Power, Approach, and Inhibition', *Psychological Review*, vol. 110, 265–84.

Kent, D. V. (2000), *Cosimo De' Medici and the Florentine Renaissance: The Patron's Oeuvre*. (Yale University Press)

Kent, J. R. (1983), 'Folk Justice and Royal Justice in Early Seventeenth-Century England: A "Charivari" in the Midlands', *Midland History*, vol. 8, no. 1, 70–85.

Kepel, G. (2006), *Jihad: The Trail of Political Islam*. (I.B.Tauris)

Kern, B. (1948), *Kingship and Law in the Middle Ages*. S. B. Chrimes (ed.) (Basil Blackwell)

Kersey, J. K. (1715), *Dictionarium Anglo-Britannicum* (Second edition corrected) (London: Printed by J. Wilde for J. Phillips, N. Rhodes, and J. Taylor)

Kesselring, K. J. (2005), 'Deference and Dissent in Tudor England: Reflections on Sixteenth-Century Protest', *History Compass*, vol. 3, no. 163, 1–16.

Ketelaar, T. and Clore, G. L. (1997), 'Emotion and Reason: The Proximate Effects and Ultimate Functions of Emotions', in G. Matthews (ed.), *Cognitive Science Perspectives on Personality and Emotion Volume 124 (Advances in Psychology)*. First Edition. (Amsterdam, Holland: North Holland Publishers), pp. 355–98.

Keynes, J. M. (1920), *The Economic Consequences of the Peace*. (New York: Harcourt Brace)

Keynes, J. M. (2011), *A Treatise on Money: The Pure Theory of Money and the Applied Theory of Money. Complete Set*. (Martino Fine Books)

Khalidi, R. (2011), Reflections on the Revolutions in Tunisia and Egypt. *Foreign Policy* online.

Khodyakov, D. M. (2007), 'Trust as a Process: A Three-Dimensional Approach', *Sociology*, vol. 41, no. 1, 115–32.

Kiefer, H. E. and Munitz, M. K. (eds) (1970), *Ethics and Social Justice*. (Albany, NY: State University of New York Press)

Kierkegaard, S. (1992), *Concluding Unscientific Postscript: Philosophical Fragments*. Revised. (Princeton University Press)

King, C. (1998), *Renaissance Women Patrons: Wives and Widows in Italy, c. 1300–1550*. (Manchester University Press)

King, M. L. (1986), *Venetian Humanism in an Age of Patrician Dominance*. (Princeton University Press)

King, S. D. (2013), *When the Money Runs Out: The End of Western Affluence*. vol. 7. (Yale University Press)

Kirby, M. (2000), 'Power and Politics', in *Sociology in Perspective*. (Heinemann), pp. 370–416.

Kissinger, H. (2014), 'The World in Flames', *The Sunday Times*, 29 August, 1–3.

Klassen, A. D. *et al.* (1989), *Sex and Morality in the U.S.: An Empirical Enquiry under the Auspices of the Kinsey Institute*. (Middletown, CT: Wesleyan University Press)

Knight, J. (1998), 'The Bases of Cooperation: Social Norms and the Rule of Law', *Journal of Institutional and Theoretical Economics*, vol. 154, 754–63.

Knighton, H. (1995), *Knighton's Chronicle 1337–1396*. G. H. Martin (ed.) (Clarendon Press)

Knights, D. and Willmott, H. (1990), *Labour Process Theory*. (Macmillan)

Knobbe, A. *et al.* (2014), 'Reconstructing Medieval Social Networks from English and Latin Charters', in *Proceedings Population Reconstruction 2014*. (Amsterdam: International Institute of Social History), pp. 1–7.

Kort, F. (1952), 'The Quantification of Aristotle's Theory of Revolution', *American Political Science Review*, vol. 46, no. 2, 486–93.

Koselleck, R. (2003), *Layers of Time: Studies Historic*. H-G. (contr.) Gadamer (ed.) (Suhrkamp)

Koselleck, R. (1985), *Futures Past: On the Semantics of Historical Time*. (Cambridge, MA: M.I.T.)

Kovarik, B. (2011), *Revolutions in Communication: Media History from Gutenberg to the Digital Age*. (Bloomsbury)

Kramer, R. M. and Wei, J. (1999) 'Social Uncertainty and the Problem of Trust in Social Groups: The Social Self in Doubt', in T. R. Tyler *et al.* (eds), *The Psychology of the Social Self* (Mahwah, NJ: Lawrence Erlboum Associates) pp.145–68.

Kreis, S. (2012), Renaissance Humanism. *The History Guide*. Lectures on Modern European Intellectual History. Available at: ahslibraryofbabel.pbworks.com/w/file/fetch/50209396/2012%20Renaissance.doc.

Krejci, J. (1994), *Great Revolutions Compared: The Outline of a Theory*. (Hemel Hempstead: Harvester Wheatsheaf)

Krentz, P. (2002), 'Fighting by the Rules: The Invention of the Hoplite Agôn', *Hesperia*, vol. 71, no. 1, 23–39.

Krieger, R. A. (2002), *Civilization's Quotations: Life's Ideal*. (Algora Publishing)

Kriesberg, L. (1992), *International Conflict Resolution: The U.S.–USSR and Middle East Cases*. (Yale University Press)

Kristof, N. D. (2009), 'Tear Down This Cyberwall!', *The New York Times*, 17 June.

Kroeber, C. B. (1996), 'Theory and History of Revolution', *Journal of World History*, vol. 7, no. 1, 21–40.

Kropotkin, P. (2008), *Mutual Aid: A Factor in Evolution*. (Charleston, SC: Forgotten Books)

Krzanic, R. (2013), '"The Ancient Greeks" and Six Words for Love'. *Yes Magazine* online. Available at: www.yesmagazine.org/happiness/the-ancient-greeks-6-words-for-love-and-why-knowing-them-can-change-your-life.

Kumar, K. (2001), *1989: Revolutionary Ideas and Ideals*. (Minneapolis: University of Minnesota Press)

Kumar, N. (1996), 'The Power of Trust in Manufacturer–Retailer Relationships', *Harvard Business Review*, vol. 74, no. 6, 92–106.

Kumar, N. *et al.* (1998), 'Interdependence, Punitive Capability, and the Reciprocation of Punitive Actions in Channel Relationships', *Journal of Marketing Research*, vol. 35, no. 2, 225–35.

Kunz, W. M. (2006), 'Why Ownership Matters', in *Culture Conglomerates: Consolidation in the Motion Picture and Television Industries* (Rowman and Littlefield Publishers, Inc.), pp. 1–15.

Kuran, T. (2005), 'The Absence of the Corporation in Islamic Law: Origins and Persistence', *American Journal of Comparative Law*, vol. 53, no. 4, 785–834.

Kurtz, P. (1994), *Toward a New Enlightenment: The Philosophy of Paul Kurtz.* (Transaction Publishers)

Kurzman, C. (2004), *The Unthinkable Revolution in Iran.* (Harvard University Press)

Kydd, A. H. (2005), *Trust and Mistrust in International Relations.* (Princeton: Princeton University Press)

Kynaston, D. (2012), *City of London: The History.* (Vintage)

Kynaston, D. (2002), *The City of London Volume 4: Club No More, 1945–2000 v. 4.* (London: Pimlico)

Lacey, W. K. (1968), *The Family in Classical Greece.* (Cornell University Press)

Lachowski, Z. (2004), *Confidence and Security Building Measures in the New Europe.* (Oxford University Press)

Laclau, E. and Mouffe, C. (2001), *Hegemony and Socialist Strategy: Towards a Radical Democratic Politics.* (Verso)

Lactantius (1984), *De Mortibus Persecutorum.* (Oxford: Clarendon Press)

Laden, O. B. (2005), *Messages to the World: The Statements of Osama Bin Laden.* (Verso)

Ladenson, R. (1980), 'In Defense of a Hobbesian Conception of Law', *Philosophy and Public Affairs*, vol. 9, no. 2, 134–59.

Lafuente, M. A. C. (2006), 'Social Imagination and History in Paul Ricoeur', in Anna-Teresa Tymieniecka (ed.), *Proceedings of the National Academy of Sciences of the United States of America* Analecta Husserliana. (Springer Netherlands), pp. 195–222.

Lagendijk, A. *et al.* (2009), 'Shifts in Governmentality, Territoriality and Governance: An Introduction', in B. Arts *et al.* (eds) *The Disoriented State: Shifts in Governmentality, Territoriality and Governance (Environment and Policy).* (Springer Netherlands), pp. 3–12.

Lagerspetz, O. (1998), *Trust: The Tacit Demand.* (Dordrecht: Kluwer Academic Publishers)

Lahno, B. (2001), 'On the Emotional Character of Trust', *Ethical Theory and Moral Practice*, vol. 4, no. 2, 171–89.

Lai, C.-C. (2000), 'Braudel's Concepts and Methodology Reconsidered', *The European Legacy*, vol. 5, no. 1, 65–86.

Laing, R. D. (1969), *The Divided Self.* (Penguin Books)

Lake, P. (2007), 'The Politics of Popularity and the Public Sphere', in P. Lake and S. Pincus (eds) *The Politics of the Public Sphere in Early Modern England.* (Manchester University Press), pp. 59–94.

Lambert, T. (2014), 'Daily Life in England in 1600s', *Local Histories*.

Lanchester, J. (2012), *What Is Money?* BBC Radio 4 Current Affairs Programme, 24 March.

Landucci, L. (1927), *A Florentine Diary from 1450 to 1516.* (J. M. Dent and Sons)

Lane, C. and Bachmann, R. (1997), 'Cooperation in Inter-Firm Elations in Britain and Germany: The Role of Social Institutions', *British Journal of Sociology*, vol. 48, 226–54.

Langland, W. (1999), *Piers Plowman*. (Wordsworth Editions)

Langlois, C. (1990), 'The French Revolution and "Revisionism"', *The History Teacher*, vol. 23, no. 4, 395–404.

Langohr, V. (2004), 'Too Much Civil Society, Too Little Politics: Egypt and Liberalizing Arab Regimes', *Comparative Politics*, vol. 36, no. 2, 181–204.

Lanni, A. and Vermeule, A. (2013), 'Precautionary Constitutionalism in Ancient Athens', *Cardozo Law Review*, vol. 34, no. 893.

Lansing, C. (1991), *The Florentine Magnates: Lineage and Faction in a Medieval Commune*. (Books on Demand)

Lantschner, P. (2009), 'The "Ciompi Revolution" Constructed: Modern Historians and the Nineteenth-Century Paradigm of Revolution', *Annali di Storia di Firenze*, vol. IV, 277–97.

Lash, S. (2007), 'Power after Hegemony: Cultural Studies in Mutation?', *Theory, Culture and Society*, vol. 24, no. 3, 55–78.

Lash, S. (2002), *Critique of Information*. Theory, Culture, and Society. Mike Featherstone (ed.) (Sage Publications)

Lash, S. and Urry, J. (1994), *Economies of Signs and Space*. Theory, Culture and Society. (Sage Publications)

Laslett, P. (1988), *Locke: Two Treatises of Government Student Edition*. (Cambridge University Press)

Laslett, P. (1956), 'The English Revolution and Locke's Two Treatises of Government', *Historical Journal*, vol. 12, 40–55.

Latané, B. (1981), 'The Psychology of Social Impact', *American Psychologist*, vol. 36, 343–56.

Latour, B. and Woolgar, S. (1986), *Laboratory Life: The Construction of Scientific Facts*. (Princeton University Press)

Latourette, K. S. (1937), *A History of Expansion of Christianity. 1. 'The' First Five Centuries*. (Harper and Brothers Publ.)

Lavery, H. (2005), *Hamlet and Elizabethan England*. Open Learn.

Lawler, E. J. (1976), 'Control Systems in Organizations', in M. D. Dunnelle (ed.), *Handbook of Industrial and Organizational Psychology* (Rand McNally)

Lawson, G. (2011), 'Halliday's Revenge: Revolutions and International Relations', *International Affairs*, vol. 87, no. 5, 1067–85.

Lawson, G. (2005), 'Negotiated Revolutions: The Prospects for Radical Change in Contemporary World Politics', *Review of International Studies*, vol. 31, no. 3, 473–93.

Lawson, G. (2004), *Negotiated Revolutions: The Czech Republic, South Africa and Chile*. (Ashgate Publishing Ltd)

Layard, R. (2005), *Happiness: Lessons from a New Science*. (Allen Lane)

Le Blanc, P. (2012), 'Lenin and Luxemburg through Each Other's Eyes', in Wuhan: International Conference on 'Lenin's Thought in the Twenty-First Century: Interpretation and Its Value'.

Le Bon, G. (2013), *The Crowd: A Study of the Popular Mind*. (CreateSpace Independent Publishing Platform)

Le Bon, G. (2009), *Psychology of Crowds*. (Sparkling Books Ltd)

Le Bon, G. (2007), *The Psychology of Revolution*. (NuVision Publications, LLC)

Le Bon, G. and MacKay, C. (1994), *The Crowd and Extraordinary Popular Delusions and the Madness of Crowds*. (Traders Press)

Leadbeater, C. (2009), *We-Think: Mass Innovation, Not Mass Production*. (Profile Books)

Leavitt, J. (2006), 'Linguistic Relativities', in C. Jourdan and K. Tuite (eds) *Language, Culture and Society: Key Topics in Linguistic Anthropology*. (Cambridge: Cambridge University Press), pp. 47–81.

Leca, J. (1994), 'Individualism and Citizenship', in B. S. Turner and P. Hamilton (eds) *Citizenship: Critical Concepts*. (Routledge), pp. 148–87.

Ledwith, S. (2013), 'Revolution in the 21st Century'. *Counterfire* online.

Lee, D. (2000), 'The Society of Society: The Grand Finale of Niklas Luhmann', *Sociological Theory*, vol. 18, no. 2, 320–30.

Lee, P. *et al.* (2010), 'Leadership and Trust: Their Effect on Knowledge Sharing and Team Performance', *Management Learning*, vol. 41, no. 4, 473–91.

Lee, R. (2007), *Contemporary Knitting for Textile Artists*. (Anova)

Lee, R. E. (2012), 'Introduction', in R. E. Lee (ed.), *The Longue Duree and World-Systems Analysis* (SUNY Press), pp. 1–8.

Lefebvre, H. (1991), *The Production of Space*. (Oxford: Blackwell)

Lehrer, J. (2010), 'Weak Ties, Twitter and Revolution'. *Wired* online.

Lehrer, K. (1997), *Self-Trust: A Study of Reason, Knowledge, and Autonomy*. (Clarendon Press)

Lehtonen, T. M. S. (1995), *Fortuna, Money, and the Sublunar World: Twelfth-Century Ethical Poetics and the Satirical Poetry of the Carmina Burana*. (Finnish Historical Society)

Lendon, J. E. (1997), *Empire of Honour: The Art of Government in the Roman World*. (Oxford University Press)

Lenin, V. I. (1989), *What Is to Be Done? (Twentieth Century Classics)*. (Penguin Books Ltd)

Lenin, V. I. (1975), 'What Is to Be Done? Burning Questions of Our Movement', in Robert C. Tucker (ed.), *The Lenin Anthology* (W.W. Norton and Company), pp. 12–114.

Lenin, V. I. (1970a), *Lenin: Collected Works*. Available at: www.marxists.org/archive/lenin/works/cw/index.htm.

Lenin, V. I. (1970b), *On Culture and Cultural Revolution*. (Moscow: Progress Publishers)

Lenin, V. I. (1965), *The Proletarian Revolution and the Renegade Kautsky*. (Foreign Languages Press)

Lenin, V. I. (1932), *State and Revolution*. vol. 7. (International Publishers)

Lenin, V. I. (1918), 'The Economic Basis of the Withering Away of the State', in *The State and Revolution: Collected Works, Volume 25* (MIA), pp. 381–492.

LePan, D. (1996), *The Cognitive Revolution in Western Culture*. (Eurospan)

Levi, G. (1991), 'On Microhistory', in P. Burke (ed.), *New Perspectives on Historical Writing* (Cambridge: Polity Press), pp. 93–113.

Levi, M. (1998), 'A State of Trust', in V. Braithwaite and M. Levi (eds) *Trust and Governance*. (New York: Russell Sage Foundation)

Levi, M. and Stoker, L. (2000), 'Political Trust and Trustworthiness', *Annual Review of Political Science*, vol. 3, no. 1, 475–507.

Levi-Strauss, C. (1963), *Structural Anthropology*. (Basic Books)

Levy, F. J. (1982), 'How Information Spread among the Gentry, 1550–1640', *Journal of British Studies*, vol. 21, no. 2, 11–34.

Lewicki, R. J. and Bunker, B. B. (1995), 'Trust in Relationships: A Model of Trust Development and Decline', in B. B. Bunker and J. Z. Rubin (eds) *Conflict, Cooperation and Justice* (San Francisco, CA: Jossey-Bass), pp. 133–73.

Lewicki, R. and Bunker, B. (1996) 'Developing and Maintaining Trust in Working Relationships', in R. M Kramer and T. R Tyler (eds), *Trust in Organizations: Frontiers of Theory and Research* (Thousand Oaks, CA: Sage Publications): 114–39.

Lewicki, R. *et al.* (1998), 'Trust and Distrust: New Relationships and Realities', *The Academy of Management Review*, vol. 23, no. 3, 438–58.

Lewis, J. D. and Weigert, A. J. (1985a), 'Social Atomism, Holism, and Trust', *The Sociological Quarterly*, vol. 26, no. 4, 455–71.

Lewis, J. D. and Weigert, A. J. (1985b), 'Trust as a Social Reality', *Social Forces*, vol. 63, no. 4, 967–85.

Lewis, K. J. (2013), *Kingship and Masculinity in Late Medieval England*. (Routledge)

Leys, R. (2011), 'The Turn to Affect: A Critique', *Critical Inquiry*, vol. 107, no. 4, 59–81.

Lichtheim, G. (1965), 'The Concept of Ideology', *History and Theory*, vol. 4, no. 2, 164–95.

Lienhard, J. T. (2015), 'A Note on the Meaning of Pistis in Aristotle's Rhetoric', *Journal of Philology*, vol. 87, no. 4, 446–54.

Lieven, D. C. B. (1993), *The Aristocracy in Europe: 1815–1914*. (Columbia University Press)

Lifvergren, M. 2011, 'The Facebook Revolution: A Content Analysis on the British Mainstream Media Coverage of the Protests in Egypt', Ph.D thesis, University of Leicester.

Lilli, E. (2011), 'Revolts in the Arab World: Is It Bad News for Islamic Terrorists?', *Journal of Terrorism Research*, vol. 2, no. 1.

Lilti, A. (2009), 'The Kingdom of Politesse: Salons and the Republic of Letters in Eighteenth-Century France', *Journal for the Study of Knowledge, Politics, and the Arts*, vol. 1, no. 1, 1–11.

Lin, N. (2002), *Social Capital: A Theory of Social Structure and Action (Structural Analysis in the Social Sciences)*. (Cambridge University Press)

Lindberg, D. C. (1990), 'Conceptions of the Scientific Revolution from Bacon to Butterfield', in D. C. Lindberg and R. S. Westman (eds) *Reappraisals of the Scientific Revolution*. (Cambridge: Cambridge University Press), pp. 1–26.

Lindberg, D. C. and Numbers, D. L. (2008), *When Science and Christianity Meet.* (University of Chicago Press)

Lindsay, P. and Groves, R. (1955), *The Peasants Revolt 1381.* (Hutchinson)

Lindskold, S. (1978), 'Trust Development, the GRIT Proposal, and the Effects of Conciliatory Acts on Conflict and Cooperation', *Psychological Bulletin*, vol. 85, no. 4, 772–93.

Linebaugh, P. (2008), *The Magna Carta Manifesto: Liberties and Commons for All.* (Berkeley, CA: University of California)

Lingren, H. G. (1995), *Adolescence and Peer Pressure.* Available at: www. experimentresources.com/sociallearning-theory.html.

Linton, M. (2015), *Choosing Terror: Virtue, Friendship, and Authenticity in the French Revolution.* (OUP Oxford)

Linton, M. (2011), 'The Terror in the French Revolution Terror'. Kingston University: Tyranicide to Terrorism in Europe, 1605 to the present, series working paper.

Lintott, A. (2014), *Violence, Civil Strife and Revolution in the Classical City: 750–330 BC.* (Routledge)

Lintott, A. (1999), *The Constitution of the Roman Republic.* (Oxford University Press)

Lippmann, W. (1963), 'Today and Tomorrow', *New York Herald Tribune*, 10 December, p. 24.

Lips, H. (1991), *Women, Men and Power.* (Mountain View, CA: Mayfield Publishing Company)

Lipsky, E. (1976), 'Comparative Approaches to the Study of Revolution: A Historiographic Essay', *Review of Politics*, vol. 38, no. 4, 494–509.

Little, M. *et al.* (2002), 'Survivorship and Discourses of Identity', *Psycho-Ontology*, vol. 11, 170–78.

Livy (2012), *History of Rome.* (Acheron Press)

Livy (2009), *Ab Urbe Condita Libri.* Reprinted (BiblioBazaar)

Livy (2006), *The History of Rome, Books 1–5.* (Hackett Publishing)

Llewellyn-Jones, L. (2003), *Aphrodite's Tortoise: The Veiled Woman of Ancient Greece.* (Classical Press of Wales)

Lloyd, D. (1668), *Memoires of the Lives, Actions, Sufferings and Deaths of Those Noble, Reverend, and Excellent Personages, that Suffered by Death, Sesquestration, Decimation, or Otherwise, for the Protestant Religion, and the Great Principle Thereof, Allegiance to Their Sov.* (London: S. Speed)

Lloyd, G. E. R. (1990), *Demystifying Mentalities.* (Cambridge University Press)

Locke, J. (1997), *Locke: Political Essays.* (Cambridge University Press)

Locke, J. (ed.) (1988). *Locke: Two Treatises of Government Student Edition.* P. Laslett (ed.) (Cambridge University Press)

Locke, J. (1980), *Second Treatise of Government.* C. B. Macpherson (ed.) vol. 8. (Hackett Publishing Company)

Locke, J. (1976), *The Correspondence of John Locke, Volume 1.* (Clarendon Press)

Locke, J. (1954), *Essays on the Law of Nature: John Locke.* (Clarendon Press)

Lockyer, R. (1959), *The Trial of Charles I: A Contemporary Account Taken from the Memoirs of Sir Thomas Herbert and John Rushworth*. (Folio Society)

Loewenstein, A. (2008), *The Blogging Revolution*. (Melbourne Univ. Publishing)

Logan, F. D. (2012), *A History of the Church in the Middle Ages*. Second Edition. (Routledge)

Loiselle, K. (2014), *Brotherly Love: Freemasonry and Male Friendship in Enlightenment France*. (Cornell University Press)

Long, H. S. (ed.) (1972), *Diogenes Laertius: Lives of Eminent Philosophers, Volume 1*. Loeb Class. (Harvard University Press)

Lopez, R. S. (1976), *The Commercial Revolution of the Middle Ages, 950–1350*. (Cambridge University Press)

Lotan, G. *et al.* (2011), 'The Revolutions Were Tweeted: Information Flows during the 2011 Tunisian and Egyptian Revolutions', *International Journal of Communications*, vol. 5, 1375–406.

Lovejoy, A. O. (2011), *The Great Chain of Being: A Study of the History of an Idea*. (Transaction Publishers)

Loveluck, L. (2011), 'The Importance of History and Process', *The World Today. Org*, vol. 67, no. 6, January, 21–23. https://www.chathamhouse.org/publications/twt/archive/view/181103.

Loyn, H. R. (1989), 'Scholasticism', in H. R. Loyn (ed.), *The Middle Ages: A Concise Encyclopedia* (London: Thames and Hudson), pp. 293–94.

Luban, O. (2012), 'Rosa Luxemburg's Critique of Lenin's Ultra Centralistic Party Concept and of the Bolshevik Revolution', *Critique*, vol. 40, no. 3, 357–65.

Lucas, R. E. (2002), *Lectures on Economic Growth*. (Harvard University Press)

Luhmann, N. (1979), *Trust and Power*. (Chichester: John Wiley and Sons)

Luhmann, N. (1982), *The Differentiation of Society* (New York: Columbia University Press)

Luhmann, N. (1988), 'Familiarity, Confidence, Trust: Problems and Alternatives', in Diego Gambetta (ed.), *Trust: Making and Breaking Cooperative Relations*. (Oxford: University of Oxford), pp. 94–107.

Luhmann, N. (1995), *Social Systems* (Stanford: Stanford University Press)

Luhmann, N. (2012), *Theory of Society, Volume 1 (Cultural Memory in the Present)*. (Eurospan)

Lukács, G. (1971), *History and Class Consciousness: Studies in Marxist Dialectics*. (MIT Press)

Lukacs, J. (2013), *A Short History of the Twentieth Century*. First Edition. (Harvard University Press)

Lukes, S. (2005a), 'Power and the Battle for Hearts and Minds', *Millennium – Journal of International Studies*, vol. 33, no. 3, 477–93.

Lukes, S. (2005b), *Power, Second Edition: A Radical View*. (Palgrave Macmillan)

Lukes, S. (1974), *Power: A Radical View*. (London: Macmillan Press)

Lundåsen, S. (2010), 'Methodological Problems with Surveying Trust', in *JSM Proceedings at AAPOR* (Alexandria, VA: American Statistical Association), pp. 5806–15.

Luther King, M. (1990), *Stride toward Freedom*. New Edition. (San Francisco, CA: Harper)

Luther, M. (1957), *Luther's Works (55 Volumes)*. Various eds. (St. Louis, Minneapolis: Concordia Publishing House, Fortress Press)

Luther, M. (1970), 'Against the Robbing and Murdering Hordes of Peasants', in E. G. Rupp and B. Drewery (eds) *Martin Luther, Documents of Modern History*. (London: Edward Arnold), pp. 121–26.

Lutri, A. (n.d.), 'A Cognitive Contribution about the Ethnographic Study of Knowledges'. *Social Anthropology*.

Luxemburg, R. (2014), 'In a Revolutionary Hour: What Next?', in R. Luxemburg., *Collected Works of Rosa Luxemburg*. (Verso) p. 554.

Luxemburg, R. (2006), *Reform or Revolution and Other Writings (Dover Books on History, Political and Social Science)*. (Dover Publications)

Luxemburg, R. (2003), *The Accumulation of Capital*. Rare Masterpieces of Philosophy and Science. John Eatwell *et al.* (eds) vol. 1. (Routledge)

Luxemburg, R. (1986), *The Mass Strike: The Political Party and the Trade Union*. (London: Bookmarks)

Luxemburg, R. (1922), 'The Russian Revolution'. *Marxist.org*.

Luxemburg, R. (1904), 'Organizational Questions of the Russian Social Democracy [Leninism or Marxism?]'. *Marxist.org*.

Lynch, M. (2011), 'After Egypt: The Limits and Promise of Online Challenges to the Authoritarian Arab State', *Perspectives on Politics*, vol. 9, no. 2, 301–10.

Lynch, T. (2013), 'Writing Up Qualitative Research: Methodology', *English Language Teaching Center*, vol. 2461, no. 2, 1–9.

Lyotard, J.-F. (1984), *The Postmodern Condition: A Report on Knowledge*. G. Bennington and B. Massumi (eds) (Minneapolis: University of Minnesota Press)

Macaskill, A. and Brown, K. (2010), 'Psychological Review of Trust – Trust Can Be Conceptualised', in *Science and Trust Expert Group Report and Action Plan: Starting a National Conversation about Good Science*, pp. 67–68.

Macaulay, T. B. (1848), *The History of England from the Accession of James II*, 5 vols (Philadelphia, Porter and Coates)

Macaulay, T. (1979), *History of England from the Accession of James II vol. 2*. (Penguin Classics)

Macaulay, T. B. (2009), *The History of England from the Accession of James the Second, Volume II: 2*. (BiblioLife)

Macdonald, S. (2003), *Expo 67, Canada's National Heterotopia: A Study of the Transformative Role of the International Exhibitions in Modern Society*. (Carleton University)

MacFarlane, A. (1979), *Origins English Individual*. (Cambridge University Press)

MacGillivray, R. C. (2012), *Restoration Historians and the English Civil War*. (Springer Science and Business Media)

Machiavelli, N. (2013), *The Discourses*. (Penguin)

Machiavelli, N. (2007), *The Prince*. W. K. Marriott (ed.) (Rockville: Arc Manor LLC)

Machiavelli, N. (1996), *Machiavelli and His Friends: Their Personal Correspondence.* J. B. Atkinson and D. Sices (eds) (Northern Illinois University Press)

Machiavelli, N. (1990), *Florentine Histories.* (Princeton University Press)

Machiavelli, N. (1965), *The Art of War.* (Bobbs-Merrill)

MacIntyre, A. (2007), *After Virtue: A Study in Moral Theory.* (University of Notre Dame Press)

MacIver, R. M. (1937), *Society: A Textbook of Sociology.* (Farrar and Rinehart)

Mackenney, R. (1987), *Tradesmen and Traders: The World of the Guilds in Venice and Europe, c. 1250–c. 1650.* (Barnes and Noble Books)

Macleod, E. V. (2013), 'British Spectators of the French Revolution: The View from across the Channel', *Groniek*, vol. 197, 377–92.

MacLeod, I. (1965), 'Quoodles', *The Spectator*, vol. December, no. 3.

MacMillan, M. (2010), *Dangerous Games: The Uses and Abuses of History.* (New York: Modern Library)

Madden, M. R. (1930), *Political Theory and Law in Medieval Spain.* (The Lawbook Exchange, Ltd)

Madden, T. F. (2008), *Empires of Trust: How Rome Built – and America Is Building – a New World.* (Dutton)

Madison, J. (1787), 'The Utility of the Union as a Safeguard against Domestic Faction and Insurrection (Continued)', *Daily Advertiser*, 22 November.

Magliocco, D. (2014), 'Review of Print and Public Politics in the English Revolution', *Reviews in History*, vol. 1614. Available from: http://www.history.ac. uk/reviews/review/1614.

Magyar, Z. S. (2009), 'How and to What Extent Were the Imperial Cult and Emperor Worship thought to Preserve Stability in the Roman World?', *Acta Archaeologica*, vol. 60, no. 2, 385–95.

Mahoney, J. and Rueschemeyer, D. (eds) (2003), *Comparative Historical Analysis in the Social Sciences.* (Cambridge: Cambridge University Press)

Mahoney, P. (2001), 'The Common Law and Economic Growth: Hayek Might Be Right', *Journal of Legal Studies*, vol. 30, no. 2, 503–25.

Maier, P. (1992), *From Resistance to Revolution: Colonial Radicals and the Development of American Opposition to Britain, 1765–1776.* Reprint Edition. (W.W. Norton and Company)

Maine, H. S. (1861), *Ancient Law.* (London: John Murray)

Makar, F. (2011), '"Let Them Have Some Fun": Political and Artistic Forms of Expression in the Egyptian Revolution', *Mediterranean Politics*, vol. 16, no. 2, 307–12.

Malatesta, E. (1998), *Anarchy.* Revised Edition. (London: Freedom Press)

Malfliet, K. and Scharpé, F. (2003), *The Concept of Russia: Patterns for Political Development in the Russian Federation.* (Leuven University Press)

Mallett, M. (1999), 'Mercenaries', in M. Keen (ed.), *Medieval Warfare: A History* (Oxford: Oxford University Press), pp. 209–29.

Maloy, J. S. (2008), *The Colonial American Origins of Modern Democratic Thought*. (Cambridge University Press)

Mandelbaum, M. (1967), 'History as Narrative', *History and Theory*, vol. 6, no. 3, 413–19.

Manela, E. (2001), 'The Wilsonian Moment and the Rise of Anticolonial Nationalism: The Case of Egypt', *Diplomacy and Statecraft*, vol. 12, no. 4, 99–122.

Manhire, T. (2012), *The Arab Spring: Rebellion, Revolution, and a New World Order*. (Guardian Books)

Mann, M. (1984), 'The Autonomous Power of the State: Its Origins, Mechanisms and Results', *European Journal of Sociology*, vol. 25, no. 2, 185–213.

Mann, M. (2012), *The Sources of Social Power: volume 1, A History of Power from the Beginning to AD 1760*. (Cambridge University Press)

Mann, M. (2012), *The Sources of Social Power: Volume 2, The Rise of Classes and Nation-States, 1760–1914*. (Cambridge University Press)

Mannheim, H. (1941), *War and Crime*. (London: Watts)

Mannheim, K. (1985), *Ideology and Utopia: An Introduction to the Sociology of Knowledge*. (Harcourt Brace Jovanovich)

Mannheim, K. (1950), *Freedom, Power, and Democratic Planning*. (New York: Oxford University Press)

Mansfield, P. (2003), *A History of the Middle East*. Second Edition. (Penguin Books Ltd)

Mansour, A. (2014), *Constitution of The Arab Republic of Egypt 2014*. (Brill)

Manz, C. C. and Gioia, D. A. (1983), 'The Interrelationship of Power and Control', *Human Relations*, vol. 36, no. 5, 459–75.

Marfleet, P. (2011a), 'Act One of the Egyptian Revolution', *International Socialism*, no. 130, 4 April. http://isj.org.uk/act-one-of-the-egyptian-revolution/.

Marfleet, P. (2011b), 'Egypt Shaped at the Grass Roots', *OpenDemocracy*, 25 June, 1–5.

Margetts, H. Z. *et al.* (2016), *Political Turbulence*. (Princeton, NJ: Princeton University Press)

Margetts, H. Z. *et al.* (2013), 'Leadership without Leaders? Starters and Followers in Online Collective Action', *Political Studies*, vol. 63, no. 2, 278–99.

Marien, S. and Hooghe, M. (2011), 'Does Political Trust Matter? An Empirical Investigation into the Relation between Political Trust and Support for Law Compliance', *European Journal of Political Research*, vol. 50, no. 2, 267–91.

Marincola, J. (2001), *Greek Historians*. (Cambridge University Press)

Markham, F. (1625), *The Booke of Honour: Or Five Decades of Epistles of Honour*. (Matthewes)

Markoff, J. (1986), 'Literacy and Revolt: Some Empirical Notes on 1789 in France', *American Journal of Sociology*, vol. 92, no. 2, 323.

Marková, I. and Gillespie, A. (2011), *Trust and Conflict: Representation, Culture and Dialogue*. I. Marková and A. Gillespie (eds) (Routledge)

Marks, J. D. (1979), *The Search for the 'Manchurian Candidate': The CIA and Mind Control*. (Times Books)

Marks, L. F. (1960), 'The Financial Oligarchy in Florence under Lorenzo', in E. F. Jacob (ed.), *Italian Renaissance Studies* (London: Faber and Faber), pp. 123–47.

Markus, H. R. and Kitayama, S. (1991), 'Culture and Self: Implications for Cognition, Emotion, and Motivation', *Psychological Review*, vol. 98, no. 2, 224–53.

Marqus, S. (2008), *Religious Tension: Exceeding Safety Levels – The Problem of National Inclusion in Egypt* (December)

Marsh, S. and Dibben, M. R. (2005), 'Trust, Untrust, Distrust and Mistrust – An Exploration of the Dark (er) Side', in P. Herrmann *et al.* (eds), *iTrust*, pp. 17–33.

Marsh, S. P. (1994), 'Formalising Trust as a Computational Concept', Ph.D thesis, University of Stirling.

Marshall, P. (2002), *Beliefs and the Dead in Reformation England*. (OUP Oxford)

Marshall, P. (2008), 'The Making of the Tudor Judas: Trust and Betrayal in the English Reformation', *Reformation*, vol. 13, 77–101.

Marshall, S. (2015), *The Egyptian Armed Forces and the Remaking of an Economic Empire* (April)

Martin L. K. Jr. (1963), '*I Have a Dream*' at Washington D.C. Civil Rights March, 1963.

Martin, S. (2005), *The Knights Templar: The History and Myths of the Legendary Military Order*. (New York, NY: Thunder's Mouth Press)

Martin, T. R. (2000), *Ancient Greece: From Prehistoric to Hellenistic Times*. (Yale University Press)

Marvell, A. and Smith, N. (2007), *The Poems of Andrew Marvell*. (Pearson Longman)

Marvin, C. (1979), 'The Printing Press as an Agent of Change – Book Review', *Technology and Culture*, vol. 20, no. 4, 793–97.

Marx, K. (1990), *Capital, vol 1*. (Penguin Books Limited)

Marx, K. (1852), *The Eighteenth Brumaire of Louis Bonaparte. Karl Marx 1852*. (New York: International Publishers)

Marx, K. (1844), 'The Power of Money in Bourgeois Society', in Marxist Organisation (ed.), *Economic and Philosophic Manuscripts of 1844. Marxist.org* online.

Marx, K. and Engels, F. (1998), *The German Ideology: Including Theses on Feuerbach and an Introduction to the Critique of Political Economy*. (Prometheus Books)

Marx, K. and Engels, F. (1975), *Collected Works*. (London: Lawrence and Wishart)

Marzouki, Y. *et al.* (2012), 'The Contribution of Facebook to the 2011 Tunisian Revolution: A Cyberpsychological Insight', *Cyberpsychology, Behavior and Social Networking*, vol. 15, no. 5, 1–7.

Masciarelli, F. (2011), *The Strategic Value of Social Capital: How Firms Capitalize on Social Assets*. (Cheltenham: Edward Elgar Publishing)

Mascuch, M. (2013), *The Origins of the Individualist Self: Autobiography and Self-Identity in England, 1591–1791*. (John Wiley and Sons)

Maslow, A. H. (1943), 'A Theory of Human Motivation', *Psychological Review*, vol. 50, no. 4, 370–96.

Mason, L. and Rizzo, T. (1998), *The French Revolution: A Document Collection*. (Houghton Mifflin)

Massey, D. (1994), 'Politics and Space/Time', in *Space, Place and Gender* (Minneapolis: University of Minnesota Press), pp. 249–72.

Massey, D. (1991), 'A Global Sense of Place', *Marxism Today*, June, 24–29.

Masson, P. (2001), *Globalization: Facts and Figures*. IMF Policy Discussion paper PDP/01/4. Available at: www.imf.org/external/pubs/ft/pdp/2001/pdp04.pdf.

Mattingly, D. J. (2011), *Imperialism, Power and Identity: Experiencing the Roman Empire*. (Princeton University Press)

Mattingly, H. (1948), *The Emperor and His Clients*. (Australasian Medical Publishing Company)

Maurer, B. (2006), 'The Anthropology of Money', *Annual Review of Anthropology*, vol. 35, no. 1, 15–36.

Mauriac, H. M. de (1949), 'Alexander the Great and the Politics of "Homonoia"', *Journal of the History of Ideas*, vol. 10, no. 1, 104–14.

Mavor, A. (2013), 'Magna Carta: A Bitter Indictment of King John's Rule?', *History Today*, online edition, 1–5.

Mayer, R. C. *et al.* (1995), 'An Integrative Model of Organizational Trust', *The Academy of Management Review*, vol. 20, no. 3, 709–34.

Mayer, T. F. (2000), *Reginald Pole: Prince and Prophet*. vol. 23. (Cambridge University Press)

Mayhew, R. (2009), *Essays on Ayn Rand's Atlas Shrugged*. (Lexington Books)

Mayhew, R. (1997), *Aristotle's Criticism of Plato's Republic*. (Rowman and Littlefield)

Mayr, E. (1990), 'When Is Historiography Whiggish?', *Journal of the History of Ideas*, vol. 51, no. 2, 301–09.

Maza, S. C. (1993), *Private Lives and Public Affairs: The Causes Célèbres of Prerevolutionary France*. (University of California Press)

Maza, S. C. (2003), *The Myth of the French Bourgeoisie: An Essay on the Social Imaginary, 1750–1850*. (Harvard University Press)

McAdam, D. (1982), *Political Process and the Development of Black Insurgency, 1930–1970*. (Chicago: University of Chicago Press)

McAdam, D. *et al.* (2001), *Dynamics of Contention (Cambridge Studies in Contentious Politics)*. (Cambridge University Press)

McAdam, D. *et al.* (1997), 'Towards an Integrated Perspective on Social Movements and Revolution', in Marc Irving Lichbach and Alan Zuckerman (eds) *Ideals, Interests, and Institutions: Advancing Theory in Comparative Politics*. (Cambridge: Cambridge University Press)

McAllister, D. J. (2013), 'Affect and Cognition Based Trust as Foundations for Interpersonal Cooperation in Organizations', *The Academy of Management Journal*, vol. 38, no. 1, 24–59.

McCarthy, J. D. and Zald, M. N. (1977), 'Resource Mobilization and Social Movements: A Partial Theory', Mayer N. Zald and John D. McCarthy (eds) *The American Journal of Sociology*, vol. 82, no. 6, 1212–41.

McClelland, J. S. (1996), *A History of Western Political Thought*. vol. 9. (Psychology Press)

McClosky, H. (1964), 'Consensus and Ideology in American Politics', *The American Political Science Review*, vol. 58, no. 2, 361–82.

McCloskey, D. N. and Floud, R. (eds) (1994), *The Economic History of Britain since 1700, vol. 1: 1700–1860: Volume 1*. Second Edition. (Cambridge, NY: Cambridge University Press)

McClosky, D. N. (2010), *Bourgeois Dignity: Why Economics Can't Explain the Modern World*. (Chicago, IL: University of Chicago Press)

McConnell, J. (2013), *David and Goliath: Individualism and Liberty in Italian Renaissance and the American Revolution*. (University of Washington Tacoma)

McCormick, M. (2001), *Origins of the European Economy: Communications and Commerce AD 300–900, Parts 300–900*. (Cambridge University Press)

McDermott, G. R. (2000), *Seeing God: Jonathan Edwards and Spiritual Discernment*. (Regent College Publishing)

McDonnell, M. (2006), *Roman Manliness: 'Virtus' and the Roman Republic*. (Cambridge: Cambridge University Press)

McElligott, J. and Smith, D. L. (2007), 'Introduction: Rethinking Royalist and Royalism', in *Royalists and Royalism during the English Civil Wars*. (Cambridge University Press), pp. 1–15.

McFadden, D. R. *et al.* (2008), *Radical Lace and Subversive Knitting*. (ACC Editions)

McFaul, M. (2006), 'Conclusion: The Orange Revolution in a Comparative Perspective', in M. Mcfaul and A. Aslund (eds) *Revolution in Orange: The Origins of Ukraine's Democratic Breakthrough*. (Washington, DC: Carnegie Endowment for International Peace), pp. 165–95.

McGlade, J. (1999), 'The Times of History: Archeology, Narrative and Non-Linear Causality', in T. Murray (ed.), *Time and Archeology*. (London: Routledge), pp. 139–63.

McGlade, J. (2006), 'Ecohistorical regimes and la longue duree: An Approach to Mapping Longterm', in E. Garnsey and J. McGlade (eds) *Complexity and Co-Evolution: Continuity and Change in Socio-Economic Systems*. (Edward Elgar Publishing), pp. 77–114.

McGrath, L. (2012), *Heterotopias of Mental Health Care: The Role of Space in Experiences of Distress, Madness, and Mental Health Service Use*. (London South Bank University)

McGregor, C. (2000), *Class Sociology: Australian Connections*. Second Edition. (Sydney: Allen and Unwin)

McKeever, D. (2012), 'The Logic of Revolt – Populist Discourse in Tahrir Square', Ph.D thesis, Central European University.

McKillop, S. (1992), 'Dante and Lumen Christi: A Proposal for the Meaning of the Tomb of Cosimo de' Medici', in *Cosimo 'il Vecchio' de' Medici*. (Oxford: Clarendon Press), pp. 245–301.

McKnight, D. H. and Chervany, N. L. (1996), *The Meanings of Trust*. Technical Report MISRC Working Paper Series 96-04, University of Minnesota, Management Information Systems Research Center.

McKnight, D. H. and Chervany, N. L. N. (2001), 'Trust and Distrust Definitions: One Bite at a Time', in Rino Falcone *et al.* (eds) *Trust in Cyber-Societies*. Lecture Notes in Computer Science. (Springer Berlin Heidelberg), pp. 27–54.

McLean, P. D. (2007), *The Art of the Network: Strategic Interaction and Patronage in Renaissance Florence*. (Duke University Press)

McLeod, J. *et al.* (1999), 'Community, Communication, and Participation: The Role of Mass Media and Interpersonal Discussion in Local Political Participation', *Political Communications*, vol. 16, no. 3, 37–41.

McLuhan, M. (1964), *Understanding Media: The Extensions of Man*. (McGraw-Hill)

McMahon, D. M. (2013), 'The Return of the History of Ideas?', in D. M. McMahon and S. Moyn (eds) *Rethinking Modern European Intellectual History*. (New York: Oxford University Press), pp. 13–31.

McManners, J. (1969), *The French Revolution and the Church*. (Greenwood Press)

McMillan, M. E. (2016), *From the First World War to the Arab Spring: What's Really Going On in the Middle East?* (Palgrave Macmillan US)

McMyler, B. (2011), *Testimony, Trust, and Authority*. (Oxford University Press)

McShane, S. L. (2006), *Canadian Organizational Behaviour*. Sixth Edition. (Toronto, Canada: McGraw-Hill)

Mead, G. H. (2009), *Mind, Self, and Society: From the Standpoint of a Social Behaviorist*. (University of Chicago Press)

Mead, G. H. (1969), *Mind, Self and Society*. (The University of Chicago Press)

Meade, R. D. and Barnard, W. (1973), 'Conformity and Anti-Conformity among Americans and Chinese', *The Journal of Social Psychology*, vol. 89, 15–24.

Meecham, P. and Sheldon, J. (2013), *Modern Art: A Critical Introduction*. vol. 26. (Routledge)

Mehta, A. and Yadav, V. (2014), 'Henry Fayol and Frederick W. Taylor's Contribution to Management', *International Journal of Innovative Research in Technology*, vol. 1, no. 5, 807–10.

Meital, Y. (2006), 'School Textbooks and Assembling the Puzzle of the Past in Revolutionary Egypt', *Middle Eastern Studies*, vol. 42, no. 2, 255–70.

Melancon, M. (2000), 'Rethinking Russia's February Revolution: Anonymous Spontaneity or Socialist Agency?', *The Carl Beck papers in Russian and East European Studies*, vol. 1408, 1–48.

Meles, M. (2007), *Understanding People's Attitude towards the Use of Wasta*. (Cranfield)

Mellinger, G. (1956), 'Interpersonal Trust as a Factor in Communication', *Journal of Abnormal Social Psychology*, vol. 52, 304–09.

Melton, J. V. H. (2001), *The Rise of the Public in Enlightenment Europe*. (Cambridge University Press)

Melucci, A. (1996), *Challenging Codes: Collective Action in the Information Age (Cambridge Cultural Social Studies)*. (Cambridge University Press)

Melucci, A. (1995), 'The Process of Collective Identity', in *Social Movements and Culture* (Minneapolis: University of Minnestoa Press), pp. 41–63.

Melucci, A. (1989), *Nomads of the Present*. J. Keane and P. Mier (eds) (Philadelphia: Temple University Press)

Melve, L. (2006), '"The Revolt of the Medievalists": Directions in Recent Research on the Twelfth-Century Renaissance', *Journal of Medieval History*, vol. 32, pp. 231–52.

Melville, H. (1992), *Moby Dick*. (Wordsworth Editions Ltd)

Mendieta, E. (2007), 'Citizenship and Trust: Political Friendship and Solidarity', in *Templeton Lecture Series* (Stony Brook University), pp. 1–20.

Mentzer, R. A. and Spicer, A. (2002), *Society and Culture in the Huguenot World, 1559-1685*. (Cambridge University Press)

Menza, M. F. (2013), *Patronage Politics in Egypt: The National Democratic Party and Muslim Brotherhood in Cairo*. (Routledge)

Mercer, J. (2005), 'Rationality and Psychology in International Politics', *International Organization*, vol. 59, no. 1, 77–106.

Merton, R. K. (1985), *On the Shoulders of Giants: A Shandean Postscript*. (Thomson Learning)

Merton, R. K. (1996), *On Social Structure and Science (Heritage of Sociology Series)*. (University of Chicago Press)

Meusburger, P. (2011), 'Knowledge, Cultural Memory and Politics', in P. Meusburger *et al.* (eds) *Cultural Memory: The Geographical Point of View*. (Springer), pp. 51–69.

Meyer, E. (2004), *Legitimacy and Law in the Roman World: Tabulae in Roman Belief and Practice*. (Cambridge: Cambridge University Press)

Micek, D. and Whitlock, W. (2008), *Twitter Revolution: How Social Media and Mobile Marketing Is Changing the Way We Do Business and Market Online*. (Xeno Press)

Michel, T. (2011), *Time to Get Emotional: Trust, Rationality and the Spectre of Manipulative Mentality*. School of Sociology, Politics and International Studies University of Bristol Working Paper no. 01-11. Available at: www.bristol.ac. uk/media-library/sites/spais/migrated/documents/michel0111.pdf.

Michelet, J. (2008), *History of the French Revolution*. (Lightning Source Incorporated)

Michelet, M. (1855), *Modern History (from the French)*. A. Potter (ed.) (Paris: Chamerot)

Michie, R. C. (1999), *The London Stock Exchange: A History*. (Oxford University Press)

Micklethwait, J. and Wooldridge, A. (2014), *The Fourth Revolution: The Global Race to Reinvent the State*. (Penguin Press)

Mielke. J. (2005), 'Fede and Fiducia: The Problem of Trust in Italian History 1300–1500', in G. A. Brucker (ed.), *Living on the Edge in Leonardo's Florence: Selected Essays*. (University of California Press), pp. 83–103.

Migdal, J. S. (1988), *Strong Societies and Weak States: State–Society Relations and State Capabilities in the Third World*. (Princeton University Press)

Mignet, F.-A. (2007), *History of the French Revolution from 1789 to 1814.* (BiblioBazaar)

Milani, C. R. S. and Laniado, R. N. (2007), 'Transnational Social Movements and the Globalization Agenda', *Brazilian Political Science Review*, vol. 1, no. 2, 10–39.

Milgram, S. (1961), 'Which Nations Conform Most?', *Scientific American online*, vol. 205, no. 6.

Milgram, S. (1963), 'Behavioral Study of Obedience', *Journal of Abnormal Social Psychology*, vol. 67, 371–78.

Miller, S. (2008), *Trust in Texts: A Different History of Rhetoric.* (SIU Press)

Millett, P. (1989), 'Patronage and Its Avoidance in Classical Athens', in A. Wallace-Hadrill (ed.), *Patronage in Ancient Society.* (London: Routledge), pp. 15–49.

Mills, C. W. (1956), *The Power Elite (Galaxy Books).* (Oxford University Press Inc)

Mills, G. (2015), *Why States Recover: Changing Walking Societies into Winning Nations, from Afghanistan to Zimbabwe.* (Oxford: Oxford University Press)

Milner, S. J. (2011), *Political Oratory and the Public Sphere in Early Quattrocento Florence.*

Milton, J. and Fowler, A. (1998), *Paradise Lost.* (Longman)

Milton, J. (1688), *Paradise Lost.* Fourth Edition. (Jacob Tonson)

Milton, J. (1649), *The Tenure of Kings and Magistrates.* (M. Simmons)

Minio-Paluello, M.-L. (2009), *Jesters and Devils: Florence – San Giovanni 1514.* (Lulu.com)

Mintzberg, H. (1983), *Power in and around Organizations.* (Prentice-Hall)

Mishler, W. and Rose, R. (2001), 'What Are the Origins of Political Trust? Testing Institutional and Cultural Theories in Post-Communist Societies', *Comparative Political Studies*, vol. February, 1–52.

Mishler, W. and Rose, R. (1997), 'Trust, Distrust and Skepticism: Popular Evaluations of Civil and Political Institutions Societies in Post-Communist Societies', *The Journal of Politics*, vol. 59, no. 2, 418–51.

Mishra, A. K. (1986), 'Organizational Responses to Crisis: The Centrality of Trust', in R. M. Kramer and T. R. Tyler (eds) *Trust in Organizations: Frontiers of Theory and Research.* (Thousand Oaks, CA: Sage Publications), pp. 261–87.

Misztal, B. (2003), *Theories of Social Remembering (Theorizing Society).* (Open University Press)

Misztal, B. (1996), *Trust in Modern Societies: The Search for the Bases of Social Order.* (Polity Press)

Mitchell, L. and Melville, C. (eds) (2013), *Every Inch a King: Comparative Studies on Kings and Kingship in the Ancient and Medieval Worlds.* (Leiden and Boston: Brill)

Mohan, A. (2010), *The Country and the Village: Representations of the Rural in Twentieth-Century South Asian Literature.* (University of Toronto)

Mokyr, J. (1993), *The British Industrial Revolution: An Economic Perspective.* J. Mokyr (ed.) (Boulder, CO: Westview Press)

Molho, A. (1968), 'The Florentine Oligarchy and the Balie of the Late Trecento', *Speculum*, vol. 43, no. 1, 23–51.

Möllering, G. (2005), 'The Trust/Control Duality: An Integrative Perspective on Positive Expectations of Others', *International Sociology*, vol. 20, no. 3, 283–305.

Molm, L. D. (1997), 'Risk and Power Use: Constraints on the Use of Coercion in Exchange', *American Sociological Review*, vol. 62, no. 1, 113–33.

Molyneux, J. (2011), 'Reflections on the Egyptian Revolution', *Irish Marxist Review*, vol. 1, no. 1, 1–21.

Mommsen, T. (1942), 'Petrarch's Conception of the "Dark Ages"', *Speculum*, vol. 17, no. 2, 226–42.

Mommsen, T. (2008), *Mommsen's History of Rome*. (Wildside Press LLC)

Montaigne, M. de. (1992), 'Man's Presumption and Littleness', in M. Mack (ed.), *The Norton Anthology of World Masterpieces* (New York: W.W. Norton and Company), pp. 1808–16.

Montefiore, S. S. (2013a), *Istanbul, Rome and Jerusalem: Titans of the Holy Cities*. (Quercus)

Montefiore, S. S. (2013b), *Rome: A History of the Eternal City*, BBC 4 online, 3 episodes.

Montesquieu (1989), *Montesquieu: The Spirit of the Laws*. A. M. Cohler *et al.* (eds) (Cambridge University Press)

Montgomery, I. (1995), 'The Institutionalization of Lutheranism in Sweden and Finland', in O. P. Grell (ed.), *The Scandinavian Reformation*. (Cambridge University Press), pp. 144–78.

Moore, B. (1967), *Social Origins of Dictatorship and Democracy: Lord and Peasant in the Making of the Modern World*. (Beacon Press)

Moore, E. W. (1985), *The Fairs of Medieval England: An Introductory Study, Volumes 72–74*. (Pontifical Institute of Mediaeval Studies)

Moore, R. I. (2000), *The First European Revolution: 970–1215*. (Wiley)

Morawski, J. G. (1988), 'Impossible Experiments and Practical Constructions: The Social Basis of Psychologists' Work', in J. Morawski (ed.), *The Rise of Experimentation in American Psychology*. (New Haven, CT: Yale University Press), pp. 37–60.

Morgan, C. (1990), *Athletes and Oracles: The Transformation of Olympia and Delphi in the Eighth Century BC*. (Cambridge University Press)

Morgan, L. H. (1877), *Ancient Society*. (Transaction Publishers)

Morgan, R. M. and Hunt, S. D. (1994), 'The Commitment–Trust Theory of Relationship Marketing', *Journal of Marketing*, vol. 58, no. 3, 20–38.

Morgan, T. (2015a), 'Introduction', in *Roman Faith, Christian Faith*. (Oxford Scholarship Online), pp. 1–39.

Morgan, T. (2015b), 'Roman Faith and Christian Faith: Pistis and Fides in the Early Roman Empire and Early Churches', in *Roman Faith, Christian Faith*. (Oxford Scholarship Online), pp. 40–87.

Morice, J. (1590), *A brief treatise of oathes exacted by ordinaries and ecclesiasticall iudges, to answere generallie to all such articles or interrogatories, as pleaseth them to propound: And of their forced and constrained oathes ex officio, wherein is proued that the sam*. (London: Richard Schilders)

Morozov, E. (2011), *The Net Delusion: The Dark Side of Internet Freedom*. (Public Affairs)

Morozov, E. (2009a), 'Moldova's Twitter Revolution', *Foreign Policy*, 7 April.

Morozov, E. (2009b), 'Iran: Downside to the "Twitter Revolution"', *Dissent*, vol. 56, no. 4, 10–14.

Morris, C. W. (2004), 'The Modern State', in G. F. Gaus and C. Kukathas (eds) *Handbook of Political Theory* (Sage Publications), pp. 195–209.

Morrow, A. and Al-Omrani, K. M. (2011), 'Muslim-Christian Unity Characterizes Egypt's Uprising'. *The Electronic Intifada* online.

Mortimer, S. (2012), 'The Civil Wars', *History Today*, vol. 62, no. 10, 1–4.

Mosco, V. (2004), *The Digital Sublime: Myth, Power, and Cyberspace*. (MIT Press)

Moss, B. H. (1985), 'Marx and Engels on French Social Democracy: Historians or Revolutionaries?', *Journal of the History of Ideas*, vol. 46, no. 4, 539–57.

Moulakis, A. (1998), *Republican Realism in Renaissance Florence: Francesco Guicciardini's Discorso Di Logrogno*. (Rowman and Littlefield)

Moulene, F. (2015), 'The Challenge of Sociology of Language: Beyond Sociolinguistics; towards Discourse Analysis', *Language Discourse and Society*, vol. 3, no. 2, 119–33.

Moussa, M. B. (2011), *The Use of the Internet by Social Movements in Morocco: Implications for Collective Action and Political Change*. (Concordia University)

Muchinsky, P. (1977), 'An Intra-Organizational Analysis of the Roberts and O'Reilly Organizational Communication Questionnaire', *Journal of Applied Psychology*, vol. 62, 184–88.

Muddiman, J. G. (1928), *The Trial of King Charles the First (Notable British Trials)*. (London: Butterworth)

Mueller, R. C. (1997), *The Venetian Money Market: Banks, Panics, and the Public Debt, 1200–1500*. (Johns Hopkins University Press)

Muilwijk, R. (2012), *Trust in Online Information: A Comparison among High School Students, College Students and PhD Students with Regard to Trust in Wikipedia*. (University of Twente)

Muir, E. (1999), 'The Sources of Civil Society in Italy', *The Journal of Interdisciplinary History*, vol. 29, no. 3 (Part 1), 379–406.

Mulcaster, R. (1970), *The First Part of the Elementary, 1582*. (Scolar Press)

Mulgan, G. (2008), *The Art of Public Strategy: Mobilizing Power and Knowledge for the Common Good*. (OUP Oxford)

Mullins, W. A. (1974), 'Sartori's Concept of Ideology: A Dissent and an Alternative in', in A. R. Wilcox (ed.), *Public Opinion and Political Attitudes* (New York: John Wiley and Sons), pp. 77–87.

Mumford, L. (1934), *Technics and Civilization*. (New York, NY: Brace and Company, Inc.)

Myers, D. and Tingley, D. (2011), *The Influence of Emotion on Trust*. Available at: https://scholar.harvard.edu/dtingley/files/emotionmanipulationm11.pdf (later published in *Political Analysis* vol. 24, no. 4, 492–500 in 2016)

Myers, S. A. and Johnson, A. D. (2004), 'Perceived Solidarity, Self-Disclosure, and Trust in Organizational Peer Relationships', *Communication Research Reports*, vol. 21, no. 1, 75–83.

Nacol, E. C. (2011), 'The Risks of Political Authority: Trust, Knowledge and Political Agency in Locke's Second Treatise', *Political Studies*, vol. 59, no. 3, 580–95.

Naef, M. and Schupp, J. (2009), 'Measuring Trust: Experiments and Surveys in Contrast and Combination', IZA Discussion Paper no. 4087.

Nagawasa, E. (1998), '1919 Revolution as Seen by an Egyptian Child', *Hermes-IR*, vol. 15, 87–98.

Nagel, T. (1989), *The View from Nowhere*. (Oxford University Press)

Naguib, S. (2011), *The Egyptian Revolution: A Political Analysis and Eyewitness Account*. (Bookmarks Publications)

Nahrkhalaji, S. S. (2007), *Language, Ideology and Power: A Critical Approach to Political Discourse*.

Nail, T. (2013), 'Zapatismo and the Global Origins of Occupy', *Zapatismo and the Global Origins of Occupy*, vol. 12, no. 3, 20–38.

Nair, M. S. (2011), *Persuasive Citizens, Unconvinced Radicals: Comparing Workers' Politics in Two Towns in Central India*. (Graduate School – New Brunswick Rutgers, the State University of New Jersey)

Najemy, J. M. (2004), *Italy in the Age of the Renaissance: 1300–1550*. vol. 4. (Oxford: Oxford University Press)

Najemy, J. M. (1982), *Corporatism and Consensus in Florentine Electoral Politics, 1280–1400*. (University of North Carolina Press)

Nanabhay, M. and Farmanfarmaian, R. (2011), 'From Spectacle to Spectacular: How Physical Space, Social Media and Mainstream Broadcast Amplified the Public Sphere in Egypt's "Revolution"', *The Journal of North African Studies*, vol. 16, no. 4, 573–603.

Naphy, W. G. (2007), *The Protestant Revolution: From Martin Luther to Martin Luther King Jr*. (BBC Books)

Nardi, J. (2012), *Istorie Della Città Di Firenze… [Italian]*. (Nabu Press)

Nassar, A. (2011), 'The Symbolism of Tahrir Square', *Arab Center for Research and Policy Studies*, vol. May, 1–8.

Natan, J. (2011), '164 *Jihad* Verses in the *Koran*'. Available at: www.webcitation.org/query?url=http://www.yoel.info/koranwarpassages.htm and date=2011-12-20.

Naude, P. and Buttle, F. (2000), 'Assessing Relationship Quality', *Industrial Marketing Management*, vol. 29, 351–61.

Neal, P. (1988), 'Hobbes and Rational Choice Theory', *The Western Political Quarterly*, vol. 14, no. 2, 481–95.

Neely, S. (2008), *A Concise History of the French Revolution*. (Rowman and Littlefield)

Negri, A. (1991), *The Savage Anomaly: The Power of Spinoza's Metaphysics and Politics*. (University of Minnesota Press)

Nelson, M. (2007), 'Revisiting Anderson's "Imagined Communities" Almost 25 Years Later', in Carleton University: ECO 5502, Other Worlds, Other Globalization, 20 April.

Nenner, H. (2009), 'Loyalty and the Law: The Meaning of Trust and the Right of Resistance in Seventeenth-Century England', *Journal of British Studies*, vol. 48, no. 4, 859–70.

Neuman, S. (1971), 'Engels and Marx: Military Concepts of the Social Revolutionaries', in E. M. Earle (ed.), *Makers of Modern Strategy : Military Thought from Machiavelli to Hitler* (Princeton: Princeton University Press), section 3.

Neumann, P. R. and Smith, M. L. R. (2005), 'Strategic Terrorism: The Framework and Its Fallacies', *Journal of Strategic Studies*, vol. 28, no. 4, 571–95.

Neustadt, R. E. and May, E. R. (1986), *Thinking in Time: The Uses of History for Decision-Makers.* (Free Press)

Neville, C. J. (2010), *Land, Law and People in Medieval Scotland.* (Edinburgh University Press)

New York Times (1919), '800 Natives Dead in Egypt's Rising; 1,600 Wounded', *The New York Times*, 25 July.

Newell, J. Q. C. (2008), 'Learning the Hard Way: Allenby in Egypt and Palestine, 1917–19', *Journal of Strategic Studies*, vol. 14, no. 3, 363–87.

Newman, I. and Radcliffe, P. (eds) (2011), *Promoting Social Cohesion: Implications for Policy and Evaluation.* (Bristol: Policy Press)

Newman, S. (2014), *Magna Carta* [online].

Newton, I. (1846), *Philosophiae Naturalis Principia Mathematica.* A. Motte (ed.) (New York, NY: Daniel Adee)

Newton, K. (2001), 'Trust, Social Capital, Civil Society, and Democracy', *International Political Science Review*, vol. 22, no. 2, 201–14.

Ng, S. H. and Bradac, J. J. (1993), *Language and Language Behaviors, vol. 3. Power in Language: Verbal Communication and Social Influence.* (Thousand Oaks, CA: Sage Publications)

Nichols Newspapers collection. Available at: https://www.gale.com/intl/c/17th-and-18th-century-nichols-newspapers-collection.

Nicholson, H. (2001), *The Knights Templar: A New History.* (The History Press: Sutton)

Nielsen, R. K. (2010), 'Mundane Internet Tools, Mobilizing Practices, and the Coproduction of Citizenship in Political Campaigns', *New Media and Society*, vol. 13, no. 5, 755–71.

Niemi, R. G. *et al.* (1989), *Trends in Public Opinion: A Compendium of Survey Data.* (Westport, CT: Greenwood Press)

Nietzsche, F. (2008), *On the Genealogy of Morals: A Polemic (Oxford World's Classics).* (Oxford Paperbacks)

Nightingale, D. J. and Cromby, J. (1999), *Social Constructionist Psychology: A Critical Analysis of Theory and Practice.* D. J. Nightingale and J. Cromby (eds) (Buckingham: Open University Press)

Nisbet, R. (1980), *History of the Idea of Progress*. (New York: Basic Books)

Nooteboom, B. (2002), *Trust: Forms, Foundations, Functions, Failures and Figures.* (Edward Elgar Publishing)

Nooteboom, B. and Six, F. (2003), *The Trust Process in Organizations: Empirical Studies of the Determinants and the Process of Trust Development.* (Edward Elgar Publishing)

Norris, P. (1999), 'Introduction', in P. Norris (ed.), *Critical Citizens: Global Support for Democratic Government pages* (Oxford University Press), pp. 1–30.

North, D. C. and Weingast, B. R. (1995), 'Constitutions and Commitment: The Evolution of Institutions Governing Public Choice in Seventeenth-Century England', in L. J. Alston *et al.* (eds) *In Empirical Studies in Institutional Change.* (Cambridge: Cambridge University Press)

North, H. (1966), *Sophrosyne: Self-Knowledge and Self-Restraint in Greek Literature.* (Cornell University Press)

Norton, A. and de Haan, A. (2013), *Social Cohesion: Theoretical Debates and Practical Applications with Respect to Jobs.* Background Paper for the World Development Report, World Bank, Washington, DC. Available at: https://openknowledge.worldbank.org/handle/10986/12147.

Nour, S. (2011), 'An Unusual Alliance', *Development and Cooperation online.*

Novikoff, A. J. (2013), *The Medieval Culture of Disputation: Pedagogy, Practice, and Performance (The Middle Ages Series).* (University of Pennsylvania Press)

Nuemann, P. and and Rogers, B. (2007), *Recruitment and Mobilisation for the Islamist Militant Movement in Europe.* A study carried out by King's College London for the European Commission (Directorate General Justice, Freedom and Security). Available at: https://ec.europa.eu/home-affairs/sites/homeaffairs/files/doc_centre/terrorism/docs/ec_radicalisation_study_on_mobilisation_tactics_en.pdf.

Nunberg, G. (1996), 'Snowblindness', *Natural Language and Linguistic Theory*, vol. 14, 205–13.

Nuyen, A. T. (1988), 'The Role of Reason in Hume's Theory of Belief', *Hume Studies*, vol. XIV, no. 2, 372–89.

Nydell, M. K. (2002), *Understanding Arabs: A Guide for Westerners.* (Intercultural Press)

Nye, J. S. (2004), *Soft Power: The Means to Success in World Politics.* (Public Affairs)

Oakley, T. P. (1923), *English Penitential Discipline and Anglo-Saxon Law in Their Joint Influence.* (New York, NY: Columbia University Press)

Oates, J. L. (1980) 'The Influence of the French Revolution on Legal and Judicial Reform'. MA thesis, Department of History, Simon Fraser University.

Ober, J. (2009), *Mass and Elite in Democratic Athens: Rhetoric, Ideology, and the Power of the People.* (Princeton University Press)

Ober, J. (2007), *The Original Meaning of 'Democracy': Capacity to Do Things, Not Majority Rule.* Princeton/Stanford Working Paper in Classics, no. 1024775.

Ober, J. (2005a), *I Beseiged that Man: Democracy's Revolutionary Start.* Princeton/Stanford Working Papers in Classics, no. 110513.

Ober, J. (2005b), 'Solon and the Horoi. Facts on the Ground in Archaic Athens', in J. Blok and A. Lardinois (eds) *Solon: New Historical and Philological Perspectives*. (Leiden: E.J. Bil), pp. 441–56.

Ober, J. (2001), *Political Dissent in Democratic Athens: Intellectual Critics of Popular Rule*. vol. 12. (Princeton University Press)

Ober, J. (1999), 'Athenian Revolution of 508/7', in *The Athenian Revolution: Essays on Ancient Greek Democracy and Political Theory*, pp. 32–52.

Ober, J. (1998), 'The Athenian Revolution of 508/7 B.C.E.', in *Cultural Poetics in Archaic Greece: Cult, Performance, Politics* (Oxford University Press), pp. 215–32.

Ober, J. (1996a), *The Athenian Revolution: Essays on Ancient Greek Democracy and Political Theory*. (Princeton, NJ: Princeton University Press)

Ober, J. (1996b), *Demokratia: A Conversation on Democracies, Ancient and Modern*. J. Ober and C. Hedrick (eds) (Princeton, NJ: Princeton University Press)

Ober, J. and Vanderpool, C. (1993), 'Athenian Democracy', *Prologue*, vol. 25, no. 2, 127–35.

Öberg, P. and Svensson, T. (2010), 'Does Power Drive Out Trust? Relations between Labour Market Actors in Sweden', *Political Studies*, vol. 58, no. 1, 143–66.

Ockham, W. (1990), *Philosophical Writings: A Selection*. P. Boehner (ed.) (Hackett Publishing)

O'Connell, C. (2011), 'Network Theory and Political Revolution: A Case Study of the Role of Social Media in the Diffusion of Political Revolution in Egypt', Ph.D thesis, San Diego State University.

Offe, C. (1985), 'New Social Movements: Challenging the Boundaries of Institutional Politics', *Social Research*, vol. 54, no. 4, 817–67.

Offe, C. (1999), 'How Can We Trust Our Fellow Citizens?', in M. E. Warren (ed.), *In Democracy and Trust*. (Cambridge: Cambridge University Press), pp. 43–87.

O'Hagan, T. (2003), *Rousseau*. (Routledge)

O'Hara, K. (2004), *Socrates, Trust and the Interne*, in Kansaigaidai, Japan: 2nd International Conference on Speech, Writing and Context.

O'Kane, R. H. T. (1999), *Revolution: Critical Concepts in Political Science*. (Routledge)

Okpala, O. (2008), 'Plato's Republic vs. Democracy', 49–59.

Olábarri, I. (1995), '"New" New History: A Longue Durée Structure', *History and Theory*, vol. 34, no. 1, 1–29.

O'Laughlin, B. (1975), 'Marxist Approaches in Anthropology', *Annual Review of Anthropology*, vol. 4, 341–70.

Olick, J. K. and Robbins, J. (1998), 'Social Memory Studies: From "Collective Memory" to the Historical Sociology of Mnemonic Practices', *Annual Review of Sociology*, vol. 24, no. 1, 105–40.

Oliver, P. E. *et al.* (2003), 'Emerging Trends in the Study of Protest and Social Movements', in *Research in Political Sociology, vol. 12* (Elsevier Science Ltd), pp. 213–44.

Ollapally, D. and Mirilovic, N. (2012), 'Conclusion: Realists, Nationalists and Globalists and the Nature of Contemporary Rising Powers', in D. Ollapally and H. R. Nau (eds)

Worldviews of Aspiring Powers: Domestic Foreign Policy Debates in China, India, Iran, Japan and Russia. (Oxford University Press), pp. 210–34.

Olsen, M. E. and Marger, M. (1993), *Power in Modern Societies*. M. E. Olsen and M. N. Marger (eds) (Boulder, CO: Westview Press)

Olson, G. A. and Worsham, L. (2000), 'Changing the Subject: Judith Butler's Politics of Radical Resignification', *JAC Journal of Rhetoric, Culture and Politics*, vol. 20, no. 4, 727–64.

O'Neill, O. (2002a), *A Question of Trust: The BBC Reith Lectures 2002*. (Cambridge University Press)

O'Neill, O. (2002b), *Autonomy and Trust in Bioethics*. (Cambridge University Press)

Ong, W. J. (1988), *Orality and Literacy: The Technologizing of the Word*. (London: Routledge)

Onodera, H. (2015), *Being a Young Activist in the Late Mubarak Era*. (Helsinki)

Onuoho, F. (2014), 'Boko Haram and the Evolving Salafi Jihadist Threat in Nigeria', in M-A.P. de Montclos (ed.), *Boko Haram: Islamism, Politics, Security and the State in Nigeria* (Leiden: African Studies Centre), pp. 158–91.

Oppenheimer, F. (2012), *The State: Its History and Development Viewed Sociologically*. Classic Reprint. (Forgotten Books)

O'Reilly, C. A. I. and Roberts, K. H. (1974), 'Information Filtration in Organizations – Three Experiments', *Organizational Behavior and Human Performance*, vol. 11, 253–65.

Origgi, G. and Sperber, D. (1984), 'Evolution and the Human Mind: Language, Modularity and Social Cognition', in Peter Carruthers and Andrew Chamberlain (eds) *Evolution and the Human Mind: Language, Modularity and Social Cognition*. (Cambridge University Press), pp. 140–69.

Orlovsky, D. T. (1983), 'Political Clientelism in Russia: The Historical Perspective', in T. H. Rigby and B. Harasymiw (eds) *Leadership Selection and Patron–Client Relations in the USSR and Yugoslavia*. (London: Allen and Unwin), pp. 174–99.

Orr, D. A. (2002), *Treason and the State: Law, Politics and Ideology in the English Civil War*. (Cambridge University Press)

Orwell, G. (2001), *Orwell in Spain*. (Penguin Books Limited)

Orwell, G. (2000), *Animal Farm: A Fairy Story*. New Edition. (Penguin Classics)

Orwell, G. (1986), *Down and Out in Paris and London*. (Penguin Books)

Orwell, G. (1949), *Nineteen Eighty-Four*. (London: Secker and Warburg)

Orwin, C. (1988), 'Stasis and Plague: Thucydides on the Dissolution of Society', *The Journal of Politics*, vol. 50, no. 4, 831–47.

Osborne, R. (2010), *Athens and Athenian Democracy*. (Cambridge: Cambridge University Press)

Osgood, C. E. (1962), *An Alternative to War or Surrender*. (Chicago: University of Illinois Press)

Oskarsson, S. *et al.* (2009a), 'Power, Trust, and Institutional Constraints: Individual Level Evidence', *Rationality and Society*, vol. 21, no. 2, 171–95.

Oskarsson, S. *et al.* (2009b), 'Making Capitalism Work: Fair Institutions and Trust', *Economic and Industrial Democracy*, vol. 30, no. 2, 294–320.

Oskarsson, S. *et al.* (2007), *Creating Trust – The Role of Power Asymmetries and Institutional Constraints*. The Department of Government Studies in Political Economy and Welfare, Working Paper Series no. 5, Uppsala University.

Ostergaard, G. (2002), '"Anarchism." The Blackwell Dictionary of Modern Social Thought', in W. Outhwaite (ed.), *The Blackwell Dictionary of Modern Social Thought*. (Blackwell Publishing)

O'Sullivan, S. (2003), *Economics: Principles in Action*. (Pearson Prentice Hall)

Ottaway, M. and Hamzawy, A. (2011), 'Protest Movements and Political Change in the Arab World', *Policy Outlook Paper: Carnegie Endowment for International Peace*, 1–14.

Owen, I. R. (1995), 'Social Constructionism and the Theory, Practice and Research of Psychotherapy: A Phenomenological Psychology Manifesto', *Psychology Bulletin*, vol. 46, no. I, 161–86.

Owen, R. (2012), 'The Year of Egypt's Second Revolution, the Balance Sheet So Far', London School of Economics, Middle East Centre Arab Uprisings lecture series, 9 January.

Owen, R. (2005), 'The Brismes Annual Lecture 2004: Biography and Empire: Lord Cromer (1841–1917) Then and Now', *British Journal of Middle Eastern Studies*, vol. 32, no. 1, 3–12.

Oxoby, R. O. B. (2009), 'Understanding Social Inclusion, Social Cohesion and Social Capital', *International Journal of Social Economics*, vol. 36, no. 12, 1133–52.

Ozouf, M. (1989), 'Revolutionary Calendar', in F. Furet and M. Ozouf (eds) *Critical Dictionary of the French Revolution* (Harvard University Press), pp. 538–47.

Ozouf, M. and Sheridan, A. (1991), *Festivals and the French Revolution*. (Harvard University Press)

Pace, M. and Cavatorta, F. (2012), 'The Arab Uprisings in Theoretical Perspective – An Introduction', *Mediterranean Politics*, vol. 17, no. 2, 125–38.

Packer, G. (2003), 'Dreaming of Democracy'. *New York Times Magazine*. 2 March.

Padgett, J. F. (2001), *Modeling Florentine Republicanism* online.

Padgett, J. F. and Ansell, C. K. (1993), 'Robust Action and the Rise of the Medici, 1400–1434', *American Journal of Political Science*, vol. 98, no. 6, 1259–319.

Padgett, J. F. and McLean, P. D. (2006), 'Economic Credit and Elite Transformation in Renaissance Florence', *American Journal of Sociology*, vol. 111, no. 5, 1463–568.

Pagden, A. (1990), 'The Destruction of Trust and Its Economic Consequences in the Case of Eighteenth Century Naples', in D. Gambetta (ed.), *Trust: Making and Breaking Cooperative Relations* (8: Blackwell Publishing), pp. 127–42.

Paige, J. M. (1978), *Agrarian Revolution*. (Free Press)

Paine, T. (1776), *Common Sense* online.

Paine, T. (1791), *Rights of Man: Being an Answer to Mr. Burke's Attack on the French Revolution...*, *Part 1*. (J.S. Jordan)

Paine, T. (1984), *The Rights of Man*. H. Collins (ed.) (Penguin Classics)

Pakaluk, M. (1998), *Nicomachean Ethics*. (Oxford: Clarendon Press)

Pallaver, M. (2011), *Power and Its Forms: Hard, Soft, Smart*. (London School of Economics)

Papacharissi, Z. A. (2010), *The Fall of Public Man*. New Edition. (Polity Press)

Papacharissi, Z. A. (2002), 'The Presentation of Self in Virtual Life: Characteristics of Personal Home Pages', *Journalism and Mass Communication Quarterly*, vol. 79, no. 3, 643–60.

Papacharissi, Z. A. (2013), 'Book Review: A Private Sphere: Democracy in a Digital Age', *Journal of Communication*, vol. 63, E1–5.

Paras, E. (2008), 'The Darker Side of Martin Luther', *Constructing the Past*, vol. 9, no. 1, 1–12.

Parenti, M. (2007), *Contrary Notions: The Michael Parenti Reader*. (San Francisco, CA: City Lights Books)

Parenti, M. (1998), *America Besieged*. (San Francisco, CA: City Lights Books)

Park, J. *et al.* (2011), 'Revolution 2.0 in Tunisia and Egypt: Reactions and Sentiments in the Online World', in Proceedings of the Fifth International AAAI Conference on Weblogs and Social Media, vol. 1

Park, R. E. (1921), 'Sociology and the Social Sciences: The Social Organism and the Collective Mind', *American Journal of Sociology*, vol. 27, no. 1, 1–21.

Parker, D. (1980), *La Rochelle and the French Monarchy: Conflict and Order in Seventeenth-Century France*. (Royal Historical Society)

Parker, G. and Smith, L. M. (2005), *The General Crisis of the Seventeenth Century*. (Routledge)

Parker, N. (1991), *Revolutions and History: An Essay in Interpretation*. (Wiley)

Parsons, T. (1967), *The Structure of Social Action: 001*, Second Edition (Free Press)

Pascoe, S. (2011), 'Overcoming the Arab Malaise', *Arena Magazine*, November, no. 112, 36–40.

Passavant, P. and Dean, J. (2004), *Empire's New Clothes: Reading Hardt and Negri*. (Psychology Press)

Patch, H. R. (1927), *The Goddess Fortuna in Mediaeval Literature*. (Cambridge, MA: Harvard University Press)

Patrick, S. (2010), *The G20 and the United States: Opportunities for More Effective Multilateralism*. (New York: Century Foundation)

Pauley, B. F. (1997), *Hitler, Stalin and Mussolini: Totalitarianism in the Twentieth Century (European History)*. (Harlan Davidson Inc)

Paulson, R. (1983), *Representations of Revolution, 1789–1820*. (Yale University Press)

Paxton, R. O. (2013), 'Vichy Lives! – In a Way', *The New York Review of Books*, April.

Payne, R. A. (2001), 'Persuasion, Frames and Norm Construction', *European Journal of International Relations*, vol. 7, no. 1, 37–61.

Peacey, J. (2013), *Print and Public Politics in the English Revolution*. vol. 14. (Cambridge University Press)

Pearson, S. *et al.* (2005), 'Persistent and Dynamic Trust: Analysis of Trust Properties and Related Impact of Trusted Platforms', in L. P. Hewlett-Packard Development (ed.), *Trust Management*. (Springer Berlin Heidelberg), pp. 355–56.

Peck, L. L. (2003), *Court Patronage and Corruption in Early Stuart England*. (Routledge)

Pelikan, J. (1990), 'Leopold von Ranke as Historian of the Reformation', in G. G. Iggers and J. M. Powell (eds) *Leopold von Ranke and the Shaping of the Historical Discipline*. (Syracuse University Press)

Pelkmans, M. (2013), *Ethnographies of Doubt: Faith and Uncertainty in Contemporary Societies (Library of Modern Religion)*. (London and New York: I.B.Tauris)

Pelkmans, M. (2005), 'On Transition and Revolution in Kyrgyzstan', *Focaal*, vol. 46, 147–57.

Pelteret, D. A. E. (1985), 'Slavery in Anglo-Saxon England', in J. D. Woods and D. A. E. Pelteret (eds) *The Anglo-Saxons: Synthesis and Achievement*. (Ontario: Wilfrid Laurier University Press), pp. 117–33.

Pennanen, K. (2009), 'The Initial Stages of Consumer Trust Building in e-Commerce: A Study in Finnish Consumers', *Business Administration Marketing*, vol. 83, 1–85.

Pennington, K. (1992), 'Medieval Law', in J. M. Powell (ed.), *Medieval Studies: An Introduction* (Syracuse University Press), pp. 333–52.

Peperzak, A. T. (2013), *Trust Who or What Might Support Us?*. (New York: Fordham University Press)

Peristany, J. G. (1965), *Honor and Shame: The Values of Mediterranean Society*. (Weidenfeld and Nicolson)

Perley, S. (2012), *Fides Romana: Aspects of Fides in Roman Diplomatic Relations during the Conquest of Iberia*. (University of Otago)

Perovic, S. (2012), *The Calendar in Revolutionary France: Perceptions of Time in Literature, Culture, Politics*. (Cambridge University Press)

Perrotta, C. (2004), *Consumption as an Investment*. (Taylor and Francis)

Perry, M. *et al.* (2015), *Western Civilization: Ideas, Politics, and Society, Volume I: To 1789*. (Cengage Learning)

Peters, P. (1970), *Reformation or Revolt or Revolution?* Available at: https://essays.wls. wels.net/bitstream/handle/123456789/3643/PetersReformation.pdf?sequence=1 and isAllowed=y.

Peters, R. (1977), *Jihad in Medieval and Modern Islam*. (Brill)

Petras, J. *et al.* (2001), *Empire with Imperialism: The globalizing Dynamics of Neoliberal Capitalism* (Zed Books)

Peyre, H. (1949), 'The Influence of Eighteenth Century Ideas on the French Revolution', *Journal of the History of Ideas*, vol. X.

Pezzolo, L. (2005), 'Bonds and Government Debt in Italian City-States, 1250–1650', in W. N. Goetzmannand and K. G. Rouwenhorst (eds) *The Origins of Value: The Financial Innovations that Created Modern Capital Markets*. (Oxford English Press), pp. 145–63.

Pfeiffenberger, S. (1967), 'Notes on the Iconology of Donatello's Judgment of Pilate at San Lorenzo', *Renaissance Quarterly*, vol. 20, no. 4, 437–54.

Pharr, S. J. and Putnam, R. D. (2000), *Disaffected Democracies: What's Troubling the Trilateral Countries?* (Princeton University Press)

Philip, M. (2011), *Britain and the French Revolution*. BBC History online, 17 February.

Philips, S. U. (1992), 'A Marx Influenced Approach to Ideology and Language', *Pragmatics*, vol. 2, no. 3, 377–85.

Phillips, E. (1720), *The New World of English Words*. (London). Available at: https://books.google.co.uk/books?id=tPaSRYRFVJUC and printsec=frontcover#v=onepage and q and f=false.

Phillips, J. (2012), 'The Arab Spring Descends into Islamist Winter: Implications for U.S'. *Policy Heritage Organisation*. Heritage.org online.

Phillips, M. S. (2014), *The Memoir of Marco Parenti: A Life in Medici Florence*. (Princeton University Press)

Pianta, M. and March, P. G. (2012), 'European Alternatives: Trajectories of Mobilisation Responding to Europe's Crisis', *Open Democracy*, March, 1–12.

Piatnitskaia, J. (1996), *Diary of a Bolshevik Woman*. (Losada)

Pickard, E. (1761), *National Praise to God for the Glorious Revolution, the Protestant Succession, and the Signal Successes and Blessings with which Providence Has Crowned Us. A Sermon Preached the First of August, 1761. at Little St. Helen's…By Edward Pickard*. (J. Johnson; and sold by S. Gardner)

Pierson, C. (2011), *The Modern State*. Third Edition. (Routledge)

Pilbeam, P. (2001), 'Chasing Rainbows: the Nineteenth-Century Revolutionary Legacy', in T. Rees and M. Donald (eds) *Reinterpreting Revolution in Twentieth-Century Europe*. (Macmillan Press), pp. 19–40.

Pincus, S. C. A. (2014), *1688: The First Modern Revolution*. (Yale University Press)

Pinson, K. S. (1966), *Modern Germany: Its History and Civilization*. Second Edition. (Macmillan and Company Ltd)

Pipes, R. (1977), *Under the Old Regimes*. (Penguin Books)

Pixley, J. (1999) 'Impersonal Trust in Global Mediating Organizations', *Sociological Perspectives*, vol. 42, no. \ 4 (Winter), 647–71.

Plato (2009), *Protagoras*. C. C. W. Taylor (ed.) (Oxford: Oxford University Press)

Plato (1992), *Republic*. (Hackett Publishing Co, Inc)

Plato (1956), *Protagoras and Meno*. W. K. C. Guthrie (ed.) (Penguin)

Plessis, A. (2003), *The History of Banks in France* (Edward Elgar Publishing Ltd)

Pliny the elder (1991), *Natural History*. J. Healey (ed.) (Penguin Classics)

Plomer, H. R. (1905), 'An Analysis of the Civil War Newspaper Mercurius Civicus', *The Library*, vol. 6, 184–207.

Pocock, J. G. A. (1998b), *The Citizenship Debates*. (Minneapolis: The University of Minnesota Press)

Pocock, J. G. A. (1972), 'Virtue and Commerce in the Eighteenth Century', *Journal of Interdisciplinary History*, vol. 3, no. 1, 119–34.

Pollock, T. (2013), *Political Prophecy in Elizabethan England*. (Victoria University of Wellington)

Polybius (2010), *The Histories*. R. Waterfield (ed.) vol. 2010. (Oxford: Oxford University Press)

Pooley, E. H. (1947), *The Guilds of the City of London: With 8 Plates in Colour and 19 Illustrations in Black and White*. (Collins)

Popper, K. (2012), *The Open Society and Its Enemies*. vol. 12. (Routledge)

Post, G. (1964), *Studies in Medieval Legal Thought: Public Law and the State 1100–1322*. (The Lawbook Exchange, Ltd)

Postan, M. (1975), *The Medieval Economy and Society*. (Harmondsworth: Penguin)

Pratt, R. B. (1978), 'Towards a Critical Theory of Revolution', *Polity*, vol. 11, no. 2, 172–99.

Price, J. J. (2001), *Thucydides and Internal War*. (Cambridge University Press)

Pritchard, D. (2015), 'Democracy and War in Ancient Athens and Today', in *War, Democracy and Culture in Classical Athens*. (Cambridge and New York: Cambridge University Press)

Proudhon, P. J. (1979) *The Principle of Federation*. (Toronto: University of Toronto Press) (originally published 1863)

Putnam, R. D. (2000), *Bowling Alone: The Collapse and Revival of American Community*. A Touchstone book. (Simon and Schuster)

Putnam, R. D., Leonardi, R. and Nanetti, R. Y. (1993), *Making Democracy Work: Civic Traditions in Modern Italy*. (Princeton, NJ: Princeton University Press)

Rahim, M. A. (1989), 'Relationships of Leader Power to Compliance and Satisfaction with Supervisors: Evidence from a National Sample of Managers', *Journal of Management*, vol. 15, 545–56.

Rahman, H. (2012), 'Henry Fayol and Frederick Winslow Taylor's Contribution to Management Thought: An Overview', *ABC Journal of Advanced Research*, vol. 1, no. 2, 32–41.

Rainnie, A. (1993), 'The Reorganization of Large Firm Sub-Contracting: Myth and Reality', *Capital and Class*, vol. 49, 53–75.

Ramsay, D. (1789), *The History of the American Revolution*. L. H. Cohen (ed.) (R. Aitken)

Ransel, D. (1988), 'The Character and Style of Patron–Client Relations in Russia', in A. Maczak (ed.), *Klientelsysteme im Europa der frühen Neuzeit*. (Munich: R. Oldenbourg), pp. 211–31.

Rapin-Thoyras, P de (1723), *History of England, written in French by* Mr. Rapin de Thoyras. Trans N. Tidal (London: Printed by J.J. and P. Knapton)

Rapin de Thoyras, M. P. (1733) *The History of England vol. II, 2nd edition*. (Printed for James, John and Paul Knapton)

Raymond, J. (1998), 'The Newspaper, Public Opinion, and the Public Sphere in the Seventeenth Century', *Prose Studies*, vol. 21, no. 2, 109–36.

Raymond, J. (ed.) (2013), *News, Newspapers and Society in Early Modern Britain*. (Routledge)

Raynes, H. E. (1948), *A History of British Insurance*. (London: Sir Isaac Pitman and Sons)

Raz, J. (1990), *Authority*. (New York University Press)

Reemtsma, J. P. (2012), *Trust and Violence: An Essay on a Modern Relationship*. J. P. Reemtsma (ed.) (Princeton University Press)

Rennick, S. A. (2013), 'Contested Meanings in the Egyptian Revolution', *Socio*, no. 2, 81–98.

Retat, P. (1985), 'Forme et discours d'un journal revolutionnaire: Les Revolutions de Paris en 1789', in C. Labrosse *et al.* (eds) *L'instrument périodique: la fonction de la presse au XVIIIe siècle*. (Lyon: Presses universitaires de Lyon), pp. 139–66.

Rex, R. (2006), *Henry VIII and the English Reformation*. (Palgrave Macmillan)

Rex, R. (1996), 'The Crisis of Obedience: God's Word and Henry's Reformation', *The Historical Journal*, vol. 39, no. 4, 863–94.

Reynolds, S. (2012), *The Middle Ages without Feudalism: Essays in Criticism and Comparison on the Medieval West*. (Ashgate)

Reynolds, S. (2007), 'Secular Power and Authority in the Middles Ages', in H. Pryce and J. Watts (eds) *Power and Identity in the Middle Ages: Essays in Memory of Rees Davies*. (Oxford University Press), pp. 11–22.

Reynolds, S. (1984), *Kingdoms and Communities in Western Europe, 900–1300*. vol. 15. (Clarendon Press)

Rhodes, P. J. (1993), *A Commentary on the Aristotelian Athenaion Politeia*. (Clarendon Press)

Ricciardelli, F. (2012), 'Violence and Repression in Late Medieval Italy', in S. K. Cohn Jr and F. Ricciardelli (eds) *The Culture of Violence in Renaissance Italy*. (Florence: Le Lettere), pp. 55–79.

Richardson, J. L. (2001), *Contending Liberalisms in World Politics*. (London: Lynne Rienner Publishers)

Richelet, P. (1680), *Dictionnaire de langue française*. (Genève: J.-H. Widerhold)

Richet, P. (2007), *A Natural History of Time*. (University of Chicago Press)

Riddiford, M. (2008), *Social Exclusion from Early Medieval Wessex*. (University of Sheffield)

Rifkin, J. (2000), *The Age of Access: The New Culture of Hypercapitalism, Where All of Life Is a Paid-for Experience*. (J.P. Tarcher/Putnam)

Rigby, S. H. (2008), *A Companion to Britain in the Later Middle Ages*. (John Wiley and Sons)

Rinuccini, A. (1978), 'On Liberty', in R. N. Watson (ed.), *Humanism and Liberty: Writings on Freedom from Fifteenth-Century Florence* (University of South Carolina Press), pp. 193–222.

Roberts, S. K. (1988), 'Juries and the Middling Sort: Recruitment and Performance at Devon Quarter Sessions, 1649–1670', in *Twelve Good Men and True: The Criminal Trial Jury in England, 1200–1800* (Books on Demand), pp. 182–213.

Rodger, N. A. M. (2005), *The Command of the Ocean: A Naval History of Britain, 1649–1815, Volume 2.* (W.W. Norton)

Rogers, J. (1998), *The Matter of Revolution: Science, Poetry, and Politics in the Age of Milton.* (Cornell University Press)

Rookmaaker, H. R. (2002), 'Western Arts and the Meanderings of a Culture', in *The Complete Works of Hans R. Rookmaaker, 6 Volumes* (Piquant Editions), Volume 4.

Roover, R. de. (1944), 'Early Accounting Problems of Foreign Exchange', *The Accounting Review*, vol. 19, no. 4, 381–407.

Rosecrance, R. N. (1986), *The Rise of the Trading State.* (New Year: Basic Books)

Rosendale, T. (2001), '"Fiery Tongues": Language, Liturgy, and the Paradox of the English Reformation', *Renaissance Quarterly*, vol. 54, no. 4, 1142–64.

Rosenthal, J. T. (1970), 'The Training of an Elite Group: English Bishops in the Fifteenth Century', *Transactions of the American Philosophical Society*, vol. 60, no. 5, 1–54.

Rosenthal, L. (1882), *America and France: The Influence of the United States on France.* (New York, NY: Holt)

Roseveare, H. (1991), *The Financial Revolution, 1660–1760.* (New York: Longman)

Ross, C. (2011), *The Leaderless Revolution: How Ordinary People Can Take Power and Change Politics in the 21st Century.* (Simon and Schuster)

Rosser, G. (2011), 'The Discovery of the World and of Man the Discovery of the World and of Man', in *Burckhardt's Renaissance, 150 Years Later.* (Oxford: Society for the Study of Medieval Languages and Literature), pp. 1–13.

Rotfeld, A. D. (2008), 'Confidence- and Security-Building Measures (CSBMs) in the Modern Context: The European Experience 1', *Korean Journal of Defense Analysis*, vol. 20, no. 1, 3–12.

Rothchild, J. A. (2007), 'Introduction to Athenian Democracy of the Fifth and Fourth Centuries BCE'. Wayne State University Law School Research Paper no. 07–32.

Rothstein, B. and Stolle, D. (2008), 'The State and Social Capital an Institutional Theory of Generalized Trust', *Comparative Politics*, vol. 40, no. 4, 441–59.

Rotter, J. B. (1980), 'Interpersonal Trust, Trustworthiness, and Gullibility', *American Psychologist*, vol. 35, no. 1, 1–7.

Rotter, J. (1971), 'Generalized Expectancies for Interpersonal Trust', *American Psychologist*, vol. 35, 1–7.

Rousseau, D. M. *et al.* (1998), 'Not So Different after All: Across-Discipline View of Trust', *Academy of Management Review*, vol. 23, 393–404.

Rousseau, J.-J. (1998), *The Social Contract.* New Edition. G. D. H. Cole (ed.) (London: Wordsworth Editions Ltd)

Rousseau, J.-J. (1856), *The Confessions of J.J. Rousseau.* (Belford)

Rousseau, J.-J. (1979), *Emile: Or, on Education.* A. Bloom (ed.) (Basic Books)

Rubenfeld, J. (2005), *Revolution by Judiciary: The Structure of American Constitutional Law.* (Harvard University Press)

Rubinstein, N. (1966), *The Government of Florence under the Medici (1434–1494).* (Clarendon Press)

Rudolph, C. (2006), *A Companion to Medieval Art: Romanesque and Gothic in Northern Europe*. (Wiley)

Ruggiero, G. (1978), 'Law and Punishment in Early Renaissance Venice', *The Journal of Criminal Law and Criminology*, vol. 69, no. 2, 243–56.

Rushworth, J. (1649), *Historical Collections* online.

Russell, J. B. (1997) 'The Myth of the Flat Earth', in *American Scientific Affiliation Conference* (Westmont College)

Rusnock, A. A. (2002), *Vital Accounts: Quantifying Health and Population in Eighteenth-Century England and France*. (Cambridge University Press)

Ruzicka, J. and Wheeler, N. J. (2010), 'The Puzzle of Trusting Relationships in the Nuclear Non-Proliferation Treaty', *International Affairs*, vol. 86, no. 1, 69–85.

Sahlins, P. (1989) 'Language, Identity, and the French Revolution: A View from the Periphery', *Qui Parle*, vol. 3, no. 2, pp. 137–67.

Said, E. W. (2003), *Orientalism*. 25th Anniversary Edition. (Penguin Books)

Salisbury, J. E. (2004), *The Blood of Martyrs: Unintended Consequences of Ancient Violence*. (New York: Routledge)

Sambrook, J. (2014), *The Eighteenth Century: The Intellectual and Cultural Context of English Literature 1700–1789*. (Routledge)

Santangelo, F. (2013), *Divination, Prediction and the End of the Roman Republic*. (Cambridge University Press)

Sapienza, P. *et al.* (2013), 'Understanding Trust', *Economic Journal*, vol. 123, no. 573, 1313–32.

Saussure, F. de. (1983), *Course in General Linguistics*. R. Harris (ed.) (Open Court Publishing)

Scarisbrick, J. J. (1991), *Reformation and the English People*. (Wiley)

Schama, S. (1990), *Citizens: A Chronicle of the French Revolution*. (Vintage Books)

Schell, J. (2003), *The Unconquerable World: Power, Nonviolence, and the Will of the People*. (New York: Metropolitan Books)

Schelling, T. C. (1984), 'Strategic Analysis and Social Problems', in T. C. Schelling (ed.), *Choice and Consequence*. (Cambridge, MA: Harvard University Press)

Scherer, K. R. (2011), 'On the Rationality of Emotions: Or, When Are Emotions Rational?', *Social Science Information*, vol. 50, no. 3–4, 330–50.

Scheuer, M. (2011), 'The Zawahiri Era', *National Interest*, September/October.

Schmidt, E. (2013), 'The Future of Revolution', in E. Schmidt and J. Cohen (eds) *The New Digital Age: Reshaping the Future of People, Nations and Business*. (Alfred A. Knopf)

Schmidt, J. (2003), 'Enlightenment: British and the Oxford English Dictionary Inventing', *History*, vol. 64, no. 3, 421–43.

Schneck, C. (2012), *Between Words: Popular Culture and the Rise of Print in Seventeenth-Century England*. (University of Central Florida)

Schneider, Z. A. (2008), *The King's Bench: Bailiwick Magistrates and Local Governance in Normandy, 1670–1740*. (University of Rochester Press)

Schwarzenbach, S. (1996), 'On Civic Friendship', *Ethics*, vol. 107, no. 1, 97.

Schwiebert, E. G. (1950), *Luther and His Times: The Reformation from a New Perspective*. (Concordia Publishing House)

Schwiebert, E. G. (1948), 'A History of the Reformation from a New Perspective', *Church History*, vol. 17, no. 1, 3–31.

Schwoerer, L. G. (2004), *The Revolution of 1688–89: Changing Perspectives*. (Cambridge: Cambridge University Press)

Scorpo, A. L. (2014), *Friendship in Medieval Iberia: Historical, Legal and Literary Perspectives*. (Ashgate)

Scott, M. (2016), *Who Were the Greeks?* BBC 2 online, 2 episodes.

Scott, H. and Simms, B. (2007), *Cultures of Power in Europe during the Long Eighteenth Century*. (Cambridge University Press)

Scoville, J. G. (2001), 'The Taylorization of Vladimir Ilich Lenin', *Industrial Relations*, vol. 40, no. 4, 620–26.

Scullard, H. H. (2013), *From the Gracchi to Nero: A History of Rome 133 BC to AD 68*. (Routledge)

Sealey, R. (1975), 'Constitutional Changes in Athens in 410 B.C.', *California Studies in Classical Antiquity*, vol. 8, 271–95.

Seigworth, G. J. (2010), *The Affect Theory Reader*. (Duke University Press)

Selbin, E. (2001), 'Same as It Ever Was: The Future of Revolution at the End of the Century', in M. Katz (ed.), *Revolution: International Dimensions* (Washington: Congressional Quarterly), pp. 284–97.

Seldon, A. (2010), *Trust: How We Lost It and How to Get It Back*. (London: Biteback Publishing Ltd)

Seligman, A. B. (1997), *The Problem of Trust*. K. S. Cook (ed.) (Princeton University Press)

Sennett, R. (2006), *The Culture of the New Capitalism*. (Yale University Press)

Sennett, R. (1980), *Authority*. (New York: Knopf)

Sexton, B. (2012), *Occupy: American Spring: The Making of a Revolution*. (Mercury Link)

Shagan, E. H. (2003), *Popular Politics and the English Reformation*. (Cambridge University Press)

Shakespeare, W. (2001), *Hamlet*. (Classic Books Company)

Shanin, T. (1985), *The Roots of Otherness: Russia's Turn of Century, Volume 2*. (Yale University Press)

Shapiro, D. *et al.* (1992), 'Business on a Handshake', *Negotiation Journal*, vol. 8, 365–77.

Shapiro, S. P. (1987), 'The Social Control of Impersonal Trust', *American Journal of Political Science*, vol. 93, no. 3, 623–58.

Sharpe, K. (1993), *Culture and Politics in Early Stuart England*. (Stanford University Press)

Sharpe, K. (1992), *The Personal Rule of Charles I* (Yale University Press), pp. 275–402.

Shaw, M. (2011), *Time and the French Revolution: The Republican Calendar, 1789-Year XIV*. (Boydell and Brewer Ltd)

Shear, J. L. (2011), *Polis and Revolution Responding Oligarchy Classical Athens*.
(Cambridge, New York: Cambridge University Press)

Shear, J. L. (2007), 'Cultural Change, Space, and the Politics of Commemoration in
Athens', in R. Osborne (ed.), *Debating the Athenian Cultural Revolution*. (Cambridge
and New York: Cambridge University Press), pp. 91–115.

Sheppard, S. (ed.) (2003), *The Selected Writings and Speeches of Sir Edward Coke*.
(Liberty Fund)

Sher, P. J. and Lee, S-H. (2009), 'Consumer Skepticism and Reviews: An Elaboration
Likelihood Model perspective', *Social Behavior and Personality: An International
Journal*, vol. 37, no. 1, 137–43.

Shirky, C. (2009), *Q and A with Clay Shirky on Twitter and Iran*. Tedblog online.

Shlapentokh, V. (1989), *Public and Private Life of the Soviet People: Changing Values in
Post-Stalin Russia*. (Oxford University Press Inc)

Siedentop, L. (2014), *Inventing the Individual: The Origins of Western Liberalism*.
(Penguin Books, Limited)

Siegel, D. J. (2010), *Mindsight: The New Science of Personal Transformation*. (Random
House Publishing Group)

Sievers, B. R. (2010), *Civil Society, Philanthropy, and the Fate of the Commons*.
(UPNE)

Silva-Vigier, A. de. (1992), *The Moste Highe Prince...John of Gaunt, 1340–1399*.
(Edinburgh: Pentland Press Ltd)

Silvert, K. H. (1961), *The Conflict Society: Reaction and Revolution in Latin America*.
(New Orleans, LA: Hauser Press)

Simpson, T. W. (2012), *Trust on the Internet*. (University of Cambridge)

Singer, P. (1980), *Marx*. (Oxford: Oxford University Press)

Sizer, M. A. (2008), *Making Revolution Medieval: Revolt and Political Culture in Late
Medieval Paris*. (Minneapolis: University of Minnesota Press)

Skinner, Q. (2008), *Hobbes and Republican Liberty*. (Cambridge University Press)

Skinner, Q. (2002), 'Moral Ambiguity and the Renaissance Art of Eloquence', in Q.
Skinner (ed.), *Visions of Politics, vol. 2*. (Cambridge: Cambridge University Press),
pp. 264–85.

Skinner, Q. (1998), *Liberty before Liberalism*. (Cambridge University Press)

Skinner, Q. (1978), *The Foundations of Modern Political Thought: Volume 2, The Age of
Reformation*. vol. 30. (Cambridge University Press)

Skinner, Q. (1969), 'Meaning and Understanding in the History of Ideas', *History and
Theory*, vol. 8, no. 1, 3–53.

Skocpol, T. (1979), *States and Social Revolutions: A Comparative Analysis of France,
Russia, and China*. vol. 18. (Cambridge University Press)

Slack, P. (1984), *Rebellion, Popular Protest, and the Social Order in Early Modern
England*. (Cambridge: Cambridge University Press)

Smith, J. H. (1970), *The Great Schism, 1378*. (Weybright and Talley)

Smith, M. R. (1994), 'Technological Determinism in American Culture', in M. R. Smith and L. Marx (eds) *Does Technology Drive History? The Dilemma of Technological Determinism*. (Cambridge, Mass: MIT Press), pp. 1–36.

Smith, P. (2004), *Cycles of Electoral Democracy in Latin America, 1900–2000*. Center for Latin American Studies University of California, Working Paper no. 6.

Smith, P. (1920), *The Age of the Reformation*. (H. Holt)

Smith, T. (1990), 'A Report: The Sexual Revolution?', *Public Opinion Quarterly*, vol. 54, no. 3, 415–35.

Smollett, T. G. (1795), *The Critical Review, Or, Annals of Literature*. (W. Simpkin and R. Marshall)

Snow, V. F. (1962), 'The Concept of Revolution in Seventeenth-Century England', *The Historical Journal*, vol. 5, no. 2, 167–74.

Snyder, R. S. (1999), 'The End of Revolution?', *The Review of Politics*, vol. 61, no. 1, 5–28.

Solomon, R. C. and Flores, F. (2003), *Building Trust in Business, Politics, Relationships, and Life*. (Oxford: Oxford University Press)

Solomon, R. C. and Flores, F. (1997), 'Rethinking Trust', *Business and Professional Ethics Journal*, vol. 16, no. 1, 47–76.

Solum, S. (2015), *Women, Patronage, and Salvation in Renaissance Florence: Lucrezia Tornabuoni and the Chapel of the Medici Palace*. (Ashgate Publishing, Ltd)

Sommerville, J. P. (1986), *Politics and Ideology in England, 1603–1640*. (Longman)

Sooke, A. (2015), *Treasures of Ancient Greece*, BBC 4 online, 3 episodes.

Southern, R. W. (1990), *The Penguin History of the Church: Western Society and the Church in the Middle Ages*. Reprint. (London and New York: Penguin Books)

Southern, R. W. (1953), *The Making of the Middle Ages*. (Yale University Press)

Southwell, R. (1822), *Marie Magdalens Funeral Teares*. W. J. Walter (ed.) (London: Keating)

Speck, W. A. (1989), *Reluctant Revolutionaries: Englishmen and the Revolution of 1688*. (Oxford University Press)

Spencer, R. (2013), *For the First Time, Egyptian Military Academy Accepting Muslim Brotherhood Activists*. JihadWatch.org online.

Speth, G. W. (ed.) (1889), *Quatuor Coronatorum Antigrapha*. Masonic re. (Keble's Gazette)

Spielvogel, J. (2014), *Western Civilization: Volume C: Since 1789*. (Cengage Learning)

Spinoza, B. de (1996), *Ethics (Penguin Classics)*. (Penguin Classics)

Spirkin, A. G. (1983), 'Consciousness and Language', in R. Daglish (ed.), *Dialectical Materialism* (Progress Publishers)

Spraggs, G. (2001), *Outlaws and Highwaymen: The Cult of the Robber in England from the Middle Ages to the Nineteenth Century*. (Pimlico)

Sprang, R. L. (2015), *Stuff and Money in the Time of the French Revolution*. (Cambridge, MA: Harvard University Press)

Spufford, P. (1970), 'Population Movement in Seventeenth-Century England', *Local Population Studies*, vol. 4, 41–50.

Stalin, J. V. (1924), Socialism in One Country. *Marxist.org* online.

Standage, T. (2013), *Writing on the Wall: Social Media – The First 2,000 Years.* (A and C Black)

Standish, J. (1556), *The Triall of the Supremacy.* (London)

Stanley, S. A. (2012), *The French Enlightenment and the Emergence of Modern Cynicism* (Cambridge University Press)

Stapleton, M. (2013), 'Steps to a "Properly Embodied" Cognitive Science', *Cognitive Systems Research*, vol. 22–23, 1–11.

Starkey, D. (2015), *David Starkey's Magna Carta*, BBC 2 online, 26 January.

Starkey, D. (1986), 'Court and Government / Which Age of Reform?', in C. Coleman and D. Starkey (eds) *Revolution Reassessed* (Oxford: Oxford University Press), pp. 29–58.

Starn, R. (1998), 'Renaissance Redux', *The American Historical Review*, vol. 103, no. 1, 122–24.

Steele, R. (1713), *The Crisis: Or, a Discourse Representing…the Just Causes of the Late Happy Revolution… With Some Seasonable Remarks on the Danger of a Popish Successor.* (F. Burleigh)

Steffen, L. (2007), *Holy War, Just War: Exploring the Moral Meaning of Religious Violence.* (Rowman and Littlefield)

Stern, L. I. (2004), 'Law: Criminal', in *Medieval Italy: An Encyclopedia.* (Routledge), p. 2160.

Stocks, C. (2015), *Fides in Flavian Literature* [online].

Stothard, T. (1786), *Harrison's British Classicks: The Connoisseur. The Citizen of the World. The Babler.* (Harrison and Company)

Stow, K. R. (1977), *Catholic Thought and Papal Jewry Policy, 1555–1593.* (Jewish Theological Seminary of America)

Strathern, P. (2003), *The Medici: Godfathers of the Renaissance.* (Jonathan Cape)

Strayer, J. R. (2011), *On the Medieval Origins of the Modern State.* (Princeton University Press)

Strickland, M. J. (1994), 'Against the Lord's Anointed: Aspects of Warfare and Baronial Rebellion in England and Normandy 1075–1265', in G. Garnett and J. Hudson (eds) *Law and Government in Medieval England and Normandy: Essays in Honour of Sir James Holt.* (Cambridge University Press.), pp. 56–79.

Strike, K.A., and Posner, G.J. (1992). A revisionist theory of conceptual change. In R.Duschl and R. Hamilton (eds.), *Philosophy of science, cognitive psychology, and educational theory and practice* (pp. 147–176). Albany, NY: SUNY Press.

Stryker, S. and Statham, A. (1985), 'Symbolic Interaction and Role Theory', in G. Lindzey and E. Aronson (eds) *The Handbook of Social Psychology* (New York: Random House), pp. 311–78.

Strype, J. (1709), *Annals of the Reformation and Establishment of Religion: And Other Various Occurrences in the Church of England; during the First Twelve Years of Queen Elizabeth's Happy Reign.* (Printed for John Wyat, at the Rose in St. Paul's Church-Yard)

Suetonius, T. G. (2004), *The Twelve Caesars*. (Digireads.com Publishing)

Sueur, P. (2007), *Histoire du droit public français XVe–XVIIIe siècle: Tome 1, La Constitution monarchique Broché*. (Presses Universitaires de France)

Sur, S. (1997), 'The State between Fragmentation and Globalization', *European Journal of International Law*, vol. 3, 421–34.

Sussman, N. and Yafeh, Y. (2004), *Institutions, Deficits, and Wars: The Determinants of British Government Borrowing Costs from the End of the Seventeenth Century to 1850*. Available at: https://pdfs.semanticscholar.org/742a/350027481ddcfbf123fddc446f40 91da127f.pdf.

Sutherland, D. M. (2008), *The French Revolution and Empire: The Quest for a Civic Order*. (John Wiley and Sons)

Sutherland, T. (2013), 'Liquid Networks and the Metaphysics of Flux: Ontologies of Flow in an Age of Speed and Mobility', *Theory, Culture, Society*, vol. 30, no. 5, 3–23.

Swithinbank, H. J. (2012), 'The Corruption of the Constitution The Lex Gabinia and Lex Manilia and the Changing Res Publica', in P. Bosman (ed.), *Corruption and Integrity in Ancient Greece and Rome, Acta Classica Supplementum IV*. (Pretoria: V and R Printing Works Ltd)

Sydow, J. and Windeler, A. (2003), 'Knowledge, Trust, and Control: Managing Tensions and Contradictions in a Regional Network of Service Firms', *International Studies of Management and Organization*, vol. 33, no. 2, 69–99.

Syme, R. (1939), *The Roman Revolution*. (Oxford University Press)

Syrjämäki, S. (2011), *Sins of a Historian. Perspectives on the Problem of Anachronism*. (University of Tampere)

Szendi, E. (2014), 'Trust in the Symposium', *International Relations Quarterly*, vol. 5, no. 3, 1–3.

Sztompka, P. (1997), *Trust, Distrust and the Paradox of Democracy*. (WZB)

Sztompka, P. (2000), *Trust: A Sociological Theory* (Cambridge Cultural Social Studies). (Cambridge University Press)

Tacitus (2007), *The Annals and The Histories*. (Random House LLC)

Tackett, T. (1986), *Religion, Revolution, and Regional Culture in Eighteenth-Century France: The Ecclesiastical Oath of 1791*. (Princeton University Press)

Tackett, T. (1977), *Priest and Parish in Eighteenth-Century France: A Social and Political Study of the Curés in a Diocese of Dauphiné, 1750–1791*. (Princeton University Press)

Tajfel, H. (1978), 'Interindividual Behavior and Intergroup Behavior', in H. Tajfel (ed.), *Differentiation between Social Groups: Studies in the Social Psychology of Intergroup Relations*. (London: Academic Press), pp. 27–60.

Tannenbaum, A. S. (1962), 'Control in Organizations: Individual Adjustment and Organizational Performance', *Administrative Science Quarterly*, vol. 7, no. 2, 236–57.

Tanzi, V. and Schuknecht, L. (2000), *Public Spending in the 20th Century: A Global Perspective*. (New York: Cambridge University Press)

Tarde, G. de (2009), *The Laws of Imitation*. E.W.C. Parsons (ed.) (BiblioLife LLC)

Tarrow, S. G. (2013), *The Language of Contention: Revolutions in Words, 1688–2012.* (Cambridge University Press)

Tarrow, S. G. (1994), *Power in Movement: Collective Action, Social Movements and Politics.* (Cambridge University Press)

Taubman, A. W. (2009), *Clergy and Commoners: Interactions between Medieval Clergy and Laity in a Regional Context.* (University of York)

Taylor, C. (1992), *Sources of the Self.* (Harvard University Press)

Taylor, F. W. (1911), *Scientific Management.* (New York: Harper Brothers)

TeBrake, W. H. (1993), *A Plague of Insurrection: Popular Politics and Peasant Revolt in Flanders, 1323–1328.* (Philadelphia: University of Pennsylvania Press)

Teegarden, D. A. (2013), *Death to Tyrants! Ancient Greek Democracy and the Struggle against Tyranny.* vol. 24. (Princeton University Press)

Teitelman, R. (2011), Don't Overuse the Word 'Revolution'. *Huffington Post*, 21 February.

Temple, W. (1814), *The Works of Sir William Temple, Bart: Life of the Author.* (F.C. and J. Rivington)

Temple, W. (1693), *Miscellanea: The First Part.* (Jacob Tonson…and Awnsham and John Churchill)

Tertullian (2005), *Tertullian, De Pallio: A commentary.* V. Hunink (ed.) (J.C. Gieben)

Tertullian, Q. F. S. (1890), *The Apology of Tertullian for the Christians.* T. H. Bindley (ed.) (Parker and Co.)

Theognis (1999), *Greek Elegiac Poetry: From the Seventh to the Fifth Centuries B.C., Volume 1.* Gerber (ed.) (Harvard University Press)

Thomas, H. M. (2008), *The Norman Conquest: England after William the Conqueror.* (Rowman and Littlefield)

Thompson, E. P. (1971), 'The Moral Economy of the English Crowd in the Eighteenth Century', *Past and Present*, vol. 50, 76–136.

Thompson, E. P. (1966), *The Making of the English Working Class.* (New York: Vintage Books)

Thorley, J. (1996), *Athenian Democracy.* (Taylor and Francis)

Thrupp, S. L. (1989), *The Merchant Class of Medieval London, 1300–1500.* (University of Michigan Press)

Thucydides (2000), *The History of the Peloponnesian War (Classics).* Revised Edition. R. Warner (ed.) (Penguin Books)

Tibi, B. (2012), 'Islamism and Violence: The New World Disorder', in *Islamism and Islam* (Yale University Press), pp. 134–57.

Tilly, C. (2006), *Regimes and Repertoires.* (Chicago, IL: University of Chicago Press)

Tilly, C. (1972), 'How Protest Modernized in France, 1845 to 1855', in R. M. Fogel *et al.* (eds) *The Dimensions of Quantitative Research in History.* (Princeton, NJ: Princeton University Press), pp. 192–255.

Tilly, C. (1922), *Modern France: A Companion to French Studies.* (The University Press)

Tiryakian, E. A. (1968), 'Typologies', in D. L. Sills (ed.), *International Encyclopaedia of the Social Sciences* (New York: Macmillan), pp. 177–86.

Tocqueville, A. de. (2012), *The Old Regime and the French Revolution*. (Courier Corporation)

Tocqueville, A. de. (1998), *The Old Regime and the Revolution*. F. Furet *et al.* (eds) (Chicago, IL: University of Chicago Press)

Todd, S. C. (1993), *The Shape of Athenian Law*. (Oxford: Clarendon Press)

Tolstoy, L. (1966), 'The Meaning of the Russian Revolution', in M. Raeff (ed.) *Russian Intellectual History: An Anthology*. (New York: Harcourt, Brace and World)

Tomkins, C. (2001), 'Interdependencies, Trust and Information in Relationships, Alliances, and Networks', *Accounting, Organizations and Society*, vol. 26, 161–91.

Tomkins, S. S. (1995), *Exploring Affect: The Selected Writings of Silvan S Tomkins*. E. V. Demos (ed.) (Cambridge University Press)

Tovey, J. (2011), 'Listen Hard for the Real Heroes in Syria', *The Sydney Morning Herald*, 15 June.

Trebizond, G. (1997), *Cambridge Translation of Renaissance Philosophical Texts: Volume 2: Political Philosophy*. J. Kraye (ed.) (Cambridge: Cambridge University Press) (Original work published 1452)

Trexler, R. C. (1991), *Public Life in Renaissance Florence*. (Cornell University Press)

Tripp, C. (2006), *Islam and the Moral Economy: The Challenge of Capitalism*. (Cambridge University Press)

Trotsky, L. (1906), *Results and Prospects: Europe and Revolution. Marxist.org* online.

Tsatsou, P. (2009), 'Reconceptualising "Time" and "Space" in the Era of Electronic Media and Communications', *PLATFORM: Journal of Media and Communication*, vol. 1, 11–32.

Tse-Tung, M. (2012), *Mao: Collected Works*. Marxists.org online.

Tse-Tung, M. (1972), *Quotations from Chairman Mao Tse Tung*. (China Books)

Tse-Tung, M. (1961), *On Guerrilla Warfare (1937)*. S. Griffith II (ed.) (Urbana, IL: University of Illinois Press)

Tubb, A. (2015), 'The Engagement Controversy: A Victory for the English Republic', *Historical Research*, 1–20.

Tuck, R. (1989), *Hobbes*. (Oxford University Press)

Tugal, C. (2013), The End of the 'Leaderless' Revolution. *Counter Punch*.

Turner, J. C. (1987), *Rediscovering the Social Group: A Self-Categorization Theory*. vol. 94 (Oxford: Blackwell)

Turner, J. C. (2005), 'Explaining the Nature of Power: A Three-Process Theory', *European Journal of Social Psychology*, vol. 35, no. 1, 1–22.

Tyler, T. R. (2006), 'Psychological Perspectives on Legitimacy and Legitimation', *Annual Review of Psychology*, vol. 57, 375–400.

Tyler, T. R. (2016), 'Trust in the Twenty-First Century', in E. Shockley *et al.* (eds) *Interdisciplinary Perspective of Trust: Towards Theoretical and Methodological Integration* (Springer International Publishing), pp. 203–15.

Uslaner, E. M. (2018), *The Oxford Handbook of Social and Political Trust*. (Oxford University Press)

Uslaner, E. M. (2008), 'Trust as a Moral Value', in D. Castiglione *et al.* (eds) *Handbook of Social Capital.* (Oxford: Oxford University Press), pp. 101–21.

Uslaner, E. (2002), *The Moral Foundations of Trust.* (Cambridge: Cambridge University Press)

Underwood, K. W. (1957), *Protestant and Catholic: Religious and Social Interaction in an Industrial Community.* (Beacon Press)

Unknown (1390), *The Regius Poem: A Poem of Moral Duties.* Freemasons online.

Upshaw, R. (2005), *Political Systems and the Nature of Freedom.* (Variocity)

Valente, C. (2003), *The Theory and Practice of Revolt in Medieval England.* (Ashgate Publishing Limited)

Vallance, E. (2007), *The Glorious Revolution.* BBC History online, 17 February.

Vanheste, J. (2007), 'Introduction and Overview', in *Guardians of the Humanist Legacy: The Classicism of T.S. Eliot's Criterion Network and Its Relevance to Our Postmodern World.* (Leiden: Koninklijke Brill)

Varchi, B. (2012), *Storia Fiorentina... [Italian].* (Nabu Press)

Varickayil, R. (1980), 'Social Origins of Protestant Reformation', *Scientist*, vol. 8, no. 11, 14–31.

Vasari, G. (1550), *The Lives of the Artists.* Oxford Work. J. C. Bondanella and P. Bondanella (eds) (Oxford Paperbacks)

Vernant, J-P. (1984), *The Origins of Greek Thought.* (Cornell University Press)

Vidino, L. *et al.* (2010), 'Bringing Global Jihad to the Horn of Africa: al Shabaab, Western Fighters, and the Sacralization of the Somali Conflict', *African Security*, vol. 3, no. 4, 216–38.

Villani, M. (2011), *Cronica Di Matteo Villani, A Miglior Lezione Ridotta Coll' Aiuto De' Testi A Penna, Volume 4... [Italian].* (Nabu Press)

Vincent, A. (2013), 'Conceptions of the State', in M. Hawkesworth and M. Kogan (eds) *Encyclopaedia of Government and Politics*, pp. 39–53.

Virgil (2014), *The Aeneid.* (Interactive Media)

Volney, C. F. (1792), *The Ruins, or, a Survey of the Revolutions of Empires.* (Johnson)

Voltaire (1953), *Voltaire's Correspondence.* T. Besterman (ed.) (Institut et musée Voltaire)

Vygotsky, L. S. *et al.* (1978), *Mind in Society: Development of Higher Psychological Processes.* (Cambridge, MA: Harvard University Press)

Walker, E. *et al.* (1896), 'A History of Banking in All the Leading Nations', *The Journal of Commerce and Commercial Bulletin*, vol. 1 Available at: http://oll. libertyfund.org/titles/sumner-a-history-of-banking-in-all-the-leading-nations-vol-1-u-s-a.

Wall, A. (2000), *Power and Protest in England 1525–1640.* (Bloomsbury Academic)

Waller, M. (2006), *Sovereign Ladies: Sex, Sacrifice, and Power – The Six Reigning Queens of England.* (St. Martin's Press)

Walsh, C. P. (2012), *Civic Friendship, Justice, and Political Stability.* Ph.D thesis, Graduate College of the University of Illinois at Chicago.

Walsham, A. (1999), *Providence in Early Modern England.* vol. 3. (Oxford University Press)

Walsingham, T. (1869), *Gesta Abbatum Monasterii Sancti Albani*. H. T. Riley (ed.)
(London: Longmans, Green, and Co.)

Walsingham, T. (2003), *The St Albans Chronicle, Volume I 1376–1394: The Chronica
Maiora of Thomas Walsingham: 1376–1394 vol 1*. Reprint. (Clarendon Press)

Walton, C. (2013), 'Reciprocity and the French Revolution', in A. Fairfax-Cholmeley
and C. Jones (eds) *New Perspectives on the French Revolution*. (e-France), pp. 25–30.

Ward, A. (1972), 'The Forging of Ore: Blake and the Idea of Revolution', *Triquarterly*,
vol. 23/24, 167–227.

Wartenberg, T. (1990), *The Forms of Power*. (Philadelphia, PA: Temple University Press)

Watson, G. (1998), 'The Idea of Conservative Revolution', in *The Lost Literature of
Socialism by George Watson*. (Cambridge: Lutterworth Press), pp. 29–42.

Watts, J. (2009), *The Making of Polities: Europe, 1300–1500*. (Cambridge University Press)

Weber, M. (2013), *Economy and Society*. (University of California Press)

Weber, M. (2009a), *From Max Weber: Essays in Sociology*. (Routledge)

Weber, M. (2009b), *The Theory of Social and Economic Organization. vol. 24*. (Simon
and Schuster)

Weidenkopf, S. (2015), *The Real Story of the Reformation*, Catholic Answers, live
broadcast, 4 March.

Weijers, O. (1977), 'Some Notes on Fides and Related Words in Medieval Latin', *ALMA
Archivum Latinitatis Medii Aevi (Bulletin Du Cange)*, vol. 40, 77–102.

Weil, F. D. (1986), 'The Stranger, Prudence, and Trust in Hobbes's Theory', *Theory and
Society*, vol. 15, no. 5, 759–88.

Weissman, R. F. E. (1982), *Ritual Brotherhood in Renaissance Florence*. (Academic Press)

Wells, H. G. (2005), *The Shape of Things to Come: The Ultimate Revolution*. New Edition.
(Penguin Classics)

Weltecke, D. (2008), 'Trust: Some Methodological Reflections', in P. Schulte *et al.*
(eds) *Strategies of Writing: Studies on Text and Trust in the Middle Ages*. (Turnhout,
Belgium: Brepols Publishers), pp. 379–92.

Welwood, J. (1689), *A Vindication of the Present Great Revolution in England*. (R. Taylor)

West, C. (2013), *Reframing the Feudal Revolution: Political and Social Transformation
between Marne and Moselle, c. 800–c. 1100*. (Cambridge University Press)

Wheeler, N. J. (2012), 'Trust-Building in International Relations', *Peace Prints: South
Asian Journal of Peacebuilding*, vol. 4, no. 2, 21.

Wheeler, N. J. (2007), 'Trust Building between Enemies in the Nuclear Age', in *All-Wales
Peace Conference* pp. 1–6.

Wheeler, N. J. (2010), '"I Had Gone to Lahore with a Message of Goodwill but in Return
We Got Kargil": The Promise and Perils of "Leaps of Trust" in India–Pakistan
Relations', *India Review*, vol. 9, no. 3, 319–44.

White, A. B. (1933), *Self-Government at the King's Command: A Study in the Beginnings
of English Democracy*. (The University of Minnesota Press)

White, H. C. (1992), *Identity and Control: A Structural Theory of Social Action*.
(Princeton University Press)

Wicker, E. (1996), *The Banking Panics of the Great Depression (Studies in Macroeconomic History)*. (Cambridge University Press)

Wickham, C. R. (2013), *The Muslim Brotherhood: Evolution of an Islamist Movement.* (Princeton University Press)

Wilbur, A. P. (2013), Pierre-Joseph Proudhon: Self-Government and the Citizen State. (Corvus Editions)

Williams, B. (1988), 'Formal Structures and Social Reality', in D. Gambetta (ed.), *Trust: Making and Breaking Cooperative Relations.* (Wiley-Blackwell), pp. 3–13.

Williams, K. (2009), *Read All about It! A History of the British Newspaper.* (Routledge)

Williams, M. and Satgar, V. (eds) (2013), *Marxism in the Twenty-First Century: Critique, Crisis and Struggles.* (Johannesburg: Witts University Press)

Williamson, O. E. (1993), 'Calculativeness, Trust and Economic Organization', *Journal of Law and Economics*, vol. 34, 453–502.

Willis, S. (2015), *Outlaws and Highwaymen: Highwaymen, Pirates and Rogues*, BBC 4 online, 3 episodes.

Winter, Y. (2012), *Plebeian Politics: Machiavelli and the Ciompi Uprising.* vol. 40. (Sage Publications)

Witt, R. G. (1983), *Hercules at the Crossroads: The Life, Works, and Thought of Coluccio Salutati.* (Duke University Press)

Wolff, J. (2006), *Trust and the State of Nature.* Open Learn online.

Wolffe, J. (2013), *Protestant-Catholic Conflict from the Reformation to the 21st Century: The Dynamics of Religious Difference.* (Palgrave Macmillan)

Woloch, I. (1982), *Eighteenth-Century Europe, Tradition and Progress, 1715–1789.* (Norton)

Wolpert, A. (2001), *Remembering Defeat: Civil War and Civic Memory in Ancient Athens.* (JHU Press)

Wood, G. S. (1998), *Radicalism of the American Revolution.* (Random House USA Inc)

Woolf, G. (1994), 'Becoming Roman, Staying Greek: Culture, Identity and the Civilizing Process in the Roman East', in *Proceedings of the Cambridge Philological Society.* (The Cambridge Classical Journal), pp. 116–43.

Woolf, G. (2002), 'Roman Peace', in J. Rich and G. Shipley (eds) *War and Society in the Roman World*, Volume 5 (London and New York: Routledge), pp. 171–95.

Worcester, K. (2010), 'The Meaning and Legacy of the Magna Carta', *PS: Political Science and Politics*, vol. 43, no. 3, 451–56.

Worchel, P. (1979), 'Trust and Distrust', in W. G. Austin and S. Worchel (eds) *The Social Psychology of Inter-Group Relations.* (Belmont, CA: Wadsworth)

Wordsworth, W. (2004), *William Wordsworth: Selected Poems.* New Edition. S. Gill (ed.) (Penguin Classics)

Wren, D. A. and Bedeian, A. G. (2004), 'The Taylorization of Lenin: Rhetoric or Reality?', *International Journal of Social Economics*, vol. 31, no. 3, 287–99.

Wright, S. (2010), 'Trust and Trustworthiness', *Philosophia*, vol. 38.

Wrightson, K. (2013), *English Society 1580–1680.* (Routledge)

Xenophon (1891), *Xenophon's Minor Works.* J. S. Watson (ed.) (London: George Beel and Sons)

Yamagishi, T. *et al.* (1998), 'Uncertainty, Trust, and Commitment Formation in the United States and Japan', *American Journal of Sociology*, vol. 104, no. 1, 165–94.

Yamagishi, T. (2001). Trust as a form of social intelligence. In K. S. Cook (Ed.). Trust in society Vol. 2 (pp. 121–147).

Yeager, R. F. (2010) 'John Gower's French and His Readers', in E. Dutton, J. Hines and R. F. Yeager (eds) *John Gower, Trilingual Poet: Language, Translation, and Tradition.* (Boydell and Brewer), pp. 304–14.

Yoder, D. (1926), 'Current Definitions of Revolution', *American Journal of Sociology*, vol. 32, no. 3, 433–41.

Young, J. D. (1988), *Socialism since 1889: A Biographical History.* (Totowa, NJ: Barnes and Noble Books)

Zagorin, P. (1973), 'Theories of Revolution in Contemporary Historiography', *Political Science Quarterly*, vol. 88, no. 1, 23–52.

Zaheer, A. and Venkatraman, N. (1995), 'Relational Governance as an Inter-Organizational Strategy – An Empirical Test of the Role of Trust in Economic Exchange', *Strategic Management Journal*, vol. 16, 373–92.

Zarrow, P. G. (1997), *Imagining the People: Chinese Intellectuals and the Concept of Citizenship, 1890–1920.* J. A. Fogel and P. G. Zarrow (eds) (M.E. Sharpe)

Zevallos, Z. (2012), *The Egyptian Revolution as a Spectacle for the West. Other Sociologist.com.*

Zsolnai (2005), 'The Rationality of Trust', *International Journal of Social Economics*, vol. 32, no. 3, pp. 268–69.

Zucker, L. G. (1986), 'Production of Trust: Institutional Sources of Economic Structure (1840–1920)', in B. M. Staw and L. L. Cummings (eds) *Research in Organizational Behavior: vol. 8.* (Greenwich, CT: JAI Press), pp. 53–111.

Index

Adamson, J. S. A. 120
Addison, J. 131
Alfonsin, R. 32
American Revolution 131, 137, 229 n. 71
Ancient Greece 2–3, 71–2, 76, 93, 216 n. 39
    Classical or Golden Age (508–322
      BCE) 62
    class struggle 67
    Cleisthenes's democratic reforms 63,
      68, 70
    direct democracy 61–2
    governance in 66–9
    Greek identity 61–4, 66–72, 77
    philosopher's writing 64, 67–8
    revolution in 63–7
    social customs 66
    transition from monarchy to
      aristocracy 70
    tribes as legends 69–70
    trust framework 63–4, 69–70
Ancient Rome
    Christianity, influence of 79–80
    citizenship in 71, 77, 80
    Etruscan rule 72
    fides (trust), notion of 71, 73–4, 76, 79
    Fides Publica Populi Romani (public
      trust of Roman people) 73–6
    first revolution 73
    forms of government 71–2, 75
    Milvian Bridge, battle of 79
    monotheism 79
    polytheism 77
    religious persecutions 78
    revolution 71–2, 75–6, 79–80
    Roman Revolution 72, 76
    Tarquinius's tyranny 72
    trust framework 74–5, 78
Anderson, C. 154
Antiphon 64, 196 n. 36
anti-Semitism 109
Arab Spring 1, 21, 149, 152–3, 159, 178 n.
    126, 240 n. 11, 244 n. 88

Aristotle 23, 170 n. 10, 181 n. 48, 187 n.
    161, 194 n. 2, 194 n. 6, 194 n. 9, 195
    n. 20, 195 n. 19, 196 n. 31, 198 n.
    55, 199 n. 75, 203 n. 128
    on city-state 81, 92
    on communal citizenship 67
    'friendships of utility', analysis of 64
    meaning of trust 64
    notion of civic friendship 68–70, 197
      n. 38
    Politics 12, 199 n. 79, 200 n. 86
    on revolution 23
Athenian Revolution 12, 67–8
    508/7 BCE 61
    conceptions of trust 62–6, 68–71
Axelrod, Robert, *Evolution of Cooperation,*
    The 48
Aylmer, G. E. 125

Bachmann, R. 57
background trust 29, 41, 163
Bagshaw, E. 125
Baier, A. C. 30, 63
Baker, K. M. 103
Barber, B. 25, 47
Barthelemy, D. 82
Barton, C. A. 74, 78
Bayat, A. 152
Bennett, W. L. 166
Berlin, I. 1
blind trust 42, 46, 138
Bodin, J. 18
Bon, Le 18
Bradley, K. 63
Brand, L. A. 73
Bradley, K. 63
Brand, L. A. 73
Braudel, F. 3–4
Brent, A. 78
Brexit 1, 153, 166
Britain in seventeenth century
    affordable print 118–20
    Engagement Controversy (1649–51)
      125

Guizot, François, reference to 'English
Revolution' 121
political life 118–19
post-Reformation society 114
Puritan movement 118
revolution, political debate and use of
term 121–2
Stuart rule 117
trust framework 124–8
trust, use and meaning of term
124
Whig politics 120
Brown, A. 84
Brunt, P. A. 74, 78
Buchanan, G. 125
Buckley, W. F. 54
Burckhardt, J. 96
Burke, E. 16
Burke, P. 132–3, 137, 139

Caesar, Augustus 75
Caesar, Julius 76
Cairns, A. 63
Cambodian Revolution 145
capitalism 20, 96, 100, 176 n. 104
Carroll, J. 107
Caskey, J. 85
Castells, M. 159
Castro, Fidel 19
Catholic Church, Council of Trent
(1545–63) 107
Charles I 15, 121–2, 125, 173 n. 61, 188 n.
180, 226 n. 11, 227 n. 28
Charles II 15, 119, 121, 227 n. 28
Charles V 106
Chartier, R. 130
Chervany, N. L. N. 7
Chinese Revolution 19, 145
Cicero M. T. 202 n. 106, 203 n. 122, 205
n. 157
de Amicita 218 n. 95
de Officiis 203 n. 126, 204 n. 148, 218
n. 83
on power and authority 54
on public trust 73–4
citizen(s)
of Florence during the Renaissance 99,
101, 104
universal laws 12
Clarendon, Earl of 15

Cleisthenes 62–3, 68–71, 194 n. 6, 194 n. 9,
195 nn. 19–20, 199 n. 74, 200 n. 80
Cleveland, J. 125
Clinton, Bill 48
Coke, Sir Edward 124
Cold War 1, 20
Coleman, C. 30
Coleridge, S. T. 132
conceptual trust 42, 155, 192 n. 70
control
definition 53
power and 52–5, 57–9
trust and 55–7
Cook, K. S. 48
Copernicus 15
1543 treatise 14
Crompton, R. 113
Crubaugh, A. 140
Crusades 22, 89, 184 n. 100, 210 n. 51, 212
n. 85
Cuban Revolution 145

Dahrendorf, R. 54
Darwin, Charles 17
Das, T. K. 56
Davis, R. C. 128
Defoe, D. 131
Deutsch, M. 54
Dickson, P. G. M. 128
Digital Age 153, 161
Drayton, Michael, *Poly-Olbion* 117
dualism and duality 56, 58, 115, 127, 192
n. 73, 192 n. 75

Egyptian Revolution 22
Ellwood, C. A. 18
England. *See also* Britain in seventeenth
century.
Baron's role 87
legal system 89
Mary I 'Bloody Mary' 114–15
Peasants' Revolt 13, 82, 91–2, 107, 212
n. 87
Reformation 105, 112
Roman Catholicism 113–15
trust framework 82–6, 89–93
Tudor rule 106, 113–14, 164
English Civil War 13
Erikson, E. H. 41
European Wars of Religion 22

Fiske, S. T. 53
Florentine Renaissance (1330–1550)
    civic institutions 101
    civil society, role of individuals in 98–9
    Compagni's account 99
    Cosimo the Elder 101, 103
    cultural movement 96
    governance system 97–102
    Lorenzo the Magnificent 101
    under Medicis 101–4
    notion of liberty 103–4
    religious and judicial practices 101–2
    Revolt of Ciompi 100
    revolution 96, 98, 102–4
    social freedom 95–6
    squitinio (scrutiny) 98
    trade and commerce 100
    trust framework 96–104
Flores, F. 41, 47
Flyvbjerg, B. 34
Foucault, M. 134
Fox, A. 132
Foxe, John, *Book of Martyrs* 114
Foyster, E. A. 128
France in eighteenth century. *See also*
    French Revolution.
    absolute monarchy, replacement of
        132
    Bourbon rule 130
    Catholicism 130, 140
    civil and religious war 105, 131
    de-Christianization 140–1
    governance 139–42
    new social order 133–5
    revolutionary calendar 133
    three estates 129–30
    trust framework 129, 135–42, 144
French Revolution 2, 9, 15–17, 108, 130–2,
    134–5, 137, 143, 145–8, 152, 161,
    164, 173 n. 61, 184 n. 107, 233 n.
    192, 235 n. 251
    disorder of events 131–2
    dramatic changes 133–5
    emergence of words 132
    use of term 131
Fuller, G. E. 59
Furetiere, A. 132

Gau, J. M. 157
Gerard, H. B. 54

Germany
    fascism 48
    Peasants' Revolt 221 n. 149
    Protestantism 105, 108, 113
    Renaissance 104
    Weimar Republic 40
globalization 1, 45, 151, 153, 159
Glorious Revolution 15, 131, 172 n. 58,
    214 n. 2
Golden Bull of Hungary 82, 172 n. 53
Gorbachev, Mikhail 48
Gray, J. M. 114
Greco, T. H. 72, 80
Greif, A. 38
Guizot, F. 120

Hacking, I. 128
Hardin, R. 31, 46–7, 49
Havel, Vaclav 21
Hawhee, D. 63
Heller, A. 95
Henrich, J. 32
Henry VIII 106, 109, 220 n. 139, 223 n.
    198, 225 n. 242
Herodotus 12, 64, 67–8, 183 n. 95, 194 nn.
    5–7, 195 n. 13, 196 n. 28, 197 n. 43,
    199 n. 74
Hexter, J. H. 97
Hobbes, Thomas 228 n. 62, 229 n. 65
    Leviathan 15
    on revolution 122–4
    on trust 126
Ho Chi Minh 19
Ho, H. L. 19
Holborn, H. 106
Holkeskamp, K.-J. 74
Holton, R. 30
Huber, T. L. 58
Huguenots 131, 220 n. 134, 223 n. 190
Hus, Jan 82, 220 n. 126
Hyndman, H. M. 18

ideational trust 43, 161
impersonal trust 38–41, 44–6, 71, 153–8,
    165–6
Industrial Age 17
industrial revolution, first and second 17
institutional trust 43–4, 146–7, 187 n. 148
interlopers 25, 48–9
interpersonal trust 34, 45–6, 90, 124, 156

Iranian Revolution 20
Islamic State 149, 152, 178 n. 128, 222 n. 163, 240 n. 10
Isocrates 64
Italian Renaissance 96
Italian Wars 103

Jackson, R. 157
James II 121–2
jihad (holy war) 20
Jihadi Spring 21, 178 n. 126
John, King of England 92
Johnson, S. A. M. 121
Johnstone, S. 63
Jones, A. H. M. 47, 128

Kargil Crisis 33
Kersey, J. K. 121
Khodyakov, D. M. 35, 37
Kiefer, Howard Evans, *Ethics and Social Justice* 15
Koselleck, R. 4–5

Lafayette, Marquis de 16
Lahno, B. 34
Laing, R. D. 41
Lash, S. 154
Le Bon, G. 18
Lendon, J. E. 74, 78
Lenin, V. I. 19, 147
Levi, M. 49
Lewicki, R. J. 47
Locke, J. 172 n. 55, 229 n. 69, 230 n. 111
    on revolutions 122–4
    theory on politics 127
    on trust 126–7, 135
    Two Treatises of Government 15
Lovejoy, A. O. 128
Luhmann, N. 25, 35–6
Luther, Martin 105–9, 110, 219 n. 118, 220 n. 129, 221 n. 151, 221 n. 156, 222 n. 178, 222 n. 184, 225 n. 227
    anti-Catholicism 214 n. 115
    notion of two kingdoms 113
    95 Theses 105

Machiavelli, N. 99, 103, 172 nn. 45–7, 188 n. 162, 188 n. 176, 215 n. 24, 232 n. 167
    The Prince 14

MacIntyre, A. 33, 37
Magna Carta 13, 80, 82, 91–2, 172 n. 53, 207 n. 3
Mao, Zedong 19
Martin, H.-J. 105
Martin, L. K. Jr. 105
Marx, Karl 17
Mayr, E. 128
McConnell, J. 97
McKnight, D. H. 7
McLean, P. D. 97
McMahon, D. M. 3
medieval times
    Church and Christianity, role of 13
    trust framework 88
    value transfer system 185 n. 122
Mercer, J. 31, 33
Michelangelo, *David and Goliath* 103
Michelet, J. 96
Michel, T. 33
Michnik, Adam 21
Middle East and North Africa (MENA) 21, 152, 160
Milton, J. 125
mistrust 44, 97
Mollering, G. 56
monarchy
    absolutist 235 n. 240
    Ancient Athens 70
    Ancient Rome 71–2
    Aristotelian concept 86, 200 n. 86
    French 132, 138, 143
    Locke's distrust of 126
    in medieval Europe 91–2, 113, 115–17
    patrimonial 239 n. 24
Montesquieu 136
Moore, B. 81, 92–3

Nardi, J. 14, 102
Neustadt, R. E. 5
non-betrayal 44, 157, 166–7

Occupy movement 151
Octavius, Gaius 75
O'Neill, O. 30

Paine, T. 16, 133, 136
Papal Revolution 87, 113
Parenti, M. 102
Patch, H. R. 85

Peasants' Revolt 13
Pelham, Henry 39
Peloponnesian War 12, 68, 79, 199 n. 74, 200 n. 92
Philip, M. 121
Phillips, E. 102
Pixley, J. 35
Plato 199 n. 75, 199 n. 79, 200 n. 86, 201 n. 99
    on civic friendship 68
    concept of revolution 12, 68–9
    doctrine of tripartite soul 34
political trust 43, 46, 127, 187 n. 157
political unrest 12–13
Polybius 12, 71, 170 n. 9, 200 n. 86, 203 n. 122, 204 n. 133, 204 n. 148
    The Histories 71
Pooley, E. H. 87
power
    authority, impact on 51–5, 57
    concepts 52–5
    control and 52–5, 57–9
    definitions 53
    objectives 51
    revolutionaries 51
    social 52
    social structure 51–2
    trust, interplay with 55–9
Protestant Reformation 87, 93, 104–16, 164
    authority and obedience 105, 107–14
    German nation, birth of 104
    Renaissance period (*c.*1400–1600) 104
    sola scripture (scripture only) and *sola fide* (faith only) 111
    trust framework 105, 110
    Tudor and Stuart reigns 105

Qur'an/Quran 21, 176 n.110, 178 n.133

Reagan, Ronald, Intermediate-Range Nuclear Forces Treaty 48
rebels 13, 84, 92–3, 123, 171 n. 28, 177 n. 113, 214 n. 112
Reformation, the. *See* Protestant Reformation.
Renaissance. *See also* Florentine Renaissance; Protestant Reformation.
    European concept of revolution 13

    medieval history 93
    trust framework 97
revolution. *See also* specific instances.
    ancient Greek definition 13
    classical *vs.* modern 151
    in communication technology 159–61
    concept 11, 19, 22–4
    contemporary notions 159–62
    economic change and scientific innovation, impact on 17
    European etymology 12–22
    examples 1, 14
    international factors 19
    Islamic concept 21–2, 151–2
    late Renaissance period 13
    modern concept 145–9
    origin, terminology 121
    permanent 18
    political phenomenon 17–18, 20, 93, 104, 122, 147, 158, 164
    role of trust and distrust in 7
    scientific 13–14
    seizure of power and 14–15
    social 71, 80, 136
    twentieth century theory and method 19
    twenty first century experience of 151–3
    violent 18
revolutionaries
    digital media, use of 154
    French 133, 139–40, 142
    future vision 16
    goal 51, 67
    Marxist/Leninist revolutionary movements 145–6
    position in state 18
    professional 19
    twentieth century 158
    Western 148
Reynolds, S. 85, 87, 91
Rinuccini, A. 103
Robespierre 16, 139, 164
Rohan, Duc de 131
Rotter, J. B. 47
Rousseau, D. M. 136
rudimentary trust 6–7, 41, 44
Russell, J. B. 49
Russian Revolution 19–20, 145

Salafis 21, 178 n. 127
Sarnay, Jose 32
Scorpo, A. L. 85
self trust 42
sexual revolution 20
Shakespeare, W. 14
   Julius Caesar, portrayal of mob 17
Sharpe, K. 128
Siedentop, L. 85
Sizer, M. A. 83, 85
Skinner, Q. 5
social influence 54–5, 191 n. 50, 191 n. 53
social life 18, 51, 73–4, 113, 187 n. 152,
   187 n. 154, 190 n. 23
social upheaval 18, 131
Solomon, R. C. 41, 47
Soviet Union, collapse of 20, 149, 158
Stalin, J. V. 19, 147
state
   absolute trust 147–8
   abstract concept 14–15
   changing notion 1, 11–12, 14–16, 18,
      23, 156–7
   citizen and 12, 157, 165–6
   global hegemony 154–5
   global politics 146
   position of revolutionaries 18
   ruler as synonymous 15
   twenty first century 46, 110
Stothard, T. 131
Syrian Revolution 22
Syrjamaki, S. 5
systems trust 43–4
Sztompka, P. 44

Tarrow, S. G. 161
Teegarden, D. A. 63
Teng, B.-S. 56
Theognis 64
Thomas, H. M. 16, 92
Thucydides 194 nn. 5–6, 195 n. 13, 195 n.
   17, 196 n. 35, 197 n. 38, 199 n. 74,
   199 n. 77, 199 n. 79, 203 n. 123
   concept of revolution 12, 64, 67–8,
     70
   on Peisistratus reign 67
   revolution in Corcyra 169 n. 5
   on trust 64
Tocqueville, A. 135–6, 138–9, 143
Trump, D. 1, 153, 166

trust. *See also specific types.*
   affective attitudes 6, 28, 30–1, 33, 49,
     87, 90, 156
   behavioural elements 6, 26–8, 49,
     156–7
   belief *vs.* 49
   betrayal of 30, 44, 48
   changing relationships of 37
   cognitive acts 6, 26–8, 31, 49, 156
   common factors 27–9
   contemporary political theorists on 137
   contemporary sociologists on 36
   control and 55–7
   co-operation *vs.* 48–9
   definitions 25–7
   distrust and 47–8
   emotional feelings of 33–5
   five dimensions of 27–9, 49
   Greek concept 63–5
   ideology *vs.* 49
   methodological approach 32–3
   modern conception 74, 135, 145–9
   money, prerequisite for 35–40
   power and control, interplay with 55–9
   process 29–30
   rationalist approaches 30–2
   reliance *vs.* 48
   social practice 35–41
   trust building approaches 26, 31–3, 73
   trustworthiness and 46–7
   twenty first century approaches 25
   types 41–4
Tunisian Revolution 22
Tyler, T. R. 157

Ukrainian Revolution 22
Upshaw, R. 167

Vajpayee, A. B. 32
Valente, C. 85
Varchi, B., *Tumulto di Venerdi* 14
Vietnamese Revolution 145
Villani, M. 14
Vygotsky, L. S. 42

Wall, A. 1
Walpole, Robert 39
Walsh, C. P. 67
Walsingham, Thomas 92, 171 n. 30, 209
   n. 26

Watts, J. 87
Weber, M. 54
  'iron cage' bureaucracy 240 n. 7
  power, definition of 54
  sine qua non of modern State 189–90
    n. 9
  on types of authority 191 n. 39
Weidenkopf, S. 108–9
Western Europe
  Black Death 82
  Cabochien Revolt 82
  Church's role 82–3, 85–90, 92–3
  Ciompi Revolt 82
  citizens 45–6
  commercial revolution 82
  feudal system 81–2, 86, 89–93
  fides (trust), notion of 82–6, 88–93
  first European Revolution 81, 92
  guilds and fraternities 86–7
  infantry revolution 89
  Jews and women, exclusion of 87

  monarchy/kingship 82–7, 89–92
  moral dilemmas 84
  Papal Revolution 87
  Papal Schism (1378–1417) 82
  Peasants' Revolt in England 82
  Rebellion of the Remences 82
  rebellions and revolts 82–4, 86, 91–3
  religious beliefs 86
  Renaissance period 96
  scholasticism, reaction against
    82
  social order 81–2, 86
  Weltanschauung 82
Westphalia, Peace of 14
Wheeler, N. J. 32–3
White, A. B. 82
White, S. D. 82
Winter, Y. 152
Witt, R. G. 97
Worchel, P. 47
Wycliffe, John 82, 220 n. 126